Cornwallis

The Imperial Years

Cornwallis

The Imperial Years

by
Franklin and Mary Wickwire

The University of North Carolina Press

Chapel Hill

© 1980 The University of North Carolina Press
All rights reserved
Manufactured in the United States of America
Library of Congress Catalog Card Number 79-9943
ISBN 0-8078-1387-7

Library of Congress Cataloging in Publication Data

Wickwire, Franklin B
  Cornwallis, the imperial years.

  Bibliography: p.
  Includes index.
  1. Cornwallis, Charles Cornwallis, 1st Marquis, 1738–1805.
2. India—History—British occupation, 1765–1947.   3. Ire-
land—History—1760–1820.   4. Statesmen–Great Britain–
Biography.   I. Wickwire, Mary, joint author.   II. Title.
DA506.C8W5   941.07'3'0924[B]   79-9943
ISBN 0-8078-1387-7

Contents

Illustrations

Preface

This second volume of our life of Cornwallis carries him from America to service halfway around the world in India. It covers his diplomatic activities on the European Continent on three different occasions, including his final service in negotiating the peace of Amiens, the only respite England enjoyed in the long struggle with France that began in 1793 and did not end until 1815. It shows him at work in the British cabinet as master general of the ordnance and engaged as lord lieutenant of Ireland in suppressing rebellion and tediously, frustratingly, carrying the Act of Union between Britain and Ireland. Finally, it follows him back to India again, where he sickened and died. Cornwallis served the empire in so many capacities during this time, worked so hard at so many different tasks, that the period from 1781 to his death in 1805 may justly be termed the imperial years.

Research for these imperial years we sometimes found as difficult as Cornwallis found his work. Part of the difficulty lay in our needing to familiarize ourselves with British India and the archives that tell its history. For the rest, we needed time to work in other areas—ordnance, Ireland, diplomacy—all of which Cornwallis entered and in all of which he made a lasting impression. Through it all we had to keep in mind the man as well as the institutions he served.

We should like to thank the many people who helped us, especially the officials of the Public Record Office, the trustees of the British Museum, and the officials of the India Office Library and Records. The India Office also permitted us to reproduce in our book photographs of Indian life from the many prints and pictures they possess. The National Portrait Gallery graciously permitted us to reproduce the portrait of Cornwallis painted in Madras, which shows, more than words can convey, the toll the campaign against Tipoo took upon his constitution.

We should like to thank Hoare's bank at 37 Fleet Street for the information given us from its records of Cornwallis's finances, and Viscount Elveden, by whose courtesy we were able to examine Cornwallis's rent rolls at Elveden Hall in Suffolk. We are also grateful to the central library at Sheffield, whose Rockingham papers proved useful for this volume.

In Edinburgh we met with invariable courtesy at the Scottish Record Office and the National Library of Scotland, making our stay there both rewarding and enjoyable.

Finally, as on previous visits, we are appreciative of the attention and consideration given us by the staff of the William L. Clements Library at Ann Arbor, Michigan.

Many friends and scholars have looked at, criticized, praised, and otherwise contributed to this volume. A former graduate student of Franklin Wickwire's, Captain Dale Pearson, suggested many of the ideas we advanced about Cornwallis's role at the ordnance in the paper he submitted to a graduate seminar entitled "Cornwallis and Richmond: A Case Study of the Master Generalship of the 1790s." It was a pleasure to have a graduate student with a creative imagination who prompted the professor to think. Three of our colleagues have always encouraged us. The first, Stephen Oates, has always been a friend, but more than that, a devoted biographer, whose literary skills we have always admired and whose portrait of Lincoln we consider one of the finest biographies in the English language. He has always been one of the three with whom we could discuss our work freely, without suffering pain from his criticism or swollen egos from his praise. The second, Robert Hart, has suffered with us the frustration of knowing we have much to say, yet often were not sure how to say it. We also owe him a tremendous debt of gratitude for his hours of labor on our maps. The third, Harold Gordon, has been a staunch, loyal, and helpfully critical friend for twenty years.

Finally, we also owe a large debt across the seas. Ian Christie, at University College, London, was the first scholar whom we met when we first went to England in 1959, and he has remained for twenty years a friend, a critic, and at the same time a ruthless searcher after honest, thorough scholarship in the period we all love the most, the eighteenth century. T. C. J. ("Bob") O'Connell, M.D., M.Ch., showed us Dublin as no one else could have. We saw not only Cornwallis's Dublin, but Shaw's and Joyce's as well. He was a courteous, gracious host, whose kindness we shall never forget.

Cornwallis
The Imperial Years

Chapter 1

A Sea of Troubles

To some aboard the *Greyhound* it must have seemed a final derisive blow from the capricious fates that had long presided over their careers in America. Only imagine! To be prisoners of war returning to England on parole and to be captured on the way by a French privateer! Before that the officers had formed part of the most active British army in America, marching and counter-marching hundreds of miles through wilderness and alien country, frequently far removed from any hope of external succor. Those who survived the battles, the hunger, the fatigue, and the icy waters had ended their soldiering at a small settlement beside the sea, daily anticipating the generous relief they had solicited. Instead the watery avenue that had so often befriended the British bore upon its tide a French fleet that interdicted escape. That they were aboard the captured transport *Greyhound* instead of the *Robust* on which they had originally sailed owed only to their sheer bad luck (the *Robust* had proved unseaworthy).

For Lieutenant General Earl Cornwallis the capture was but the most recent in a series of personal and professional misfortunes. He could not yet know that those misfortunes would not prove complete disasters. Most immediate in his memory loomed the unpleasant interview he had had in November in New York with his commander in chief, Sir Henry Clinton. On either side, wounded professional pride had confronted injured innocence. Cornwallis had blamed Clinton for not coming sooner with relief; Clinton had blamed Cornwallis for expecting him to come at all. Clinton had deplored the choice of Yorktown for a post; Cornwallis had deplored the order that had led him to choose Yorktown as the best of a bad bargain. The mutual distrust and strain

3

between the two generals increased to the point that by December
they would communicate with each other only by formal letter.
The arguments and counterarguments grew complicated and detailed.[1] They did not end even with the Peace of Paris, for Clinton
had had his own defense printed in pamphlet form, a copy of
which he carried with him to show to persons he encountered
over the years. Indeed, he had become obsessed. Several months
after Cornwallis's departure from New York, Clinton called a
young captain about to return to England and had his secretary
read passages from that pamphlet to the hapless junior officer.
Clinton added to the reading a verbal diatribe intended "to excul-
pate himself from all blame" and, having made the young man an
hour late boarding his ship, dismissed him by wishing him well
and a happy voyage.[2]

Whatever might await Clinton, Cornwallis at least could
look toward the future with some pleasurable anticipation. The
grief he had felt over the loss of his wife had naturally faded
somewhat with the passage of years. His daughter and son, now
aged twelve and seven, respectively, would have changed much in
the almost three years since he had last seen them. He would also
be glad to see his brothers and his mother, his friends, and, not
least, his country home. Nor need he fear too much the reproba-
tion of king and country for his surrender at Yorktown—his
activities had throughout the war won the approval of government and he did not make a good scapegoat for the growing
opposition.

His immediate problem was this capture by the French
privateer *Boulogne*. Normally, Cornwallis and his fellow officers on
parole could have expected to land in some French port, where the
authorities would condemn the *Greyhound* as a prize. Having first
removed the British transport's crew to the privateer, the *Boulogne*'s first lieutenant, Julien Durontois, boarded the *Greyhound*
with a skeleton French crew to sail the prize to Morlaix or Saint
Malo. Weather took a hand, however, and those plans vanished in
a gale. For three days and two nights, the French officers and
crew struggled against the violent winds and weather, but even
with the assistance of their British prisoners they could not navi-
gate the ship. All had grown too exhausted to continue the un-
equal battle, and less than one butt of water remained aboard the

Greyhound. Furthermore, the wind bore the appearance of increasing rather than diminishing. Under these circumstances, Lord Cornwallis and the other British officers, together with the *Greyhound*'s master and passengers, urged Julien Durontois to put into England for assistance "in order to the preservation of our lives." They agreed that he and his prize would be allowed to sail on to France and that they would "consider themselves prisoners in the same situation as if they had arrived in France."[3] Thus, Cornwallis next set foot on English rather than French soil. Because of the kind treatment he had received from the French privateers, Cornwallis later used his influence on behalf of two French officers who had been "plundered of everything" following their capture by Admiral Richard Kempenfelt.[4]

Following his landfall at Torbay, while the *Greyhound* went on to France, Cornwallis proceeded in a triumphal journey to London, lionized along the way. People at Exeter even carried him on their shoulders. He reached the capital on 22 January and moved into the house on Mansfield Street that he had purchased several years earlier. Soon he discovered that the local sentiment that overwhelmed him on the trip to London reflected national opinion among all classes of people with all sorts of political views. No one really seemed to blame him for Yorktown. The ministry in power, on the verge of leaving in disgrace, bore him no ill will. King George III said that he did not "lay anything at the charge of Lord Cornwallis" and that the earl should therefore be presented at the king's levee at Lambeth.[5]

Once back in England, life did not immediately return to normal for Lord Cornwallis. He was still technically a prisoner, and as such he was constrained by his "parole of honor." He therefore avoided attendance at the House of Lords and any conversations that concerned the war.[6] His complete return to usual civilian activities was also prevented by all the unfinished business generated by the American Revolution. Writing a tribute to an officer killed at Yorktown (for the benefit of the man's widow and children), supplying the treasury with lists of the losses sustained by the German troops in Virginia, and dealing with the endless tangle of loyalist pleas and claims all occupied Cornwallis in the months after his return to England.[7] The issue of loyalist claims proved particularly troublesome to him—as a man of conscience he naturally felt both compassion and a sense of responsibility toward them. He indulged in some private charity, but his means were too limited to admit of a great amount of such activity. Fully two years after his return to England, he wrote to his intimate friend and former aide-de-camp, Lieutenant Colonel Alexander Ross: "I am still plagued to death and impoverished by starving Loyalists; but I am now determined to shut the purse, except in the most moving instances of misery."[8] After another half year, however, he reported that he was "as usual pestered to death every morning by wretched starving loyalists."[9]

Yet another war-related matter engaging Cornwallis's attention in the months following his departure from America was his attempt to get himself exchanged. Until that happy occurrence, he remained a prisoner on parole and subject to recall across the Atlantic by the new American government—a whim Congress seemed intent on pursuing during the summer of 1782.[10] Sir Guy Carleton, who succeeded Sir Henry Clinton as commander in chief in America, thought that the Americans practiced "a studied incivility."[11] Cornwallis hoped to get himself exchanged for Henry Laurens, president of the Congress, whom the British had captured while he was en route to Europe to negotiate a treaty with Holland. The exchange did not take place, however, and the earl remained a prisoner on parole even though the British released Laurens from his imprisonment in the Tower. Not until the signing of the Peace of Paris, which released all prisoners on both sides, did Cornwallis regain his freedom.

If his technical status as a prisoner for a time prevented his taking an active part in the House of Lords, he could at least solace himself by renewing his acquaintance with his beloved son and daughter, whom he kept with him whenever he could.[12] He took a father's usual interest in their education and growth. In order to do well by his children, however, he had to improve his depleted finances.

Lacking a substantial income, he had begun dabbling in land transactions in 1769. That year he bought estates in Huntington that in 1772 he sold for £66,000 to a Mr. Flavell. Had the sale worked properly, Cornwallis would probably have made a tidy profit. But Flavell could not raise sufficient cash; the earl therefore held a mortgage from him for £30,000 and kept for himself the woods, fee farm rent, and prebendal lease. Flavell could not, unfortunately, even keep up his interest payments. During the years from 1780 to 1783, when the interest of 5 percent on the mortgage should have brought Cornwallis £4,500, Flavell managed to pay a mere £900. Later, other arrangements would make for prompt and regular payments, but meanwhile the unemployed lieutenant general felt the pinch. Because of expenses in America, he had already sold land in 1777 and 1779. By 1782, he was annually depositing less than £4,000 in Hoare's bank and withdrawing £3,000. For an earl, the sums were beggarly.[13]

The cure for an empty purse was full employment. Impecuniosity alone did not urge the earl toward finding a new appointment in 1782: his was a restless soul that craved activity and responsibility. He had, as well, professional pride in himself as a soldier and wished to see his career recover from the blow that Yorktown had given it. Despite the king's assurances that he did not hold Cornwallis to blame for the military disasters in America, the earl nevertheless tested the wind by taking the honorable course and offering to resign as constable of the Tower (an office whose income he very much needed). The king replied that he did not wish Cornwallis to think of it.[14]

Probably the king's continued trust in Cornwallis owed to the latter's high personal morality. But, however vital the king's trust for political survival in the eighteenth century, a man also needed other support. The earl seemed to have such support from many sources. Charles Townshend commented to William Cornwallis that "very few disapprove Lord Cornwallis's conduct."[15] Perhaps the corporation of Leicester's offer of the freedom of the borough to Cornwallis for his "very gallant & distinguished behaviour and meritorious services in America" expressed better than Townshend the feelings of the nation at large.[16] As for politicians, they liked him because he did not angle for cabinet posts, yet seemed always willing to serve king and country. The North government when in power had blamed Clinton for doing nothing and had encouraged Cornwallis to his Virginia venture, while the opposition had blamed the North government for not giving the earl sufficient support.

Though he did not intrigue in the usual fashion of eighteenth-century politicians, yet he had an ability to cultivate friends among the political opposition. He had early in his career associated with John Wilkes. Now, almost as soon as he arrived in England, he began to keep company with the Earl of Shelburne, who would in March join with Rockingham to form a government to replace that of Lord North. Shelburne possessed an unsavory reputation, whether or not he merited it. In an age noted for political deals, "Malagreda" or the "Jesuit of Berkeley Square," as his contemporaries dubbed him, supposedly conspired and intrigued even more than his peers. Perhaps for that reason, Cornwallis, the man of known principle, attracted him. Shelburne at any rate would soon have the power to help Cornwallis and would use it. The two men had known each other a long time. In 1780, Shelburne had asked Cornwallis to do a favor for one of his friends in America, an impecunious physician in Florida.[17]

When he took office, Shelburne meant to return the favor. In late April or early May of 1782, he proposed that Cornwallis go to India as governor general. Cornwallis liked the offer. He thought his status as a prisoner of war—the only obstacle he saw in the way of accepting the opening—might be easily removed. "I have now," he wrote his brother William, "a prospect of being speedily exchanged, and, if any service offers, of being employed, as there are few of our generals who wish to quit their easy chairs, unless it is to command an English camp."[18]

The collapse of arrangements for his exchange, however, did not alone prevent the earl from accepting the governor generalship. Political developments also delayed the appointment. Another fact of eighteenth-century life was that even the support of the king and prominent politicians might not prevail if luck turned against a man. Such an event for Cornwallis was Rockingham's death in July of 1782. Shelburne then installed his own administration with only minimal political support. Harassed on all sides, he could barely sustain himself in power. Charles James Fox, who had taken over leadership of much of the Rockingham group, refused to serve with "Malagreda" and began to work with the faction led by the former premier, Lord North. Together they mustered more votes in the Commons than Shelburne. Had the latter followed tradition, he would have tried to entice some of the opposition into his administration. But Shelburne held noble though scarcely realistic political views. He believed in a nonparty or nonfactional system and thought the best individuals should rally to government regardless of their political affiliation. He was well-intentioned. He wanted to make economic reforms. He wished for a peace that would not only heal old wounds but also keep a free flow of commerce between the United States and Britain. These goals he planned to obtain by granting all the concessions America demanded. Indeed, in the preliminaries signed in February of 1783, Americans enjoyed the rights of Englishmen with respect to trade. But by this concession Shelburne overreached himself. He had gone too far with too little political support. "The country would accept peace," the historian Steven Watson has noted, "because it needed it, but then condemn the man who made it." [19] In late February, Fox and North combined to defeat Shelburne's peace proposals and bring him down. He resigned on 24 February. Fox and North then forced themselves into office, much to the chagrin of George III. They ratified the peace treaties, but repudiated the commercial arrangements.

These developments left Cornwallis's prospects up in the air. Anxious all the while for an appointment, he nonetheless remained away from politics as much as he could.[20] Although the earl admitted to his friends at the time that his "partiality" lay toward the opposition to Fox-North, he would not act with that opposition. He still somehow believed the government was committed to giving him command in India.[21] But he could not run with the hare and hunt with the hounds. He could not be a friend of Fox-North and remain the king's friend. George III hated the coalition, employed them only because he had no alternative, and intended to dump them as soon as he found one. Fox, the fat, jovial, good-natured wastrel, who had inherited a fortune that he did his best to gamble away, displeased the ascetic George in two unforgivable ways: he led what his sovereign considered an immoral private life; and in politics he had steadily opposed the prosecution of the war in America, in what the king regarded as almost a personal vendetta against him. Lord North, once the king's favorite minister, the man who had lost America, had also committed two unforgivable sins: he had left office, thus deserting King George; and then he had tried to come back in alliance with the detestable Fox.

In October and early November of 1783, Cornwallis heard

rumors that the king had talked to North, that the ministry had proposed him for governor general, and so forth, but by the middle of November he began to awaken to reality. The ministry had not approached him about being governor general before it introduced a bill to revamp the government of India. "I cannot possibly conceive," the earl noted, "but that if Administration had any serious intention of employing me, they would have sounded me before the matter was brought into Parliament." [22]

Now the peer who had previously shunned politics changed tactics and acted politically. Since he could not get his desired office from this ministry, he no longer had any reason to hold himself back from joining the opposition toward which his own inclinations lay. He knew also that the king hated the coalition and would welcome his general's conversion, a notion the ousted Shelburne reinforced. [23] Thus, in mid-November, Cornwallis decided to become active in opposing the Fox-North ministry. Perhaps its successor would employ him.

Meanwhile, George III drifted with the coalition until Fox's India bill passed the House of Commons in November, to the dismay of the East India Company. In early December, a group of professional administrators, forerunners of the civil service, calculated the chances a new ministry would have of acquiring and maintaining power against the coalition. They deemed those chances good, once the new administration could hold a general election to improve its base of support. Leaders of the opposition informed the king of these calculations. They added that they had found just the right man, William Pitt the younger, son of the great war minister, the Earl of Chatham, who was ready to take over should George III dismiss his present government. Armed with this information, the monarch could at last do battle with his despised ministers. Accordingly, he instructed the House of Lords, which had not yet voted on the India bill, to reject it. George allowed Earl Temple to spread it about that "whoever voted for the India Bill was not only not his [the king's] friend, but would be considered by him as an enemy." [24]

Cornwallis, never one to disobey his sovereign, came down from his country seat to help defeat the measure. The Lords subsequently refused it with a majority of nineteen. The king had won. Fox-North had lost. On the morning of 19 December 1783, William Pitt became "prime minister" (technically, first lord of the treasury and chancellor of the exchequer).

In the midst of these political changes and uncertainties about his own prospects, Cornwallis experienced trouble in making up his mind what actions he should take. It was not merely that he had to make calculations about what would prove the most fruitful political course for him to follow. He also underwent very real torments of conscience, finding himself tugged and pulled in opposite directions by many internal forces. Thus, just as his sense of generosity toward the loyalists and the children of a feckless friend had wrestled with his sense of duty toward his own children, so his sense of honor and dignity wrestled with his need for money.[25] Could he with honor retain the post of constable of the Tower, a political rather than military appointment, after he had helped defeat the ministry under which he had held that office? Even before he had known of the change of ministry, he had determined to resign the Tower.[26] Indeed, he later admitted that he probably should have quit that office as soon as the Fox-North coalition came in.[27] Having finally made the decision to resign, he declared that he felt "at least the satisfaction that I have no humiliating sensations to undergo, and that although I shall have lost a much greater part of my income than I could afford, I have lost no character, which is more than most of the *dramatis personae* can say."[28]

Whether his actions were motivated purely by considerations of principle, they did not in fact work to his disadvantage politically. By voting with the opposition against the Fox-North India bill, he had undoubtedly won the gratitude of the king as well as the new ministry. Furthermore, Cornwallis's resignation called attention to himself just at a time when Pitt, running a government that commanded only a minority in Commons, needed friends desperately. Pitt immediately tried to press the earl into service.

The service offered, however, was not in Calcutta but in Dublin. On 26 December, Pitt proposed to the king that Cornwallis should have the lord lieutenancy of Ireland—an idea the king liked, but doubted the earl would accept. A week later, the rumor had reached Cornwallis that "there is a possibility of its being proposed to me to go to Ireland," but he deemed it "merely wild conjecture" since not a single official syllable had reached him from the members of the government.[29] When the offer came, through the home secretary, Lord Sydney, Cornwallis replied with the greatest discretion: "I should refuse with reluctance any situation in which the present Ministry think I can be serviceable to them, and . . . my secrecy on such an occasion might be most perfectly depended on. I know it is not pleasant to have employments refused."[30] The earl declined Ireland, as the king had predicted.

India, however, was another matter. The government continued for the first seven months of 1784 to dangle in front of Cornwallis the prospect of his going there. He did not regard the prospects so dangled as a carrot. Again some intense soul-searching took place, as Cornwallis's private wishes to remain at home "at his ease" with his beloved children warred with his sense of duty and public service. At the same time, his love of military service and his professional ambitions found their counterbalance in a cautious attitude toward military and political realities. He had no intention of going to India unless he had supreme power in both the civil and military (unless, in other words, he combined the offices of governor general and commander in chief) and unless he could overrule his council, a right denied previous governors general, including the unfortunate Warren Hastings. Without such powers, he could not serve his country and could only expect to ruin his own reputation. His natural inclinations urged him to decline an appointment as fruitless as he deemed India.[31]

By late May 1784, the government apparently decided to meet Cornwallis's terms, for when Lord Sydney again pressed him to go to India, and he again objected to the limited powers of the military command without the civil command as well, Sydney assured him that Pitt wished him to have both. With this impediment seemingly removed, Cornwallis underwent yet stronger torments of conscience than before. He still did not want to leave the comforts of home and family, but he promised Sydney he would carefully study the final India bill brought in by the government, and if it seemed to answer his objections, he "might perhaps be induced to sacrifice every prospect of comfort and happiness in this world, to the service of my country and the advantage of my family."[32]

His mental agitation was great. Even should the final plan put forward for the government of India prove to offer him the chance for useful service there, he found that

inclination cries out every moment, Do not think of it; reject all offers; why should you volunteer plague and misery? duty then whispers, You are not sent here merely to please yourself; the wisdom of Providence has thought fit to put an insuperable bar to any great degree of happiness; can you tell, if you stay at home, that the loss of your son, or some heavy calamity, may not plunge you in the deepest despair? try to be of some use; serve your country and your friends; your confined circumstances do not allow you to contribute to the happiness of others by generosity and extensive charity; take the means which God is willing to put into your hands.[33]

This heroic wrestling match between desire and duty, which ended in a decision for duty, ultimately proved not a championship bout but a practice round. The East India Bill brought forward in August kept the military and civil commands separate. Cornwallis could have one or the other, whichever he wished. The earl refused either: should he become governor general he would "abandon a profession to which I have from my youth wholly turned my thoughts"; should he, on the other hand, take the military command, the circumscribed powers of that position would enable him neither to earn credit for himself nor to render service to the public.[34] After his flat refusal to serve without both commands, he heard no more from the ministry about India and by September deemed "that business as absolutely and finally concluded."[35]

Now the earl sat back and waited for the mountain to come to Mohammed. He did not, would not, could not grovel and bootlick among the politicians for a post.[36] Besides, had he not been assured by Lord Sydney that the government of Pitt as well as the king himself regarded with favor his desire for a military appointment? Fully expecting to receive the governorship of Plymouth when its keys passed from the dying Lord Waldegrave's hands, Cornwallis could not believe that the government did not bear toward him the gratitude he plainly felt they owed him. He could not bring himself to ask for Plymouth, thinking it "indelicate" to request "anything specific."

His disappointment and disillusionment were complete by November, when the ministry granted to other persons the next two military "plums" that fell vacant: Plymouth and the colonelcy of a regiment of Grenadier Guards. Deeply wounded (more than at any other time of his life) in his professional and personal pride, he reacted with uncharacteristic anger and vehemence on his own personal account. He held two stormy conferences with Lord Sydney on 3 and 6 November. The home secretary tried to spread oil on the waters. He protested, at the end of the second meeting, that they could not part on such terms, to which Cornwallis answered, "We can part on no other," and stalked from the room. What hurt Cornwallis most was "the contempt and neglect" with which he had been treated: the government had never even considered his name for the vacant military appointment. The earl imagined that "every fool I met in the street condoled with and pitied me." He had now "done forever with Kings and Ministers," he announced.[37]

But two days later he considered it his duty to inform Pitt directly of what had happened and of his own reactions to those occurrences; theretofore his only communications with the government had taken place through Lord Sydney, with whom he was now more than a little dissatisfied.[38] Thus Pitt took on the task at which Sydney had failed: to mollify the aroused earl. Disclaiming on the part of government any intention of slighting so valued a servant and friend, Pitt offered Cornwallis the constableship of the Tower, a position that had by now (since Cornwallis's last tenure of it) been declared a military rather than a civil one. This sop the earl allowed himself to be talked into accepting.[39] He deemed it "in point of income and security . . . as good as Plymouth," although he still felt "most sensibly and seriously mortified." Nonetheless, he determined to put past events behind him.[40]

The misunderstanding and disappointments, as well as the ultimate reconciliation, of that autumn served to illustrate afresh the realities of eighteenth-century British politics (if not of all politics through the eras): ministers tend to reward persons who put themselves before ministerial eyes rather than those to whom a debt of gratitude may be owed; and the squeaky gate gets the oil. On the one hand, Cornwallis's feelings of delicacy, which prevented his pushing his case and caused him to sit back and wait for the government to offer him positions, almost ensured that the administration would ignore him. On the other hand, his outrage over his treatment almost ensured that the administration would find something to offer him.

Although not preoccupied chiefly with politics and certainly not a consummate politician, Cornwallis yet could see ministerial chicanery well enough. Thus he recognized that the cabinet were trying to use him as a pawn to patch up disputes among themselves, when, in February of 1785, Pitt again urged him to go to India, promising some alterations in the bill if he would accept. The earl refused.[41]

The homework he had done to prepare himself for Indian command must now have seemed a barren labor.[42] Fortunately, other activities had occupied some of his time since his return from America, so that all fronts did not present merely wasted effort. He had done "military reading" to broaden his understanding of his profession.[43] Also, as became an eighteenth-century earl, he had cultivated his parliamentary influence at Eye, maintaining almost open house for a month each year at Brome, getting his brother William elected to Parliament by the Eye constituency, and carefully drafting a letter to the Gentlemen of the Corporation of Eye to explain his (at one time) intended departure for several years in India.[44] Of course, as head of the house, he concerned himself a great amount with his motherless children, worrying especially about the sometimes fragile health of his son and about his widowed and aging mother.

Spring of 1785 found him engaged in more immediately professional activities as a member of a Board of Land and Sea Officers inspecting the fortifications at the seaports. The board worked long hours—sometimes thirteen hours a day—and considerable disagreement occurred among the members about what Portsmouth and Plymouth needed in the way of improved defenses. Cornwallis did not find much enjoyment in the work, probably more because of his colleagues than because of the long hours. "Suppose to yourself," he wrote, "the utmost of all human misery, and your supposition must fall greatly short of our condition . . . God only knows when our misfortunes can end; I think they may last two or three months. Tell all my friends that they must not expect to hear from me, and to be satisfied if they do not see in the papers that I have hanged myself." [45] While thus disagreeably engaged in proceedings "the most extraordinary and the most tiresome that you can conceive," the earl decided to visit the Continent during the summer to attend the Prussian military reviews. [46]

He was not allowed, however, to go in a purely private capacity. The British government impressed him for a diplomatic mission to the court of Frederick the Great to sound out that monarch's sentiments on a possible alliance between England and Prussia. Presumably, the errand had some chance of success, owing to Cornwallis's high reputation and unofficial station and owing to the Prussian minister, Count Lusi, having said that Frederick would like to talk with some "confidential person" from England. Because neither country genuinely desired an alliance and because Frederick was struck by illness immediately after the interview with Cornwallis, it is understandable that no lasting diplomatic gains accrued to either country. The interlude served, nonetheless, to introduce the earl to the toils of diplomacy and to the stuff of intrigue. Neither appealed to him. His written instructions from the secretary of state, Francis, Lord Carmarthen, arrived by way of a messenger disguised first as a common traveler and later as a valet-de-chambre. [47]

The Prussian expedition acquainted Cornwallis with diplomacy and secrecy and also gave him an opportunity to take the measure of one of the sons of George III, the Duke of York, who would eventually become commander in chief of the British forces. York was with the earl in Berlin and later in Hanover. Cornwallis liked the young royal duke, who was only twenty-one at the time, but thought his military ideas "those of a wild boy of the Guards," an opinion the duke's later conduct did nothing to dispel. Cornwallis nevertheless maintained cordial relations with York and corresponded with him regularly thereafter. [48]

The earl returned home having enjoyed himself less than he had originally anticipated and having been little enlightened in any aspects of his military profession. He had had an unflattering reception from Frederick's court in which a marked preference had been shown for Lafayette. He had found that monarch's Prussia a "sandy desert" and the maneuvers of his infantry "ridiculous."

He also returned home to family troubles. His son, Lord Brome, attended Eton; his daughter Mary, now seventeen, sometimes visited with her great aunt Caroline, widow of the archbishop of Canterbury (Cornwallis's uncle), but often lived at Culford. When a young captain in the guards, Mark Singleton, visited Culford, he fell in love with Lady Mary as soon as he cast eyes upon her. Despite warnings from his parents that the match was unsuitable and that he could never get the earl's consent to a marriage, Singleton persisted in his attentions. After he learned that Cornwallis had traveled to Europe in the summer of 1785, he decided to visit Culford and propose to his love in the absence of her father's constraining influence. He discovered Mary as eager as he for marriage, and the pair eloped to Gretna Green in Scotland and wed. The affair soon became known all over Great Britain. Lady Mary Lindsay wrote to the wife of Archibald Campbell, soon to be Cornwallis's subordinate in India, that it was a "bad business for both."[49]

When he learned of this "bad business," the earl exploded with anger. The boy's father should have prevented the marriage. Mr. Singleton, deeply embarrassed and also contrite, agreed, even though Mark was a second son, to give him a decent settlement and to clear his debts. Cornwallis also eventually reconciled himself to the inevitable and settled on Mary stock worth £400 a year, a sum similar to that given to Mark by his father. But Cornwallis never forgot the elopement and never fully forgave Captain Singleton. In his will he left £10,000 in bank annuities. Interest on these dividends, the will stipulated, should go solely to Lady Mary "exclusive of the said Mark Singleton and any future husband." On her death the stock would revert to her children according to her wishes. During her life she could use it, if she chose, to advance their careers.[50]

Cornwallis had thus had several years and more than his allotted share of uncertainties and disappointments, when, in February of 1786, Pitt again pressed him to go to India. This time, at last, the government met his terms, promising an amending act (which followed in April of 1786) to allow the governor general to hold the additional rank of commander in chief and to override his council. On 23 February 1786, Cornwallis assented to take the supreme command: "Much against my will, and with grief of heart, I have been obliged to say yes, and to exchange a life of ease and content, to encounter all the plagues and miseries of command and public station."[51]

He obviously had to make many preparations, not least regarding his "family" of officers and his financial affairs. The ever faithful Ross gave up his own comfortable establishment as adjutant general of Scotland to accompany his former chief on this new adventure.[52] Cornwallis gave up not only his ease but also some of his new salary: despite his straitened circumstances, he refused the salary of commander in chief, accepting only that of the governor general (a substantial sum of £25,000 per year).[53]

Not everyone thought him a good choice for the new position, but perhaps the most ominous prophecy came from his old comrade in arms, Lord Percy:

By the by [he wrote George Rose], I see the papers announce an intention of sending Lord Cornwallis out to command-in-chief in India. I believe I have often told you my opinion of his lordship. He is a worthy, honest, brave man; but more than all that is necessary to make a good general. I know him well; and I thought since the last business in America, everybody else had known him also. One thing I will venture to foretell (and I beg you will remember it) that if this step is determined upon he will lose his reputation—and we, our territories in that part of the world. He is as fit to command-in-chief as I am to be Prime Minister.[54]

It was just as well the earl knew nothing of this discouraging forecast. He had endured enough trouble getting the post, and he did not need prophets of doom now.

His preparations complete and his business settled, he boarded ship and, following repeated delays owing to contrary winds, he left England in early May 1786. After years of whispering from the shadows, at long last the East beckoned openly.

Chapter 2

The Anglo-Indian Scene

Cornwallis now entered a world very different from any he had known. Earlier European arrivals had found in India a civilization not inferior to their own. For scores of years the Mogul Empire had held sway over the vast and teeming subcontinent. Moslem law and Moslem taxes reached to the millions of Hindus, who outnumbered their conquerors. Indians made their own brass cannon, sometimes far superior to the iron cannon that prevailed in Europe. They had good steel in their swords. They possessed a rich melange of religious, literary, and artistic traditions. And the Westerners were few and weak.

By the middle of the eighteenth century, however, the great political organization that had given strength to Moslem rule had perceptibly declined. Many local chiefs, whether Hindu or Moslem, whether sultans, ranis, or maharajas, had shaken off imperial restraints and established themselves as virtually independent rulers. Personal rivalries and territorial ambitions further divided one region from another. Clever and determined Westerners might play upon local jealousies and manipulate the Indian chiefs to their own advantage and to the disadvantage of Europeans of another country. Thus rivalries and military alliances thrived, and imperial order languished. The Westerners—especially the French and the British—slowly began to grow in numbers and strength. They long remained aliens, however, unwelcome visitors clinging to a tenuous hold along the coast, touching only upon the fringes of Indian culture. Whatever adapting needed doing was for the aliens to do.

Adapt they did. Therein lay one of their greatest strengths. Clothing, diet, exercise, sports, manners—all felt the impact of

India's uncompromising climate and ancient traditions. Nor did the realm of morality remain unaffected. Whatever their previous contact with bribery, intimidation, and judicial discrimination, in none of their countries had they seen them practiced so thoroughly, so constantly, and so skillfully as in India. Many of the newcomers had little trouble adapting to the new morality. Having come as adventurers—was there another reason?—and having found that great prizes awaited the bold and resourceful, should they adhere to foreign codes and customs and thereby surrender to others the plucking of the bright fruits? India had great wealth: no European monarch or nobleman could compare in his personal estate to the richest of Indian maharajas. That the Westerners sought to accomplish a redistribution of Indian wealth owed nothing at all to European loyalties and traditions. Those who succeeded returned with fortunes. They were the storied "nabobs," of whom Thomas ("Diamond") Pitt was one of the most famous but not exceptional.

They succeeded in the nick of time. Changed circumstances and changed regimes would end forever British complacency toward such Indian-made fortunes. An important step in this process of change was the winning by the British East India Company in 1765 of the right to collect taxes in Bengal, Bihar, and Orissa. For with the collection of taxes went administrative powers and duties; and the British public began to ask whether it was right for a commercial company to exercise such powers over millions of people who lived thousands of miles away. The unregulated days of "John Company" thus ended, and the days of most of the quick and easy fortunes were numbered. To accomplish such a change, the British would need a man of courage and integrity. They found him in the second Earl Cornwallis.

Landfall at Madras

If he felt cultural shock upon his arrival at Madras on 21 August 1786, he did not admit it. His laconic report to Henry Dundas, head of the board of control, mentioned only that he had had "a most prosperous and expeditious passage."[1] Nowhere has he recorded his thoughts and impressions of that strange land which had for so many years loomed large in his thoughts and plans. Thus it is from other travelers that we have descriptions of the Coromandel coast south of Madras, "with a few straggling coconut trees rising out of the haze of the tropical horizon." Perhaps as his ship made its way northward, beyond the settlements of Britain's European rivals—Dutch Negapatam with its symmetrical squares and canals, Danish Tranquebar, and French Pondicherry—he pondered chiefly about the problems of maintaining his nation as the paramount power in India. That he had much to learn of the local situation before he could make important decisions would have become clear as the new sights of the harbor and city spread before him. First came the multitude of catamarans that pushed off from shore and struggled through the triple line of breakers toward his ship when it anchored in the open roads off Madras. Once ashore, he found himself immersed in a bewildering array of colors, sights, and smells and a vast assortment of people speaking a babble of tongues: Hindu merchants in long, flowing robes, natives struggling to advance themselves as chief factotums to the new arrivals, palanquins shoving about. And over everything lay the summer heat like a suffocating blanket. An earlier traveler, the prolific memoirist and rake William Hickey, had found the Coromandel coast "so intensely hot that I could compare it only to standing within the oppressive influence of the steam of a furnace."[2] Cornwallis, who had, after all, campaigned in South Carolina in the summer, would not feel the torments of heat in Madras and Calcutta that plagued so many other Englishmen. Even if not flattened by the heat, however, one wonders whether he reacted to Madras as did a later traveler, John Blakiston, who deemed it the "most dreary spot in existence" yet a welcome one after so long a voyage.[3]

Probably he did not, for he had to look at Madras with a soldier's and administrator's eyes. He also could chat about old times with his former comrade in arms in America, Sir Archibald Campbell, now governor of Madras. The new governor general's tour would have commenced with the East India Company's headquarters of Fort St. George, which contained the government offices, warehouses, and counting houses of merchants. To a military eye it must have seemed a well-engineered defensive fortification, with its outworks, drawbridges, and deep moats. Yet the views to the west and north would give concern to the same mili-

1. India House
   Published 1 August 1809, by W. H. Wyatt, London.

2. Western Entrance of Fort St. George, Madras
   From Thomas Daniell, *Oriental Survey*, II, plate vii.
   Reprinted by permission of the India Office Library and Records, London

tary eye. To the west lay a sandy plain where the English population lived in beautiful one- or two-story white houses pleasantly
surrounded with trees and gardens but without any defenses. To
the north lay Blacktown, a city almost three miles long, with perhaps three hundred thousand people, mostly natives, but containing a sprinkling of English, Dutch, French, and Portuguese.[4] If
the British faltered in their rule and the natives determined to oust
them, the inhabitants of Blacktown alone overwhelmingly outnumbered the English population. Fort St. George would then
need its strong fortifications.

Cornwallis's brief time in Madras was not all business.
Lady Campbell entertained him at the governor's house, next to
a bridge just outside the fort. She made his stay there a pleasant
introduction to Anglo-Indian life, as he later acknowledged. She
herself constituted his introduction to that group of remarkable
people, known to history as the Anglo-Indian imperialists, who
thrived in the eighteenth and nineteenth centuries. Lady Campbell
had almost single-handedly brought British civilization to Madras.
She managed the local theater and sustained an asylum for children. Her presence and influence seem to have restrained Europeans from the "scandalous" behavior that prevailed after her departure.[5] Eventually she received an annuity of £1,500 for life
from the nabob of Arcot and the Carnatic, the titular ruler of
the territory that included Madras.[6] Unfortunately, Cornwallis in
his letters proved as reticent about this remarkable woman as
about many other aspects of the Indian scene, saying only that she
made his stay at Madras "agreeable."

Perhaps administrative problems already occupied his
mind. The new governor general did not long tarry, even in the
company of old friends. He left Madras within two weeks, sailing up the coast to Bengal and the approaches to Calcutta, where
he would take up his new command. At Diamond Harbor his
ship anchored and took on a pilot to guide them around the sand-
banks at the mouth of the Hughli River. At Fulta the earl disembarked and continued the rest of the way on a budgerow, a
long, heavy boat propelled by oars. Had not darkness intervened,
he could have clearly discerned, as he made his slow passage
upstream, evidences of the British impact. The area on both sides
of the river for several miles below Calcutta had earned the name

"Garden Reach." Here were elegant garden houses and the large residence occupied by the superintendent of the Company's botanical garden, which extended along the edge of the river. On the other bank of the river were handsome villas with English-style gardens. Cornwallis's view of Garden Reach would have to wait, for he anchored during the night of Monday, 11 September 1786, at Calcutta.

The morning would reveal to him the shipping of all sorts that plied the river. From his budgerow he had his first view of Fort William, the strongest fortification in Bengal, which defended the Company's position. He could also glimpse the famous Esplanade that extended inland or eastward from the river, at right angles to a line between the fort and the town.[7] And, of course, he saw the governor's bodyguard drawn up at quayside to welcome him formally.

At long last he set foot in Calcutta, the "city of palaces," the capital of Bengal and of British India. He walked the short distance to Fort William, where acting governor John Macpherson received him with formal ceremony, the troops under arms and on parade. With his commissions duly read, Cornwallis officially became the governor general and commander in chief of all British India. He went in to breakfast with John Shore, a Company servant who had made the voyage with him, and his military "family," Alexander Ross, Henry Haldane, and his nephew Spencer Madan.

Calcutta Life

Getting to know the people, habits, and places of Calcutta obviously formed an essential part of his official duties. But here duty could combine with pleasure, for he could meet many of the people on social occasions and see many of the places on his daily rides. Certainly the city, where he would spend so much of his time in the next seven years, was an interesting one. Although some adaptations to Indian climate and conditions had been necessary, the British had contrived to bring much of their familiar world with them. Their architecture followed the symmetrical, graceful, neoclassical lines of the Georgian style. The Esplanade, with its row of public buildings, was Calcutta's pride. There stood the governor's palace, government house, the court house, the council house, and the writers' building where the Company had its administrative offices. Yet the city offered sharp contrasts. The squalor of native dwellings huddled cheek by jowl against the splendid façades of the European ones, since, unlike Madras, Calcutta did not set its black and white towns apart. From the Maidan, the area cleared around Fort William to afford the artillery an ample field of fire, the city also gained a park. Like the English aristocracy of the sixteenth century, who built their magnificent homes along the Thames River from London to Westminster, the Company's servants of the eighteenth century constructed theirs along the Hughli from Garden Reach to Barrackpore (where Cornwallis eventually resided). They used stuccoed brick, painted it white, and had venetian blinds to keep out sun and folding doors to keep out dust. They imported the best furniture they could find, walked on splendid carpets, and slept in the large beds characteristic of the time.

The wonderful mix of Europe and Asia must have immediately struck Cornwallis. The artist Thomas Daniell, in his views of Calcutta, plate 2, portrayed a typical street scene along the Esplanade. Although both courthouse and writers' building have pillars and porticoes, the graceful arches in the one contrast with the long, symmetrical rows of windows in the other. The street itself is a hive of activity. In the foreground a European lady reclines in a palanquin borne by natives. Behind her follows another native leading two braces of dogs. Another lady, in a large coach pulled by two horses, with rider in front and coach boy behind, gets directions through the coach window from a European riding alongside on horseback. Down the street appear the ever-present bullocks, carts, Indian merchants strolling, and idlers talking to a sepoy.

Like the aristocrats at home in Britain, Calcutta's rulers surrounded themselves with servants. Many of the Company's personnel, who could never have afforded many domestics in England, easily employed them in India, where labor was plentiful and cheap. According to a pair of European observers, the average gentleman required for his needs a professor of languages, a native officekeeper, clerks, a barber, a baton bearer and pole bearer (both of whom announced guests and received and delivered notes and

3. Old Court House and Writers Building, Calcutta
From Thomas Daniell, *Views of Calcutta*, plate ii.
Reprinted by permission of the India Office Library and Records,
London

4. The Return from Hog-Hunting
From Williamson Howlett, *Oriental Field Sports*, plate vii.
Reprinted by permission of the India Office Library and Records,
London

messages), a head servant, a messenger, table servants, a head of household, torch bearers, a khelassy to keep the punka going, a man to purchase as well as to receive and disburse moneys, a pipe bearer, a snake catcher, a tailor, and for some gentlemen, dancing girls.[8]

Although households graced with a European mistress probably lacked the dancing girls, her presence would dictate a host of other servants, over whom she presided as at court. In 1782, an Indian artist depicted the domestic life of Mrs. Elijah Impey, wife of the justice. In a corner of her boudoir stands a cagelike crib with netting over it to protect her baby from insects. Two ayahs, or nurses, tend the child so that Mrs. Impey can devote her time to other concerns. The management of an army of servants required considerable time and attention to details. In her room, with its typical high ceiling, plush carpeting, wainscoting, and probably the usual lime-washed walls, Mrs. Impey receives and gives directions to her gardeners, her milliner, her tailors, and the punka boy with his fan, a total of fourteen servants. Cornwallis, indeed, showed conservatism in this regard, for in his day government house employed only fifty-seven servants.[9]

This multitude of servants obviously required supervision, but they also afforded the Anglo-Indians a great amount of leisure time in which to enjoy themselves. Like Englishmen everywhere, they were avid sportsmen. They bet freely on their horse races and spent freely to construct suitable buildings next to the racecourse, such as the marvelous Georgian assembly rooms at Madras. They played squash and cricket. In addition, some of the sports they engaged in were indigenous to India. Swaying in their howdahs atop elephants, they hunted tigers. Fearless riders, they pursued wild pigs on horseback, armed only with a spear. They also indulged in the cruel "sport" of pitting animal against animal in a fight to the death and would watch from grandstand seats above a stockade while a buffalo gored a tiger. One time at Lucknow, to celebrate Cornwallis's victory over Tipoo, the nawab put on a show that featured fights between elephants and fights among deer, rams, bears, bullocks, and buffaloes.[10]

The British had brought with them to Bengal not only many of the sports, but also many of the refinements of their life back home. They put on concerts and amateur theatricals. They created clubs of all sorts. Young men took tea with young ladies in the afternoon.

Even these recreations and diversions together with their official work for the Company did not consume all their hours. They still found time for scientific and humanitarian undertakings. Charities and circulating libraries flourished in British India. Such individuals as Sir William Jones did monumental work in making Indian culture known to the Indians as well as to the British. The botanical garden experimented with fruit, seeds, and plants. Indeed, one of Cornwallis's commissions was to send from Calcutta and other parts of India such "fruits, seeds, and plants, as may be sufficiently valuable to be transported to St. Vincents," which also had a botanical garden.[11] This fascination with botanical experimentation had unexpected results: in the same year as the order to Cornwallis, it led the *Bounty* to the Pacific and the most famous mutiny in history.

The British performed all their various activities in a frenetic atmosphere, never certain whether they would survive the climate to return to the British Isles. Survival and return home were the most important goals for most of the Company's servants. Life in England was precarious and cheap, but it was far more so in India. Bengal witnessed even more (per capita) robberies, assaults, and murders than did rowdy, lawless England. Dacoit (robber) bands roved in the thousands. Housebreaking and kidnapping were common. Nor did crime in India confine itself to the native population. Westerners who lacked official positions and responsibility robbed other Westerners and assaulted them mercilessly. In 1791, the police superintendent caught eight men, all Europeans, who had committed robbery and murder.[12] "Portuguese" gangs, deserters from ships, and others made life extremely hazardous for the ordinary Company servants, civil or military.[13] Officers were not safe once away from their commands. Even these dangers, however, paled before the constant threat of death from snakebite, cholera, typhus, typhoid, or other disease. Everyone in Calcutta knew that many, many Company people who had come out to India would leave their bones there.

Not surprisingly, numerous British lived each day as if it was their last on earth. Too often, what began as decorous dinners or balls ended with drunken debaucheries, quarreling, and duels. People understandably took the attitude that they must make their fortunes quickly so they could return to England before India claimed them. Thus vice mingled daily with refinement. Many people determined to use any means possible—fraud, deceit, chicanery—in order to make money. With callous indifference they cheated, lied, beat the native inhabitants, and sired illegitimate children whom they never took care of.

A New Example

Cornwallis gave life in British Bengal a new tone. As governor general he took official measures to stop the lawlessness, the riot, and the fraud. A plainspoken man with simple, even ascetic, tastes, he expected those who served him to practice the same honesty that he himself did. Thus he set new standards for the rulers. But his private acts proved even more important than his public ones in changing Calcutta's habits. By his own example he led English society away from the prevailing evils of drunkenness, callousness, and dishonesty. In their place he substituted dignified assemblies, charitable work, honesty, sobriety, courtesy, and an end to pompous display. Yet he took care to retain the ceremony and the pageantry proper to rulers whose power over their subjects depended as much on moral force as on military force.

Cornwallis, of course, did not alone accomplish the reform of British India. Part of the change owed to the arrival in Bengal of larger numbers of wives and daughters. The women had something of a sobering effect on the men's manners and entertainments. The satirical observer John Blakiston later noted that "petticoats" still remained scarce, making the matrimonial market compare to the one for livestock. The unmarried women invariably attended the balls, and any bachelors aspiring to wedded bliss had to act with at least a modicum of manners. Had a lady any charms, she could take her pick, and "she must be a hapless virgin indeed, who might be compelled to put up with an ensign of native infantry, with whom she would spend a honeymoon in a hill fort."[14]

Cornwallis's tenure thus coincided with the beginning of a

more refined society, a refinement he urged and hastened. Indeed, remarkable changes occurred in the seven years he held office. When he first came to Bengal in 1786, men still played the female parts in theatrical productions (as in the England of Shakespeare, rather than that of Dr. Johnson). By 1789 women began appearing on the stage. The next year actresses regularly played female roles in the Calcutta playhouses.[15] Some of the women were quite remarkable. Mrs. John Bristow, for example, erected a private theater in her house in Calcutta, where she delivered the prologue to the *Poor Soldier* and acted the part of Nora. She rode astride like a man and beat some of the best jockeys in horse races. She shot with the best and rarely missed her bird. She even understood the science of pugilism, knocking down anyone who insulted her. In addition, she bore four children.[16]

In the same period, another touch of refinement, circulating lending libraries, began to spread out from Calcutta into the interior. Although the English in India had for years been playing their decorous sport of cricket, during Cornwallis's time cricket clubs began to organize, thus in a sense ritualizing the game.[17] Typically English social clubs also flourished. Cornwallis's staff immediately became members of the Bachelors' Club in Calcutta, and the earl himself became an original member of the Eton Club in 1790.[18]

If such developments seem inevitable, Cornwallis speeded up the process and made them a firm part of British India. Hickey noticed the changed atmosphere almost from the moment the new governor general alighted from his budgerow. Soon after Cornwallis's arrival, the paymaster general of His Majesty's forces, William Burke, invited the earl and his staff to dinner. Everyone drank a good deal of wine during the meal. Around eight o'clock Burke excused himself for a few minutes. In his absence Cornwallis ordered his carriage, but just as he started to enter it his host reappeared and pleaded with him to remain, arguing that it was too early to break up such a splendid party. The earl steadfastly refused, declaring that he had already drunk too much, more than he had consumed in years, and that he had no intention of incapacitating himself for business next day. He had become sufficiently mellow, however, to tease his "family" into lingering on. When the paymaster bodily tried to prevent Ross from entering the carriage behind his chief, the latter applauded: "Aye, aye, that's right, that's right. Keep Ross. I don't want him nor any one of the family. Keep them all Burke." And he clattered away alone without troopers or even a servant behind the carriage. Ross and the others remained, drinking toast after toast until one o'clock. That particular evening with Burke was the nearest to inebriation Cornwallis ever allowed himself to come and the one and only time during his stay in India that Ross "committed a debauch."[19]

The new governor general's ideas on the proper order of society soon manifested themselves in other ways. In 1788, Cornwallis ordered that the Company's old courthouse must no longer serve as a tavern "or for any other purpose whatsoever" without his "particular" permission. At the same time he informed the managers of concerts, public assemblies, and all societies of "ladies and gentlemen of the settlement" that they would "always" receive his permission to use the rooms for their purposes. He set about refurbishing the building and its furnishings so as to fit it for its proper use as a place for public gatherings rather than for tavern brawls.[20]

Cornwallis shunned ostentation as much as he endorsed the social amenities. He dropped public breakfasts as an unnecessary waste of time and money and instead ate with his staff.[21] Immediately upon coming to Bengal he established regular hours, from eight to ten on Tuesday and Thursday mornings, for his public receptions or levees.[22] Though he later reduced these affairs in number, he always remained open to private application.[23]

He frowned upon displays of bad manners at the receptions. Hickey tells what happened at one levee when Colonel Auchmuty, a boisterous and uncouth Irishman with three sons in the Company service, approached the earl. Cornwallis, who made it a point to talk to everyone, opened the conversation:

"You must have good friends in Leadenhall Street, Colonel, to get so large a proportion of your family provided for in this part of the world." To which the Colonel replied, "Faith and you may say that, my Lord. By my soule, I had many friends there sure enough, staunch ones too; no fewer than five thousand, my Lord!" Lord Cornwallis looking greatly astonished, the Colonel said, "You seem surprized my Lord, but it's very true for all that, no fewer, by Jesus, than five thousand, my Lord, all bright shiners! Shiners I assure you, my Lord!" accompanying the latter words with the action of his hands as if counting money from one to the other.

Cornwallis perfectly understood Auchmuty's meaning, yet could not believe the colonel would brazenly discuss bribery with the very man who had made it part of his official policy to stop such practices. After a pause, the governor general continued the exchange of words:

"Upon my word, Colonel Auchmuty, I do not understand you, your language is perfectly incomprehensible to me." "Auch!" (roared Paddy), "not understand me. That's droll *Bathershun* (which is Irish for *may be so*). Why, then, my Lord, though I thought I fully explained myself, I'll spake more plain. I gave the lads of Leadenhall Street five thousand guineas, true sterling, Gold British Guineas, no less nor more, my Lord, for the writerships in Bengal, though they wanted to fob me off with a Madras one, for my two eldest whelps, and so in the generosity of their hearts they threw a Cadetship into the bargain, for my youngest spalpeen!"

At this outrageous outburst, according to Hickey, Cornwallis "turned upon his heel and abruptly left the Colonel." [24]

Auchmuty's boorishness was an unusual display, for not many people so flew in the face of Cornwallis's obvious expectations regarding decorum and honesty. In all ways he tried to set a good example to the other British. He subscribed to all sorts of charitable work and was one of the first to donate money when Lady Campbell at Madras planned an asylum for female Protestant children, white and nonwhite. He gave handsomely toward the expenses of building a new church in Calcutta and attended its consecration. He contributed to the "Associates for extending the fisheries and improving the coast of the kingdom," to the establishment of a free elementary school, to a fund to assist a dentist who had served Calcutta for eleven years and then lost his sight, and indeed to practically every worthwhile charity in British India. [25]

That he could do so owed only in part to his new wealth, the salary of £25,000 as governor general. It also owed to his simple, unostentatious life, which avoided such extravagances as gambling, pompous hospitality, and excesses in food and drink. He did enjoy wine and had it shipped out from England, along with other assorted spirits necessary for entertainment. He also received from home his uniforms, boots, books, magazines, newspapers, and even toothpaste. But he carefully accounted for all expenses and did not spend lavishly. His greatest personal indulgence, for he liked to read at night, was his collection of books.[26] According to one historian of British India, his house at Barrackpore was "of inferior pretensions to many that were held by the leading servants of the Company."[27] During the hot weather, he slept at night on the special barge he normally used to take him to his house.[28]

His daily routine was so simple and regular that it attracted the notice of most Calcutta residents. He was "rigidly constant" in his exercise, getting up at dawn every morning to ride on horseback six or seven miles.[29] Then he would breakfast, address himself to government business before and after lunch, and in the evening drive out, usually accompanied by Ross, in his phaeton. After that he would read or write, sit down with his officers for some fruit or a biscuit, and get to bed by ten. "I don't think the greatest *sap* at Eton," he told his son Lord Brome, "can lead a duller life than this."[30]

Yet this life, though abstemious, was rarely as dull or desk-bound as he described it. He wished to set an example, but to do that His Majesty's chief representative could not isolate himself in government house. His duties often carried him afield. In July of 1787, he took a trip upriver in his barge to visit British military posts in Bengal, Bihar, and Oudh. When he docked at various points, natives often flocked aboard to press upon him their suits.[31] Once when he left his barge to go into a smaller boat, a sudden squall nearly capsized it; help, had it been needed, was far away.[32] On the same trip he worried about ceremonial, the proper salutes, and so forth. He periodically reviewed the artillery at Dum Dum, where they performed drills, maneuvers, and demonstrations of firing.[33] He received ceremonial visits from important native potentates and fretted about the proper gifts to give them.[34] On one occasion he tried to find the smallest full-grown elephant in India as a gift for the peshwa of Poona. The earl hoped he would appreciate it as a curiosity.[35]

As head of government all manner of concerns fell within his cognizance. Worried about the possibility of fire in Fort Wil-

liam, in 1787 he ordered that illumination there should henceforward utilize only candles, not torches.[36] His concern proved
justified but the precaution insufficient. In March of 1789, during
his morning ride, a huge conflagration started in the artillery
artificers yard, which was surrounded by buildings two stories
high filled with various stores. The fire burned up one building
and all its stores. That morning, at least, the governor general's
ride was scarcely "routine."[37]

That he led society as well as government necessarily involved him in social affairs: entertainments, balls, masquerades,
and receptions. Cornwallis never shirked this duty, whether it
consisted of ceremonial for himself or entertainment for the Company servants. He received the Order of the Garter shortly after
his arrival in India. In the presence of the Europeans invited to
witness the occasion, Charles Stuart ceremoniously invested him
with the Order, while Fort William fired a twenty-one gun salute.[38] Again, when Cornwallis returned from his successful war
against Tipoo in 1793 and learned that the king had elevated him
to a marquisate, he formally received the honor at government
house with full ceremony—as Hickey said, with "great pomp
and state."[39] The governor general regularly entertained Calcutta
society with balls and suppers, and he supported those entertainments, exhibitions, and charities which he did not originate.
He consistently and conscientiously patronized the theater and
had printed in the Calcutta Gazette, the government newspaper,
a public apology when business forced his absence from a performance.[40]

A typical invitation in the Gazette would run to the effect
that "Lord Cornwallis presents his compliments to the Gentlemen
of the Honorable Company's Civil and Military Service, and requests the favour of their company on Monday, the 18th December, at the Old Court house to a Dinner, and to a Ball and Supper
in the evening." The busiest social season occurred from December through February, when he gave such entertainments nearly
once a week. Although he spent enough on entertaining at these
public assemblies to rival or even surpass, for taste and elegance,
those held in the past, their character was altered. According to
the historian John Kaye, previous to Cornwallis's arrival in Calcutta, people had rarely danced after supper. "The gentlemen-

dancers," Kaye noted, "were commonly too far gone in drink to venture upon any experiments of activity demanding the preservation of the perpendicular. But when Lord Cornwallis set his mark on Anglo-Indian society, all this changed."[41] The drinking did not stop, but fewer and fewer people overindulged in it, and dancing came to surpass drink as an entertainment. At one typical affair in January of 1788, dancing of the minuet continued until almost midnight. The guests then partook of an elegant supper, after which they danced again until four in the morning. Most of the ladies and gentlemen "partook in the pleasures of the dance, though a few votaries of Bacchus kept their places."[42]

Some of these parties were lavish and expensive. Perhaps the most elaborate one Cornwallis himself ever gave occurred in July of 1789, when he wished to celebrate George III's recovery from an illness that had threatened him with permanent insanity. At sunrise on Tuesday, 28 July, the artillery from Fort William fired a salute. At one o'clock that afternoon the ships with guns lying off Calcutta fired another salute. At three o'clock the earl gave a dinner attended by the governors of the Dutch, French, and Danish settlements. At sunset another salute of twenty-one guns boomed out from the fort, followed by a feu de joie performed on the Esplanade by the artillery and by two companies of the 76th regiment and the 4th battalion of the Company's European infantry. That night the inhabitants illuminated the town with mottoes such as "God save the King" (though rain dampened the splendor). There followed a concert, fireworks, and supper.[43]

The commemoration of the Seringapatam victory, which Cornwallis dutifully attended from beginning to end, dwarfed even the earl's largest display. Given by the principal officers of the Company's civil service on 6 February 1793 at the Calcutta theater, it attracted a huge crowd of spectators, whose palanquins pushed one against another. The theater held paintings depicting various heroic moments in the campaign. The boxes and galleries were gay with canopies of silk, banners, and military trophies, a giant transparent view of Seringapatam, and transparent pictures of all the principal forts the commander in chief had captured. Flowers, laurels, and foil decorated the ceiling and entwined the pillars. Mirrors ornamented the walls. At eleven in the evening the dancing began; each lady was attired in a uniform dress of white satin and gold fringe. An hour later the company adjourned to the supper rooms with their splendidly decorated tables and afterward returned to dance the night away.[44] Hickey estimated the cost at somewhere in the vicinity of £7,000, "an enormous sum for a single night's amusement."[45] However little such extravagance suited the governor general's taste, he remained to the end, as behooved his position.

With his emphasis on entertainments at once elegant and properly decorous, Cornwallis set an example for future governors general. Shore, who succeeded him, thought he could do the official work as well as or better than anyone alive, but he doubted whether he could ever set the social tone as well.[46] He could not, for he was neither a nobleman nor a victorious general. But he wanted to do so, because he realized that the social atmosphere the governor general created might be as important as the calculation of revenues. When Richard, Lord Wellesley came, he continued and vastly expanded on the Cornwallis tradition, which became an integral custom of British India.[47]

Chapter 3

Reform and Expansion

The East India Company had done well as a profitable trading organization from its inception in 1601 up until the middle of the eighteenth century. Its financial troubles had their origins in the decline of the Mogul Empire, which began to break up early in the eighteenth century. To defend its right to trade, to stay in India despite the French efforts to oust it, and to preserve its independence from domination by any one native power, the Company had increasingly concentrated its attention on defense and administration, to the detriment of trade. Defense and administration cost money. Even so, in the 1730s the Company profited from its exports to England of cotton piece goods, raw silk, pepper, saltpeter, coffee, tea, chinaware, and drugs. The Company paid for these goods (the "investment") with silver, base metals, and woolens. At this time, also, the interests of the directors and their employees did not differ basically. The directors paid their servants very low salaries, but allowed them to earn additional money by trading on their own, an arrangement that worked profitably for both sides, because the servants then were primarily traders at the "factories," or trading posts. Within a few decades, however, the Company's situation underwent dramatic changes.

Commerce and Communications

Beginning in the 1760s, profits from Bengal fell so drastically as to put the Company in debt. Indeed, when Cornwallis went to India the Company owed £11,800,000 in Britain and over £9,700,000 in India—staggering sums for the eighteenth century.

37

Several factors accounted for the debt. As the industrial revolution took hold in Britain and her exports of textiles to Europe increased, Bengal nearly stopped exporting altogether to Europe. More important, by this time the Company had taken on an entirely new role with vast new responsibilities and vast new expenses. It had conquered Bengal completely and had won the right to collect taxes there. This right to gather revenue had convinced the directors that they could now dispense with sending silver from England to India to pay for the investment; instead they could pay for it from Bengal revenue. They did not seem to realize that the conquests they had made and the rights they had established would entail enormous additional expenditures. John Company now had a large army, an increased number of civil servants, and an increased number of creditors. The costs associated with this administrative and military expansion far outpaced the Bengal revenues—and the debt increased.

The new Company servants, furthermore, had very little interest in the increasingly unprofitable commercial trade from Bengal to Europe. The Company paid their salaries and still allowed them the same privileges, but they no longer concerned themselves with making the factories thrive. Indeed, the only really profitable factory in Cornwallis's day lay not in India, but at Canton in China, to which the British at first sent silver, then later cotton and opium in return for their purchase of tea.

Other developments had also muddled the financial waters. By the earl's day, trade had grown in many directions. It went not only to Europe and China, but also to the Persian and Arabian gulfs and to the Malay archipelago. The three presidencies at Bengal, Bombay, and Madras carried on trade with each other (though that had declined by Cornwallis's time), and Bengal traded with the interior. A network of European agency houses had also grown up to invest the money of the servants in the "country trade," that is, trade to Asia.[1]

In this complex situation, for East India servants to make profits for the Company and for themselves required a considerable business acumen. For example, one had to guess at the rates of exchange for a great many different kinds of currencies. Company agents had to pit their wits against Indians often as clever and resourceful as they. In fact, not too many men did make their fortunes in India, although enough of them did so from the 1730s through the 1760s to foster the impression that India contained boundless wealth, which for venturesome Britons was theirs for the taking. It was to the interest of the organization's servants to perpetuate that impression so as to maintain confidence in the Company's credit. If that confidence wavered, indebted as John Company was, many Europeans in India would be ruined.

In the 1780s, however, the directors did not think that Company servants should profit while the Company itself tumbled ever deeper into debt. As long as the Company thrived, they had not cared if a writer (clerk) made a personal fortune. But when the Company ceased to profit while the writers continued to do so, the directors logically tended to conclude that the servants stole from the Company or at least put their private interests above those of the organization they supposedly served. In 1784, for example, the "Company's goods brought home by *The Earl of Oxford* . . . realized only 1s 10d the current rupee, [yet] the goods sent home by the Company's servants on their own account produced on an average 2s 6d per rupee."[2] Directors who were themselves not above corruption, intrigue, and self-serving manipulation naturally suspected their employees of similar activities, especially in the light of such statistics.

The Company charged Cornwallis to reverse the trend. He should dismiss from service those men who had cheated the Company, retrench and reform, and secure the soundness of the Company's credit. In particular he should investigate the silk contractors, men who helped secure the investment by offering contracts to the native manufacturers who offered the best bids. Earlier, when the Company had purchased goods directly from the manufacturers, it had turned a profit. Now the Company no longer earned a profit, and the directors suspected that the contractors were in collusion with the board of revenue to ensure that the Company's loss became their own private gain.

Cheating on a large scale did indeed hamstring John Company. Soon after he arrived in India, however, Cornwallis discovered that fraud extended far beyond the silk contractors. In pursuit of his mandate to root out corruption and put the Company on sound financial footing, he found that his predecessor, John Macpherson, was one of the Company's biggest disasters.

Before he could discharge other miscreants, he felt it necessary to discredit Macpherson and disown his measures.

Macpherson as acting governor had attempted to bring all trade along the Hughli under British control and had begun to abolish customs duties at British Indian ports, because he believed a freer trade the best way to solvency. But whatever the potential gain in the future, the immediate result was a loss of revenue from customs. He had also allowed the Company's servants to ship large amounts of goods home in Company ships as an inducement for them to serve the Company—a policy that had instead induced them to serve themselves. Because the recent war against the French and the sultan of Mysore had drained Bengal of silver, his and other servants' wealth was in paper, bills of exchange on the Company, Bengal bonds, and Bengal treasury orders. He had slashed civil and military budgets, thus encouraging the poorly paid servants to speculate even more in the paper. Macpherson, in summary, had involved himself, the Company, and its agents in an ever-deepening financial morass and then worsened the situation by condoning all sorts of jobbery, collusion, and favors for friends at Company expense. Someone warned Cornwallis before he left for India that Macpherson was a "dark, designing, cunning knave, open to every species of corruption."[3] Certainly his record supported that judgment.

His first contact with the earl confirmed it. Macpherson greeted Cornwallis cordially enough and promised him "the most zealous support and assistance." But he then tendered the earl a thirty-three-page letter of advice on how to treat the Mahratta confederacy and Tipoo Sultan.[4] The advice immediately aroused Cornwallis's suspicion and distrust of his predecessor. Contrary to the express orders of the directors not to involve the Company in the politics of the native state, Macpherson advised pledging aid to the Mahrattas.[5] From then on, Cornwallis's opinion of his predecessor grew increasingly unfavorable, especially when the earl learned that the smiles masked deceit and that Macpherson's pledge of cooperation while in India turned into backbiting and intrigue upon his return to Britain.

Macpherson (by now Sir John Macpherson, Baronet) arrived in England in August of 1787 and immediately connived to get Cornwallis removed from office and himself back in. Some of Sir John's friends tried to argue with Dundas the illegality of Cornwallis's appointment. A parliamentary act gave the governor general the right to hold his position for five years, which Macpherson had not done. Cornwallis, they persisted, was fully aware of this fact and thus knowingly acted illegally.[6] Macpherson's vindictiveness showed itself when he spread the rumor, which Dundas evidently believed, that Cornwallis intended to marry a sixteen-year-old girl, a Miss Philpot, the sister of an artillery officer residing in Bengal. That rumor gained credence throughout Calcutta, along with another one, which Macpherson again encouraged, that he was coming out to replace Cornwallis as governor general.[7]

When it seemed to the earl that the British government really believed Sir John's bile, he hastened off to Dundas the fieriest and most indignant letter of his life. Never before on paper had he spoken so vehemently against the character of a single individual. Macpherson represented everything that Cornwallis detested and that the directors had charged him to eliminate: intrigue, jobbery, the amassing of a private fortune at the expense of employers, misuse of power, and in general debasing the British character in the eyes of the native inhabitants. Cornwallis boiled:

Why does he [Dundas] not tell him [Macpherson], when he talks of grievances and pensions, that he may think himself well off that he is not impeached? That he was guilty of a breach of an Act of Parliament in the offer which he made of aid to the poonah [Mahratta] government; and that he was guilty of basely degrading the national character, by the quibbles and lies which he made use of to evade the performance of it. That his Government was a system of the dirtiest jobbing; that besides a number of other stipulations, he bought General Sloper's [previous military commander in India and member of the council] vote by making Mr. ——— [James Grant, collector of Benares] give a quarter of the plunder of ——— [Benares] to Mr. ——— [Pellegrine Treves] and that his conduct in Oude was as impeachable, and more disgusting to the Vizier, than Mr. Hastings'.

. . . Mr. Dundas chose to believe a report, which, if he had been at the trouble of inquiring, he must have been soon convinced could have no sort of foundation, that Lord Cornwallis, at the age of forty-nine, forgetting the serious task which he had undertaken, and forgetting likewise his gray hairs and rheumatism, had married a girl of sixteen.

If this had been true, no very flattering hopes would have been indulged
respecting the future conduct of the Governor General, and it is not
probable that Sir J. Macpherson's coming out could have done any material harm, as Lord Cornwallis' government would have been in no
great danger of being either weakened or degraded.[8]

In another letter of August 1789, the earl told Dundas that Macpherson was guilty of "flimsy cunning and shameless falsehoods."
If that villain were ever appointed again to a position of trust,
Cornwallis warned, "Under his management a relaxation of authority in Government and a system of mean jobbing and peculation, would immediately take place, and if in my time we shall
have recovered any part of the national character for sincerity and
honour with the native powers, you may depend upon it that his
duplicity and low intrigues amongst them would soon completely
demolish it."[9]

    Macpherson did not return to mismanage and corrupt Brit-
ish India. But what of the servants just like him still there? The
directors had ordered prosecutions, though in so doing they intended to punish men for acts the directors had formerly con-
doned. Cornwallis believed in fairness as well as honesty, and
many of these prosecutions smacked of a vendetta. One could no
more encourage honesty by hounding temporary backsliders than
by allowing corrupt individuals to continue unchecked. In regard
to the silk contractors, he proposed suspending inquiry:

All these Gentlemen [he observed] were in office under the Board of
Trade, & the Salaries allowed them were notoriously insufficient for
their subsistence; and even the continuance of these, as well as their
appointments, depended upon the pleasure of the Board, under which
they served.
    In this situation they were reduced to the singular predicament
of acquiescing in the terms prescribed to them, or of forfeiting, by a
refusal, their present appointments & future expectations. The proper
line of conduct which their public duty required them to pursue is obvious, & I by no means contend that a deviation from it can upon any
principles be completely justified; But the circumstances of their situation admit of some palliation for submitting to propositions which afforded present & future advantage, under the countenance of that authority, which the commercial servants were bound to obey.
    . . . Most of the Gentlemen named in your letter are now em-
ployed by this Government in different departments, & whatever their

conduct may formerly have been, are entitled to praise for the zeal & assiduity of their present exertions. The prosecution of an enquiry into their conduct, if effectually undertaken, must commence with a real injury to your service by depriving them of their Offices, in which they are at present so usefully employed.

    . . . The great object for the Government, is by a few striking examples of the punishment of delinquency, to prevent the repetition of it in future.[10]

The few "striking examples," Cornwallis believed, should come from the superiors of the silk contractors, the members of the board of revenue. Cornwallis fervently believed that persons in power must set an example of responsible action. He could not excuse those who had not. Thus, by late December, he was ready to file bills in equity against several of them. Early in the new year, on 15 January, the first letter went out. He informed the recipients of the "painful" course he had to follow, but stated that he could not let "private considerations . . . interfere with the discharge of what I conceived to be my public duty."[11] After that the legal process took over, with the eventual result that three escaped prosecution when the bills against them were dropped, one individual won his case at enormous expense to himself, and three had to pay considerable sums back to the Company.

In contrast with his negative policy of punishing the corrupt were the positive actions Cornwallis undertook for enhancing the commerce and prosperity of the Company. The governor general laid down an elaborate set of restrictions on the commercial residents to ensure that they put the Company's investment before their own private trade. Indeed, he would have preferred to forbid their engaging in private commerce had they been granted adequate salaries.[12] To reform administration of the salt monopoly, he put salt to public auction rather than leaving it to the previous jobbery which, he thought, had let the Company's money go into the pockets of "judges, secretaries, whores, and hangers on of all kinds."[13] He gave the directors a long, detailed history of the returns on their investment by the agency or contract method and opted for the continued use of the commercial agents (although he found it impossible to prevent private individuals from sending home their own trade goods in Company ships).[14] He continued cultivation of indigo despite the directors' orders against it because he thought it might turn a profit.[15] He made new arrangements about supplying the Company with opium for sales to China, although he thought an opium contract "even in the best hands, must be a severe and cruel burthen to any country."[16] The earl concluded, after considerable difficulty and haggling, a commercial treaty with Oudh.[17]

Healthy commerce demanded uninterrupted communication between the various parts of British India. In Cornwallis's day, those parts included political residencies at Benares, Lucknow, Delhi, Gwalior, Hyderabad, Nagpur, Goa, and Poona, plus a deputation at the French island of Mauritius. The Company had army posts spotted here and there. In the center division of the army along the Malabar Coast, for example, there were stations at Fort St. George, Walajaubad, Arnee, Arcot, Poonamalee, Vellore, and other places.[18] To the north, in Oudh, the Company stationed one regiment of its own troops at Lucknow and both its own and regular regiments at Cawnpore and Futtyghur.[19] It had troops in Bengal and a regular establishment in Bombay. Overcoming the slow and uncertain communications thus became vital for both civil and military purposes.

That it took something like six weeks for news from Hyderabad to reach Calcutta rendered efficient decision making difficult.[20] In an age of sail, one could do little about communications between Calcutta and England, which on the average involved nearly a year's delay between the sending of a letter from Calcutta to England and receipt of England's response. Wind and weather defied man's puny efforts.[21] But in the interest of the Company's commerce and the British Empire, one could speed up overland communications and thus promote "the speedy and regular literary intercourse of the British possessions in India."[22]

Though Charles Ware Malet originally proposed a new postal route and secured the Mahrattas' consent to its implementation, Cornwallis approved and instituted the plan. The new route ran from Bombay through Poona to Masulipatam, where it joined the great post road between Madras and Calcutta.[23] Cornwallis was the first governor general to link the three presidencies of Madras, Bombay, and Calcutta by overland mail.

He also reformed the general post office, doubling the salary of the postmaster general and increasing the number of lesser servants in that department. By adding a number of cross-postal routes to the four main ones, he made collection and distribution more efficient than in the past.[24] Although he never mentioned it in his letters, it seems likely that his experience in America contributed to his interest in rapid communication. In South and North Carolina he had always suffered both from inadequate and interrupted communications and from poor intelligence. He would not let that happen to him in India. Before he visited the military stations up the Ganges, he tried to ensure that he would have "early information of every material occurrence" in Calcutta,[25] so that he would never be out of touch as he had been in America.

Imperial Expansion

Improved mail routes between Bengal, Madras, and Bombay, together with consolidation of administration, prepared the way for imperial expansion. Cornwallis's first acquisition, however, proved remarkably unspectacular: the Guntoor "fief," one of the six districts composing the Northern Circars. Ownership of all six would nearly link Calcutta to Madras by land. Robert Clive had acquired five of these districts, but not Guntoor (or Guntor), which consisted of several petty zemindars. By treaty with the nizam of Hyderabad in 1768, Guntoor should have gone to the Company upon the death of the nizam's brother in 1782, but the Company had not yet acquired control of it. To be sure, John Company had at first taken the "fief" but had then given it back as the price of an alliance with Hyderabad when the British were militarily hard pressed after Colonel William Baillie's defeat in 1780 in the second Mysore War. The directors had expected Cornwallis to reassert the Company's claim when he arrived in India. But the earl had not wanted to pressure the nizam while at the same time trying to arrange a peace with the sultan of Mysore in early 1787. Cornwallis also thought that, in light of the money the British already owed the nizam, taking the Circar seemed grossly unfair. By the summer of 1788, however, the nizam seemed secure financially and militarily (the Company had agreed to the entire defense of the Carnatic, with Hyderabad contributing to the cost). Cornwallis then asked for and received the "fief." He sent Captain John Kennaway to request formal cession, and by early fall the nizam had complied. Thus, without hostilities, the Company added another revenue-producing area to its territories.[26]

Cornwallis seemed particularly pleased with the smooth completion of these negotiations. In one of his rare moments of self-congratulation, he wrote Dundas that "we have got the Guntoor Circar without any danger of a war, & without being likely to pay much for it, & that we are assured of the assistance of the Marathas in case of a war with Tippo, without any embarrassing engagements on our side." Sir Archibald Campbell called the acquisition "a most masterly stroke in the politicks of India."[27]

Perhaps it was masterly because it achieved one of Cornwallis's major tasks and in the process avoided war, entangling alliances, and extensive Company commitments of any sort to the native powers. The governor general not only disapproved any further Company involvement in the affairs of the native powers, but also disapproved lending British officers to Indian princes already allied with the Company, a past practice that he believed had helped account for "the wretched province of Oude." British officers tended to overextend their influence when serving a native prince. They might lend him money, demand control of his policy if payment was not prompt, and become indeed the de facto rulers of a province, which would eventually involve the Company in the province's affairs. The Company would then have to intervene to stop the "terrors and oppressions," which had, in Cornwallis's estimation, "cruelly disgraced the British name in Hindostan."[28]

Avoiding complications in Hindostan, however, in no way inhibited the governor general from using diplomacy to extend Company influence elsewhere. Diplomacy cost less than war and might prepare the way for trade. One of the earl's more significant efforts in this direction in the 1780s would have important consequences for the British armies of the future. In 1788, the earl requested the ruler of Nepal to consider opening trade with the Company's dominions.[29] Nepal, then fighting the Chinese on behalf of Tibet, countered with a request for British military assistance. Cornwallis, of course, refused, but offered to send an envoy to mediate the dispute. Though the Nepalese made peace on their own, they agreed to receive a British representative. The earl then chose one of his former aides-de-camp, Captain William Kirkpatrick, to head the mission, which also included an assistant, a surgeon, and assorted servants. Kirkpatrick was an odd choice, for though familiar with native customs and culture and an accomplished linguist, he had already failed once at diplomacy. As resident with the Mahratta chief Scindia he had been tediously longwinded, a stickler for the finer points of ceremony, overly conscious of the Company's "rights," and determined to uphold what he deemed British honor and prestige in the face of Mahratta slurs. He had expressed contempt for Scindia, whom he considered a friendless and unscrupulous conniver, shifty and secretive, bent on destroying British influence. He had insisted on all the ceremony due a British resident, but had taken every opportunity to slight Scindia. Scindia had responded in kind by refusing the ceremony Kirkpatrick believed so important, by persecuting Kirkpatrick's servants in Agra, and by forbidding his people even to sell them goods from shops. The trouble that inevitably followed left one sepoy wounded, but Scindia failed to punish the offenders. Endless other incidents took place, many of them trivial, which Kirkpatrick found necessary to detail in a sixty-page letter. These incidents were of precisely the sort Cornwallis wished to avoid, and he had asked for Kirkpatrick's resignation, admonishing him for losing his temper in matters "very nearly deserving of the epithets of frivolous & insignificant."[30] Yet he chose to send this man to Nepal. Why?

Perhaps he wanted to give him another chance. Perhaps he thought a man of Kirkpatrick's aggressiveness would best serve in opening up relations with a power hitherto aloof from the British. Perhaps Kirkpatrick's nice sense of British honor would impress the Nepalese. At any rate, this odd choice proved singularly suitable. Kirkpatrick went off to Nepal in 1792 and arrived there in January of 1793. The Nepalese received him favorably, and he got along with them cordially.[31] In years to come, those same Nepalese would become some of the fiercest units in the British army, the dreaded Ghurkas.

Cornwallis pushed just as forcefully to extend British influence by sea as he did by land. The governor general had a strategic as well as a commercial interest in exploring various islands in the Bay of Bengal. The British lacked safe, deep harbors on the east coast of India, where they could securely anchor their ships to ride out the monsoons. Bombay had dockyards, but the British reasoned that to withdraw entirely to the west during monsoon season left the east coast unprotected (although where a British man-of-war dared not venture, no other sail would). Bombay also was expensive to maintain. Cornwallis accordingly formulated plans from the beginning of his tenure to remedy the deficiency. "I shall take measures this year," he wrote Dundas in March of 1787, "to examine with more attention than has ever been bestowed by the government the neighboring countries & islands to the eastward. If good and secure harbors for ships of war can be found in that quarter, which I think by no means impossible, it may perhaps become a future indication whether Bombay & Bencoolen are of substantial use to the Company." [32]

For the purpose of this exploration, the earl found an extremely compatible naval commander, his own brother, Captain William Cornwallis, commodore of His Majesty's Indian fleet. Even before he arrived in India, William had sent out an expedition that had claimed and settled one harbor in the Andaman Islands,[33] but he did his most extensive exploring much later, in September of 1789.[34] He scouted the islands in the Bay of Bengal, including the Nicobars (which belonged to the Danes), Prince of Wales' Island, and the Andamans. As a result he recommended a port, which his brother established with suitable stores, in the southeast end of the Great Andaman Island.[35]

The earl also settled Penang, an island north of the Straits of Malacca, just off the Malayan coast. Although the king of Keda had ceded Penang to the Company before the earl arrived in India, Cornwallis, after reading all reports about it, decided to keep it and wholeheartedly approved the expedition already gone to take possession. Later the king regretted the cession (he had thereby lost revenue) and tried to stop all trade with the English on the island, threatening them with starvation. Commodore Cornwallis sailed to their relief. Eventually the ruler of Keda accepted Company terms and lifted the blockade. Thereafter the settlement continued to grow.[36]

The governor general also wanted to expand Company trade with the ancient empire of China. Dundas suggested a mission for that purpose, which Cornwallis approved. Lord Macartney eventually led the mission there. Though at the time it failed to enlarge the commercial ties between India and China, it pointed the way toward future trade.

Thus, in the name of trade, Cornwallis enlarged the Company's influence and its empire. New worlds opened up with ever greater possibilities for increasing trade. Britain now floated a greater number of commercial vessels than any of her rivals. The British navy, though challenged by the French during the American Revolution, now reigned supreme in Asian waters and would continue to do so for another century. The possibilities for commercial and imperial expansion seemed limitless.

Directors and Appointments

Yet Cornwallis viewed all these attempts at commercial reform and expansion as mere measures. Their success in the long run would depend on the ability, honesty, and integrity of the men who carried them out. Be they collectors or commercial residents, civil or military officers, if the Company's servants were not honest and industrious, looking to the good of the Company and the British Empire in India, no amount of lawmaking or prosecutions or adjusting of administrative arrangements would help. He pointed out in a long letter about the Company's investment on 1 November 1788 that whatever arrangements were made, whatever machinery came into operation, "the Company's interests may yet in the execution be sacrificed. This result in a word, can be prevented only by a *faithful intelligent and attentive conduct in their Commercial Servants*. If this be suppos'd wanting, hardly any System can be tolerable."[37]

Solvency lay not merely in altering institutional arrangements, but in encouraging merit, disavowing patronage appointments, and creating a climate of integrity and disinterested service: if the Company had honest servants it would get honest profits. The most important institutional changes, therefore, should be ones designed to encourage trustworthiness and loyalty. As Cornwallis told the directors:

Under the views therefore, with which I undertook the management of your affairs, it seem'd particularly ineligible to lay it down at the Outset as a determin'd point, that fidelity was not to be expected from your Servants, and on the other hand most desireable and important in every view, that a principle of honour should be excited and diffus'd among them as the principle of their service. I had reason to believe that the Establishment was not without men thus actuated, and that by a due application of the power and influence of government, evincing a determin'd resolution on the one hand to tolerate no irregularities, and on the other, setting the example of that fair and liberal conduct which it requir'd, not a few would willingly exchange the temptations, dangers and discredit of the former system of conceal'd emolument for an open and reasonable compensation of honest service.[38]

For the servants to receive that "open and reasonable compensation," however, the directors themselves would first have to start mending their own ways. "The first fault was in the court of directors," the earl told Dundas, and in 1787 berated them in a letter to their chairman, pointing out that instead of suppressing the "shocking evils" they knew existed in the Hastings era they quarreled about whether their friends or those of Hastings "should enjoy the plunder."[39] And they had erred badly in other ways: they had tended to appoint men to responsible positions solely on the basis of jobbery, using their patronage to employ their friends, cousins, and nephews. Unfortunately, they still continued the practice in the Cornwallis era. Though they repeatedly expressed their goodwill toward their governor general and their desire to aid him, they nonetheless constantly saddled him with councillors whose judgment he distrusted and upon whom he could not rely. In 1789, for example, they elevated Peter Speke to the supreme council. Cornwallis considered him a "miserable counsellor . . . very weak, and open to the solicitations of individuals to support their most ruinous jobs, and totally unacquainted with all the business of this country, except making silk."[40] Time confirmed the judgment. Three years later he wrote to Dundas: "There is no hold whatever on a man so wonderfully eccentric, neither a regard for his interest and character, nor the public welfare and the honour and faith of Government, would weigh an instant against some absurd and pernicious caprice which interested men may have had art enough to work on his vanity to adopt."[41] Again, although Cornwallis requested Dundas to pressure the directors to replace Shore (who went to England on sick leave) with Jonathan Duncan as a councillor, and although he wrote as well to the chairman, they appointed somebody else.[42] In 1791, when he learned that councillor Charles Stuart was leaving, Cornwallis once more appealed to Dundas to speak out for Duncan. "Remember," he said, "that I speak not for Duncan, but for the public."[43] Instead, the directors picked Thomas Graham, an even worse choice than Speke in the earl's view. He fumed: "Of all the Company's servants, out of the degree of total inability, I really think Graham, even independent of his bankruptcy, the most unfit for a seat in Council. He has no fixed or steady opinions on any points of the public business, and he is now a bankrupt and by continuing his engagements in a commercial house, after he had, to save his seat at the board of revenue, made a public declaration he had quitted it; but what is worst of all, with a strong propensity to jobbing and intrigue, he has formed connexions with the worst black people in Bengal."[44]

Not only did the directors thwart their governor general's wishes in these major appointments, but they also did so with regard to subordinate positions. In 1789 they paid no attention to professional qualifications or seniority in three appointments, and in 1792 they repeated the same error.[45]

How could the Company hope for solvency, let alone profit, if it continued in this way? "A government therefore," the earl wrote the Prince of Wales, "which has the power & inclination to select the best instruments may do a great deal, but it is by an attention to this point alone that the national honor and interest can be promoted."[46] The directors had so continually erred that Cornwallis gradually concluded they should lose their patronage rights altogether. When the Company's charter was coming up for renewal, Dundas asked Cornwallis if the government should not indeed take over most of the Company's patronage. In 1790, the governor general for various reasons had not thought so.[47] Two years later, after the directors had climaxed six years of bad appointments with their elevation of Graham, Cornwallis in despair changed his mind. He was prepared to acquiesce in the total abolition of the directors' rights of appointment. "If the Court of Directors cannot be controlled," he wrote, "I retract my opinion in favour of their continuance after the expiration of the Charter."[48]

The earl felt as strongly about the directors' miserliness

as about their jobbery. Time and again he pointed out to them, to Dundas, and to others that failure to pay decent salaries to men in positions of authority invited those men to remunerate themselves in other ways, usually by oppressing the native inhabitants on the one hand and cheating the Company on the other. He wrote Dundas in 1787: "I never can or shall think it is good economy to put men into places of the greatest confidence, where they have it in their power to make their fortunes in a few months, without giving them any salaries. If it is a maxim that no Government can command honest services, and that pay our servants as we please they will equally cheat, the sooner we leave this country the better." He repeated the same observation a year later: "No reduction can be made in the civil establishment of Bengal that would in reality promote economy—those persons who hold offices of great labour and great responsibility must be well paid, or they will for the most part betray their trust."[49]

Small salaries not only corrupted Company servants, but also, in Cornwallis's view, damaged British honor. If God had called upon Britain to rule Bengal, then rule Britain should. But rulers had a deep responsibility to their subjects. If the British in India forgot that responsibility and oppressed the natives, then they were not fit sovereigns and should get out. "The whole system of this Presidency [Madras]," he observed to Dundas, "is founded on the good old principles of Leadenhall-street economy—small salaries and immense perquisites, and if the Directors alone could be ruined by it, everybody would say they deserved it, but unfortunately it is not the Court of Directors but the British nation who must be the sufferers."[50]

Setting the Example

Despite his repeated attempts to get the directors to mend their own fences, his exhortations fell largely on deaf ears. What he could do was to set an example for his successors in India to follow. He could live up to those precepts of honesty and faithfulness he had urged upon others. If his words could not alter the directors' thinking perhaps his example could.

First he tried to influence the directors to appoint the right sort of person to the most important position in British India, that of governor general, to replace him at the end of his term. Without honesty and dedication to duty in the governor general, what could be expected of subordinates? But these two characteristics, important as they were, were not enough. The governor general should also have two other qualifications: disinterest in serving one faction of men or another and a sufficiently high place in society to command respect from all. In other words, the supreme government should never again go to a Company servant, because that servant would find it nearly impossible to set the example he should. Having deliberated equally with others on the council for years, he could not suddenly command respect and obedience in his new position as governor, no matter what powers the Company vested in him. His colleagues would have been familiar with him for too long, and instead of according him respect, they were likely to nurse jealousy. Many would ask themselves: "Why did he get the position instead of me?"

Indeed, many men felt thus toward Shore, who succeeded Cornwallis. The earl would have preferred someone of the upper classes from Britain, though he admitted Shore was "an exception to a general rule."[51] Shore, despite his demonstrated abilities, had difficulties that proved the wisdom of Cornwallis's suggestion about the type of men who should serve as governors general. Partially because Shore lacked Cornwallis's prestige and authority, the officers of the Bengal army nearly mutinied against his government. Thereafter the British administration usually followed the Cornwallis maxim in selecting its supreme governors. Subsequent appointees usually came from the ranks of the landed aristocracy, had no previous connection with India, and served for five years (the original term Cornwallis had set for himself). Commanding more authority, they undoubtedly directed British India in a far more effective way, for good or ill, than a Company servant (or later a member of the famed India Civil Service) would have. The expansion under Richard, Lord Wellesley and Francis, Lord Hastings, the reforms of Lord William Bentinck, the policies of the first Marquis of Dalhousie that contributed greatly to the Mutiny, the tenures of Lords Curzon and Minto: all shaped British India.

The earl also set a worthy example both in his private life and in his official work. In the midst of all the opulence, partying, heavy drinking, and gambling of the British society in India, he lived a spartan existence, as contemporaries noted. He was equally fastidious in his official work, careful never to allow even the slightest suspicion that he could be bribed or otherwise corrupted. He was even chary of accepting the perquisites that by custom, without any taint of illegality, usually came to a governor general. Gift giving and receiving, for example, was universally practiced. Yet Cornwallis thought the exchanges so lavish as to encourage corruption. As governor general he tried to reduce the cost and extravagance of such exchanges. What protocol demanded, he did. Thus he presented jewels, cloth, and elephants to the peshwa at Poona and received presents from him as well as from the king of Siam and other heads of state. But beyond protocol he would not venture. He would take no presents whatever from private citizens, whether native or British. His private secretary returned one such gift to a certain Mustapha with the remark: "It is a fixed regulation of his lordship's not to accept anything in the form of a present, & if he was in any instance to deviate from this general rule, it would entail upon himself much trouble and be offensive to many respectable persons whose presents he has already refused."[52] Samuel Turner, captain of his bodyguard, thought this determination to resist temptation so inflexible that the earl would not accept some "trifling presents of fruits" from the subjects of one nabob, since he had "unexceptionally" declined every "tributory compliment offered him both by the inhabitants of this town [Calcutta], the Nabob Mobaruk ud Dowlah [of Bengal] and the minister [Hyder Beg Khan] of the Vizier [of Oudh]." In the end, however, the earl accepted them because protocol demanded it: "Their rejection would have been deemed . . . ·such a mark of indisposition that no explanation that could have been devised would have served to satisfy."[53]

Indeed, the earl went so far in removing monetary temptations from the governor general's office that he paid out of his pocket the expenses of all public entertainments for the acting governor during his own absence from Calcutta in the campaign against Tipoo. He hoped thereby to ensure that Councillor Stuart, the acting governor, could not be tempted to divert an entertainment allowance to his own pocket.[54] Though Cornwallis could certainly have used to good purpose the salary of commander in chief in India, he turned it down, contenting himself with his admittedly handsome salary as governor general. To take more than that would give the appearance of greed, of serving in India only to make money, the very attitude he hoped to eliminate.

He disliked the abuse of patronage by the directors and refused to abuse the patronage at his disposal. No matter from whom the request, he chose merit as the prime consideration in making appointments. That is not to say that if two men of equal abilities sought the same employment, he would not favor one recommended by a friend or an important official over one lacking such a recommendation. He would naturally favor the protégé of a friend or colleague over an unknown, but only if the person merited the position. As he told Sir Robert Sloper: "The eyes of the nation are opened about India, and governors & commanders in chief must now relinquish the idea that they have a right to serve their friends and relatives in an irregular manner. That system has lasted long enough to ruin our affairs in this country.

5. Embassy of Hyderbeck to Calcutta
Reprinted by permission of the India Office Library and Records, London

It is high time it should have an end."[55] Though some of his most intimate correspondence was with Dundas, whom he regarded as a firm friend and a warm advocate of his administration in India, Cornwallis even refused Dundas's patronage requests. He refused those of the Prince of Wales as well and was appalled that the prince wished Cornwallis to take care of a person not in Company service. He pointed out to Charles Fitzroy, first Baron Southampton, the consequences that might ensue should he honor the royal plea: "If I was to create office, or extra-offices, which is a term I do not very well understand, I should not only disgrace myself and undo everything I have been doing since I landed in Bengal, but I should render a very short-lived service to the person for whom they were created: for if I was to forget my duty and betray the trust which is reposed in me, the Court of Directors would not forget theirs, and they would undoubtedly annul such appointments the instant they heard of them."[56] To the prince he wrote directly that he could not "even in the most moderate degree provide for him." "When I seriously consider how impossible it is," he observed, "that our affairs in this country could prosper, if the practice which so long prevailed was to be again revived of sending persons of ruined fortune to be provided for in India, I feel it incumbent upon me, during the remainder of my stay, to persevere in the principles that I have hitherto followed, & to endeavour by that means to establish strong & obvious checks upon the abuse of patronage in the Governor General."[57]

In his campaign to appoint and reward men of merit, Cornwallis did not entirely lack success. He recommended and had the satisfaction of obtaining baronetcies for Charles Ware Malet, resident at Poona, and for Captain John Kennaway, resident with the nizam of Hyderabad.[58] As a positive inducement to good service, for those less dedicated than Mallet or Kennaway, he tried time and again to secure sufficient salaries despite the directors' miserly intransigence. Warren Hastings had tried and failed, but Hastings had lacked the earl's prestige and authority. Finally, in exasperation with his superiors, Cornwallis defied them by using that prestige and authority to increase the salaries of the revenue collectors.[59] Perhaps he foresaw that they would choose to acquiesce in their governor general's actions rather than repudiate him.[60] The earl also managed to raise the salaries of his private secretary and of Edward Hay, secretary to the supreme council.[61]

Once he had secured them adequate salaries, Cornwallis had no sympathy for men greedy for more, and he would not condone any attempts by decently paid Company servants to gain added income. He issued strict orders that the revenue collectors should under no circumstances engage in any private commercial activities. He promised Dundas that collectors who violated the rules imperiled their positions. "I promise you," he said, "that I will make an example of the first offender that I can catch."[62] Cornwallis considered that he had made a "liberal provision" for Hay's department, yet Hay continued to engage in commerce. "I do not approve," the earl told him, "of the secretaries being concerned in commerce or other business & . . . I wish they would take the earliest opportunities of disengaging themselves from any connexions of that kind."[63] Hay, secretary to the secret and political department of the supreme council, nephew of the eighth earl of Kinnoull, might have resented this admonition. His uncle had obtained "jobs" in England, and Hay knew perfectly well what had gone on previously in India. Yet he promised to yield a "ready and cheerful" obedience to the injunction.[64]

Thus Cornwallis set the example and enforced it. Undoubtedly his doing so helped change attitudes in India. Contemporaries noted the change for the better as his tenure progressed. Captain Turner believed the earl's conduct "raised throughout the [military] service a general spirit of progressive emulation."[65] George Forster, who performed intelligence services for Cornwallis at Lucknow, commented to Dundas: "You made a happy choice in Lord Cornwallis, who, standing far above the reach of corruption, unincumbered by powerful claimants on his favor, and directed by a sound discerning judgment, must be the source of essential benefits to a country which has long groaned under the weakness and wickedness of its governors."[66] An engineering captain observed that Cornwallis "seems to wish every person to have justice done them."[67] Dundas heard from an anonymous observer in November of 1786 that "even our morals [in Calcutta] will insensibly correct from the good example of our chief ruler."[68] Artillery colonel Thomas Pearse told Warren Hastings:

"Cornwallis has made us all happy as he becomes more known he rises in the respect of the natives; they see the revived Hastings in him, they expect good, a firm and upright government resolved on doing what is right." [69] Sir William Jones wrote: "In my opinion the country was never so justly and so mildly governed as it is now by Lord Cornwallis and Mr. Shore." To another correspondent Jones stated that "Lord Cornwallis and Mr. Shore are justly popular, and perhaps, the most virtuous govenors in the world." [70]

Thus the testimonials by distinguished and undistinguished contemporaries measured the earl's success at "setting the example." The Indian Civil Service, founded decades later, followed that example, becoming famous for its tradition of honest men dedicated to their task, always the rulers but always trying to rule in the interests of the native inhabitants. Cornwallis initiated the concept of the British Empire in India as one dedicated to securing good government (but not self-government) for its subjects. The implementation of this concept by his successors constituted a significant change in the British rule in India.

Chapter 4

The Permanent Settlement

Another significant change in the British position in India followed from the expansion of the East India Company's territory and interests. The Company had necessarily enlarged its armies to defend its position in India, especially against the French. Had it not triumphed, its French counterpart would have, because after the collapse of the Mogul Empire no native power possessed the organization or the economic resources of the Europeans. The success of Clive's arms paved the way for vast changes. By 1765, a private British business enterprise governed and administered justice to an alien people in a distant land.

When Cornwallis arrived there, the East India Company's actual territorial control still extended only to Bombay, the land around Madras, and Bengal, Benares, Bihar, and Orissa. But in these areas John Company ruled as sovereign.

Bombay and Madras (the latter was much the larger) were not much more than Company settlements containing a contingent of Europeans, their governments subordinate to Calcutta. But Bengal, Bihar, and Orissa, together with Benares (which Warren Hastings seized from the nabob of Oudh in 1775) included not only the capital city of Calcutta but also an area of two hundred thousand square miles and a population in the late eighteenth century estimated at twenty-four million people.[1] Bengal's civil servants totaled around three hundred, including a mere twenty commercial agents to handle the Company's trade and thirty-five collectors to gather its revenue. The army that protected them was now much enlarged, numbering more than fifty thousand men in Bengal, near fifty thousand in Madras, and about fifteen thousand in Bombay. The overwhelming majority of these soldiers were native Indians: the European military contingent consisted of only about thirteen hundred officers and five thousand enlisted men.

When Cornwallis arrived in Bengal, the European community probably did not exceed five thousand. It included the Company servants, the military, an assorted group of Europeans who did not work for John Company, and, of course, the families of many of them. The officials had vast responsibilities administratively and (more important from the directors' point of view) economically.[2]

The acquisition of Bengal had altered not only John Company's territorial control but also its revenues. Before Clive's conquests, the Company had sent money from Europe for its agents in India to invest in Asian (especially Chinese) goods, which in turn went back to England to be sold (it was hoped) for a profit. Clive's victories supposedly meant that this "investment" would no longer have to come from Europe. In 1765, the Company obtained the right to collect taxes and administer civil justice in the provinces of Bengal, Bihar, and Orissa in return for an annual payment to the now merely titular Mogul emperor of India, whose capital lay at Delhi.

It appeared to all that the Company had gained a tremendous financial windfall. The directors naturally thought that they could apply the revenues gained through taxation of the native inhabitants to the purchase of goods for shipment to Europe, thereby decreasing the capital contribution that England made toward the investment. Accordingly, they demanded a greater Bengal contribution. The Company's servants at first hesitated to displace the traditional collectors (who for the sake of convenience, though not with total accuracy, may be termed zemindars) in order to meet this demand. A wholesale dismissal of established native officers and departments would have invited hostility at the very time when Britain held but a precarious position in Bengal. Furthermore, the Company's servants did not yet have the local knowledge necessary to become collectors.

The directors demanded more and the Company officials tried to produce more, creating a system fraught with inequities. Between 1765 and Cornwallis's tenure in 1786, the Company's

servants tried one taxation expedient after another with only vary-
ing degrees of success. At first they made use of native collectors,
who in time-honored Indian tradition oppressed the peasants. At
first, the British tended to care much less about such oppression
than about the contribution it brought to the investment. But as
early as the 1760s, some of the more responsible officials began to
realize that the power they now held carried responsibilities to the
governed as well as to the directors. Richard Becher, the resident
at Murshidabad, had carefully studied the system, and in 1769
he suggested that English supervisors replace natives. The English
would arrange long-term assessments, not annual ones based on
crop yields. The Calcutta government accepted the suggestion,
and from 1772 to 1774 European supervisors worked in the interior. Unfortunately, the new system began just when a great
famine rolled over Bengal—perhaps three million people perished
—and nullified what might have been a promising experiment.
Furthermore, supervisors turned collections over to the highest
bidders, which led to rack renting. The Company then tried
working through provincial councils, with a return to annual
assessments and the elimination of farming out collections to the
highest bidders. Warren Hastings, the last governor general before
Cornwallis (save for the interim appointment of Sir John Macpherson), in 1781 tried yet another expedient by establishing a
committee of revenue to improve collection. It also failed marked-
ly. Thus Cornwallis faced the still unsettled question of the best
way to collect the revenue for maximum return to the Company
and minimum distress to the tillers of the soil, or ryots.[3]

The directors had already hinted at the sort of system they
favored before he left. In a letter to the governor general and
council of 21 September 1785, they deemed it "essential" for the
board of revenue in Bengal to adhere to "just and uniform principles in the transactions with the Zemindars and other land-
holders." They had already perused revenue suggestions of some
Company servants and at the time were consulting their "most
able and experienced servants who are now in England."[4]

One of the ablest of these servants was the thirty-four-
year-old John Shore. Shore had come from a Derbyshire family,
had attended Eton, learned bookkeeping at Hoxton, and at the age

of seventeen had gone to Calcutta as a writer (clerk). He now
bore the look of a benevolent, dignified gentleman. His personality matched his appearance: he tempered intelligence with humanity, dignity with self-reliance. He possessed an energy that
derived from an inner purpose rather than physical robustness.
His pious, dedicated commitment to Christianity drove him to
labor unsparingly in the service of his employers and the natives of
India. Unlike many of his contemporaries, he never cheated the
Company or netted large profits in private transactions. During
his first five years in the service, he had never earned more than
£500 a year and had saved nothing at the end of ten years.[5] He
neither drank nor womanized. He enjoyed music and cricket, but
his real passions were the classics and studying the languages,
customs, and people of India. He translated Persian and Sanskrit
works into English.

As a Company official, Shore had risen from work in the
secret service to become an assistant to the revenue board at Murshidabad and eventually chief of the revenue board at Calcutta.
He had worked tirelessly from 1780 to 1785 on Bengal revenues,
going on special missions to Dacca and Bihar. Had Shore been a
different sort, he might have added, according to his own estimate, £100,000 from his mission to Dacca alone. Yet he had refused the opportunity and remained genuinely dedicated to the
welfare of the native inhabitants. They knew and appreciated his
dedication. "One day, when I was walking in the fields," he later
recalled, "weak in body and uneasy in mind, a poor native, whose
sufferings I had relieved, was proceeding in the same path; and I
heard him exclaim, 'May God prolong thy life, and restore thy
health, for thou has saved the lives of the poor!' This indeed was
a reward for all my exertions; and I felt the force of it with a
satisfaction I would not have bartered for thousands."[6]

Such unstinting labor had undermined his constitution. He
suffered from bilious disorders and chronic insomnia. In the very
year of Cornwallis's appointment he had decided to return to
England to regain his health. He landed in June of 1785 and visited
his brother, where he met and married Charlotte Cornish, the
daughter of a doctor in Teignmouth. Though he did not really
wish to return to India, the directors so appreciated his abilities
that they offered him a seat on the supreme council in Bengal.

They expected him to help their new governor general gain an understanding of Indian affairs.

Shore had reluctantly accepted. He sailed in company with Cornwallis to India, and during the voyage each took the other man's measure. They became fast friends, each valuing the other's personal qualities and dedication to duty. Cornwallis soon came to trust Shore implicitly, realizing he would never betray that trust, nor use their friendship to secure favors either for himself or others. Shore reciprocated the trust and respect. He expressed their relationship clearly after he had taken his seat on the council: "With Lord Cornwallis I have had the happiness to live constantly on terms of the most intimate confidence; and on this account, as well as by a knowledge of his character, I am precluded from asking any solicitations, but such as are warranted by the strictest propriety." [7]

If Shore's sense of propriety made it impossible for him to ask for anything extra for himself, Cornwallis's sense of what was fitting prompted him to solicit just rewards for this able man. Accordingly, he wrote a letter to Henry Dundas as soon as he landed at Madras, asking that the Company remunerate Shore for "his expense in fitting out and passage." Otherwise this "deserving and valuable man" would not receive any money until December. [8] The directors complied so far as to vote £1,000.

Another individual who won Cornwallis's esteem was Charles Grant. He was born in 1746 and attended Elgin school. His father, Alexander, the "swordsman," was one of the romantic figures of the 1745 rebellion, as was also Charles's cousin Alexander. Despite the failure of the Jacobite cause, it indirectly helped Charles get his start in life. His cousin, who had served the Pretender even to the disaster at Culloden, had afterward fled to India, where he became an officer in Clive's Bengal army. Later Alexander returned to Britain to become a partner in a mercantile house in London. When it was time for him to go back to India, where he had valuable contracts for supplying transport and food for the army, he got his younger cousin Charles Grant to look after his London interests. Thus Charles's connections could help him secure a coveted appointment in 1767 as a cadet in the Company's army. He found, however, that soldiering did not suit him. When he arrived in Bengal in 1768, he left the army to become the agent of Richard Becher, resident at Murshidabad, who, in accordance with then Company policy, carried on private commercial activities of his own.

From that beginning, Grant learned a great deal about the commercial activities of the Company and its servants. Indeed, he became an expert. He left Bengal with Becher in 1771, but in 1772 secured another appointment with the Company as a writer. In 1774, he became secretary to the board of trade, where he further increased his knowledge of the operations of the Company's commercial transactions. After six years as secretary, in which he elevated that office to more than a clerical position, he became commercial resident at Malda. When Cornwallis became governor general, he prevailed upon Grant to take a seat on the board of trade in 1787.

Grant, like Shore, was ruled by religion, piety, and a devotion to duty that manifested itself in hard work. Perhaps their similarities explain why Grant was Shore's best friend. They had probably first met in Murshidabad in 1770. Unlike Shore, Grant in his youth had been rather wild (understandable enough considering his adventurous family). He had gambled and lived far above his income. His attempts at private trade had brought him losses, which his reckless gambling increased. The death of his two children by smallpox, however, had at once damped his excesses. He came to believe that God had singled him out as "an object of . . . just displeasure."[9] In desperation he had turned to Shore in 1774 for books to afford him religious consolation. From then on their friendship had grown very close. Recognizing Grant's ability, Shore no doubt took the first opportunity to press his friend's qualifications for a seat on the board of trade.[10] But meanwhile Cornwallis had also learned something of Grant's ability. When he had first arrived in Bengal, he had requested Grant's opinions on how to improve the investment. Grant had answered fully and promptly.[11] Shortly thereafter, the earl had described Grant to Dundas as a "man of abilities and the most acknowledged worth and integrity." By 1788, he told Dundas that Grant was one of the three best men in the country.[12]

Thus Cornwallis, Shore, and Grant—three men of Victorian morality and temperament in a non-Victorian age—together worked out the terms of the permanent settlement. By far the heaviest burden fell on Shore. Indeed, he drew up several minutes, one of which in June of 1789 stretched to 562 paragraphs and covered nearly 90 pages of print.[13] But none of the three men worked in a vacuum. Many others tackled the problem as well, collectors and residents. Solicited and unsolicited opinions poured in.[14] A captain in the Indian army even volunteered to survey all the Company's lands in anticipation of a permanent settlement.[15] As Cornwallis told Dundas: "I have spared no pains to obtain the most useful information. There is not a man of character and ability in the service that has had experience in the real business of the country, whom I have not consulted."[16]

Influenced by the dozens of responses of others of the Company's servants to the problem, guided by the past history of revenue collections, applying the considerable information he had received of local conditions, but relying the most on Shore, by the summer of 1789 Cornwallis arrived at an elaborate set of regulations for a settlement of the land revenue in Bengal.

In essence, this settlement would make the zemindars hereditary landholders. Government would work out with them the value of the land and the taxes paid on it. Once determined, the zemindars would pay the government only the agreed amount. Cornwallis wanted the system to be permanent. Shore, on the other hand, wanted an arrangement for ten years only. He reasoned that the value of the land would increase by the end of that period, and the British should accordingly increase their taxes. A ten-year settlement, he insisted, would afford the zemindars sufficient security of tenure and incentive to work to improve the value of their holdings. He stuck to this position, reiterating it once again just before he left India on sick leave in December of 1789.[17]

Cornwallis thought differently. He believed the past so troubled, tax gathering so uncertain, and, most important, the peasants so sorely oppressed by the tax collectors' rack renting and extortion that only a permanent settlement would restore confidence in the British government and prompt the zemindars steadily to improve the cultivation of their lands.

As it happened, the two good friends, Shore and Grant, went home to argue the opposite sides before the authorities. Grant not only favored Cornwallis's permanent settlement, but believed in it fervently. Shore left India in December of 1789 for reasons of health—he was often ill while working on the permanent settlement—whereas Grant left in February of 1790 because of his surviving children's illness. Shore headed for the court of directors to appeal for a ten-year settlement, but he never had a chance of winning his case. In a letter to Dundas of 7 November 1789, Cornwallis noted that collectors W. A. Brooke, Robert Bathurst, Thomas Law, and Archibald Seton all favored a permanent settlement.[18] In another letter of 5 December 1789, he pointed out that other knowledgeable Company servants as well favored it: Jonathan Duncan, the resident collector at Benares of whom Cornwallis thought highly; William Cowper, a member of the revenue board; and Thomas Law's assistant, George Barlow, whom Cornwallis had employed to draw up a commercial treaty with the nabob of Oudh two years previously.[19] Furthermore, although he lauded Shore's abilities, the earl particularly recommended Charles Grant to Dundas. "I must beg of you for my sake to receive him with all possible kindness and attention," the governor general said, "and I should recommend it to you for your own, to converse with him frequently upon every part of the business of this country."[20]

Dundas, president of the board of control, close friend of Pitt and his adviser in all East India matters, was entirely sympathetic to Cornwallis's proposals and lent a ready ear to them. "You may rest assured," Dundas wrote in 1790, "I will not fail to pay every attention to everything you state relative to the Bengal settlement." In May of 1791, Dundas wrote that the court of directors wanted to "postpone the consideration of the great question of the land revenues . . . but I do not mean to indulge them in that disposition." With Grant as his technical adviser, who "staid with us a great part of the time," Dundas met with Pitt for ten days at Wimbledon in August of 1792 and swung the chief minister's opinion in favor of the permanent settlement. Pitt had interest in India, especially in matters connected with its finances. Faced with the solid backing of the board of control and the British government, the directors acquiesced to the permanent settlement.[21] It became a part of the extensive new regulations Cornwallis promulgated a year later and was extended to Benares in 1794.

Although the permanent settlement was by no means the most important of Cornwallis's reforms, it seems to have generated the most historical controversy. Its opponents have damned it as wrong and wrongheaded and have even described it as immoral, while its defenders have admitted some of its weaknesses but have argued its utility for the era in which it operated.

One of its first and most vehement critics, the philosophical radical James Mill, father of the more famous John Stuart Mill, scathingly criticized it in his groundbreaking *History of British India*, which first appeared in 1818. A disciple of Jeremy Bentham, Mill disliked the English aristocracy, whom he considered parasites upon the land. He insisted that the permanent settlement was an example of the British applying their own social structure to India. "With this turn of mind, it was to be expected," he stated, "that they would, if possible, find a set of land-holders, gentry, and nobles to correspond with those in England." Since the zemindar had some of the traits of a landholder, Mill argued, "it was inferred without delay" that the zemindars "were the proprietors of the soil, the landed gentry and nobility of India." Thus, he continued, the British did not consider that the zemindars were merely rent collectors and nothing more, "that if they governed the ryots, and in many respects exercised over them despotic power, they did not govern them as tenants of theirs," and that the ryots had hereditary rights to their lands. Instead, Mill affirmed, "full of the aristocratical ideas of modern Europe, the aristocratical person now at the head of government, avowed his intention of establishing an aristocracy, upon the European model." In drawing up the permanent settlement, the English did not look to the history of India but to "abstract theory" that they had "commonly drawn from something in their own country, and either misdrawn or misapplied." In the forefront of English political reform, Mill in effect did precisely what he accused the Company's servants of doing: he based his assumptions upon abstractions rather than upon experience. His hatred of the landed aristocracy in England preconditioned him to hate a settlement in India that vested power over the land to a hereditary group.[22] He thus assumed that the English did so in order to copy their own class system without consulting India's past, when in reality they had studied that past far more than had Mill. If any arrangement was ever based on history and recent experience instead of abstraction, the permanent settlement was.

In 1914, W. S. Seton-Karr's short study of Cornwallis defended his administration. He pointed out that the British knew the difficulties in bestowing a settlement upon the zemindars because they knew perfectly well that zemindari rights varied. Seton-Karr noted, for example, that J. H. Harrington, secretary to the board of revenue and collector of Calcutta in Cornwallis's time, had a century previously described the zemindars as accurately as anyone had. Harrington defined a zemindar as a receiver of territorial revenues from ryots and undertenants. He succeeded to his zemindari by inheritance, but he generally had to receive his title from the sovereign. He also had certain powers of sale and other rights. Harrington added that Cornwallis did not give the zemindars absolute rights in the soil. As his minutes made abundantly clear, the earl reserved some protection for the ryots. Seton-Karr admitted that Cornwallis did not fully understand the zemindars' past role, but asserted that most of the Company's servants supported the earl in giving zemindars the right to control the land. Seton-Karr's major objection was that instead of a permanent one, Cornwallis should have made the settlement for ten years, as Shore wished, in order to allow for periodic reassessment.[23]

Philip Mason, a retired Indian civil servant, wrote in 1953 that, in fact, the actual historical position of the zemindars varied and that their rights had originated in several different ways. Although the Company's servants knew that only one class resembled English landlords, "the district officers welcomed the settlement; almost to a man they were convinced that a long-term settlement was required." Indeed, with but a single exception, they all "agreed that the settlement should be made with the zemindars."[24] Thus Mason did not criticize Cornwallis for establishing the arrangement with the zemindars. In the face of nearly unanimous advocacy of it, the governor general had little choice. Mason did add, however, that Shore was probably right in asking for ten years instead of a permanent settlement. His chief criticism of Cornwallis was of the racist policy he established.

H. R. C. Wright, who examined the permanent settlement in an article in the *Economic History Review* in 1954, in general did not disparage it. He argued that it was an act of deliberate self-denial that forsook future revenues in the interest of maintaining rural peace. The history of past attempts to tax had resulted in oppression, discontent, and uncertain revenues. Wright argued that a permanent settlement seemed necessary not only to collect the revenue but also as the only way to protect the ryots. The Company was not, of course, a welfare state: it wanted an assured revenue for defense, administration, and the investment.[25]

B. B. Misra, who in 1959 wrote a detailed study of the East India Company's central administration, also noted that the Company's servants wanted a settlement with the zemindars and that Cornwallis, fully aware that by making it permanent he might deprive the Company of further revenues, yet thought it the best way to ensure rural peace and a steady revenue. But Misra added that the earl seemed to envisage a new class of zemindars, a new social element in India. Misra concluded that under the permanent settlement the ryots, far from being protected, suffered more than under the previous methods.[26]

Argument and counterargument continue unceasingly. But one must consider Cornwallis's decisions in perspective, examining what pressures he faced for such a settlement and what alternatives, if any, he had. The directors who appointed the earl expected a settlement with the zemindars and expected the governor general to work it out. Cornwallis sailed out to his new command with the one individual whom he admitted influenced him most in his thinking, Sir John Shore. Though in the end Shore wanted a settlement for only ten years, he favored above all else an arrangement with the zemindars. When Cornwallis got to Bengal, he ordered the collectors to report their views on a just and beneficial revenue arrangement. These reports, James Mill notwithstanding, showed full realization of the complexities of revenue collection in the past and how the position of the zemindars had differed in different areas.[27] Yet as Cornwallis twice remarked to Dundas, the collectors were almost to a man in favor of a permanent settlement with the zemindars.

Indeed, the near impossibility of discovering all the complexities within any reasonable compass of time made them opt under the circumstances for an arrangement with the zemindars. How else could thirty-five collectors administer a land with twenty-four million people? They would have required hundreds of additional people merely to gather statistics. The English government still had neither an extensive central administration to gather statistical information about Britain nor any intention of creating one. Why should a private concern think of it? Cornwallis operated in the years before the Indian Civil Service, the British Civil Service, and parliamentary reform.

The collectors argued, furthermore, that a permanent settlement would benefit the ryots as well as the zemindars. Their reports did not argue abstractly in favor of an English-type landlord class. W. A. Brooke, the collector at Shahabad, pointed out on 8 May 1789 that "the exultation with which the Zemindars, and I may say the Ryots, as their Interests are reciprocal, would receive Intelligence of the Sanction of Government, to a Quit-Rent in perpetuity, would be beyond description." Thomas Graham, a member of the revenue board, who came to the supreme council in Bengal in 1792, stated that the principles upon which the permanent settlement were founded were good, "and it has been no small object of my attention to promulgate them in such a manner amongst the natives as to impress them with a conviction of their permanency, as whilst doubts exist in their minds on that score, their operation will be slow and uncertain. The measures of past government have been so fluctuating that it is difficult to inculcate a belief that the existing ones will have greater stability." The collector at Burdwan, Lawrence Mercer, regretted that he did not have more information about the rights of the zemindars, or at least more knowledge of past accounts, but he had no objections to the settlement being "immediately concluded." Although Robert Bathurst, the collector at Tyrhoot, at first opposed it, by October of 1789 he favored a permanent settlement. "I entertain no doubt," he said, "of making a considerable encreáse upon the jumma [tax] of last year, & at the same time spreading general confidence & satisfaction." A summary of the collectors' reports concluded: "The collectors in general were decidedly of opinion that the future settlement for the revenue of the lands should be made with the zemindars."[28]

Thus, when Cornwallis urged a permanent settlement with the zemindars, he did no more than follow the advice of the Company's servants, men with far more experience in India than he.

Because the court of directors had pressed such a settlement even before he departed for India, he carried out their instructions as well. Even then he did not infer "without delay" that the zemindars should be proprietors. Far from it. He postponed the decennial settlement in Dacca for one year because of the "mismanagement" of the two collectors there.[29] In fact, Cornwallis did not particularly like the zemindars, whom he damned in 1787 for "alienating the government land."[30] He simply found no alternative to them.

As a landed aristocrat Cornwallis certainly favored the position and privileges of the landed aristocracy in Britain, although he was never self-conscious about it. He was so assured of the permanency of the landed aristocracy as an institution and of the attachment of all classes of Englishmen to it that he always took his position for granted. One may certainly question, however, that his main motivation in reaching the permanent settlement was to transplant to India a replica of Britain's class structure. He said at one time that "A regular gradation of ranks . . . is nowhere more necessary than in this country for preserving order in civil society."[31] But he spoke in the context of an already graded Indian society. Indeed, the Hindu caste system separated people far more than the English class system. One could never escape one's caste in India. Cornwallis, rather, had two basic goals: a steady, assured revenue and the improvement of the land and the lives of the ryots who tilled it. His minute of 1789 expressed both aims clearly:

In a country where the landlord has a permanent property in the soil it will be worth his while to encourage his tenants who hold his farm in lease to improve that property; at any rate he will make such arrangement with them as will prevent their destroying it. But when the lord of the soil himself, the rightful owner of the land, is only to become the farmer for a lease of ten years, and if he is then to be exposed to the demands of a new rent, which may perhaps be dictated by ignorance or rapacity, what hopes can there be, I will not say of improvement, but of preventing desolation? Will it not be his interest, during the early part of that term, to extract from the estate every possible advantage for himself; and if any future hopes of a permanent settlement are then held out, to exhibit his lands at the end of it in a state of ruin . . . ? I may safely assert that one-third of the company's territory in Hindostan is now a jungle inhabited only by wild beasts. Will a ten years' lease induce any proprietor to clear away that jungle, and encourage the ryots to come and cultivate his lands, when at the end of that lease he must either submit to be taxed *ad libitum* for the newly-cultivated lands, or lose all hopes of deriving any benefit from his labour, for which perhaps by that time he will hardly be repaid? . . . Although . . . I am not only of opinion that the zemindars have the best right, but from being persuaded that nothing could be so ruinous to the public interest as that the land should be retained as the property of government, I am also convinced that, failing the claim of right of the Zemindars, it would be necessary for the public good to grant a right of property in the soil to them, or to persons of other descriptions. . . . It is immaterial to government what individual possessed the land, provided he cultivates it, protects the ryots, and pays the public revenue.[32]

Protecting the ryots meant as much to Cornwallis as assuring the public revenue. He did not devise his system only to raise money and please the court of directors. He once remarked to Archibald Campbell that though the directors merited "respect and consideration" and though government should give satisfaction to the king and his ministers, "the great object of our being here is to serve the public at large."[33] That public at large in India was, overwhelmingly, the cultivators of the soil, for whom he time and again expressed concern. In the midst of his campaign against Tipoo he could still be "anxious . . . for the success of the revenue settlement, from which I trust we shall enjoy the pleasing reflexion of having conferred happiness upon millions."[34]

More effective, however, than high-sounding phrases, was the very real legal protection that he included in the final document announcing Company policy. Government reserved the power of "enacting such Regulations as it may deem necessary for the protection of dependent Talookdars and cultivators, and no objection to be made on that account to the punctual discharge of public revenue." The zemindars were to make arrangements with the cultivators for the same period as the term of their own engagements and to keep a record which they would turn over to the collectors. They were not to increase rents arbitrarily, and they had to be specific as to the conditions under which a cultivator held and paid for the land. The zemindars could not extort. The ryots were entitled to demand and receive from the zemindars "pattahs," stating specifically the rents or conditions.[35]

That the zemindars later grew rich and that many ryots

continued to suffer oppression was not the fault of Cornwallis. He did not remain in India to implement the regulations. That task went to his successors. In any event, the ryots certainly fared as well in most instances as they had before the regulations. In addition, the measure brought rural peace, improved the lot of the zemindars, and returned an assured revenue. It also established as a permanent fixture the resident collector in Bengal, a man of whom honesty was required, who must refrain from becoming a landholder himself, and who must under no circumstances trade on his own.[36] Even were Cornwallis alive today to reflect upon the permanent settlement, he would probably consider it, despite the criticisms, a moderately successful measure.

Chapter 5

Justice

Cornwallis had just as much interest in reforming the native system of justice and police as he had in attending to the Company's revenues. He found native justice biased and brutal, and he considered the police inefficient and dishonest. Lawlessness permeated Indian society, and yet Europeans could scarcely approve the manner in which Indian justice dealt with those criminals its police did apprehend.

Criminal Justice

The England from which the earl came scarcely offered an example to emulate in either its execution of justice or its police procedure. Highwaymen and smugglers were folk heroes. Death penalties had proliferated so as to cover even the most minor offenses, with no discernible improvement in public order. Save for the Bow Street Runners, whose jurisdiction was limited, London had no effective police force. The countryside had none at all. Mobs frequently disrupted life, as in the recent Gordon Riots of 1780, when in a savage mood they had burned and looted London for a week.

And yet a spirit of humanity and reforming zeal had grown steadily in Britain during that same lawless century. James Oglethorpe had tried to help the debtors and had founded Georgia as a refuge for them. John Howard's investigations of prison conditions had done much to arouse the public conscience. Jeremy Bentham thundered endlessly against the inequities of the law. Cornwallis, a product of the new spirit, was naturally appalled

74

by the lawlessness and cruelty that seemed to prevail everywhere when he arrived in Calcutta.

The Europeans, to his chagrin, often seemed as guilty as the native inhabitants. Reports poured in of the misdeeds of Europeans, which in his view made them doubly culpable, because they should set an example of upright conduct. Cornwallis discovered that one man, a self-styled Englishman, followed the army's artillery to Dum Dum, where he set up a spirit shop that sold cheap liquor to soldiers and caused a high rate of desertion. Many European sailors deserted their ships and "having no visible means of maintenance became dangerous members of society." At Sylhet the Company's own collector seized people working for the agent of a Greek merchant trading to China and would not let them go until they agreed to work for him. The collector at Chittagong sent to Fort William under a guard of sepoys in 1789 a person of "indifferent character" who was said to have "seduced and plundered" a woman in Dacca.[1] One of Cornwallis's countrymen told the earl a long story about how a fellow Britisher had held him illegally.[2] The earl even learned of Portuguese gangs living in Calcutta who committed burglary at Chitpore.[3] In 1791, the superintendent of police reported that crime increased consistently in Calcutta, particularly among Europeans not in Company service. The council told the directors it "cannot but regret that the police of Calcutta should still continue upon a footing not only inadequate to the purpose of restraining the bold attempts of the licentious and desperate, but unauthorized, in its active exertions by any legal sanction whatever."[4]

Yet this European disruption, however shameful, was easier to bridle than was native lawlessness. Europeans for the most part could be identified and apprehended. They stood out as a relative few in a population of millions. The depredations among those millions seemed frightful and endless. Nearly every issue of the *Calcutta Gazette* for 1789 noted dacoit outrages. Dacoits even robbed European officers in the Esplanade.

The collector at Furrackhabad, John Willes, in early 1787 described a "banditti of near 2000 thieves." Willes had troubles with individuals as well. One Somier Sing, not a zemindar but a man who rented lands yielding 6,000 rupees per year, refused to pay his rent and grew bolder in defiance. Willes took Sing's son as hostage for payment. In retaliation Sing led a band of people to kidnap the lieutanant of a sepoy battalion stationed at Futty-ghur as he rode on a pleasure jaunt and then carried the hapless officer into a fort that Sing had built illegally. Willes of necessity exchanged the son for the lieutenant.[5]

Other examples of crime abounded. Captain Thomas Welsh reported to Cornwallis that at Futtyghur on the night of 31 January 1786, two hundred dacoits forced the small guard at his bungalow, opened his treasure chest, and stole 3,000 rupees.[6] Colonel Gabriel Harper reported in February of 1787 the assassi-nation of a rajah by the servant of a man whom the rajah had "confin'd and dishonor'd for a trifling balance of twenty thousand rupees." To right this illegality, the rajah's servants had murdered both the servant and the master.[7] The collector general in Thana (on the west coast) complained to the Bombay board that the parliamentary act of 1784 had denied collectors the right to serve as magistrates or justices of the peace, but that he had felt com-pelled to do so anyway as the only method of maintaining order. He had sentenced a native to a whipping for riotous behavior. He explained his sentiments: "By the inadvertency perhaps of Parliament they [collectors] do not now possess those powers legally, but the strong necessity of the case compel them still to exercise them in all petty matters that tend to preserve the peace in order that the people might feel there was a power ready and prompt instantly to punish offenses. By these fears the innocent and the peaceful can be alone protected in a country where the generality of the people are restrained by fear alone."[8]

The collector might order a whipping, which he con-sidered rough but equitable justice. Those native miscreants de-livered to native magistrates for native justice, however, did not receive even that, at least as Europeans viewed it. Moslem crim-inal law, which predominated in India, identified "crime" with "sin," thereby violating all European sensibilities. Furthermore, although the Koran served as the fountainhead for all criminal law, its interpretations differed according to the different schools of jurisprudence that had developed it. In Moslem law, a crime was a sin against God, the sovereign, or an individual. If against an individual, the aggrieved party rather than the sovereign punished the wrongdoer. But if friends of a murdered man feared the murderer and did not prosecute, he could go unpunished. One school of jurisprudence maintained that no one committed willful homicide unless he did it with a deadly weapon. Thus a man who drowned a girl and stole her clothes and ornaments, yet used no weapon save his hands, would suffer only a fine. Most Hindus did not even know the contents of Moslem penal law, and most Moslems could escape serious punishment under it. Willful homicide could not be proved on the testimony of women, slaves, or non-Moslems. Nor could a Moslem be convicted on the evidence of a non-Moslem, although a Moslem's evidence sufficed to convict a person of any religion.[9]

Most criminals escaped apprehension. Calcutta did not have a legally organized, effective police force. Those caught usually suffered in the pocketbook, with fines. Yet Moslem justice, if carried out to the full extent of the law, inflicted horrible punishments. The *Calcutta Chronicle* of 19 February 1789 described the fate of fourteen dacoits brought to the south bank of the Hughli near the orphan house. Apprehended for housebreaking, they endured the prescribed punishment of mutilation. They must have trembled in awful anticipation as one after the other they were tied to the ground and gagged, with only their right hands and left legs left free. The public executioner then proceeded to saw off, with something like a carving knife, their right hands and left feet. He took six to eight agonizing minutes with each man. When he had finished, their stumps were thrust into boiling ghee, and the amputated limbs thrown into the river. Apparently only four of the eight died from the treatment.[10] But what of the others? If they had not earned an honest living before, they now had no way to earn a living at all and became pitiful burdens on their friends, families, or the community.

Under these circumstances, Cornwallis naturally advocated reforming criminal justice, which he termed "oppressive and beyond measure corrupt." "Whilst we call ourselves sovereigns of the country we cannot leave the lives, liberty, & property of our subjects unprotected," he observed.[11] One of the first steps toward such protection came with a petition to the directors to allow the governor and council broader powers to amend the judicial system in Calcutta.[12] He told them in August of 1789 that he felt himself "called upon by the principles of humanity and a regard for the honor and interest of the Company and the nation, not to leave this Government without endeavouring to take measures to prevent in future, on one hand, the cruel punishments of mutilation, which are frequently inflicted by the Mahomedan law, and on the other to restrain the spirit of Corruption which so generally prevails in native courts, and by which wealthy offenders are generally enabled to purchase inpunity for the most atrocious crimes." [13]

From then until he completed his plans in 1792,[14] he moved ahead methodically, utilizing expert advice as he had with the permanent settlement. This time he relied upon the brilliant Welsh orientalist, Sir William Jones, a dedicated scholar and linguist. Cornwallis considered Jones "by far the most capable in that [judicial] line," whose "cordial assistance" would help right long-standing inequities.[15] A consuming intellectual curiosity had possessed Jones all his life. As an undergraduate at Oxford, he had provided board and lodging to a young Syrian in order to learn Arabic from him. From that beginning Jones had attained fluency in thirteen languages and acquainted himself with some thirty more. A lawyer from the Middle Temple, a fellow of the Royal Society, friend of Burke and Gibbon, he had become a judge in the supreme court at Calcutta in 1783. He had founded the Asiatic Society, and he and others had contributed to the *Asiatic Miscellany*. He had rediscovered Hindu culture (long forgotten or ignored by most Hindus) and had pioneered scientific archaeology. Yet Jones did not flaunt his intellect nor abuse his gifts. He fitted the pattern of those Cornwallis selected as his most trusted advisers. Like Grant and Shore, he was an honest Company servant, a pre-Victorian Victorian. He was a man of high purpose, sincerity, and "ferocious integrity." Not for him nautch girls and drunken parties. He had married for love and remained faithful to his wife, whom he had brought out to India.[16]

Jones, Shore, and Grant thoroughly adhered to the ideal of selfless devotion to duty that Cornwallis had set for himself in effecting his reforms. Whatever crass commercial motives sent the first agents of John Company to Hindustan, the aims of Cornwallis and the men whom he trusted made them the first of the new breed. He probably expressed the goals of the other three when he wrote to his son, shortly after he took up his duties, that "the reasonable object of ambition to a man is to have his name transmitted to posterity for eminent services rendered to his country and to mankind."[17]

Certainly Jones echoed Shore's regard for Cornwallis and his intimacy with him. He told George, the second Earl Spencer that he never asked patronage of Lord Cornwallis, "even for those whom I wish to serve, because if I did, the publick might think, that I returned the favor by partiality in my judicial character which ought to be above suspicion."[18] And to Dundas, Jones confided that Cornwallis had "nothing at heart but the public good" and for that reason was anxious to promote judicial reform.[19]

The governor general promoted judicial reform in two ways: by encouraging Jones to compile a digest of native laws and by promulgating with Jones's help new laws designed to ensure equitable justice and a more efficient police. The first project began in March of 1788, when Jones asked permission of Cornwallis to compile a digest of Hindu and Moslem laws for the use of English judges trying native cases.[20] Jones deemed the undertaking necessary because Europeans would not learn Sanskrit or Arabic, where the Hindu and Moslem laws were "locked," because such knowledge would not help them advance in the service. As a consequence, they relied upon native interpreters, who might twist the law any way they wished (for a price). Cornwallis not only agreed to the idea, but actively encouraged it, promising to pay the expenses of the undertaking.[21] Jones completed the Moslem section by 1792 and most of the Hindu section before his death in 1794.

Cornwallis consulted Jones while he was working on the second project, the governor general's new judicial regulations. In 1790, for example, he sent some judicial propositions to Jones for his consideration and "earnestly" recommended that Jones "use no ceremony with them but scratch out every part that you do not approve."[22] As he worked on the new criminal code, Cornwallis naturally had to familiarize himself with the legal and police systems, both as they had existed under the Mogul government and as they had been adapted by the British. Both systems were complex. In order to bring criminals to the courts, the Mogul government had established a variety of magistrates. The faujdars served as district police superintendents. Under them worked the kotwals, who oversaw the town police and represented government executive authority (the nawab), but had no judicial authority. They could, however, appoint officers to aid them. The faujdar ran an entire district and commanded anywhere from five hundred to a thousand sepoys. Yet another authority existed in villages, where two types of watchmen functioned as police: those who helped in the collection of revenue and conveyed it to the district collector and who also guarded ryots and their property; and the paiks or chaukidars, whose duty was to apprehend offenders and to prevent breaches of the peace. As the zemindar class became powerful landlords, the village police in many areas tended to come under their control, though the faujdars continued to function independently. By the time the Company assumed the right to collect the revenue in 1765, the zemindars controlled most rural police, though the nawab's police under the kotwals continued to hold authority in the towns. The zemindars became notoriously lax in law enforcement, partly because the British refused either to prod them or to accept the responsibility of police and justice, which should have gone with the new right to tax. Instead, the British allowed formal authority for criminal justice and police to remain with the nawab of Bengal's deputy, Mohammed Reza Khan. He, too, did nothing, and robber bands thrived.[23]

Hastings had begun to reverse British indifference in 1772. He established criminal courts in each district of Bengal, with native judges and legal officers, and a superior criminal court at Murshidabad, later moved to Calcutta. The district courts had jurisdiction over such felonies as murder, theft, and assault and could inflict corporal punishment, hard labor, or fines, subject to the approval of the superior court, or Sadar Nizamat Adalat. Only the superior criminal court could inflict capital punishment.

The European collector in each Bengal district tried to oversee the district court, but he was not a member of it. Hastings took over direct supervision of the judges in the superior court at Calcutta from 1773 to 1775, but then lost this control when his council stripped him of power and returned supervision to Mohammed Reza Khan. Meanwhile, according to the Regulating

Act of 1773, a new supreme court of judicature, intended primarily to deal with Europeans, had begun to function in Calcutta. Its four crown-appointed English judges (of whom Jones was one) administered British, not Indian, law to all "British subjects."

From 1776 to 1781, Mohammed Reza Khan again ran the native courts and police. He returned the superior court to Murshidabad, reorganized the district courts, and expanded the police with headquarters at the principal towns of every large district and the chief police office at Murshidabad. Yet he hamstrung the district police, who had no real authority to punish. They could only report the conduct of an unruly zemindar, a report that might eventually reach the governor general in council.

In 1781, Hastings again changed the system. He abolished the district police superintendent, or faujdar. The Company's servants now began to act as civil court judges and as magistrates, who could apprehend alleged criminals and commit them to the district criminal courts. The problem was that these courts, still with Moslem judges, now had no control over their European police, who supposedly worked with the help of the zemindars. Another European, the remembrancer of criminal courts, had the power to receive court and magistrate records, supposedly in order to coordinate the unwieldy police and judicial branches. Hastings, in the name of economy, reduced the number of district courts and also created new native establishments to help the European magistrates in their duties. These new police, numbering anywhere from 25 to 150, depending on the district, carried swords, shields, and sometimes matchlocks. With this force at their disposal, the European magistrates could not call out the sepoys without the permission of the local commanding officer, but they might ask a zemindar to maintain additional police stations at the zemindar's own expense.[24]

That was the system when Cornwallis arrived, and he proceeded to change it in several ways. First, he gave more authority to European magistrates. On 27 July 1787, they received the power to try persons accused of petty offenses and to inflict corporal punishment to the extent of fifteen lashes, or a fine of not over 200 rupees, or fifteen days in jail.[25] The collectors, already civil judges, thus became criminal judges with limited powers.

Through the work of these collector-judges, Cornwallis began to acquire the necessary information for instituting other changes, notably in establishing more equitable criminal justice.

He ordered them to report on the law courts in their districts and to give information on the average length of detention before trial, the punishments for robbery and murder, the monetary allowances of court officers, the effectiveness of Moslem law in suppressing crime, and so on. The answers did not give the earl any reason for satisfaction with the native justice, for the reports spoke time and again of unpunished murders and robberies, mutilations, prolonged imprisonments without trials, dishonest judges, and the constant suffering of the masses.[26]

These reports particularly impressed the aristocratic Cornwallis, whose confirmed belief in noblesse oblige, a benevolent paternalism in government, held even more in India than in his native England; he saw the suffering Indian masses as far less able to better their lot. The British administrators in Bengal should for the good of the people initiate and themselves manage a new judicial system. He told the directors in 1789: "I conceive that all regulations for the reform of that department [criminal justice] would be useless and nugatory, whilst the execution of them depends upon any native whatever . . . and that two or three respectable Company's servants should be selected to act as superintendents of the criminal trials, which may be conducted, under their inspection, by native judges . . . in strict conformity to the laws and customs of Hindustan."[27] He wrote to Dundas in March of 1789 that "three or four judges for Bengal and Bahar from the Company's senior servants . . . should go the circuit twice a year and superintend the trials and be particularly careful that the sentences should be executed on those who are found guilty and that the innocent should be released."[28] Thus Europeans alone would hold ultimate responsibility for equitable justice for the inhabitants of Bengal. "Although," he said in 1793, "we hope to render our subjects the happiest people in India, I should by no means propose to admit the natives to any participation in framing Regulations."[29] He would not upset the natives by overthrowing their laws or customs, for such a change would scarcely benefit either Indians or British. But he would eliminate what he considered the worst abuses in native law or custom and would make both conform to what he considered the best parts of English law. And he would rely entirely on British scrutiny and supervision.[30]

The governor general began laying down a new set of criminal regulations in December of 1790. He asserted that motive, not method, would determine the sentence in murder cases and that a murdered man's relatives could not pardon the murderer. He took the criminal courts away from Mohammed Reza Khan and put them in English hands. The governor general and council would now run the superior criminal court, which would meet in Calcutta at least once a week. It had the power of review over district courts, though the governor general alone had the right of pardon in his executive capacity. Cornwallis also replaced the old faujdari district courts with four provincial courts of circuit, three for Bengal and one for Bihar, each presided over by two European judges from among the Company's servants. The courts would move in turn to each district headquarters and after a complete circuit would fix themselves at Calcutta, Dacca, Murshidabad, and Patna, there to try prisoners interned by the city magistrates.

Cornwallis made European subjects answerable only to the supreme court of judicature at Calcutta. This principle of letting only Europeans try other Europeans he had enunciated in 1786, almost as soon as he got to India. "I am however willing to acknowledge myself," he said in November of that year, "averse to suffer the Europeans of any nation to be tried by the Mahommedan tribunals. How far it may be prudent to relax from the established practice of the native government in this instance, you will be better enabled to judge from what follows. If it should be relinquished, I am clearly of opinion that we ought then to preserve this power to ourselves, and that the French if this point be acceded to them should be tried for offenses committed by them against the peace of the country by the court of justice in Calcutta."[31]

In conformity to a principle he constantly stressed—that decent pay instead of gratuities, or presents, would encourage honesty among Company servants as well as among Indians —he gave the new judges and their Indian assistants adequate salaries.

During 1791 and 1792, he instituted yet more reforms: he altered the law of evidence so that Moslems were now subject to the death sentence on the evidence of non-Moslems; he gave magistrates power to try cases of petty theft except by notorious criminals; he demanded that magistrates pay witnesses in need of financial assistance a daily sum and traveling expenses for the circuit courts (more than England did for witnesses during this time); he ordered a month's subsistence for prisoners released after long confinement to tide them over until they could support themselves (again ahead of England); and he abolished the practice of attaching the property of prisoners awaiting trial. These and other measures went into the Cornwallis Code of 1793, which also abolished mutilation of limbs, established definite court procedures, and deprived the collector of his power as magistrate.

The police, too, changed, in accordance with rules Cornwallis set down in December of 1792. He first disbanded the police run by the zemindars and forbade them to maintain any police establishments in the future. He divided the districts into police jurisdictions of twenty to thirty miles each. A native government officer in each of these districts became a salaried daroga of police with regularly defined and established subordinates. The daroga, who secured his position on recommendation of a magistrate, had to possess a certain amount of property to qualify him for office, and he acted directly under the magistrate's authority. To encourage zealousness, the new rules allowed him a 10 percent commission on the recovery of stolen property. The rural police became subject to the daroga's orders, and the zemindars were required to help him. The principal cities of Dacca, Patna, and Murshidabad received special establishments. Natives still filled the police jobs, but now they became the direct instruments of the Company government under the British magistrates. In Calcutta itself, a new superintendent, the preparer of reports, and two deputies headed the police. They lost all judicial powers, but they and their subordinates received substantial salaries to encourage their honesty.[32]

Finally, Cornwallis improved the jails. Even by the low standards of contemporary English jails, the ones in India were shamefully wretched and overcrowded when the earl arrived there. One contained, in a room seventy-two by forty-eight feet, 179 prisoners, who were locked in stocks at night to give each of them twenty-five inches of space. Jails located on river banks were frequently swept away in the rainy season. Debtors, murderers, robbers, men, and women often sweltered together in the same cell. Some buildings were so rotten that heavy winds blew them down. Rooms in some jails swam knee deep in water. The disgraceful account went on and on.

In 1790, the governor general transferred management and control of jails to the European magistrates in each district. Conditions still did not improve, however, so the earl manifested his intention to rebuild every jail in the province to protect the health, morals, and safety of the prisoners. He promised inexpensive repairs after the admittedly heavy initial costs of building. He planned to construct five brick prisons each year (instead of the conventional ones of mud, straw, or bamboo) until a sufficiency existed and to segregate sexes, types of prisoners, and prisoners of different religious persuasions.[33] He thus began in India the type of humanitarian reform his distinguished contemporary John Howard had passionately advocated in England. But, unlike Howard, Cornwallis could effect his proposals because to do so he did not have to overthrow an entrenched interest group of his own countrymen.

Civil Justice

In the area of civil justice, Cornwallis encountered more opposition to his attempts at reform. Directors, the Company's erratic past performances, indeed the very nature of civil justice— all worked to confound the new governor general's efforts. Civil justice involved all manner of contracts, wills, property disputes, tax matters, and so on. In India, as the Mogul government had declined, civil justice had fallen into the hands of men in charge of revenue collection. When, therefore, the Company received the diwani in 1765, it almost of necessity received the responsibility to administer civil justice.

As in many other matters, Warren Hastings had taken the lead in attempting to make the Company live up to this new responsibility. In 1772, he established a civil court in each district and a supreme civil court (the Sadar Diwani Adalat) in Calcutta.

European collectors presided over the former and a Company servant over the latter. Indian officials helped the presidents, whose courts administered Moslem and Hindu law. The supreme civil court, because of troubles with the supreme court of judicature, did not function at all between 1774 and 1780 and only poorly from then until 1786.

In 1773, the court of directors altered Hastings's arrangement by replacing the collectors with six provincial councils of revenue, which also sat as civil courts, at Calcutta, Burdwan, Murshidabad, Dacca, Dinajpur, and Patna. Elsewhere than in these six provincial seats the directors returned both revenue collection and the district courts to the natives.

Hastings disliked the revenue councils and in 1777 appointed a Company servant unconnected with them to oversee the court of civil justice at Dacca, thus separating civil justice from revenue collection. In 1780, he appointed Company servants to preside similarly over the five remaining provincial courts, independent of the revenue councils. The six revenue councils remained as courts for trying revenue cases, but the six new courts tried all other civil causes.

All of Cornwallis's personal efforts were required to make the supreme civil court function well. He issued an order on 13 November 1786 that the governor general and council would sit once a week as the Sadar Diwani Adalat. By 1787, he reported that the court functioned regularly and got through the business brought before it.[34]

In 1788, the directors again altered the civil judicial system. On Shore's advice, they abolished the provincial revenue councils and reestablished the collectors, to whom they also gave judicial powers. Shore had deemed it almost impossible to draw a line between revenue and other civil matters and feared that if they clashed, justice, or revenue, or both, must suffer. The collector thus acquired despotic power as judge, magistrate, and revenue gatherer. The board of revenue in Calcutta became the court of appeal from the decisions of the collectors and in 1790 a court of review as well.

When Cornwallis altered this system in 1793, he probably did so more on the basis of abstract principle, that is, his conception of the English common law and the English constitution, than for reasons of practical experience. A cornerstone of the English common law—one for which Parliament had struggled against the king in the seventeenth century and which it had eventually gained in 1701, when the Act of Settlement rendered judges independent of the crown—was that no man should judge in his own cause. Yet the revenue collectors, acting as civil judges in cases often relating to the revenue, possessed power the English king had lost decades before, that of acting as arbiters in their own cause. This situation Cornwallis thought intolerable and inequitable. By the early 1790s, he had determined to change it. "I have been for some time employed," he wrote to Sir Charles Oakeley at Madras in December of 1792, "in preparing a plan for separating the judicial authority from the collection of revenue."[35] He wrote the directors in March of 1793 explaining in some detail why he wished to strip collectors of judicial powers: "Where the power to redress oppressions, and functions that must always have a tendency to promote or screen the commission of them, are united in the same person, a strict adherence to the principles of justice cannot be expected, and still less can it be hoped that the people will feel a confidence of obtaining justice."[36]

Thus, in the Cornwallis Code of 1793, collectors lost their judicial powers and reverted to the business of collecting alone. The code abolished the distinction between civil and revenue causes and gave the district courts the power to hear all civil causes. It set up appeal courts with English judges, who also presided over the criminal courts of circuit in the same town.

Cornwallis in effect created a class of Indian lawyers—a class that would eventually become instrumental in pushing for self-government—by his regulations providing for licensed Hindu and Moslem vakils, or pleaders, to serve as legal representatives for people unfamiliar with the law who might wish the services of experts in litigation. To prevent gouging, rules further stipulated precisely the fees that pleaders could charge, according to the nature of the suit. Indeed, some thirty-nine clauses dealt with these pleaders.

The code also made the collectors—hitherto unrestricted—subject to law. No matter what a collector did, a native until now had possessed no legal recourse against him other than that of petitioning the governor general. Regulation three, however, now rendered collectors, commercial residents, and all other servants of the Company subject to the courts for their official actions. No British subject—aside from king's officers and Company servants —could move more than ten miles inland from Calcutta unless he would submit himself to the jurisdiction of the civil courts in any suits brought against him. As one modern Indian student has noted: "The code of 1793 may be characterised as the very bed-rock of modern Indian judicial system."[37] Another scholar states that "for the first time in British India a Government Regulation laid down the principle of the sovereignty of the law."[38] Perhaps an early biographer of Cornwallis summed up best the code's impact: "The Cornwallis Code, whether for revenue, police, criminal and civil justice, or other functions, defined and set bounds to authority, created procedure by a regular system of appeal guarded against the miscarriage of justice, and founded the Civil Service as it exists to this day [1914]. This Code has been the basis of every attempt to introduce law and order into each succes-sive acquisition of districts and kingdoms."[39]

White Rule and Racism

But the good government that Cornwallis insisted upon es-tablishing in India was not to be self-government. Indeed, the earl thought that in India the two were mutually exclusive. Thus he deliberately excluded the native inhabitants from any significant participation in their own government. Until the twentieth centu-ry, the Indian Civil Service and the army officers would all remain white Britishers, a policy Cornwallis began. On 5 November 1789, he wrote to Sir George Yonge at the war office, proposing this policy of exclusion. He noted that many of the English fathered children by the "black women who are natives of this country," educated them at considerable expense, and then solicit-ed ensigncies for them in the king's regiments in India. He admit-ted that many of these young men had the education of "gentle-men" and might acquit themselves with "propriety in a military character." Yet, he continued, "as on account of their colour & extraction they are considered in this country as inferior to Euro-peans, I am of opinion that those of them who possess the best abilities could not command that authority and respect which is necessary in the due discharge of the duty of an officer. And that by far the greatest part of them would be held in utter contempt by soldiers of His Majesty's regiments." Cornwallis added that, although he had refused all applications from these unfortunate half-castes, he feared that future commanders in chief might have difficulty in doing so should requests come from people high in the Company's service. He therefore recommended "that the King will be pleased to issue such orders and establish such regulations as will in future effectually bar the introduction of any persons but those who can furnish the clearest proofs that both their parents are European born or descended from Europeans without any mixture of the blood of natives of this country, as officers or even soldiers into any of the British regiments that are now or that may be hereafter employed in India."[40] The king and the war office agreed, and Yonge instructed the earl to inform his successor of his policy and the reasons for it and to pass on to him a letter containing the king's express orders to follow a similar policy of exclusion.[41] But it was not only the regular army that was thus affected. A standing order of 19 April 1791 stipulated: "No person, the son of a Native Indian, shall henceforward be appointed by this Court to Employment in the Civil, Military, or Marine Service of the Company."[42]

The earl thus institutionalized racism. The rulers of India henceforth would be lily-white (insofar as the Indian sun allowed). That policy, of course, has not only generated criticism, but also has infuriated many observers of the British role in India. One should, however, consider the policy in historical perspective. Cornwallis's recommendation against appointing a half-caste as an officer was as much a reflection of the thinking of his society as his recommendation that the governor general come from the aristocracy. In each instance, his chief consideration was that those in authority must be able to command the respect and obedience of all their subordinates. There were other historical aspects that bore as well upon the policy of exclusion. In the early days of John Company relations between British and native inhabitants were more informal than by mid-eighteenth century. Thereafter relations grew more and more formal. Cornwallis, in essence, only formalized them even more. Naturally, in the 1730s and 1740s the English could not afford that superiority they later affected because they still held their territory only tenuously and confronted native powers and the French, who might at any time oust them from India. By Cornwallis's day, the British had bested their European rivals and mastered Bengal. They had won by force of arms, using native soldiers to defeat native powers. Victors usually think themselves superior to losers and do not, therefore, often adapt themselves to the ways of the losers. In any event, no matter how freely and easily British and Indian society mixed in the earlier days, they never truly blended. Indeed, how could they, when Indian society maintained sharp cleavages within itself? Religion stopped the native Moslems from marrying or even socializing to any extent with the Hindus, just as it stopped Hindus from one caste marrying Hindus of another, or even eating with them. The British came upon an established caste and class society to which they merely added another class and caste, based upon the Christian religion and a white skin. The argument that earlier the British had taken Indian girls as mistresses, or even married them, scarcely proves a merger of the two societies. Britishers did not wed native girls, take them back to Britain as legal spouses, establish them in a residence in some country home purchased with the wealth of India, and father by them heirs to the estate. A British resident, such as William Hickey, who took an Indian mistress, no more regarded Indians as his equal than a southern plantation owner who took a mistress among his slaves regarded the black people as his equal.[43] One of the forces that kept the British Empire alive was a British conviction of superiority: the superiority of Christianity over other religions, the superiority of British culture and institutions over all alien ones, the moral superiority of the British over other peoples. Indeed, without that conviction of one's own rightness and righteousness, can one ever undertake to acquire and maintain an empire?

Cornwallis had no doubt that certain classes in the world naturally ruled and others naturally obeyed them. In Britain, the aristocracy and gentry ruled, and in India the British. The system worked, he believed, because the classes at the top were much fitter to govern than those at the bottom. He had a low opinion of the intelligence, ability, or honesty of natives, though he often credited them with a low cunning. Undoubtedly his outlook was sharply influenced by his military perspective of them: as a British general he viewed British regulars as superior to sepoys and British-trained sepoys as superior to soldiers of native chiefs, such as those of the nizam of Hyderabad. In the midst of his campaign against Tipoo of Mysore he wrote of his native allies: "I need hardly state to you that in transacting business with people differing so much from ourselves in language, manners, and customs, so unsystematic in their natures, *so ignorant of the military science* [italics ours], and so liable to be biassed from the pursuit of a general good by private and selfish views, many difficulties are unavoidably experienced."[44] On another occasion he expressed himself yet more strongly. "Your experience must have convinced you," he told Edward Otto Ives, British resident at Lucknow in Oudh, "that nor princes or men of rank in this country are capable of holding open and manly language, but that when they are pressed, they will palliate weak or unguarded acts by disavowals or evasions of any kind."[45] To the British military commander in Madras, General William Medows, he wrote: "Let me earnestly recommend it to you to pursue that system so adapted to the genius of the east, and always prefer the Golden Key to the Iron one when you have an opportunity of doing it."[46] In other words, the "genius of the east" consisted of a society always open to bribery. No doubt he felt that this "eastern" trait had corrupted Company servants who might otherwise have been honest.

Yet Cornwallis might not have established such ironclad exclusionist rules had men of importance and influence in the Company opposed the policy. None did. Directors, civil and military officers, commercial residents, revenue collectors—from highest to lowest, they, too, were convinced of the necessity for the British to rule the natives. The directors had made their position clear more than a year before Cornwallis arrived in India. On 21 September 1785, they wrote to the governor general that natives should not be employed to do the business of "writers and others in our service." Natives, they emphasized, could only copy papers and be employed in "other subordinate occupations."[47] More than any European in India, Sir William Jones understood and appreciated the Indian cultural achievements and tried to get his fellow Europeans to understand them. Yet even Jones never considered making the Indians equal partners in the rule of Bengal. Although he had completed a tract on what he considered the essentials of good government, "that substantial freedom is both the daughter and parent of virtue," he admitted as he was sailing to India that he would "certainly not preach them [his doctrines of freedom] to the Indians, who must and will be governed by absolute power." [48] Firsthand acquaintance with Bengal in no way altered this opinion. To the American Arthur Lee he wrote on 1 October 1786:

I shall never cease thinking, that rational liberty makes men virtuous; and virtue happy: wishing therefore ardently for universal happiness, I wish for universal liberty. But your observation on the Hindus is too just: they are incapable of civil liberty; few of them have an idea of it; and those, who have, do not wish it. They must (I deplore the evil, but know the necessity of it) they must be ruled by an absolute power; and I feel my pain much alleviated by knowing the natives themselves as well as from observation, that they are happier under us than they were or could have been under the Sultans of Delhi or petty Rajas. [49]

Three years later, his thinking had not changed in the slightest. To his friend Walter Pollard he wrote: "Let not my Americans, therefore, be like the deluded, besotted Indians, among whom I live, who would receive Liberty as a curse instead of a blessing, if it were possible to give it to them, and would reject as a vase of poison, that, which, if they could taste and digest it, would be the water of life." [50] Charles Ware Malet, the highly trusted resident with the Mahrattas, for whom Cornwallis secured a baronetcy, also deprecated the Hindus: "A Bramin Politician," he told the earl, "will gladly submit to the imputation of Chicane to avoid the appearance of weakness." [51] Sir Archibald Campbell, like Cornwallis a veteran of the American war, and governor of Madras much of the time Cornwallis served at Calcutta, echoed these sentiments. Campbell wrote Henry Dundas in May of 1787 that he thought well of Cornwallis, who had acted with "truth and justice," but feared the earl might trust the Indians too much. Campbell added: "I hope, however, he will not put too much faith in the Natives who are connected with us. They are a faithless set of men, and all of them wholly indifferent to the performance of their engagements, when they cease to be desireable or convenient to themselves." [52] The natives, then, were "faithless," "deluded," "besotted." With such a climate of opinion, who can wonder that the earl believed in British rule?

Furthermore, the thought may have struck him that if in many ways he was instituting reforms in India along English lines, if he was straightening out the bureaucratic tangle to make it conform more closely to the English system of administration (scarcely a good model), then why not employ Englishmen, who knew about such a system, instead of Indians, who did not?

Cornwallis gave the power to the British, but he repeatedly stressed, repeatedly urged, the duties and responsibility that went with the power. "The White Man's Burden," a phrase Rudyard Kipling coined over a century later and that the opponents of empire have quite understandably derided in the twentieth century, was a real and pressing challenge to men such as Cornwallis. Indeed, it offered to them one of the strongest justifications for the British presence in India. If honest Britishers, such men as Jones of sincere goodwill and good intentions, could not in any way help the people they had conquered, could not in any way improve their lot, then the British might as well go home.

Cornwallis demonstrated, time and again, in ordinary matters of everyday life as well as large matters of state, his concern for the welfare of individual Indians as well as for the whole society. In a private way he showed this concern when he severely rebuked a British lieutenant of the 52d regiment, for abusing a native creditor. The lieutenant beat one Perseram with a stick when Perseram came to ask payment for a "just debt," already seven months overdue. The lieutenant beat him a second time, "which divided the poor man's ear," when Perseram returned after complaining to the commanding officer. Cornwallis said that the officer's conduct partook "both of ferocity and injustice." It was "no less unworthy of the manners of gentlemen than disgraceful to the character of officers." Cornwallis then ordered the regimental commanding officer not only to discharge the original debt by deductions from the lieutenant's pay, but also by the same method to make available a sum of money "to be given to Perseram, as a small compensation for the barbarous treatment that he has received."[53]

He assisted the helpless, whether groups or individuals, in every way he could. He noted the past sufferings of native weavers who had been oppressed by the commercial officials of the Company. These officials had forced the weavers to accept small advances and then made them "work throughout the year at a price that could not support themselves & their families." As a result many of them had either fled Bengal or tried to find different occupations.[54] Accordingly, Cornwallis set down in his commercial regulations of 1793 elaborate rules for the protection of native weavers. Section twenty-eight of commercial regulation thirty-one provided that "natives aggrieved by any act done in opposition to this regulation, by any commercial resident, or officer in charge of a residency" had a legal means of redress.[55] Another manifestation of his concern was the establishment in Benares of a Sanskrit college for Hindus. Opened in 1791, this college was the inspiration and child of Jonathan Duncan, but Cornwallis approved it wholeheartedly.[56] The earl's deep interest in the welfare of the indigenous population even emerged in the establishment of a mint for new coinage. Bengal had many different coins, each valued differently. One could encounter there the Sicca rupee, the Arcot rupee, the "sonaut" rupee, the Bombay rupee, Bengal mohurs, Madras star pagodas, Spanish dollars, Dutch florins: all told, in Bengal there flourished some twenty-seven different species of coins. The values fluctuated constantly, especially in Calcutta, between the Arcot (or Madras) rupee and the Sicca rupee, a fact that puzzled one observer, who could "not see any good reason for it."[57] Hastings had tried to reform the system, but the Company refused to shoulder the expense of minting a standard coin. Cornwallis gave two reasons for his determination to end this monetary confusion. In the first place, Company commerce suffered from the fluctuating exchange rates, and he told the directors that a general coinage of all the silver into rupees of the same denomination would produce "many solid advantages to the Company's interest." But just as important, a standard coinage would relieve the "vexation and extortion" the peasants, who were the "most industrious and useful part of the inhabitants of their territories."[58] It would help the ryots and discourage the leeches who prospered from their suffering. The earl wrote to Dundas that the "batta, or exchange on the different silver coins, is a great grievance & distress to the poor ryots, & is a great source of emolument to the shroffs [native bankers] & I fear some collectors."[59] As a result, he intended to issue new coinage (the Company had that right under the 1677 charter of Charles II) and to establish new mints, especially at Patna. In 1792, he appointed a mint committee to have general control over the mints and to find a way to standardize the monetary system. On the basis of this committee's findings, his successor Shore established one legal tender for public and private business.[60] This standardization, aside from its importance as a beginning of modern Indian currency,[61] and even aside from its promotion of internal commercial stability, contributed to the welfare of the natives, a project as important to Cornwallis as the Company's commerce.

Unquestionably, however, the most humanitarian of his reforms did not even pretend to relate to commerce. It dealt with slavery. Shortly after the earl reached Calcutta, he received an appeal to right the situation of "those miserable and deserted objects," children who were sold into slavery and tortured or otherwise ill treated, especially by "lower class" Englishmen.[62] The earl's military secretary, Henry Haldane, received an anonymous letter a year later telling much the same tale. Because of the "distresses of their parents," free-born native children were carted off to Mauritius and the Cape of Good Hope and sold into slavery. Captain William Kirkpatrick, whom Cornwallis would later entrust with an important mission to Nepal, confirmed the report in a letter from Barrackpore. Kirkpatrick damned this "shocking and Depopulating" traffic, though he believed it carried on by "native Portuguese living under the protection of the British government," rather than by the "lower class" Englishmen mentioned in the earlier complaints.[63]

Cornwallis could not, by himself, end slavery. Moslem law sanctioned it. Furthermore, it was still practiced in other parts of the British Empire, especially in the West Indies. But he did not like it, and he considered trafficking in innocent children "infamous" and "shocking to humanity." Though he did not have the power to stop slavery, he could and did stop the trade in children.[64] On 27 July 1789, by proclamation in council, he served notice that in the future anyone concerned directly or indirectly in this "inhuman and detestable traffic, shall be prosecuted with the utmost rigor in the Supreme Court at the expence of the Company, and, if British-born subjects, shall be forthwith ordered to Europe." He commanded the proclamation to be read in Calcutta and throughout Bengal and then reread on 1 January of every year. He not only instructed the courts to enforce the proclamation, but he also offered a reward of 100 Sicca rupees (about £11) to anyone who discovered an offender who was subsequently convicted before the supreme court of judicature or the magistrate of the district, and he offered a further bonus of 50 rupees for each person of either sex liberated as a result of the discovery. He also took steps to ensure that children could not be smuggled aboard ship.[65]

A Proud Record

Cornwallis thus went far in "Anglicizing" Bengal and in making the Company's affairs prosperous, efficient, and honestly managed. All the changes he introduced and the reforms he advanced reflected a trend characteristic of eighteenth-century Britain, a sort of "creeping" professionalism in all branches of government. Just as Shelburne and Pitt and Charles Lennox, the third Duke of Richmond (at the ordnance), were trying to shape a more efficient administration at home, so Cornwallis was attempting it in the service of the East India Company. He was formalizing functions, organizing the bureaucracy, and establishing a judicial system, all designed to function regardless of the vagaries of wayward individuals.

He was also interested in a sort of balanced constitution for India, somewhat like that of Britain, although as chief executive in India he exercised far more power over the area he ruled than did George III over the British Isles. If, as is certainly true, some of his ideas about the proper method of governing Bengal came from his observation of the British government, wherein lay the harm? What security had there been for life, liberty, property, justice, or the right to enjoy the fruits of one's own labor before he came? If the answer was very little, then some new system would have to be found, and some of its features would naturally be English. In his British approach to reform he both acted within a past tradition and set a pattern for the future. Certainly his successors—Wellesley, Hastings, Bentinck, Dalhousie, and Curzon, to name a few—were just as completely British in their conceptions of proper government. G. H. Barlow summed up what he thought Cornwallis's changes had meant when he wrote to the former governor general in 1795:

I conceive the distribution of the legislative, executive, and judicial powers, described in my letter of the 24th ultimo (which, as stated in that letter, has for its object no specific law or regulation but generally to ensure by its own operation the enaction of just and politic regulations, and the impartial administration of them when enacted) forms in the Bengal constitution the *sure*, *solid* and *presiding principle* which Mr. [Edmund] Burke points out as the proper object for those who have any concern in framing the government of a country; and that the operation of this principle described in the thirty second paragraph of that letter shows its 'prolific energy.'[66]

And yet none of the changes the earl advanced, none of the system he created was as important as the nature of the man himself. Cornwallis was a racist who did not believe in democracy. But he did believe in justice, honesty, integrity, and decency, a legacy he left behind him. The *Oxford History of India* has summed up the earl's accomplishments admirably:

The constructive work of Cornwallis was one of which any man might have been proud. Though the Permanent Settlement had serious defects, it gave tranquillity to the countryside and stability to the government: though the reorganization of the services was marred by the exclusion of senior Indians, it established a service distinguished for both efficiency and integrity; though the courts were blocked before long by massive arrears of business, they were capable of improvement and embodied the great principles of the separation of powers and the rule of law. Taking it all in all, Cornwallis had set the Company's ship of state on a new course, and had brought in justice and integrity to redress corruption and power politics.[67]

Chapter 6

The Army

Cornwallis was first and foremost a soldier, and the army came closer to his heart than any other institution. Despite his significant reforms in other areas, he spent the greatest part of his time studying the condition of the army and planning its reform, as his Indian papers show. Nonetheless it was in this field that he confronted the most opposition to his reforms and that he had the least success in effecting them. Perhaps it is for this reason that historians have paid little attention to his administrative work in the area of the military.[1]

Cornwallis hoped above all else he might achieve in India to straighten out the confusion, disorganization, waste, duplication, and inefficiency he discerned in the Indian army. He wanted the Company to offer better pay and conditions to its officers, and he wanted to transform the Company's European army into one that better conformed to the standards of the regular British army. Some of his earliest ideas, such as that of amalgamating the Company's and the king's armies, he abandoned once he reached India and learned of the actual conditions there. To understand what he confronted and what he had to undertake, one must first look at the forces that held British India for the Company.

By far the largest part of the military establishment consisted of regiments of native, or sepoy, infantry, commanded by British officers in the Company service. After the Company commissioned its cadets as officers, it promoted them strictly on the basis of seniority. The officers cherished this promotion by seniority, because they often lacked the influence and the money that could gain them rapid promotions in the regular British army.

Although pay in the Company army was not particularly good, neither was it in the regular army, whose officers were expected to be "gentlemen" of independent means at least. The officers in the sepoy army could supplement their income with several Indian perquisites and various legal allowances. If a man could withstand the Indian climate and the ravages it did to his constitution, he could by means of seniority work his way to the top, accumulate a tidy fortune, and retire to Britain.

Opportunities to accomplish that goal seemed to increase in the eighteenth century as the army grew rapidly in numbers, expanding from 18,000 in 1763 to more than 115,000 in 1782. By Cornwallis's time it numbered around 55,000 men in Bengal, 50,000 in Madras, and 18,000 in Bombay.[2] Opportunities, however, did not keep pace with growth. To be sure, the directors increased the number of officers, but only at the lower levels of subalterns and captains. By 1784, the entire Indian army had perhaps only ten colonels and thirty lieutenant colonels and no general officers, though if a colonel became commander in chief at one of the presidencies he sometimes received a generalship. (After Cornwallis's time, regular British officers tended to become commanders in chief.) Thus, while a captain in the Indian army commanded a battalion, one in the regular army, by contrast, led only a company, and command of a regular battalion went to no less than a lieutenant colonel. Although Company officers received neither furlough nor retirement income, they provided for their own future from opportunities available to them on the Indian scene.

These Company officers led good soldiers. The sepoys had won victory after victory, had held British India during the dark days of the American revolutionary war, and would prove the force most instrumental in future British expansion. Yet the composition of these regiments made problems for the Company: they contained Hindus of different classes, as well as Moslems, all of whom had different eating habits imposed by their religion. Thus a sepoy army needed a complicated and extensive messing arrangement and a huge train of camp followers. When Cornwallis campaigned against Tipoo, for example, he apparently had four hundred thousand people with him, although only eighty thousand of them, or one-fifth, went in a military capacity as members of the Company's army, British regulars, and the allied troops.[3] Archibald Campbell once noted: "The tribe of supernumerary servants, sutlers, and taylors which follow a battalion in the field are certainly among the greatest curses attending the movements of an Indian army."[4] A further complication faced the commander in chief with regard to the Company's Bengal army: the vast majority were Hindus, many of them high-caste Brahmins, who hesitated to serve outside their native states of Bengal or Oudh for fear of losing caste.

Cornwallis thus needed to act cautiously with the sepoys, especially when he wished them to serve outside Bengal. As long as he honored their religious customs and paid them with reasonable regularity, he could depend upon their loyalty. Most of them could make a better living by parading in the Company's uniform than by working in any other occupation. Their white officers, unlike the regular officers of the British army, knew their language and understood their customs. When trained by these officers in European tactics, the sepoy regiments became more formidable than any other infantry in all of India, save for the British regulars. "A brigade of our Sepoys," Cornwallis told the Duke of York, "would easily make anybody Emperor of Hindostan."[5]

In addition to the sepoys and their officers, the East India Company maintained twelve battalions of European infantry, half of them in Bengal. Though each battalion supposedly should have numbered around five hundred, returns to Cornwallis often indicated that the battalions had less than half their normal complement. Their insufficient numbers owed in part to difficulties in recruiting. The Company could not compete on equal terms with the regulars, had neither programs nor depots for recruiting, and depended almost entirely upon agents in England to sign up men who would come East on India-bound ships. The British also enlisted French, Portuguese (a term then frequently used to denote a half-caste), Dutch, and any other Europeans floating around in India. Naturally enough, these latter additions to the European infantry were not the best human material. It was axiomatic that British regulars were the "scum of the earth," recruited in grog shops, back alleys, and sometimes impressed. How much worse, then, were the privates in the Company's European army? To go to India with a military cadetship or a civilian clerkship in the Company's service held the possibility of promotion, riches, fame, retirement to England, a country house, and even perhaps Parliament. But who would wish to become a private in the Company's European army, the lowest of the low, with none of the opportunities yet all of the dangers of India? For these and other reasons Cornwallis found the European battalions remarkably deficient as military units and thought poorly of the men who filled their ranks.

The Company maintained its own engineer corps and an artillery unit of six battalions, which, since it required more skill, attracted the best of the European recruits. The Company also had sixty-seven native artillery companies, though it at one time forbade their employment in Bombay.[6] Sepoy cavalry were so few in numbers as to be negligible for a major campaign. During Cornwallis's time, the Company employed seven cavalry regiments, one in Bengal, one in Oudh, and five (numbering about two thousand men) in Madras.[7] Nor did these regiments make up in efficiency for their small numbers. The commandant at Cawnpore said of the Oudh cavalry that the men could not "fire from their horses. Neither does this regiment attempt the practice of it, altho they have wore out two sets of arms."[8] Because of its deficiency in cavalry, the Company's battle formations differed from those in Europe. Colonel Thomas Dean Pearse, who commanded the artillery at Fort William, wrote to Cornwallis in 1787: "The total want of cavalry obliges us to rely on cannon for the protection of our line. For this reason two guns in every interval and two on each flank will I believe always be a necessary arrangement in Hindostan."[9] The Company's shortage in this area had a significant effect on Cornwallis's campaigning, forcing him to the unsatisfactory expedient of relying on his native allies for cavalry support.

The king hired some of his British regulars out to the Company to supplement its forces. After reinforcement by four regiments of regular infantry in 1788 (and considerable acrimony between the government and the Company over it), Cornwallis commanded nine regiments of British foot and one of British dragoons, numbering approximately 7,500 men.[10] Unfortunately, the regular battalions, like the Company's European battalions, remained chronically understrength.

Cornwallis commanded no regular artillery until 1791, when the government sent him two companies of the royal regiment, each numbering about 6 officers and 114 men.[11]

This odd assortment did not quite complete the roster of men who served the East India Company in a military capacity in India. King George III of England was also Elector of Hanover, and he had absolute command over that German principality's armed forces. During the American Revolution, after Hyder Ali had defeated Colonel Baillie in the Carnatic and threatened to oust the British from India, the king's English cabinet had decided to hire Germans to serve in India.[12] Their efforts resulted in the raising of two Hanoverian regiments, the 13th and 14th, which went to Madras. They served there to the consternation of Archibald Campbell, who estimated their maintenance cost the Company no less than £50,000 annually.[13]

A hodgepodge thus comprised the British military establishment in India. Yet it alone, as every civil and military servant of the Company knew, made possible the Company's rule in Bengal, Madras, and Bombay and its increasing prestige elsewhere.[14] The British held their portions of India by virtue of their military superiority over the forces of native rulers.

The directors, of course, worried about losing that superiority if they could not improve, perhaps completely reorganize, their military service. At the same time, they had to ensure that the Company's sepoy and European forces increased in numbers. Growth demanded more officers for the army, which in turn required more cadets. An enlarged army, in other words, meant an enlarged patronage. As a result, the directors only reluctantly accepted the king's troops, over whom they exercised neither control nor patronage. When the Duke of Richmond, master general of the ordnance (which commanded the royal artillery), sent two companies of royal artillery to India in April of 1791, he mentioned to Cornwallis the directors' reluctance: "It was at all times proper that the king's troops in India should have a corps of the royal artillery attached to them. He [Dundas] however, found great reluctance in the Court of Directors to consent to this Measure, possibly from the loss of Patronage they would suffer if this corps should either occasion the reduction of a like number of their own artillery, or render an augmentation of them unnecessary." [15]

The British government, by contrast, wanted to bring all the military forces in India under its own control. Patronage, of course, figured in the government's concern, as it did in that of the directors, but the government's wishes went beyond patronage. As one scholar has stated: "Concern over the defense of British India, prejudice against the Indian army, the friction between the British and Indian services, the clashes between the civil and military authorities in India, and the (partly imagined) precariousness of London's control over the Anglo-Indian community, all were combining into a fixed resolve that the Indian Army should be brought under the control of the Crown." [16]

Dundas accordingly pondered several schemes, none of them really workable, for amalgamating the Company's forces with those of the crown even before Cornwallis left for India. Cornwallis himself, before he took up his governor generalship, also advanced a plan of "reform" (but not amalgamation), making the Indian army a separate part of the king's army, its officers to have a commission valid only in India. Once he had acquired experience of actual conditions in India, he never attempted to implement this initial idea, which, as he admitted, was "hastily put together." [17] The government's interest in the Indian army persisted to the extent of offering the earl nearly a free hand to effect reform. Dundas wrote to him in July of 1786 that "we have laid the foundation of your reporting your sentiments as to the arrangement of the military in India and in that report you can give us the ground for adopting any system you shall devise." [18]

He went to work on the army. He assiduously studied the relationship between the king's officers and the Company's, but could not arrive at a satisfactory method for amalgamating the forces so as to place all officers under the crown. Indeed, four months' experience in India convinced him of the impracticability of this aim. He told Dundas in February of 1787 that after "more mature deliberation" he had discovered "several objections" to joining all the forces into king's troops. He preferred instead "to establish equality of rank amongst the King's and Company's officers." [19] He repeated this view in August: "The more I reflect, the more I am convinced of the danger of giving King's commissions to the officers. It would produce an idea of appealing to His Majesty in cases where they thought themselves aggrieved by this government & lessen their respect for the civil authority."[20]

Despite his advice to the contrary, the government seemed not to understand, for it continued to think of amalgamation and it allowed the officers of the Company's sepoy and European troops the chance to become part of the original establishment of the four regular regiments going out to India. The Company's officers did not wish to join, for by doing so they would lose authority and command. Cornwallis explained the situation in identical letters to Sir George Yonge at the war office and to William Pitt:

I have expressed my doubts to Mr. Dundas of the success of the plan for the consolidated corps. If the Company had only a European force in this country, nothing could be more easy. But we have in Bengal only, near four hundred officers serving with the native troops; these are, in general, the best and most deserving officers in the army, they are acquainted with the language, manners, and religious customs of the Sepoys, their emoluments are greater than those of the officers of the European corps, and it is the reward of the best captains and subalterns to be appointed to Sepoy regiments.

It is hardly probable that a captain, who actually has command of a Sepoy battalion, or who is likely soon to be promoted to it, will choose to become one of the youngest captains in a consolidated regiment; and indeed I should think it would be as difficult to persuade a Lieutenant-Colonel or an old Major who has served in and is well seasoned to the climate, and who may expect in five or six years more to be a Colonel with an income of between seven and eight thousand pounds a year, to remove to the bottom of the long list of Lieutenant-Colonels in the King's service, where, without interest or connexions, he could not expect to get a regiment in twenty years.[21]

In face of this determined opposition, the government finally gave up pressing for consolidation, or indeed, for any major changes. Cornwallis, nonetheless, did not rest contentedly with the military establishment as he found it. A reformer by nature, he undertook many changes that would have a cumulative effect in India.

He, or indeed, anyone would find it difficult to change the jealousy and rivalry between king's officers and Company officers. Cornwallis and Archibald Campbell, though both king's officers with a natural preference for the regulars, tried to accommodate both sides by maintaining impartiality. They had very little success in quelling emotions of jealousy and stilling cries of favoritism. The regulars, for example, complained to Campbell in March of 1788 that the Company directors had deprived them of positions as barrack masters and as town majors in Fort St. George without stating the reasons for this arbitrary action: "And it is more particularly to be apprehended at present [Campbell told Cornwallis], when in consequence of the late very rapid promotion among the higher ranks in the Company's service, as well as by the appointment (however temporary) of acting field officers, many of his majesty's officers are daily suffering the painfull mortification of being superseded by those whom they have commanded."[22] Again, in a memorial to Cornwallis in 1791, in the midst of a war with Tipoo, the regular officers complained that the Company officers in the Bengal service received higher pay than the regulars, which made "the officers of His Majesty's own regiments in India seem to be ranked as a secondary class of men."[23] Their complaint in fact had little merit. No one but a fool joined the king's army as an officer with the intention of earning a decent living by his pay. The regular army was an avocation for gentlemen, whereas the Indian army was a career. At any rate, when Cornwallis could not alleviate the regulars' grievances, he acquired the reputation of partiality toward the Company's men. General William Medows, who headed the army at Bombay in 1788, complained to Dundas that "civil as well as military, Lord Cornwallis leans wonderfully to Company's officers."[24]

In actuality he did not. Indeed, the Company officers had so many of their own grievances that they tended to think the governor general favored the regulars. One of their greatest complaints was that regulars of relatively little experience could command Company officers of long service because commanders in the presidencies tended to advance the regulars rapidly with brevets of local rank. Thus a lieutenant could quickly rise locally to captain. Furthermore, regular officers automatically assumed seniority over their Company counterparts of the same rank even though the latter usually had far greater experience of important command. Thus a lieutenant in the regulars who might never even have led a company outranked a lieutenant in the East India service who might have—indeed probably had—commanded a battalion. The government removed a part of this grievance when it abolished local brevets after an organization of Company officers in London had pressured the board of control.[25]

Cornwallis had involved himself only marginally in this issue, though he had written the directors pointing out the "impropriety" in brevet rank. He applied himself directly and vigorously, however, to another problem. The Company allowed officers who had spent a long time in England on leave to return to India with their rank when a lucrative position seemed likely to open up. When they did so, they displaced men who had remained in India and served the Company faithfully, which Cornwallis thought manifestly unfair. He told Dundas of a captain with an "ample fortune" who had gone home, remained there for twelve years, and now wished to come back. According to Company policy, he could return as a lieutenant colonel just as if he had served those years in India and earned his seniority.[26] Cornwallis deemed this promotion thoroughly unjust and campaigned hard against the policy that allowed it. This time he won, for the directors abolished the practice after 1788.[27]

Company officers also complained that their employers did not pay them enough, a complaint Cornwallis found justified. He pressed for adequate salaries for the military of all ranks, applying equally to the military as to the civil service, on the principle that fair salaries usually eliminated the need for peculation. He also prodded the Company to institute pensions and a regular retirement policy. Without these benefits, he feared that many officers would retire in India because they could not afford to go home. There they would grow indifferent to the mother country and her interests, perhaps even hostile toward them.[28] He wanted the directors to continue to grant passage back to Britain to deserving officers, a practice foreshadowing the Company's future policy of regular leave.

Although he thus championed their cause on various issues, Cornwallis did not always push for things the Company officers desired. For example, he disliked promotion by seniority in the military service. They, on the other hand, cherished this policy as the only way men without "interest" could reach the top. Every humble cadet who entered the Company's military service had an equal chance, providing he lived long enough, of attaining high command, although patronage did help some men to acquire lucrative posts. At the same time that they upheld seniority, however, the Company officers complained bitterly that they could not rise as quickly in rank as the regulars serving in India. A Company captain who commanded a battalion might be junior in rank to a captain in the regulars who had never commanded more than a company. The regulars could get to the top more easily and quickly than the Company men because of that very "interest" the latter decried (Cornwallis had reached the rank of lieutenant colonel at age twenty-three). Yet they could not have it both ways. The Company's servants could never hope for the rapid promotion the regulars enjoyed as long as they stuck rigidly to the seniority system.

Cornwallis wished to change that system, but not abolish it, in favor of "interest." Rather, he favored promotion by merit, as he explained clearly to Campbell. "I do not mean in my recommendations," he noted, "to adopt invariably the rule of regimental succession, or of seniority in the line. Sometimes when superior merit is very evident I might even disregard both these claims to succession."[29] To the directors he elaborated upon this position:

And it is no less proper to offer to your observation, that unless the officers of this [sepoy] army can have it in their power to obtain promotion by some other means than that of seniority alone, the ability and spirit of exertion which many of your officers at present eminently possess, will be of little value to the public at the period of their service when it would be most particularly desireable, I mean in the rank of Colonel, at which it is impossible that the officers who are now about the middle part of the list of the army can arrive by regular promotion, before they are entirely superannuated.[30]

The governor general faced the concerted opposition of those whose interests he had in mind. The Company's officers wanted seniority retained and objected every time he tried to alter it, no matter if the result was senile, feeble colonels and generals, unfit for high command.[31]

The governor general also strove, largely without success, to effect improvement in the European battalions. If he seemed to devote a disproportionate amount of his time and energy to them, the future would bear out his concern (especially the Mutiny in 1857). Cornwallis saw as clearly as anyone, and more clearly than most, that ultimate authority in India depended upon the bayonets of white European troops. In November of 1786, soon after he arrived, the governor general pointed out to the Duke of York that the defense of India might one day depend entirely upon European infantry.[32] In August of 1787, he reiterated this point to the directors:

I think it must be universally admitted that without a large and well-regulated body of Europeans, our hold of these valuable dominions must be very insecure. It cannot be expected that even the best of treatment would constantly conciliate the willing obedience of so vast a body of people, differing from ourselves in almost every circumstance of laws, religion and customs; and oppressions of individuals, errors of Government, and several other unforseen causes will no doubt arouse an inclination to revolt. On such occasions it would not be wise to place great dependence upon their countrymen who compose the native regiments to secure their subjection.[33]

Cornwallis hoped, therefore, to improve the quality of the European regiments and bring them up to strength (although they were usually no more understrength than the regulars).[34] He was especially concerned with quality, for the Europeans in Bengal struck him initially as in a "wretched state."[35] His visit from July through November of 1787 to the various military stations in Bengal and Oudh (the farthest lying one thousand miles from Calcutta) confirmed that impression. He told the Duke of York that the ranks of the Company's European regiments were filled with "miserable subjects." He called them "contemptible trash" in a letter to the adjutant general and described them to the directors as in "the most wretched condition." He doubted if he could fill one complete battalion of "serviceable soldiers" from the whole lot.[36]

He found several glaring faults. First, they lacked "discipline and even subordination," the most essential qualities in an army.[37] That lack owed to several other factors, most important among them drunkenness, desertion, and invalidism. Desertion rates were high,[38] and many of those who did not desert were so chronically ill as to be of no use to the Company's service. Battalions were filled, as one colonel pointed out, with "a great number of men under size, ill limbed & weak," not one-third "fit for service." In 1788, over a thousand men were invalids in the Bengal presidency alone.[39] Though the cream of the recruits went to the artillery, invalidism was high even there. Colonel Pearse reported in February of 1787 that one-third of the garrison at Fort William was unfit for duty.[40]

Absenteeism among the Company officers, to be sure, compounded the other problems of lack of discipline, drunkenness, desertion, and invalidism,[41] but the root cause of all the troubles with the Company's European infantry was the low quality of the human material in the ranks. Poor recruiting practices had resulted in poor recruits. Though the British regular army somehow managed to do so, the Company found it difficult to turn poor recruits into good soldiers.

Cornwallis determined to correct as many deficiencies as he could. He put the sale of liquor under the direct supervision of commanding officers at the military stations.[42] He discharged a number of invalids from both the Bengal and Madras forces and sent them back to Britain. Even so, he thought he probably had discharged only half of those who should be released for the good of the service:

I did not think myself justified in putting the Company to the expense of pay, clothing, barracks, hospitals &c &c for all those wretches who would in fact have been left here for the sole purpose of getting drunk [arrack was cheaper in Bengal than elsewhere]. I therefore directed their cases to be attentively examined & after selecting those who had particular claims on the Company for long services or who were objects of compassion from having large families, to the amount of about four hundred, I ordered the remainder to be embarked on board of the ships of the season, recommending those who were entitled to it, for the pension in England.[43]

Indeed, he felt himself "more open to censure for those I have kept than those I have sent away." Keeping one "useless, licentious drunkard" on the Company's payroll cost more than "three pensioners" in England.[44]

He gathered together the worst of these "useless, licentious" drunkards, formed them into a special battalion, and shipped them to Chunar, where at least they could do the Company little harm. His own account of the affair seems amusing:

I found a disorderly mass of debauched invalids living in Fort William almost without officers & without regulation of any kind corrupting, of course, all the recruits & all the other Europeans in garrison. Compassion for many who had brown families & for a number of Frenchmen with whom the caprice & infatuation of Sir Eyre Coote had filled this army, prevented my sending them all home, which in justice to the Company & the service I ought to have done. I formed therefore a battalion of those who had the strongest pretension to live upon arrack for the remainder of their days & sent them under some appearance at least of military form to Chunar.[45]

Having sent to Britain or to Chunar the worst of the lot, Cornwallis could ill afford to lose the men who remained. Yet lose them he did, for desertion plagued the army as much as drunkenness. The army's recruitment in India from among the drifters of all nationalities there—French, Portuguese, Danish, and Dutch—apparently contributed to the lack of discipline and the endemic desertion rate. Cornwallis tried to stop desertion with a number of positive actions. In one instance, he followed in Bengal what Campbell had done at Madras. Convinced that the French encouraged others to desert, as well as being the chief deserters themselves, the Madras governor had allowed a discharge to all non-British Europeans who requested it, had forbidden the reenlistment of all non-British Europeans at the end of their terms of service, and had forbidden any European in the future to enlist without his permission.[46] Captain Kirkpatrick from Agra suggested other means to prevent desertions: prompt payment of the Company's promised reward for the apprehension of deserters, buying information from peasants, and stationing sepoys in various places to apprehend Europeans without passports. Cornwallis also implemented these suggestions immediately.[47]

Invalidism compounded the problems of the Company's European army. It thinned the ranks nearly as much as drunkenness and desertion. The incidence of debilitating sickness was appallingly high, owing largely to inadequate medical facilities and personnel. The head surgeon of Berampore, for example, represented to the governor general the wretched state of the hospital for Europeans (and for sepoys as well). A thatchroofed, timbered structure, it had been built five years previously and not repaired since. It was so unsafe during the monsoon season that then the Europeans went into the sepoys' hospital. But this latter building, with its mat walls, mud floors, and lack of apartments either for operations or for examining patients in private, was nearly as bad. Furthermore, the hospital was located such a long distance from the cantonment that surgeons who had no carriages took two hours to reach it.[48] At Dinapore, the Company soldiers received little attention because of the scarcity of trained personnel: the head surgeon had only one mate to attend to two hundred invalids.[49]

Cornwallis tried to correct these lamentable inadequacies as soon as he discovered them. He put the Berampore invalids into a clean, dry, empty barracks and ordered a general inspection of all the hospitals of all the military stations. He also instituted a program of preventive medicine. He encouraged, with some success, a mass inoculation against smallpox, the greatest killer of the eighteenth century.[50] Although these measures undoubtedly helped prevent disease and ensured better care for the ill, they could not overcome the basic problem of lack of knowledge. The medical profession was so ignorant of the causes of so many diseases that all the measures the governor general took could still not check the terrible ravages of malaria, typhoid, and cholera, to say nothing of venereal disease, which, if the surgeon at Dinapore is correct, infected 71 out of 126 men of the 6th European battalion admitted to and discharged from hospital in May of 1788.[51]

Not only the poor hospital facilities, but the poor state of other buildings, ones that the soldiers either lived in or used regularly, contributed to invalidism. Cornwallis discovered in 1787 that all the roofs of the officers' barracks, privates' barracks, ordnance, and storehouses at Dinapore needed repair. During the monsoons, their interiors were subject to cold drafts and dripping rains.[52] At Berampore in 1787, the field officers' barracks had been constructed with fewer than one-third the rafters and beams necessary to support the roof. White ants had eaten many of these away. Even Fort William itself lay in a ruinous condition: kitchens and offices in the south barracks "past repair," drains stopped up,

casemates leaking, and broken and irreparable locks.[53] Again
Cornwallis tried to effect repairs, not only to remove this disgrace
to the Company, but also thereby to improve the health of his
troops.[54]

The higher rate of drunkenness, desertion, and invalidism
in the Company's European troops than in the other military units
owed, in Cornwallis's view, to one outstanding deficiency: the
poor quality of men recruited in the first place. That the Company's rank and file should be "better recruited," he wrote Dundas in 1787, "is so essential a point, that without it we can have
only the name of an European army. I can assure you that the
Bengal part of it does not deserve that name."[55] Cornwallis
wanted the Company to recruit on an equal basis with the British
army in Britain. He hoped to establish its own recruiting depot to
supersede the nearly useless Carisbrooke Castle on the Isle of
Wight. "The Company must have permission to raise recruits
publickly," he urged, "these recruits must be properly examined
and subjected to martial law, and placed under the command of
their own officers until the time of their embarkation."[56] Although Cornwallis knew the regular army would oppose such
competition from the Company, he pressed for it nonetheless
throughout his tenure as governor general. Unfortunately, his efforts seem to have had relatively little effect. One can discern very
little improvement in the quality of the Company's European
forces during his administration.

Perhaps the governor general worried too much about
their "quality." The ranks of the British regulars, after all, came
from the dregs of society. If they fought better than other forces
in India, it undoubtedly owed to their harsh discipline and to the
far more binding king's regulations and laws that governed them.
Indeed, Cornwallis could never be satisfied with the Company's
European ranks unless and until their officers drilled the men in
the same fashion as did officers of the regular army.

He also found the sepoys wanting in discipline, though he
thought them better physical specimens than the European privates (probably because high-caste Hindus joined the army eagerly
rather than as a last resort). Accordingly, he worked to improve
discipline. Shortly after he arrived in India, he corrected a drill
book given him by the adjutant general, Sir William Fawcett, sent

copies to Madras and Bombay for distribution, and printed the infantry regulations in the *Calcutta Gazette*.[57] He hoped for the Company's sepoy army to drill as did the regulars, to be "uniform in all the presidencies," and to have "an exact uniformity in the two services."[58] In this endeavor he achieved some success, which afforded him a degree of satisfaction.

Cornwallis was, of course, most satisfied with the drill and discipline of the regulars. "The King's British regiments," he told Dundas, "must not be parted with; we have in reality nothing else, except the corps of artillery, that deserves the name of an European force."[59] Yet even the regulars presented some problems. Absenteeism among the officers deprived these well-trained and disciplined enlisted men of experienced leadership. In April of 1787, for example, from only six regiments (the 19th dragoons and the 36th, 52nd, 71st, 72nd, and 73rd infantry regiments) three lieutenant colonels, three majors, thirteen captains, eleven lieutenants, one cornet, nine ensigns, one surgeon's mate, and two chaplains were in Europe.[60] This list of absentees did not include the men of the additional companies detached for recruiting in Britain. The enlisted men, furthermore, hardly qualified as responsible citizens. Even in the regulars, desertion rates were high,[61] and recruiting was inadequate. One batch of men shipped out from Gravesend were felons and deserters who had gone aboard ship in fetters.[62] Yet the greater discipline in the regular army made up for the deficiencies in the human material, and Cornwallis never worried as much about the regulars as he did about other branches of the service.

These other branches included the Hanoverians, to which he paid little attention. They served in the Madras presidency at too much expense, he believed, for their worth.[63]

Tinkering

Although he paid little attention to regulars or Hanoverians, he constantly worried about the condition of the Europeans and sepoys, in matters great and small. As a result, he worried them with all sorts of measures. For example, nearly every issue of the *Calcutta Gazette* for 1787 prescribed some new rule or regulation. Cornwallis tried to straighten out the military bazaars, or markets, to end "grievous oppressions." He even reprimanded the colonel in charge of the Cawnpore bazaar and passed over the colonel's aide for command of a sepoy battalion.[64] The governor general took a survey of all the elephants the army used.[65] He instituted reforms in the office of the Company's quartermaster general in order to prevent that official from pocketing money at public expense.[66] He provided for rotation of regular and Company troops in the various military stations.[67] He appointed a special committee to study and improve the military ordnance.[68] He locked horns with some of the Company's engineers, one of whom complained to Dundas that Cornwallis did not use them.[69] He distrusted their integrity and deprived them of fees, gratuities, and similar emoluments which they had hitherto pocketed during the construction of public works. Instead, he gave them better salaries.[70] Finally, the governor general tried gradually to accustom the sepoys to the idea of service overseas, a practice upon which the Hindus frowned. He reasoned that if he could only get them to serve outside Bengal proper, such as in the Bay of Bengal during peace, they would more willingly volunteer to serve away from the province in war. He believed that he had attained some success with the sepoys in this endeavor.[71]

The Reforms of 1794

All these changes were but details, however. They did not achieve what the governor general wished deeply: a comprehensive overhaul of the entire military forces in India. Only through such major reform could he obtain the better, more efficient army he wanted. To that end, in 1793, Cornwallis circulated a questionnaire about changes in the army to regular British officers and a few of the Company officers in Madras. He did not, however, consult the Bengal officers.[72] Combining the questionnaire results with his own experience of seven years, he used the enforced leisure of his long voyage home to draw up a comprehensive plan for "new modeling" the army in India.[73] This plan went to Dundas for his consideration and action.

Surprisingly, Cornwallis advocated bringing all the forces in India under the crown, an amalgamation he had opposed in the past. His experience in war with the army organization as it was under the old system must have helped change his mind. At any rate, he now believed "that the Company's possessions in India cannot be secured without the assistance of a considerable body of His Majesty's troops."[74] He also recommended that the Indian establishment contain more officers of higher rank. Colonels should command two-battalion regiments, each battalion led by a lieutenant colonel. He proposed a regular retirement plan for all officers and regular leave in Europe with full pay. He again addressed himself to the pesky problem of rank between Company and regular officers and suggested a sweeping series of changes in perquisites, gratuities, and emoluments for the Company's army.[75]

Though Dundas approved the plan, the proposed reforms ran into solid opposition. In the end they failed of implementation for various reasons, including the cabinet's procrastination. More important, some Bengal officers resented the idea of amalgamation and attacked the British administration because they thought it intended other "bad" measures as well, perhaps because the administration never made its intentions clear. Their resentment ran so deep that these officers verged on mutiny in 1796. Shore, Cornwallis's successor, lacked the exalted status of a peer, the authority that went with years of command, and the prestige of having led the military to a brilliant victory over Tipoo. As a result, he conciliated the officers instead of standing firm. Finally, Henry Dundas, pressured at home by agents representing the Bengal officers, opposed by the Company directors, and doubting the reliability of an insecure governor general, withdrew the controversial aspects of the Cornwallis plan.

By 1795, the Bengal officers had obtained most of what they wanted. New regulations did, however, include some of Cornwallis's proposals. For example, regiments had two battalions, each regiment commanded by a colonel and each battalion by a lieutenant colonel. The number of captains and subalterns increased, and each presidency had a general. The regulations granted a three-year leave with pay after ten years' service, passage money home for subalterns, and retirement after twenty-five years with pay at the rank then held.

The amalgamation failed and the seniority system remained unaltered. Officers retained most of their allowances.[76] The Indian army would remain basically the same until the great mutiny of 1857. Cornwallis's prophecy that the British could not hold India without a large establishment of regular troops was borne out in ghastly fashion by that mutiny. Regulars, in the end, saved India for Britain and crushed the uprising (with some help from loyal sepoy regiments). Thereafter the British never allowed the percentage of regulars to drop as low as it had before the Mutiny.

Though the Company's officers had resented his attitude, Cornwallis had tried, he hoped impartially, to improve their performance. He had realized their just grievances and was instrumental in getting them leaves, passage money, and retirement pensions. He wanted to eliminate their fees, gratuities, and perquisites, as he had done with the civil servants. He thought decent salaries openly paid obviated the temptation to garner illicit wealth. He wanted to change the seniority system, not from a desire to elevate men with "interest" to the top commands, but because he believed seniority stifled merit, and he wished to reward merit.

Indeed, the governor general would need merit in the army during his last years in India. For war would test that army's mettle.

Chapter 7

The First Campaign against Tipoo

From the moment of his landing, Cornwallis found the brilliant Indian sunshine darkened by the shadow of war with the ruler of Mysore, Tipoo (or Tipu) Sultan. Anticipating conflict at any time, yet hoping it would never come, the earl determined to offer no provocation to hostilities. Yet, as governor general of British India, his duty would dictate a course that inevitably offended the ambitious head of Mysore.

Tipoo Sultan

In the 1780s, Tipoo had little reason to fear the English. They were few and their area of control was small. British India, that jewel of empire in the nineteenth century, did not yet exist, nor could anyone predict that it would. Unlike the overweening self-confidence and exclusiveness of the later Victorian rulers, who called themselves the "Raj" or "paramount power," the eighteenth-century British had a humility born of knowledge of their own relative weakness. Despite Clive's triumphs, they believed that at any time they might be pushed into the sea. The Company, therefore, wanted to avoid trouble, to isolate itself from the complexities of Indian diplomacy. It wanted trade and profit, not risky and expensive war. The British government agreed. Pitt's India Act of 1784 expressly forbade the Company's servants in India from making treaties with native powers that might lead to war or from embarking upon hostilities:

Whereas [the act read] to pursue schemes of conquest and extension of dominion in India are measures repugnant to the wish, the honour, and

117

policy of this nation . . . it shall not be lawful for the Governor-General and Council . . . without the express command of the said Court of Directors, or the Secret Committee of the said Court of Directors, in any case, except where hostilities have actually been commenced, or preparations actually made for the commencement of hostilities, against the British nation in India or against some of the princes or states dependent thereon, or whose territories the said United Company shall be at such time engaged by any subsisting treaty to defend or guarantee, either to declare war or commence hostilities, or enter into any treaty for making war against any of the country princes or states in India, or any treaty for guaranteeing the possession of any country prince or states.[1]

This stringent injunction owed not only to government conviction, but also to the past practices of Company servants in Bengal, Madras, and Bombay. They had made all sorts of engagements with various native princes, some of them mutually contradictory, which had involved the Company and its soldiers in hostilities at great expense in lives, effort, and money.

Native princes and their principalities dotted India by the hundreds as they did Germany in the days of the Holy Roman Empire. Yet in India, just as in Germany, a few large and powerful states emerged. After the breakup of the Mogul Empire in the eighteenth century, and after the French defeat in the Seven Years' War, three native Indian states came to dominate the rest. The Mahrattas, a confederacy of Hindu horsemen, were loosely governed by the peshwa at Poona. But the Mahrattas had many powerful, nearly independent chieftains, such as Scindia at Gwalior. They roamed across central India raiding and plundering. The Mahratta boundaries could be defined only approximately in Cornwallis's day, but their domain comprised the largest chunk of territory in India, running from the east coast between Bengal and the Northern Circars, across India south of Bengal, Oudh, and the Mogul territory at Delhi, over to the west coast and down toward Goa. Though they had lost disastrously to raiding Afghans at Panipat near Delhi in 1761, they soon recovered because the Afghans had returned northward with their loot instead of following up their victory. Cornwallis had special awareness of the Mahrattas' military potential because their power lay in the cavalry, an arm in which he was weak.

A second state, Hyderabad, was headed by the Nizam Ali.

Described in 1787 as addicted to "intrigue and dissipation, principally the latter," the nizam ruled by means of a "feeble" and "arbitrary" administration and a small army of "disorderly troops."[2] Hyderabad also had arisen from the ruins of the Mogul Empire. The viceroy of the Great Mogul, called the subadar of the Deccan, had made himself hereditary ruler, and his descendants even to modern times call themselves the nizams of Hyderabad. This Moslem state was bordered on the east by the Northern Circars and the Carnatic (whose nawab, Muhammed Ali, was, for all practical purposes, under British control), on the north and west by the Mahratta dominions, and on the south by Mysore.

Mysore, the third important kingdom, was the only "permanent" native foe the English had in India. Throughout turbulence, shifting alliances, and intrigues, from the time Hyder Ali (Tipoo's father) grasped control of Mysore by storming the capital at Seringapatam with the aid of Devraj (a member of the family of "hereditary" rulers) until Tipoo's death, the kingdom remained belligerently anti–British. That belligerence mingled fear with contempt. Mysore had spasmodically tried to extend its boundaries eastward into the Carnatic. It had also periodically wrestled with its neighbors to the north, the Mahrattas and Hyderabad. Ruled by the usurper Hyder Ali, Mysore had undergone a continuous succession of wars, two of them with the English, before Cornwallis arrived in Bengal. Friendly toward, but suspicious of, the French, it had allied with them and had employed French officers in various military capacities to fight the British.

The initial fight, the first Mysore War, began after the nizam of Hyderabad, who had signed a treaty with the English and had allied with the Mahrattas to attack Mysore, listened to Hyder's diplomats, joined himself to Mysore, turned his back on the Mahrattas, and in concert with Hyder attacked the English, whose soldiers he had previously employed. The rulers jointly aimed to gain control of the Carnatic. In 1767, they descended the ghats, or passes, from the plateau of Mysore to the flatlands of the Carnatic with sixty thousand men. Hyder captured a number of coastal strongholds and even reached the outskirts of Madras. Then, his resources apparently strained and the English eager to cease hostilities, the two powers made peace in the treaty of Madras. But an article fecklessly inserted in the treaty stipulated that either

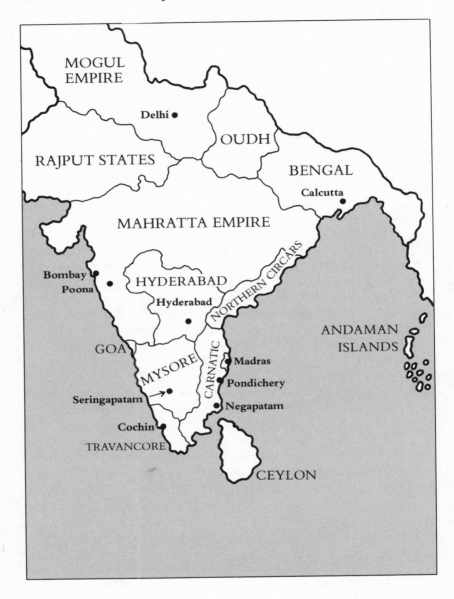

1. India about the Time of Cornwallis
   Based on a map by T. Kitchin, 1779.

side would assist the other in case of attack by a third party. Neither side honored this article.

Tipoo, born in 1759, had risen to military command during this war, though he had participated very little in it. Yet he had seen Mysore defeat the English and ever after thought it could do so again. The British slapdash method of making the treaty of Madras had furthermore excited his contempt.

Shortly after the conclusion of the first Mysore War, the Mahrattas invaded Hyder's domain for the fourth time in twelve years to support the peshwa's claim for tribute. When Hyder approached the English to support him against his foes in accordance with the Madras treaty, they refused. Instead, the Madras council held to a course of strict neutrality, which the nawab of the Carnatic had urged and his agent in London had worked to get the government to support. That Mysore had to fight alone, in Tipoo's view, owed solely to English perfidy.

The war seesawed back and forth, but by 1778, Hyder and his son had extended their land's boundaries, particularly against Hyderabad and the Mahrattas. In that year France entered into war against England in support of the American war for independence. The British then seized the French post at Pondicherry and determined to take the Guntoor Circar, from which they had been excluded by the treaty of 1766. The ruler of this fief, brother of the nizam of Hyderabad, agreed to cede Guntoor and dismiss a French force there in return for military aid. The English now angered Hyder not only by marching their forces through his territory, without his permission, but also by leasing Guntoor to his enemy, Muhammed Ali, nawab of the Carnatic.

Hyder and his son (now almost an equal partner) reacted swiftly by marching into the Carnatic in 1780 with 100,000 men. Affairs again went badly for the British. Aided by the French, the Mysore forces won a spectacular victory over Colonel William Baillie at Pollilur, where they killed or captured his entire small force of about 700 Europeans and 3,521 sepoys.[3] Only the heroic efforts of Warren Hastings as governor general and the military abilities of Sir Eyre Coote enabled the British to hold their own until the death of Hyder in 1782 and the withdrawal of French support in June of 1783, when their forces in the Carnatic learned of the Peace of Paris. The British and Tipoo worked out another treaty, that of Mangalore, to end this second Mysore War in early 1784. It mutually restored conquests, those by the English along the Malabar Coast and those by Tipoo in the Carnatic, and promised that neither side would fight the allies or help the enemies of the other.[4]

Tipoo now ruled a state that had twice defied the English and twice given as good as it received. His name meant "tiger," and it suited his sense of humor to symbolize his implacable hatred of the British in a curious device. French craftsmen constructed for him a mechanical toy in the form of a prostrate Englishman being mauled by a tiger. While the tiger emitted savage roars, the victim feebly moved an arm and moaned. Legend has since clouded the picture of this ruler, legend to which the English contributed considerably. Prisoners captured by him or his father, who later escaped or gained their release, told horror tales of dungeons and torture. Cornwallis himself received narratives from escaped British prisoners.[5] These stories, published in Calcutta and London, turned the public against Tipoo, who became to many the archetype of Oriental cruelty. Yet he seemed a figure of romance and intrigue as well, typical of the exotic East and its mysterious ways.[6] Wilkie Collins's great detective novel, *The Moonstone*, used the storm of Tipoo's capital at Seringapatam by Colonel Arthur Wellesley and the loot of treasure there as an essential ingredient in the plot.

But Cornwallis's view of Tipoo's character did not owe only to escaped prisoners. The governor general maintained a regular intelligence network that spied on Tipoo and magnified his malevolence. Not untypical was a memorandum describing in detail the sultan's human and material resources and his barbarous acts, in effect depicting Tipoo as a monster and a religious bigot. He killed in cold blood men who would not conform to Islam and then executed their widows. "The cruelties exercised on his unhappy subjects," the memorandum observed, "rivet the principles of disgust and detestation. . . . I myself have witnessed a sight of barbarity unknown in any civilized nation, where the unfortunate widows have been hanged by dozens on trees by the roadside, or suspended in hedgerows."[7]

Yet Tipoo was more than a cruel Oriental despot and less

than the monster the British believed him. To his French ally he was no monster, but rather a hero for his persistent opposition to the British. If he could be ruthless, so could the British. He rose to the top in trying circumstances. His father, a military adventurer, had seized the central authority in Mysore (though he ruled in the name of the hereditary family) by his military ability. That same ability not only saved Mysore in its endless wars with the country powers but even enlarged its boundaries. Tipoo grew up a good soldier. His efforts to strengthen the military forces of his land achieved some success, for he had more numerous and heavier artillery than the British. Anyone who studies the British conquest of India will recognize as but a myth the persistent argument that the British triumphed over their foes because of superior military technology. In Cornwallis's day, the only technological superiority of the British lay in their control of the sea, which admittedly played a significant role in his campaign. But Tipoo had more guns, more men, more horses, and more cavalry than the British, and his material equipment was at least as good as theirs, if not better. He did not use them as well because he had not created an administrative organization equal to that of his enemies, and he had not instilled into his soldiers the same discipline the English had drilled into the sepoys. Thus the military superiority the British acquired rested upon administrative skills or what one might term political organization and moral authority.

Tipoo tried, however, to improve both organization and discipline. Perhaps he depended too heavily on his French advisers to mold his army, for, lacking any loyalty to him or his cause, they deserted him at critical moments. Certainly he tried to organize his state, but his letters show him as an administrator overly inclined to look after every detail, no matter how insignificant, to the neglect of larger issues. That he sometimes let his political objectives interfere with the best economic course for his country gives him something in common with many governments, even in the twentieth century. As a ruler, Tipoo, a devout Moslem, did not believe in nor extend to other faiths that broad toleration characteristic of his father. Accordingly, his wars against the English tended to take on the nature of holy wars against the infidel, the type of conflict that creates the most bitter animosity and hatred.

Cornwallis, typical of his time in his distaste for religious enthusiasm, thought Tipoo had a "general character of bigotry to his religion, and jealousy and hatred of Europeans."[8]

His nature molded by war, the sultan despised the "unmilitary" characteristics of indecision, cowardice, disloyalty to superiors, and so on. He ordered his share of summary executions. He sometimes murdered prisoners, including Europeans. He tortured and mutilated Indians, either his own subjects or those of his enemies. Although not excusable, his acts probably did not much (if at all) exceed in cruelty those of other parties in other wars throughout time. But such measures were abhorrent to a man of Cornwallis's temperament, essentially humane and devoted to the "rules" of war. He knew that Europeans could be cruel and arbitrary, but he comfortably believed such methods untypical of Europeans and typical of Indians.

Tipoo had, however, many pleasing characteristics. A muscular man, about five feet seven inches tall, he had black eyes, "large and penetrating," a long neck and face, a thick black mustache, and a tendency to obesity, so that like Cornwallis in his later years he grew fat with a double chin. Yet he had delicate hands more suited to the harpsichord than the saber.[9] He wore elegant clothes—colorful turbans interwoven with threads of gold, a "dressing gown" fastened with a diamond button—and followed a daily routine in peacetime that included a massage, a bath in seclusion, breakfast, official audiences, consultation with astrologers, and the lengthy conduct of public business in the hall of public audience. In the afternoons he inspected the army and in the evenings listened to literature and read by himself before retiring. Despite his fiery military reputation, he was personally modest and highly cultured. Though a mystic and a dedicated Moslem, he was yet a cynic with a satiric wit and realistic enough to use Christians to serve his state. A patron of literature, a promoter of trade, industry, and agriculture, he might have passed on to his posterity a strong, united Mysore, free from all foreign control.

He might have, had he not cultivated the arts of war, which destroyed him. Yet for him war was inevitable. He grew up in it, reveled in it, and believed it the only way to final independence for his country. He matured hating the English because they had violated a treaty and because they were Christians as well.

He did not fear them because he and his father had beaten them more than once. The attitude he felt toward the English he felt almost equally toward their allies, because these allies occupied land all around Mysore, some of it, in Tipoo's view, his own.

Although he never really knew Tipoo nor understood the depth of his character, Cornwallis was certainly aware of his military record, his military ambitions for his state, and the threat he posed to the English. Indeed, the governor general's first diplomatic initiatives involved Mysore. In addition to trying to undo other acts of his predecessor Macpherson (the same man who had earlier served as agent in London for the nawab of the Carnatic), Cornwallis also had to stop British involvement in the still-lingering war between Tipoo and the Mahrattas. The Bombay government had promised Company troops to aid the Mahrattas, though it had stipulated that they could not enter Mysore. Immediately after his arrival, Cornwallis took steps to pull the British out. Their involvement, he insisted, would violate the treaty of Mangalore and would expressly disobey the stipulation in the act of Parliament against outside engagements. He informed the Mahrattas of his decision.

Disentangling Bombay from this particular affair with Tipoo, however, by no means ended English interest in the affairs of Mysore. Cornwallis kept up a large intelligence network, as did Campbell at Madras. The earl sent a Company servant, George Forster, disguised as a native, through Mysore to gather intelligence.[10] He also received constant reports of Tipoo's military strength, some of them wildly exaggerated. One in October of 1787, for instance, informed him that Tipoo was ready on the instant to march into the Carnatic with 25,000 native cavalry, 1,500 European cavalry, 53,000 regular infantry, 50,000 irregular infantry, 30,000 artificers, and 2,000 pieces of artillery.[11] It indicated British apprehensions regarding Mysore that the *Calcutta Gazette* published this report as an established fact of Tipoo's strength.[12] Captain Alexander Read, who commanded at the frontier station of Amboor, sent the earl constant descriptions of Tipoo's military forces, broken down into the minutest detail, but often extreme examples of hyperbole.[13] Another intelligence estimate gave Tipoo an army of 153,000 in 1789.[14] The earl even got word from England that an American vessel was loading ammunition and other supplies at Ostend to take to Tipoo "and that other vessels are fitting out for the same purpose in different ports of Europe."[15]

Cornwallis read this information, but he did not really believe much of it, especially since some of his operatives tended to contradict others and a few actually disclaimed or disparaged the work of their fellows. Indeed, he once commented that British officers had "got into the habit of transmitting foolish and incredible reports as actual intelligence," which had "greatly embarrassed and impeded all our business, and given a general alarm from Bangalore to Madras." In the course of three weeks, Captain Read, for example, had "conjured up no less than three armies of from twenty to forty thousand men, and although a moment's reflection must have convinced him of the impossibility of their existence has acted in every respect as if he had really thought them to be where they were reported."[16] Though Cornwallis discounted many of the fantasies, they steadily reached him, reminding him constantly of the all too real presence of a powerful enemy eager to enlarge his dominions at British expense.

He therefore began preparing for war the moment he took office. Throughout the late 1780s, he and Campbell at Madras discussed contingency plans should hostilities erupt. They agreed that armed conflict would most likely come if Tipoo invaded the territory of a British ally, the rajah of Travancore. Malet wrote from Poona in 1787 that the British could not let Travancore fall to Tipoo, for it would hurt the British interest on the Malabar coast and cause the loss of the pepper trade.[17] Campbell observed: "Although I am not of opinion, that Tipoo would of himself wantonly quarrel with us for the acquisition of the Travancore Country yet it is by no means unreasonable to suppose, from his general political principles, that if he saw a good Opportunity to seize the Travancore Country while our hands were otherwise engaged, he would not fail to embrace it and he would glory in the event if his attempt proved successful."[18] Campbell therefore urged alliances with the nizam and the Mahrattas in the event of war and discussed the construction of defensive posts and the manner of organizing the army to fight Tipoo when he chose to invade.[19] For his part, Cornwallis assumed that war was inevitable. He would not start it, but "as soon as war is commenced,

I would by no means advise that we should confine ourselves to defensive measures, but that every engine should be moved to carry it on in such a manner as to secure the honor of the nation, & to be the most likely to bring it to a speedy conclusion."[20] Here the ghost of America may have haunted his thinking. This time, however, he had supreme command and could exercise fully that offensive spirit he had displayed on the North American continent. He would move swiftly from the beginning and not let himself bog down in the fashion of Howe and Clinton.

Although armed conflict came later than anticipated, Tipoo did not disappoint the governor general's expectations.[21] As in most wars, blame for the commencement of hostilities did not lie entirely on one side. That Tipoo was an aggressive ruler out to enlarge Mysore at the expense of others not even the sultan himself would have denied. His state was an armed camp, alert for any opportunity of aggrandizement. But Cornwallis also had anticipated war and had prepared for it, even though he believed himself acting on the defensive. Furthermore, at least in Tipoo's view, his diplomacy seemed particularly designed to isolate and humiliate the sultan. When the governor general took over the Guntoor Circar in 1788, he reactivated the treaty of 1768, which contained clauses stipulating that the British would provide the nizam of Hyderabad with troops. Cornwallis did not want to give troops, feeling that it would violate the treaties made with Hyder and Tipoo. Nonetheless, he sent Hyderabad two battalions, and he omitted Tipoo from the list of country powers against whom he forbade the nizam to employ these troops. Even if not quite an alliance, this arrangement certainly rubbed against the grain with Tipoo and with the spirit of the India Act of 1784. General William Medows, Campbell's successor (after John Holland) at Madras, later wrote a public letter saying the arrangement was absurd, not from a political, but from a military point of view. Medows's letter embarrassed Cornwallis no end and caused him to fire off a long epistle to his subordinate explaining his actions and his interpretation of the 1768 treaty, "a most jesuitical performance on our part."[22] Indeed, Cornwallis took the Circar in 1788 instead of earlier or later because he thought the moment offered perfect conditions: the nizam "ill prepared for war, and by disposition adverse to it," the state of his government "disordered," and Tipoo not really ready for a fight over the issue. "The recovery of the Guntoor," he said, "can in reason afford no pretence for the interference of Tipoo. If prepared for a war and determined upon it, he will never want a pretext nor will he wait for it."[23] Hyderabad did not really suffer, for the British paid the money owed and the nizam secured two full-strength battalions of better troops than any he commanded. The earl got the better of the deal, however, for he now had Hyderabad in his pocket and committed to him should hostilities erupt. Tipoo probably did not interpret the matter in such a light. In his eyes, the British had annexed territory and allied themselves with an enemy on his borders, even to the extent of furnishing that enemy with troops.

The other enemy of Mysore, the Mahrattas, Cornwallis had dallied with ever since he came to India. When he first arrived in Bengal, he immediately canceled, because it violated Pitt's India Act, the agreement the previous government had made to furnish the Mahrattas three battalions from Bombay.[24] Yet he constantly kept in mind an alliance with them in the event the Company had to fight Tipoo. He respected their military strength and figured he could use their cavalry, in which his forces were deficient, to good advantage. In 1787, he told Major William Palmer, resident with the Mahratta chief Scindia, to deal circumspectly with him (the British could not give Scindia troops), but to assure him that in the event of a rupture with Tipoo "we would be inclined to form a close connexion & alliance with the Maharatta. While a reinforcement of useful Cavalry or a powerful diversion on the northern side of Tipoo's dominions would no doubt be of great value to us, they on their side might certainly derive the most solid advantage from such a connexion."[25] Palmer reported in January that Scindia pressed him for a British defensive alliance with the Mahrattas, and Cornwallis again pointed out that existing treaties forbade it. The earl did not mention, however, his private belief that if once granted the alliance, the Mahrattas would deliberately provoke Tipoo into attacking them, so they could bring in the British to help them dismember Mysore.[26] Instead he diplomatically reassured Scindia that the British would support the Mahrattas against Tipoo should a European power (France) assist Tipoo against them or against the Company.

The governor general, in fact, seemed fairly sure that he

could count on Mahratta friendship toward the Company in any war with Tipoo. They had repeatedly manifested their desire to chip away at Mysore, and they had pressed him for the alliance steadily. By the late 1780s, the worst he could expect from them was neutrality.

Although British dealings with the Mahrattas and Hyderabad were bound to arouse Tipoo's suspicions, both sides understood that the issue most likely to cause open war related to the rajah of Travancore whose lands lay south of Mysore, at the tip of the Indian peninsula. The earl persuaded the rajah to take on loan and pay for two battalions of sepoys from Madras for his own protection. The earl was particularly pleased that Campbell had acquiesced in the measure, which Cornwallis thought vastly preferable to the past practice of sending Company officers to command the rajah's troops, "or in other words to ruin both him & this country which has universally been the case whenever that plan has been adopted."[27]

Tipoo chose in December of this same year of 1789 to attack the rajah's very strong defensive lines, constructed between 1761 and 1766, which ran for about forty miles.[28] Hyder and his son had always desired to control Travancore, but Tipoo had for various reasons waited until now to achieve his father's ambition. The rajah had recently directly provoked Tipoo not only by accepting Company troops, but also by purchasing two forts from the Dutch. The sultan asserted that the Dutch had no right to sell, that they only held the forts on lease from one of his own tributaries, the rajah of Cochin (though it turned out that Tipoo had put in a bid to purchase them himself).[29] Tipoo now discovered with rage that he had been the butt of a diplomatic trick. The Dutch had been in no position to defend the forts had Tipoo cared to attack. The Dutch governor commanded only a few thousand militia and regulars, among whom were only a few Europeans. But if the Dutch governor sold the forts to Travancore and Tipoo then attacked, the British would come to Travancore's aid. So, at the instigation of a wealthy Jewish merchant of Cochin, the territory changed hands, though in fact no money transaction took place at the time. Travancore merely promised to supply two and one half lakhs of rupees worth of pepper to the Dutch within four years.[30]

The old soldier Archibald Campbell had by this time gone home because of ill health, to be replaced as governor of Madras by John Holland, a Company servant. Campbell, who suffered from bilious complaints, might nonetheless have remained had he not been furious with the court of directors. Convinced he had made good appointments who would serve them well, he grew livid when the directors appeared to believe anonymous reports that favoritism had guided his choices.[31] Campbell had worked reasonably closely with Cornwallis on many matters, and his sudden departure may also have influenced Tipoo's timing. It was one thing to go adventuring against the civilian John Holland, quite another to confront a veteran soldier and intimate of the governor general.

At any rate, Holland now faced the crisis. He was aware of the deal between Travancore and the Dutch. He was also a principal creditor of the nabob of Arcot, and he believed Cornwallis would suspend payments to the nabob's creditors in the event of war with Tipoo. Yet Holland also knew very well the earl's views about Tipoo and Travancore, and Campbell surely had briefed him on the exchanges between himself and Cornwallis. The Madras governor, caught in the conflicting interest of his own finances and his superior's wishes, hesitated and vacillated after Tipoo launched his attack.

The indecision at Madras, once war had come, infuriated the earl. He told the secret committee of the court of directors that Holland had been guilty of "criminal disobedience of our orders, which directed him to consider Tipoo as at war with the Company if he should attack any part of the ancient possession of the Rajah of Travancore and to make preparations accordingly for carrying it on with vigor."[32] To Medows, Holland's successor, he seethed: "If Mr. Holland had not practised the oeconomy of making no preparation for war after he was attacked for which his brother seems to take credit in the minute he has transmitted to us, you might have got a good hold of the Coimbatour Country before the rains; It is God's Mercy that he did not carry his oeconomy so far as to disband his Army."[33] Cornwallis now saw red at the very mention of the name Holland and prepared to journey to Madras to take personal command of the government and army.

Before he could do so, however, William Medows succeeded Holland in the Madras government and took command of the army there. Like most of the senior officers who served in India during Cornwallis's tenure, Medows had learned his trade during the American Revolution. He had served in America with the earl during the northern campaigning, before Cornwallis went to South Carolina. Medows had commanded the brigade that had repulsed Comte d'Estaing, at St. Lucia. His fellow officers accounted him a good soldier with an unusual ability to manage troops and an excellent tactician. Like Cornwallis, he received the overwhelming loyalty of his soldiers. According to one anecdote, when he received orders for America upon being appointed to a new regiment, the government permitted him to take as many from his old one as would volunteer. The story goes that Medows then drew up the regiment in line and said: "Let all, who choose to go with me, come on this side." To a man they volunteered. Again like Cornwallis, he was always in the thick of the fight. At Brandywine he was wounded in his right arm, fell from his horse, and broke his collarbone. He also, like the earl, had a reputation for gallantry and chivalry. "An enemy in our power," he once said, "is an enemy no more." He even, according to one account, issued an order at St. Lucia to the effect: "As soon as our gallant and generous enemy [the French] are seen to advance in great numbers, the troops are to receive them with three huzzas, and then to be perfectly silent and obedient to their officers."[34] Highly in favor with the king and Dundas in 1787, Medows received his own regiment from George III. The general had served at Bombay before his move to Madras.[35]

Though he had a good record and many fine qualities, Medows also possessed some traits that served him ill as a soldier. He was an impulsive man, given to fits of moody introspection and excessive worry about whether or not he followed the right course. Fearless in a fight, he tended to indecision in planning. It remained to be seen whether the gallantry and courtesy that had distinguished him in fighting Europeans and Americans would serve him well in India.

Cornwallis decided to find out. He thought it only fair to give his subordinate a chance, so he remained in Calcutta. As he told his old comrade in arms, Francis, Lord Rawdon (also a future governor general): "As I could not with propriety supercede him in his Government, I have been obliged, 'tho' not without regret, to relinquish the conduct of the war, and content myself with the more humble station of Commissary of Supplies."[36]

The "commissary of supplies," however, did more than forward goods to Medows. In June of 1790, the governor general concluded treaties of alliance with the nizam of Hyderabad and the Mahrattas, who would now support the Company against Tipoo in the war.[37]

Unfortunately, under Medows's supervision the war did not go well for the British. Although the blame for its lack of success rests squarely on Medows's shoulders, one cannot but feel sorry for the general. Cornwallis cajoled, scolded, hinted, upbraided, demanded, and otherwise treated his subordinate like a naughty but favored child throughout Medows's conduct of the campaign. The earl alternated between cautioning Medows against hasty action on the one hand and "pep talks" on the other. He had bombarded Medows with such missives long before their unfortunate recipient took up the Madras command. After telling Medows in January of 1788 how pleased he was that the general had accepted the Bombay government—"nothing could give me greater satisfaction"—Cornwallis cautioned him against rash ideas of reforming the army without consideration for charters and acts of Parliament. The earl frankly expressed the hope in 1788 that Medows could succeed him as governor general in 1791, in 1789 called him "a pattern to all good governors," and yet could not help censuring him for attacking Jonathan Duncan and for the ridiculous complaint that Calcutta had sent Bombay more money than it could use. Finally, when Medows took up his commission as governor of Madras in 1790, Cornwallis, though he hoped the new chief executive would "spare no pains" to bring the "delinquent" Holland to justice, cautioned him "not to act on this, or indeed on any other occasion precipitately, or under the impulse of the first impression."

Such admonitions, scarcely designed to improve Medows's self-confidence, increased in frequency as the general undertook operations. Cornwallis nagged, cautioned, and advised him. He disagreed that one of Medows's subordinates had done well in the Travancore country. He cautioned him to use discretion in his speech with strangers. In August, the governor general pointed out in a long, long letter that Medows had embarrassed him greatly not only by indiscreet conversation but also by indiscreet public letters. Cornwallis assured himself that the general "meant nothing offensive to me," but observed that even some of the "best and most friendly" of the Company's directors had noted "with concern the advantage which the indiscretion of your letters gave to their opponents." Medows took all of this in "good humor," but, given as he was to fits of despondency in any event, Cornwallis's constant injunctions must have affected his judgment and eroded his self-confidence. He needed both in the campaign he now undertook for the Company against Tipoo.[38]

Unfortunately for the general, he disagreed with Cornwallis from the beginning as to how the campaign should proceed. Cornwallis reluctantly let him have his way, but not freely. As "commissary of supplies" the earl forwarded from Calcutta a stream of reinforcements, money, gunpowder, and ordnance,[39] but accompanied them with endless criticism. He found several flaws in his subordinate's strategy as well as in his logistical dispositions. As the war progressed, the earl's migivings, arising in part from thoughts about similar mistakes made in America, increased.

Medows's plan of war, based on a scheme presented by one of his subordinates, called for a triple attack upon Mysore. The main army from Madras would march to the Coimbatore district (south of Mysore). There it would gather supplies preparatory to hurling itself northward through the mountain passes into Tipoo's territory. While the main army thus occupied itself, a second one from Bombay would march from the west coast of India eastward into Mysore. A third force, chiefly from Calcutta, would assemble at Arnee near Madras and march westward into the enemy's country. This complex plan required a degree of coordination not easily obtained in the vast expanses of India in a day of slow communications. Furthermore, it anticipated that the enemy would wait passively for these forces to converge upon him, an expectation that Tipoo's past history in no way justified.

Cornwallis pointed out to Medows from the beginning the difficulties involved in approaching Mysore from the south, a move he compared to Howe's operations in Pennsylvania. Attacking Mysore by way of Coimbatore, Cornwallis averred, was "very like our going round by the head of Elke, to conquer America, and I do not think our success on that occasion gives much encouragement." The governor general preferred a fast march west from Madras.

If, despite the earl's objections, Medows chose the southern route, Cornwallis urged that he hasten his preparations in order to ascend the passes into Mysore before the monsoons halted his advance. That Medows did not, and because of his supply arrangements could not, march immediately to Coimbatore constituted another of Cornwallis's objections. His subordinate did not plan to move until he had collected forty days' provisions and thirty thousand bullocks. Slow to start, he would also be slow to arrive, for an army so heavily laden would take much longer to reach its destination than one traveling unencumbered. Cornwallis could not understand why Medows wished to lose those extra days of campaigning by burdening himself in such a fashion. Again the earl referred to America: "I must own that this amazing proviant train puts me in mind of the unfortunate and ruinous system which we pursued in America, when we thought it necessary to carry as much provisions with us through the fertile plains of Pensylvania [sic], as if we had been to march from Aleppo to Bussorah."

Marching from "Aleppo to Bussorah" (with the huge baggage train requisite) would devour so much time that Medows might be unable to file through the passes before the monsoon set in. The earl feared that such a delay would give Tipoo a chance to seize the initiative. Should that happen, Cornwallis predicted dire consequences: the Mysore ruler would "send his rabble of cavalry to watch and harrass [sic] you, and lead the flower of his army to the borders of the Carnatic, from whence unless you detach a considerable force to oppose him, he will have six months to ravage that Country."

This prophecy proved only too accurate. Medows's delays gave Tipoo every opportunity to seize the initiative. Although rebuffed at the Travancore lines, Tipoo left his tableland in September, ravaged the Carnatic, and harassed Medows's army. Indeed, he came within an ace of bagging a large detachment of that army (about one-third of the main force), which Medows sent north. He threatened but failed to engage the relatively small Calcutta force, choosing instead to plunder and terrorize the whole of the Carnatic.

Cornwallis followed these events with increasing apprehension. He perceived a number of errors in Medows's conduct of operations remarkably similar to those the earl had himself committed in America. Medows did not keep enough men under his own command, did not procure adequate intelligence, and did not use his allies effectively. The earl reminded his general of the dangers that menaced a fragmented command: "You have as well as myself so often seen the ill effects of hazarding small detachments and being beat in detail." Several months later he expressed his hope that should rains force the southern army to abandon an offensive, Medows would "think it right to leave only a sufficient force for a secure defensive plan in Coimbatore, and withdraw a considerable part of the troops, especially of the artillery and cavalry, in order to form an army at Wallajahabad at the head of which you might confidently march towards Bangalore and Seringapatam, and would have nothing to fear from any force that Tippoo could bring against you." [40]

Despite these representations, Medows not only separated his southern and center armies, but even split the former into detachments. As a result, Tipoo chased and almost captured one unit, inflicting 436 casualties upon it and taking six of its guns. [41]

That his enemy could so surprise Medows illustrated another weakness in the conduct of his operations—inadequate intelligence. For his campaign to succeed, Medows needed accurate information at least of his own detachments. Cornwallis knew full well the necessity for several sources of intelligence to arrive at something approaching accuracy concerning the disposition, location, and strength of the enemy. He had previously remarked upon Medows's weakness in this respect. "And as the passes in your front have hitherto been totally unknown to Europeans, and you have as yet not been successful in obtaining intelligence, I cannot help feeling some uneasy sensation." [42] Unsure both of the terrain and of the situation of his detachments, Medows also failed to follow the movements of his adversary. He had the greatest difficulty in keeping track of Tipoo once the sultan left Mysore. He could not save the garrison of Darapooram, which surrendered to Tipoo on 8 October, and he became so confused that on 15 November he mistook Tipoo's army for a reinforcement from Calcutta.[43] As Cornwallis wrote to the Duke of York, Medows's "Principal embarrassments have been occasioned by his almost total want of intelligence."[44]

Total want of allied cooperation also helped ruin the British offensive. Cornwallis had taken pains to secure alliances with the nizam of Hyderabad and with the Mahrattas and to prod them into active support of Company forces. Indeed, he had even promised the nizam a complete company of European artillery, three companies of European lascars, and a brigade of sepoy infantry to act with the Hyderabad army.[45] The earl, of course, did not hold the martial prowess of his allies in any high esteem, yet he believed they might prove useful if handled properly. "I know it very easy to make all armies abuse the supineness and want of exertion of their Allies," he pointed out. "But surely it can answer no wise purpose, nor tend to support our public credit or the confidence of our troops, to undervalue our confederates. . . . We cannot deny that even their appearance in the field must distract and intimidate Tipoo, and of course be productive of great advantage to our own operations."[46] Medows disagreed. "I put not my trust in princes," he once said, "and have very little expectation from the zeal and activity of our allies."[47] Thus the British general did not encourage the nizam to act vigorously in the north to divert Tipoo from his plan of moving on Coimbatore and into the Carnatic.

Though the constant stream of advice undoubtedly undermined Medows's confidence, the advice was in the main sound. Cornwallis still had much to learn about supply problems and the usefulness of allies, but most of the measures he suggested, and nearly every move he cautioned against, Medows would have benefited from heeding. The general chose, however, to follow his own path, and it led him only into the wilderness of confusion and defeat. After his subordinate suffered continuous reverses without any appreciable gains, the governor general determined to take over operational command. On 20 October, he warned Medows of his intention of coming to Madras for that purpose unless his subordinate won "some very important advantage over Tippoo."[48] Medows stumbled along without winning that advantage. On 9 November, Cornwallis sent Captain Alexander Kyd and Lieutenant G. A. Robinson to Madras. He instructed Kyd to learn the "nature and face of the country, and the centre and southern armies" and "to obtain the most accurate information possible of the number and precise situation of the passes into Tippoo's country." He also enjoined Kyd to acquaint himself "for my information when I arrive at Madras, with the state of the country and roads, as well as with the distance and means of communication between what may then be the respective situations of the center and southern armies." He ordered Robinson to secure all possible information about supplies: how much money would be available for buying provisions and paying the troops, what ordnance, military stores, and camp equipage was on hand; how much grain had been or could be collected and stored for the army; how many draft and carriage cattle could be obtained; and how well staffed and supplied the hospitals were.[49]

The earl then prepared to leave Bengal to engage once again in war, bringing more reinforcements and supplies with him. Shortly before his departure, three hundred gentlemen of Calcutta sent a note thanking him for his "zeal for the nation" and for undertaking to run a war upon whose success depended the prosperity of the country, the "honor of our arms," and the "stability of the British power in the east."[50]

New Direction

The governor general left Calcutta on 6 December aboard the *Vestal*, a stout naval frigate, capable of weathering the heavy monsoon seas that beset him all the way to Madras, where he arrived nine days later.[51] He immediately applied himself to the war, outlining his own plan of campaign to the frustrated Medows: no more flanking maneuvers, no more splitting of forces, no more indecisiveness. "I have," the earl told Medows, "after long & very mature reflections on the safest & most practicable means of invading the Mysore dominions finally resolved to do it by the passes which lead into that country from the center of the Carnatic." He would drive straight west toward the enemy's capital, daring Tipoo to challenge him. On their way, the Company's forces would assault Oussore and Bangalore in the hopes of luring Tipoo into a fight, if he had not challenged them before that. Even if Tipoo refused the bait, the two fortified cities would be of great value to the British: they would yield supplies and would serve as depots for the accumulation of further stores. He directed the armies from Madras and those of Medows in the field to unite close to Madras "in order to render so large a convoy of money, artillery, stores, and provisions perfectly safe."[52]

He ordered the participation of the commander at Bombay, Brigadier General Robert Abercrombie, another "American" general, who had led Cornwallis's last desperate sortie in the trenches at Yorktown. To avoid the danger that the Bombay army, numbering only about 6,500, might be "beat in detail," Cornwallis sent the 73d regiment of British regulars to reinforce it.[53] He instructed Abercrombie first to reduce the coastal fortress of Cannanore, and then to proceed eastward into Mysore by way of the Coorga passes or any other convenient ones, joining the grand army outside Seringapatam. The brigadier should not approach Tipoo's capital alone, but wait until the main army was "close at hand" to support him.[54]

His plans outlined and his orders given, the earl turned to his most demanding task, that of forwarding reinforcements and accumulating enough supplies to feed, clothe, and arm the vast multitude he intended to lead into Tipoo's heartland. He told Medows at the beginning of the new year: "we can only be said to be as nearly independent of contingencies as can be expected in war, when we are possessed of a complete battering train, and can move it with the army; and whilst we carry a large stock of provisions with us that ample magazines shall be lodged in strong places in our rear and at no great distance from the scene of our intended operations."[55]

To move a "complete battering train" was a herculean task for which India offered a solution unavailable in America: elephants. Indeed, Cornwallis was the first British commander to use elephants extensively for hauling artillery.[56] In late February at Pallomanor (or Palamanair) he received from Bengal sixty-five of these valuable beasts.[57] Others came at regular intervals (in July of 1791, one hundred arrived at Vellore), so that he was soon served by several hundred elephants.[58]

They certainly proved their worth. Lieutenant Colonel Patrick Duff of the Bengal artillery said they did "wonders" by hauling his twenty-four-pounders out of mud "up to their axle-trees."[59] The deputy adjutant general of the king's forces, Alexander Dirom, discovered them indispensable in the siege of Tipoo's hill fortresses and "of such evident and essential advantage, that they will in future be considered of the first consequence in all operations that require a train of heavy artillery."[60]

But several hundred elephants answered only a part of the army's logistic needs, which literally stagger the imagination. For example, 27,000 draft and carriage cattle started with the army on its march, as well as tens of thousands of camels. All—elephants, cattle, camels—needed forage. The camp followers, as well as the army, had to eat. An Indian campaign inevitably seemed to require four civilians for each soldier. Major James Rennell, an engineer in the expedition, observed that in a campaign in 1778–79, some 19,779 camp followers trailed only 103 European and 6,624 native troops. He emphasized that the "difficulties that a general has to surmount in that country [India]; and particularly in the article of feeding his army and its myriads of followers, and beasts of burden, are more than most European officers can readily conceive."[61]

The army actually needed some of the civilians. It required cattle drivers to the extent of about one man for every two or three bullocks. Bearers carried rice for food. Elephants and camels needed attendants. Every cavalry trooper used two men to serve him. Palanquin and dooly bearers conveyed the sick. Field officers had forty servants, captains twenty, and subalterns ten. The soldiers employed their own attendants, particularly as cooks. Sepoys often brought their families, and, of course, merchants and their servants trailed along behind. Finally, an army on the move attracted adventurers who were not overly careful about whether the loot they garnered came from foe or friend.

Certainly the amount and variety of equipment for the army might tempt the avaricious: over a hundred thousand muskets, flints, pistols, two thousand barrels of powder, thirty-one

different tents for Cornwallis and his staff, extra canvas for repairs, drums, swords, mortars, shovels, axes, picks, eighteen-,
twenty-four-, and thirty-two-pound siege cannon, colors, billhooks, sandbags, spike nails, and much more. The governor
general procured many of these provisions from Calcutta, which
also supplied him quantities of money (which he had always
lacked in America), horses, draft bullocks, and other necessaries,
as well as reinforcements.[62]

Just assembling an army presented problems unique to
India. The sepoys had to come from Calcutta to Madras by ships,
and, according to Hickey, they hated even the thought of it.
"But," he noted, "their extraordinary respect for Lord Cornwallis and attachment to his person proved sufficient to induce
them to surmount long-established prejudices." Once aboard
ship, they needed special accommodations. Moslems required
quarters separate from Hindus, and Hindus separated themselves
by caste. Hindus could not eat food prepared aboard ship, so they
had to bring their own dried fruits and grain and their own water
casks sealed by Brahmins.[63]

While grappling with logistics (a term not then in use),
Cornwallis had to consider his allies as well. He dispatched Company forces to help the nizam, kept communication open between
his and the nizam's forces, and tried to hasten Hyderabad's fifteen
thousand cavalry under Rajah Teige Wunt to a junction with the
Company troops.[64] He desperately wanted the Hyderabad and
Mahratta cavalry. Indeed, he considered himself so deficient in
that arm that he formed a corps of dismounted cavalry out of
some sepoy battalions as a protection for Madras before he joined
the army at Velhout.[65] He also sent a battery of artillery to the
Mahrattas.[66]

With his six sepoy battalions of reinforcements from Bengal, Cornwallis joined Medows's southern army at Velhout and
there took personal command on 29 January. He reviewed the
army the same day. In a general order, he praised it for its appearance and hoped for a speedy campaign. According to Lieutenant
Roderick Mackenzie of the 52d regiment, Cornwallis's presence
as well as his words boosted the morale of the entire group:
"When exalted and illustrious characters whose virtues have
gained the confidence and esteem of mankind, forsaking situations

of ease and comfort, step forth upon arduous occasions, on the purest principle of patriotism, to encounter danger and fatigue, it is wonderful to contemplate the effect that the example has upon the minds of the people. . . . Whilst all ranks of men were lost in admiration of the noble spirit that dictated this resolution, the army seemed affected by it to a peculiar degree."[67]

The army so affected was an impressive force. Cornwallis now commanded directly six regiments of regular British infantry, one of regular cavalry, seven regiments of Bengal sepoys, one battalion of Bengal artillery, six battalions of Madras sepoys, two battalions of Madras artillery, and five battalions of Madras native cavalry, along with engineers and pioneers. The army totaled around fifteen thousand men with sixty thousand camp followers.[68]

How the sights, sounds, and smells of this large assemblage must have assaulted the senses! Merchants peddling wares, women screaming, the sick moaning in doolies, thousands and thousands of animals trumpeting and braying and grunting, bullocks yoked two abreast straining at the eighteen-pounder guns, a scene of chaos, noise, dirt, and manure, made more oppressive by the heat. One pities the last person to march in this procession, who could hardly avoid what must have been a river of filth nearly to the ankles. Cornwallis, however, ignored the chaos and concentrated, with what Major Dirom, the deputy adjutant general, called "assiduous and indefatigable attention," on moving his command forward. He started the army in one long column, most of the cavalry in front, infantry and baggage next, and battering train in the rear. The train fell steadily behind, as one might expect, to the considerable worry of the one cavalry regiment detailed to act as rear guard. This whole cumbersome array lumbered toward the ghats, or passes, that gave access to the tableland of Mysore. Throughout the war, it could never make much better than twelve miles per day.

Cornwallis carefully supervised every aspect of the march. He personally instructed officers he sent on detached service and personally saw them on their return. Once the army camped, his headquarters tent became a hive of activity. In it, with the faithful Ross at his side, he dictated dispatches to coordinate the movements of the other armies involved in the war and received dispatches from all over India. This energetic conduct greatly impressed Major Dirom, who wrote: "His Lordship's tents, and the line of headquarters, appeared more like the various departments of a great office of state, than the splendid equipage that might be supposed to attend the leader of the greatest armies that, under a British general, were ever assembled in the east."[69]

The leader of "the greatest armies" immediately discovered that the greatest of plunderers marched with him. Mackenzie, who had no sympathy for whites who considered Indians "innocent natives" or "injured people," noted that several hundred camp followers made their fortunes on this march "by the most shameful or barefaced plunder that ever took place in a civilized country."[70] They stripped some of the regular officers of all their gear and stole some of the earl's equipment. As an example, Cornwallis hanged pillagers who were caught, but even this measure did not halt the "disgraceful outrages."[71] One subordinate, Dirom, actually approved the looting, saying that it helped supply the army! He believed that those bent on loot searched for and found pits of grain in the fields and villages that would otherwise remain undiscovered and brought in cattle that would otherwise not be collected.

So the army inched forward. Although its destination was Bangalore, some two hundred miles from Madras, Cornwallis wanted to deceive Tipoo with regard to his intentions before the sultan thought to close the passes to Mysore, about sixty miles away. The earl left Velhout on 5 February and reached Vellore on 11 February. He halted there two days to refurbish the battering train. He then dodged and feinted. Instead of moving by the passes of Amboor and Baramahal, he turned north and west and ascended the pass of Moogla or Muglee, about 110 miles from Bangalore. This was wild country of rocks and jungles (which necessitated his changing the order of march and forming the army in two divisions). But no one stopped him, and he reached the tableland of Mysore without firing a shot.

Climate and terrain now changed. Though the days were hot and dry, the temperature fell during the night. Cornwallis especially appreciated the "great comfort" of these "cold nights" (around 55° at five in the morning) because of the furnace-hot days. The temperature might climb to near 100° by one in the

2. Cornwallis's Campaigns against Tipoo, 1791–1792
   Based on a map by Lieutenant R. H. Colebrooke (in PRO, MR 386).

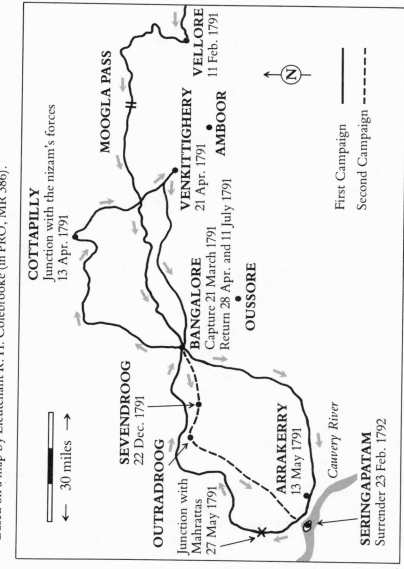

COTTAPILLY
Junction with the nizam's forces
13 Apr. 1791

MOOGLA PASS

VELLORE
11 Feb. 1791

VENKITTIGHERY
21 Apr. 1791

AMBOOR

BANGALORE
Capture 21 March 1791
Return 28 Apr. and 11 July 1791

OUSSORE

SEVENDROOG
22 Dec. 1791

OUTRADROOG

Junction with
Mahrattas
27 May 1791

ARRAKERRY
13 May 1791

Cauvery River

SERINGAPATAM
Surrender 23 Feb. 1792

30 miles

First Campaign
Second Campaign

N

afternoon and in the headquarters tent sometimes reached 110°.[72] The land, though rocky, had many streams. Because the natives stored water in tanks to irrigate their crops, the troops did not go thirsty. The land grew much grain, which the villages stockpiled and the army gobbled up. The earl had no difficulty in procuring supplies.

He moved toward Bangalore against very little opposition. Some of the Poligyar chiefs, their cavalry armed with spears and pikes, even offered their services personally to him. Two small forts in the army's path surrendered without firing a shot, and he reached Bangalore on 5 March, exactly on schedule according to the timetable he had set for himself.[73] Only then did Tipoo act. Lieutenant Colonel John Floyd of the cavalry, on a scouting expedition, espied what he believed was the rear of Tipoo's line and in sufficient confusion to attack it with his six regiments. The sultan, however, had baited a trap into which Floyd charged headlong. Tipoo's small diversionary force retreated until his main army cut Floyd off from the Company's forces. Then the sultan counterattacked in overwhelming numbers and trounced Floyd soundly, killing two hundred men and three hundred horses, neither of which the earl could afford to lose.

Success seems to have made him complacent, however, for Tipoo now sat back content to watch events. Cornwallis considered the loss only a temporary check and proceeded methodically to besiege Bangalore. Tipoo spasmodically cannonaded his enemies in hopes of drawing them off, but Cornwallis ignored the fire and concentrated on the siege. On the morning of 7 March, eighteen-pounder guns opened a tiny breach in the walls. A lieutenant who was slight of stature thought it large enough and charged through with reckless abandon. Cornwallis noticed his movement and immediately ordered troops to "support the little gentleman." The army then surged forward everywhere. Soldiers pushed scaling ladders against the walls and scampered over them in a rush. The demoralized foe fell back so quickly that Cornwallis soon controlled all of Bangalore save for the fort itself. This he immediately besieged, digging his parallels and bombarding ceaselessly. He soon breached its walls in several places. Then, at eleven o'clock on the still moonlit night of 21 March, the British forces stormed and carried this last enemy stronghold. Regiments of British regulars led the attack, supported by a battalion of sepoys. Carrying scaling ladders, they ran down into the ditch in the fort's front, scampered back up, pushed the ladders against the wall, clambered over, and carried the position in two hours. Tipoo did little but watch from a distance and shower his enemy with rockets in ineffectual attempts to lure them away. His relative inactivity probably confirmed the earl's opinion of the inferior military ability of the native powers. He, on the other hand, despite Floyd's loss, had besieged and carried his objective. One observer commented that at Bangalore Cornwallis had proved his military abilities: "a most able general, adored, and justly so, by every man in the army." [74]

In Bangalore, he discovered ordnance, ammunition, a large quantity of grain, and an "immense" depot of military stores, including about 120 cannon. He repaired the breaches in the walls and ordered his heavy artillery refitted. Then on 28 March he

6. The Death of Colonel Moorhouse at the Storming of Bangalore, 1791
Engraving by E. Stalker from a painting by Robert Horne.
Reprinted by permission of the India Office Library and Records, London

pushed on after Tipoo, falling upon his rear guard about eight miles from Bangalore.[75] Unfortunately, the British commander now found himself so deficient in cavalry that he could not pursue Tipoo's own army quickly enough to force it to action. The rear guard engagement netted him only one brass gun, which he had to leave behind when its carriage broke down. He now gave up pursuit and, instead of moving toward Seringapatam, swung directly away from it toward the north and east in order to junction with the cavalry of Hyderabad. The earl hoped these horsemen would improve his army's mobility. They could scout for it, gather forage, and protect the flanks. Yet the nizam's forces, under the leadership of Rajah Teige Wunt, had dawdled and dillydallied on one pretense or another, particularly fearful that Tipoo might surround and destroy them. Fear, instead of hastening them toward the sheltering arms of the British forces, had apparently rendered them incapable of movement at all. Cornwallis, naturally anxious to effect a junction as soon as possible, boiled with indignation over their slow progress. He threatened to turn around and attack Seringapatam alone, leaving the Hyderabad horse to their own devices.[76] The two groups, however, eventually junctioned near Cottapilly on 13 April, some sixty miles directly north and east of Bangalore, but ninety-three miles from there by the circuitous route the Company's forces had taken.

When Cornwallis beheld this fifteen-thousand-man "reinforcement," he immediately had misgivings. He commented that the men were "extremely defective in almost every point of military discipline," indeed, had no idea of it.[77] Certainly they presented a curious sight, armed with their bows and arrows, spears, pikes, swords, and matchlocks, some wearing armor, some carrying shields, some without either but carrying loaded rockets. "Each moved," one British subaltern noted, "as if he himself had been sole commander. In short, scampering in every direction, they appeared like mountebanks tilting their weapons in the air, as at a joust or tournament."[78]

These "mountebanks" now exacerbated the Company forces' supply problem, while failing to increase the army's mobility. The nizam's rabble had arrived without provisions of their own. While their horse devoured forage that was not replaced, their men consumed Company rations. The earl again had to alter his plans. Instead of returning to Bangalore, he moved south and east toward Amboor, where Lieutenant Colonel John Oldham had stockpiled sheep, cattle, arrack, salt, rice, and gunny sacks.[79] But before the provisions he had ordered Oldham to send from Amboor could reach Cornwallis's grand army at Venkittighery on 21 April, the bullock masters walked out of Oldham's camp with their hundreds of loaded bullocks.[80]

The situation now became desperate as the earl once again turned west. He had two hopes: first to garner yet more supplies from Bangalore, and then to depend upon Abercrombie, whom he would meet near Seringapatam, for further provisions. He knew that Abercrombie was at the Courga pass some thirty-five miles from Tipoo's capital.[81] Cornwallis reached Bangalore on 28 April, replenished himself scantily with military stores and provisions, and hauled out his heavy artillery. He marched south from the town on 3 May with the battering train, the nizam's cavalry, the 19th dragoons, five regiments of native cavalry, six regiments of British regulars, one of the Company's European regiments, seventeen batallions of sepoy infantry, and twenty days' provisions for the soldiers only.[82]

The march became a nightmare. Terrible weather bogged them down. The monsoons came early, the wind blew up, and rain soaked the men every day. In the earl's path, Tipoo destroyed villages, forage, straw, anything his enemy might use. Instead of scouting ahead or riding the flanks to protect followers and baggage or performing any of the other functions of cavalry, the nizam's troopers remained in the rear in an "unwieldy mass," devouring provisions. Before he left Bangalore, the earl had offered to let them have what they needed from a supply depot in his rear, but they had even refused to send draft bullocks to take advantage of this largesse.[83] "We may remark," later grumbled Major James Rennell, his engineer, "by the way, that if, instead of his cavalry the Nizam had sent an equal number of fresh draft and carriage cattle, the army would have received a more effectual reinforcement."[84] Twice Cornwallis appealed directly to Teige Wunt, on 8 May and again on 10 May, to bestir himself. But the nizam's cavalry remained worse than inactive.[85]

All now suffered privations. Toward the end of April, officers had had to abandon much of their equipment. The captains began to sleep two and the subalterns four to a tent and to carry a proportion of shot with their private baggage.[86] The officers had given most of their private cattle and carts to the army to assist in transporting shot and stores from Bangalore. They now found themselves so reduced that many of them requested the same allowance of food as private soldiers, but the private soldiers were drawing only half rations of rice. Tents and clothing wore to shreds, incessantly pounded by the rains. Smallpox struck. Cattle died in the thousands, victims of an epidemic. The animals that remained were not of much use. The "putrid flesh" of the dead ones, at least, provided some sustenance for the camp followers,[87] as did the numbers of horses that the officers and cavalry troopers had to shoot.

By 9 May, just six days out of Bangalore, only the exertions of the sepoys and British infantry, their "good will" as Cornwallis put it, enabled the army to continue. The sepoys dragged the provision carts, harnessed like bullocks, while the European infantry carried the entrenching tools.[88]

One wonders if these conditions, so similar to his privations in South Carolina, made Cornwallis remember those ghastly marches through the back country of America. There, too, men had hitched themselves to wagons and hauled them. There, too, the army had always remained short of wagons and animals to pull them. There, too, the enemy had not given battle but had sniped at the flanks. There, too, there had always seemed to be one more river to cross.

The river Cornwallis now desperately needed to cross was the Cauvery. He had to get to its south bank, either above or below Seringapatam, so as to junction with Abercrombie and his precious provisions. The Cauvery rose in Mysore, coursed on both sides of the island of Seringapatam which bisected it, and finally entered the Bay of Bengal in Tanjore. Tortuous in course, with a rocky bed, high banks, and luxurious vegetation, it presented a formidable obstacle to an army the size of his, whose men now hauled siege guns and carriages. As in Carolina, the rains worked for his enemy and against him. The unusually heavy downpours so flooded the Cauvery as to make it impassable. Cornwallis heard from various people that the army could wade it with heavy artillery. But he personally looked in several places for fords, sent out detachments for the same purpose, and found none. His last chance, seemingly, lay in the village of Arrakerry, or Arickery, about ten miles downstream from Seringapatam. But when he arrived there on 13 May and examined the terrain above and below it, he again found no passable fords. Tipoo, who had carefully watched his adversary's progress, now shrewdly chose this minute to offer him battle.

The sultan drew up his army in sight of the earl's on 13 May near Arrakerry, with his right flank on the river and his left on a rugged mountain. The governor general now had his first view of his enemy in full battle array prepared to fight. What a sight it must have been, for Tipoo's forces were as colorful and motley as any that ever gathered in India! He had some regular cavalry, decently uniformed and drilled, but the mass of his troopers came from all corners of the subcontinent. Each of the irregulars supplied his own mount and dressed exactly as he pleased. Tipoo even commanded a group of horsemen who wore nothing but a loincloth and turban, rode ponies too small for battle, served without pay, and looked for plunder to reward their exertions. His regular infantry, dressed with turbans, cummerbunds, white jackets and breeches, armed with muskets and led by foreign officers, had some of the training and discipline of the sepoys. They might prove formidable. But Tipoo's irregulars, armed with anything from old matchlocks to scimitars, dressed and drilled as they wished, and also sought their reward in plunder.[89] This motley army, with artillery dug in all along the front, now awaited the earl's pleasure.

Cornwallis hoped to scramble around the sultan's left flank, on the other side of the mountain, and then cut him off from his capital. He ordered his best cavalry (the 19th dragoons and three sepoy regiments), six battalions of regular infantry, and twelve battalions of sepoy infantry to prepare themselves for that purpose. But, like so many others, rain spoiled these plans. It poured, with thunder and lightning, "the most violent," the earl complained, "that I have seen in this part of India." As a result, he had to stop operations. Regiments lost line of march, bullocks weakened, and he could not move before dawn revealed his position to the sultan.

Tipoo now moved artillery, cavalry, and infantry to the

heights on his left. Cornwallis then altered his tactics, forming his army in two lines to charge the enemy's front, and sending two battalions of sepoys and the 52d regiment to take the heights. The cavalry, including the nizam's, he kept in reserve. During this maneuvering, Tipoo's guns mauled the Company's forces. Finally, Lieutenant Colonel Maxwell stormed the heights with fixed bayonets and carried them without firing a shot, taking three of the enemy's cannon. The earl's entire battle line surged forward, and Tipoo retreated. The retreat soon turned into a rout, while Cornwallis loosed his cavalry to cut up the broken enemy. But the sultan managed to get back to his island with most of his soldiers, where they sheltered under the guns of the fort.

This battle, which lasted about four and one-half hours, again showed Cornwallis as an excellent tactician. But it did not win the war.[90] As in Carolina, supply problems prevented the earl from following up his success, even though his casualties had been light.[91] He could not settle down to besiege Seringapatam for the simple reason that he would not be able to eat while doing so. Although his army finally found a passable ford, the Kannimbaddy or Coniambuddy, to the northwest of Seringapatam, the late season and shortages of supplies obliged him after the victory to turn back toward Bangalore. He ordered Abercrombie on 21 May to return to Bombay and outlined to him his own desperate situation: "I cannot move forward a step to favor you without exposing this army to the certain state of perishing by famine." The allies, far from helping, had proved an "intolerable burden," and the camp followers added to his troubles by plundering the public stores. So the earl destroyed his battering train, "a mortifying necessity," and marched back toward Bangalore on half rations of rice.[92] Abercrombie fell back on 24 May, also destroying some of his own artillery.[93]

When news of the Company's retreat eventually reached England, the public assumed that the earl had to abandon this first campaign because of bad weather, the chief reason that in Europe active campaigning rarely took place in the winter. But one cartoonist depicted the monsoon as Tipoo standing in his capital and urinating over its walls onto the army before him, a vulgarity of which Cornwallis was fortunately unaware.

The allies now proved just how "intolerable" they could

be. On the first day's march north, after a wearisome journey of six miles, a party of alien horsemen cantered up to meet the army on its baggage flank. Many at first thought them enemies, but they turned out to be an escort of Mahrattas, accompanied by the paymaster of the Bombay army. To everyone's amazement, the paymaster assured them that one Mahratta army of twenty thousand horse and foot commanded by Perseram Bhow and another of twelve thousand horse under Hurry Punt were ready to join in the assault on Tipoo's stronghold. Furthermore, they had ample supplies for themselves and for the Company's forces.[94] Imagine Cornwallis's chagrin when on the next day, 27 May, the Mahratta and Company armies met, but he no longer had his battering train. His best intelligence had placed them some 150 miles to the

7. The Coming-on of the Monsoons; or The
Retreat from Seringapatam
Published 6 December 1791, by H. Humphrey, No. 18 Old Bond
Street, London.

north. One can appreciate that he felt some bitterness: "If the Mahrattas had actually arrived in this neighbourhood three weeks sooner, I think we might have taken Seringapatam, and if I had been assured ten days ago [he was writing on 2 June] that they were well advanced on the road, I could have brought Abercromby forward, and perhaps we might have done by blockade what the loss of our cattle, the desolation of the country, and the criminal inactivity of the Nizam's cavalry prevented our doing by force." [95]

At least, the Mahrattas were not disposed to abandon the campaign entirely. They promised to work with the Company in harassing Tipoo. Meanwhile, the earl trudged along in "wretched dependence upon the Maratta Bazar," [96] a situation particularly galling since he did not think much more highly of the new companions than he did of the nizam's forces. One wit described the Mahratta cavalry as thirty thousand men mounted on broken-winded mares. Half the cavalry wore ragged clothes and the other half wore scarcely anything. Some carried spears, and some carried blunt, worn-out scimitars. The infantry, he said, resembled nothing so much as sepoy raw recruits. [97] Another British observer described the infantry as composed of "black Christians and despicable poor wretches of the lowest cast, uniform in nothing but the bad state of their musquets, none of which are either clean or complete." [98] They had neither sufficient ammunition nor accouterments and were commanded by half-caste Portuguese and French dressed in antiquated lace. Another observer described their appearance as that of a "banditti." [99]

Their artillery park also astounded the Europeans because the gun carriages were made almost entirely of iron, mounted on large, solid, united pieces of wood. The guns themselves, painted in all sorts of bizarre colors, they had named for various gods. Many of these cannon were useless, but the Mahrattas dragged them along anyway. On the march they made these monstrosities yet more unwieldy by piling them high with stores and baggage. Because they had no pioneers to clear and repair the roads, the Mahrattas sometimes used as many as 150 bullocks, strung in pairs, to pull one gun, the drivers sitting astride the yokes and urging the beasts along at a trot.

When this motley group broke camp, the horsemen simply

rode roughshod through the infantry, baggage, and guns, while the chiefs sat on the ground, placidly puffing their hookahs. Then each chief, followed by his aides, mounted and took his own route.

Appearances to the contrary, however, the Mahrattas were shrewd people. Their two major leaders, Hurry Punt and Perseram Bhow, though not military commanders in the European tradition, knew their own interests as well as any European. Punt was a Brahmin about sixty years old, of medium height and weight, fair, with gray eyes on an intelligent-looking face. Bhow, who had lost a battle to Tipoo in 1784, was a small, dark man with black eyes, about forty years old, and full of nervous energy.[100] The two leaders had the earl at their mercy for provisions, at least until he reached Bangalore, and they did not hesitate to profit from it. The Company's forces and camp followers flocked to the Mahratta camp by the thousands, happy to purchase grain at any price. The price rose so high that a subaltern's pay could scarcely purchase enough to feed his horse.[101] Furthermore, the Mahrattas dictated the pace of the army. The earl wanted to move as rapidly as possible back north, leaving behind their present campgrounds, now dirty and empty of forage. But his allies politely refused to move after their junction, at least for one day, insisting that it was unlucky to march on the ninth day, and they had already traveled for eight. Later, near Oussore, Cornwallis again had to postpone his march because of their religious ceremonies.[102]

Despite these delays, he approached Bangalore in easy stages by a northern road, dotted with hill forts, along which Perseram Bhow had established a provision depot. The Company's army finally reached Bangalore on 11 July.

Chapter 8

The Second Campaign against Tipoo

Bangalore now became headquarters for the next campaign. From there Cornwallis sent a stream of letters all over India. He had much to do. This time he intended to prepare himself thoroughly before advancing on the sultan's capital. He needed badly, for example, to improve his intelligence operation. Had it served him better in May, he might not have had to abandon the campaign, for he would have been aware of the movements of the Mahratta army. He needed far better information than he possessed about the terrain of Mysore. "As the inhabitants," he observed, "are driven from all the villages for several coss on each side of the road, we had but an imperfect knowledge of the country and even the distance to Seringapatam."[1] With improved knowledge of the routes, Cornwallis could march more swiftly and surely than during the first campaign. His concentrated efforts in this direction eventually paid handsome dividends, for he learned in detail Tipoo's movements and the size and strength of his army, information invaluable to him when he actually moved south for the attack.

Cornwallis also needed to work out a better understanding with his allies. If they would participate wholeheartedly, they might actually help instead of hinder him. Failing that cooperation, perhaps they would at least act vigorously enough outside Seringapatam to draw off a part of Tipoo's army, thus weakening the defenses inside the capital. At the worst, if they would not help, Cornwallis hoped to keep them out of the way. He had only partial success.

154

Supplies

His most immediate need was to accumulate sufficient supplies so that the final campaign had no chance of ending in the humiliating fashion of the first one. He would again use the supply base he had previously established at Amboor.[2] Throughout June he urged the Madras government to forward to Amboor, as well as to the army directly, carriages, bullocks, rice, gunny sacks, gunny, arrack, camp equipment, money, guns, and clothing—the last two to come from Bengal, which also furnished the siege train. Madras complied, even to the extent of building special platform carriages for transporting the clothing and camp equipment.[3] To pay for these and the other provisions he would need, he appropriated enough bullion from the China ship to coin twelve lakhs of rupees.[4]

Cornwallis had initially disliked the military auditor general at Calcutta, Colonel John Murray. Now Murray proved his worth. He had volunteered to help before the earl left, and he now took charge of forwarding supplies from Calcutta to Madras for the Company army. Murray worked hard and on the basis of his own experience systematically estimated the supply needs of an army of eighty thousand men (twenty thousand soldiers, sixty thousand followers) for a month in a country with little forage for the animals or food for the men. He compiled numerous tables of estimates. In one, he calculated that such an army needed nearly eighty thousand bullocks to transport the rice, ordnance, forage for three thousand cavalry and three hundred elephants, and the loose shot, musket balls, spirits, and camp equipment.[5]

Obviously, Cornwallis needed drivers in greater numbers than before. He himself worked out a similar equation, estimating that just to carry from Madras to his army the battering train, ammunition, and tools for siege operations would require 1,361 draft bullocks and 1,186 carriage bullocks, plus, of course, their drivers.[6] To obtain them he resorted to several expedients. He authorized the Madras government to employ agents to procure the cattle if the contractors could not furnish a sufficient number. Anyway, he believed the contractors had cheated: the contract was "drawn so much in favor of the contractors and so much against the public, that it is impossible to establish any effectual check or control."[7] Next, the commander in chief ensured punctual payment to the drivers—"that most useful class of people"—so as to encourage their continuance with the army and discourage desertion. In the past campaign, some of them had played him false, deserting their escort and causing the army to lose some hundreds of loaded cattle.[8] To make sure, finally, that a core of drivers always remained loyal, he authorized Bengal to send down three to four hundred lascars to serve in that capacity.[9]

To lessen the need for bullocks and their drivers, Cornwallis increased the number of elephants. Proportionate to the food they consumed and the work they did, elephants had proved a more efficient means of transport than bullocks. In August he sharply raised his demands for the big beasts. The agent at Fort William had never before shipped more than 71 elephants per month to his commander, but in August he sent 148 and after that never fewer than 106 per month.[10]

All these animals needed forage, of course, which presented yet another problem. During the summer and fall of 1791, the army had to move constantly to new camps in a never-ending search for forage. As Cornwallis noted: "The remarkable dryness of the season distresses us so much in the article of forage that we can scarcely remain two days in the same camp and it falls particularly hard upon the Maratta horses."[11] But by movement and gradual stockpiling, he overcame the forage problem.

To provide food for his animals proved relatively easy when compared to the much more formidable task of feeding his people. Although the British regulars could slaughter some of the cattle to eat, Hindu sepoy and Mahratta armies could not, for religious reasons, eat beef. The grand staple, therefore, was rice, on which an Indian army moved in the eighteenth century. Cornwallis not only had to find a means of transporting enough rice to keep his army going, but also to accumulate a surplus in the event of an emergency. As he told his brother William: "It is no easy task to feed between two and three hundred thousand men, one hundred thousand horses, and twice that number of bullocks, besides elephants and camels, in a country which nature intended for a desert, and which Tippoo has, with the assistance of our friends the Mahrattas, rendered a complete one." [12] So Cornwallis turned to the one resource India had in abundance and which the Mahrattas and Tipoo had long used: swarms of people. He decided to depend upon human beasts of burden, or binjarries, to carry the food for his forces. He differed from Tipoo and the Mahrattas, however, in that he paid the men well and promptly. As a result, he got much more satisfactory service than either his allies or his enemy. The captain of the governor general's guard, Samuel Turner, noted that as the army fell back from Seringapatam in the first campaign, binjarries tended to gather around it. By the time the army was ready to commence its second advance, the binjarries numbered fifty thousand men and were "constantly employed in bringing in every species of provision for the subsistence of the troops and the vast multitude of followers." "Indispensibly necessary," they remained loyal to the Company's service and faithful in their duties because of "plain and fair dealing free from exaction of any nature whatsoever." [13] Indeed, according to Dirom, the binjarries "spoke highly in his lordship's praise; and said he always kept his word with them; and that they never came away disappointed." [14] When the rains fell, crops ripened, and the Carnatic markets promised supplies, the binjarries transported food steadily to the army, much to Cornwallis's surprise and pleasure. [15]

That he had brought sufficient specie to pay the army partly accounted for his successful supply efforts and also enabled him to economize in other ways. Instead of issuing the sepoys their full allowance of rice, for which they would have paid by deductions from their wages, the earl gave them half allowances, without making them pay for the grain, and paid them money in lieu of the other half. The regulars also received half their ration of arrack and money in lieu of the other half. "The Sepoys," explained Dirom, "bought coarser grain with the money they received for the half of their allowance of rice; and the soldiers who preferred more liquor to the money might buy it in the bazars [sic]; so that, without murmur or hardship, the public stores of grain and arrack were made to last double the time by this arrangement." [16] The commander in chief also gave relief to the bullock department by offering to pay the regular officers a monthly allowance if they would carry and provide their own tents and sepoy officers the same if they would provide for the carriage of ammunition and stores for their units.[17]

Thus Cornwallis utilized on a huge scale the vast resources of India in preparation for the final drive on Seringapatam. One awestruck commentator marveled at the abundance of material and food the army acquired before the march south because of the earl's efforts. "The department of military stores," he noted, "is complete in every respect and exhibits a capital display of the implements of war in an astonishing abundance." Behind his artillery park, Cornwallis had "an almost incredible proportion of carriages." His ordnance included substantial numbers of iron and brass guns, the heavy siege ones from Bengal, howitzers, mortars, tumbrils, and ample ammunition. The bazaars were "overstocked with all kinds of provisions" and even included the "luxuries of life." They could be purchased at "prices little more advanced than those which they are selling at the presidency." The draft cattle were "in such high order that they literally came in with the heavy guns on a gallop! The carriage cattle are equally good."[18] Indeed, the earl supplied himself so well that he allowed his allies to purchase freely in his own bazaars from Mysore to the Carnatic.[19]

More important, he kept his supply lines open so that provision trains could reach his army wherever he went. As he himself remarked: "Being sufficiently sensible that a failure of regular supplies for the support of the vast multitudes of which our armies will be composed, might render the ultimate success in the object of the campaign exceedingly precarious, I have spared no pains to open and secure our communications to the northward and eastward of Bangalore."[20] He knew the binjarries would continue to bring grain to his forces after they moved beyond Bangalore toward Seringapatam only if that part of their journey "to and from the army can be rendered as secure as it is at present."[21]

To make the route secure, he dispatched an expedition that captured the Policode pass, the most direct route for the supply trains from Madras to the army and the hill forts that protected it.[22] To provide the binjarries with armed guards while they brought supplies to Bangalore from Amboor and other points, he posted allied cavalry in different stations along their routes and detached groups of sepoys to convoy the binjarries. Although the allied cavalry never proved completely trustworthy, by the middle of November supplies flowed into Bangalore "without obstruction."[23]

The Hill Forts

To ensure that his supply lines from Bangalore to Seringapatam would remain unobstructed, he determined to seize the important hill forts that lay between the towns, especially along the northernmost road.

In July, the earl began operations systematically. He bribed one hill fort into surrender.[24] In October, he carried the extremely strong fort of Nundydroog, built on the summit of a mountain seventeen hundred feet high, inaccessible save from one direction and there protected by an outwork that covered the gateway. The Company's forces built a gun road and, using their elephants, without which the siege guns could never have been dragged up, laid siege to the fort.[25] Defended by seventeen guns and a garrison of about seven hundred, it ought to have held out for a long period. Instead, it fell in three weeks. After it refused his summons to surrender, Cornwallis brought his whole army against it. By 18 October, he considered that the artillery had made a sufficient breach in the defenses to make an attack feasible. He ordered the assault for the rising of the moon that night, and his troops carried Nundydroog with little opposition. Indeed, to their astonishment, they saw many of its defenders leap over the precipices at the rear of the fort to evade capture.[26]

After this success the earl moved against Sevendroog, the hill fort he thought more necessary to take and hold than any other. It afforded, he observed, "such ample and convenient protection to the enemy's parties that no Binjarry whilst it remains in Tippoo's possession will venture to travel on any of the roads leading from Bangalore to Seringapatam without larger escorts than it is probable we shall be able to furnish."[27] Yet Sevendroog seemed nearly impregnable. The earl did not move on it until December: the countryside around Nundydroog furnished plentiful supplies, which in turn afforded him leisure to study the obstacle confronting him and to bring up heavy guns from Amboor.

His reconnaissance, certainly, can have given him little

comfort. Sevendroog was a large mountain of rock, about half a mile high. It tapered to an east–west length of some two miles, intersected with deep ravines. Covered by walls on every side, it was reinforced by cross walls and barriers wherever Tipoo's army thought it possible someone might climb. The whole mountain, dotted with fortifications and forts, was also divided by a ravine that separated the upper part into two hills, each of which had forts on the eastern and western ends that could operate independently of the works lower down. They also provided a final retreat for the garrison below. At the base of the mountain, the country offered a natural barrier to attackers in the form of a thick jungle of thorn, bamboo, and tall trees. Natives believed that bears and tigers roamed these jungles, eager to pounce on the unwary traveler. Cornwallis could not invest Sevendroog closely, because the rock, surrounded by jungle and desert hills, altogether made a circle of some twenty miles. Samuel Turner summed up the British view of the place as they prepared to go against it: "In the estimation of the Sultan and his subjects this fortress was deemed impregnable, such was its fame all over Indostan, for there is a tradition here in the reign of the ancient Rajas of Mysore it resisted a siege of 12 years." Turner added: "Few places in the world I believe have more works about it." It seemed to deserve its ominous name, "rock of death." [28]

Cornwallis soon moved against Sevendroog as methodically as he had against Nundydroog. He sent his chief engineer and other officers to find a suitable place for attack. They chose the north face as the most practical. After their report, he moved forward the 52d and 72d regiments of regulars, four sepoy battalions, artillery, and flank companies of the 71st and 76th regular regiments. He posted allied cavalry to right and left to prevent the enemy interrupting communications during the siege and then took up position with the main army about eight miles to the north. The pioneers hacked a road through the jungle along which the army could march and drag its heavy guns. By 10 December, the troops had cut their way through to the base of the fortress. Then they climbed the mountain and occupied a position within 250 yards of the walls of the eastern fort. The heavy guns followed them and, after being positioned, opened fire on 17 December. For four days the artillery pounded away at the walls, opening a breach for the troops to storm through. Though he preferred to attack at night, he could not on this occasion because his soldiers might lose their way, so he watched until the next morning, the twenty-second. By ten o'clock the heavy fog had lifted and he launched his assault. The grenadiers and light infantry led the charge and so frightened the defenders that they fled the eastern fort without firing a shot. Some of the Company troops on the right flank of the assault group chased the enemy all the way to the gates of the western fort. Its defenders panicked and ran. Now terror possessed Tipoo's men everywhere on Sevendroog. Some jumped to their deaths to avoid British bayonets: perhaps two hundred men lost their lives in this fashion. Others scrambled down the hill wherever they could. Cornwallis sent two battalions to try to intercept the routed enemy on the far side of the mountain, but most of them escaped, slithering down the many paths, precipices, and ravines. In this entire operation, the Company's forces lost only one wounded soldier in the actual assault, plus another seventeen officers and men killed in the construction of the approaches and the artillery batteries.[29]

After the astonishingly easy victory over Sevendroog, most of the other hill forts surrendered, many of them offering little opposition. Only at Outradroog did the defenders use some imagination. They stampeded wild bullocks toward their attackers, which in addition to wounding some thirty of their enemies delayed the conquest and bought the defenders time to escape. But Outradroog fell anyway. Only a few hill forts now remained on the earl's line of march from Bangalore to Seringapatam, and these he planned to take on the way.

Before investing Seringapatam, he rested his army and undertook to improve his knowledge of the capital's defenses. He charged officers commanding foraging parties to report fully on the terrain and activities of the enemy.[30] He also began slipping reliable spies into Tipoo's encampment, whence a stream of information came to the British. During the last week of December, after he had taken Sevendroog, and the early weeks of January 1792, the earl received frequent reports on the strength of Tipoo's infantry, cavalry, and auxiliaries and of any new works under construction.[31] Like all intelligence, however, some of the information proved faulty, especially the "extremely incorrect and imperfect" reports about Seringapatam.[32] Yet he acquired a fair map of the outer works and accurate estimates of their size and strength.[33]

The Allies

Cornwallis also tried to reach a working agreement with his allies. The Mahrattas proved obstinate. He had to bribe them just to keep them in the field. Thus some of the cash from the China trade went as an ostensible "loan" to Hurry Punt and Perseram Bhow, who had made it clear that unless they received regular sums, their cavalry would vanish to the north.[34] Even though Cornwallis paid their blackmail, he never secured their willing cooperation. Hurry Punt threatened just before the final siege to negotiate with Tipoo, saying that the British had refused to furnish his men with enough grain, and Perseram Bhow inclined toward raiding for plunder rather than assisting military operations.[35] Nevertheless, the Mahrattas helped somewhat. They protected supply trains, and Perseram Bhow's raids drew off some of Tipoo's forces, thus serving to weaken the capital's defenses.

Cornwallis failed to procure even this much assistance from the nizam's cavalry. He barely managed, in fact, to keep them from hindering his own operations. Throughout the entire campaign, the Hyderabad horse had depended on British supplies and had dared not move from the magazine at Bangalore. Even after the earl took Sevendroog, they still remained in Bangalore, to Cornwallis's annoyance. The nizam's army "could not be detached even for a few days to any considerable distance," he later remarked, "from our bazars [sic] and our northern communications without exposing it to suffer great distress from want of provision."[36] Thus he was not overjoyed when, in a burst of enthusiasm, the ruler's second son volunteered to bring yet more cavalry to join the Company's army. One observer described this seven-thousand-man reinforcement as a "disorderly rabble," that was "not very creditable to the state of military discipline at Hyderabad." It resembled "more than any other scene I ever witnessed, an Irish fair after the commencement of a quarrel."[37]

No doubt it helped that these questionable reinforcements lagged behind the grand army and did not join it until shortly before the assault on the outer works of Tipoo's capital.

Triumph and Tragedy

With the allies at least in hand, Cornwallis marched from Sevendroog toward Seringapatam on 25 January. Abercrombie moved rapidly from the other coast toward the same goal. The governor general had now prepared for every eventuality. Experience had taught him to revise his order of marching and his transport. The heavy guns, so cumbersome a delay to the army before, now kept up. Duff yoked his bullocks four abreast, instead of two, and carried the chain that yoked them clear back to the gun (instead of the limber) axle, which raised the chain to a level nearer the yoke. Furthermore, he now had all the elephants he needed to help him. The army marched in three parallel columns, the heavy guns and heavy carriages in one; the infantry and field pieces in a second on a road already made for them a hundred yards to the right of the artillery; and the smaller carts and private baggage carts on the left of the battering train in a third, beyond which the great mass of baggage was carried by elephants, camels, bullocks, and men, servants of the army and members of sepoy families. As they marched, the baggage master prevented the multitude of followers from surging ahead of the column. Cavalry and infantry flanked the whole, and a regiment of cavalry, the bodyguards, and some infantry marched in front. The allies followed as they chose.[38] Meanwhile, Perseram Bhow, detached from the main army to cover its right flank and to aid Abercrombie in crossing the river, had, with the assistance of one Bombay battalion, plundered to the west. At least he was out of the way.

From Sevendroog, Cornwallis marched to Outradroog. He halted there to meet the nizam's reinforcement under his second son.[39] A "slight indisposition" prevented the earl from paying the ceremonial compliments the occasion demanded when the two forces junctioned, but on 30 January he visited his allies and next day they returned the compliment. As usual, they were late. They had promised to review his army at ten in the morning, but did not come until two in the afternoon. Thus the troops had to stand for four hours in the Mysore sun until their convalescent commander could finally conduct his allies' review party down those sweating ranks.

At dawn the next morning, 1 February, the entire mass moved out. Tipoo's cavalry annoyed them as they marched but did not really impede them. Even the sultan's policy of burning the country in their front did not prevent their gathering sufficient forage nor burning green trees for firewood. The army captured whatever fortifications lay in the path, and Cornwallis detailed sepoys to hold them. By 5 February, when the advanced guard reached the plains in front of Tipoo's army, about seven miles from Seringapatam, the earl had completed a chain of posts from eight to twelve miles apart to protect the supplies all the way back to Bangalore.[40]

As the earl's army emerged from the jungle and came onto the plains, it presented a colorful panorama. As he turned about to view it, Cornwallis could see column after column of infantry extended along the front and left flank, ready to charge any who dared present themselves aggressively. The artillery train and heavy carriages moved parallel to them about one hundred yards to the right. Further yet to the right, public and private carriages loaded with goods of all sorts lumbered along. "Elephants, camels, buffaloes, bullocks" and "myriads of followers that defy description" flanked this baggage train. The nizam's horse followed in the rear. Colonel Floyd's cavalry ranged from front to rear of the colorful procession, and swarms of irregular horsemen branched out from it "as far as the eye could reach." In the middle of this sea of animals and humanity, thousands of binjarries drove many thousands of cattle loaded with grain, while their women "groaned under the additional burden of infants clinging to their sides." A few selected people drove bullocks loaded with delicacies that the Europeans had reserved for themselves. On all sides camp followers ran and jostled, cursed and yelled, stole and plundered. Horses whinnied, whips of baggage masters cracked sharply above the noise, while bullocks, strained to the uttermost, refused still greater burdens and twisted out of their harnesses. It almost seemed that the whole of India was on the move, an inexorable force coming to overwhelm Tipoo.

The sultan, in his turn, began to shower the Company's troops with rockets, but so erratically as to do little damage. Nonetheless, the barrage convinced Cornwallis that he must quickly drive his enemy back within the walls of Seringapatam.

The earl rose at dawn on 6 February and set out to scout the Mysore position, spending the better part of the day at it. What he saw, combined with various intelligence reports, made him aware of his adversary's strength. He estimated that Tipoo had forty to fifty thousand troops, while the Company fielded only twenty thousand, not including the allies, who as usual remained in the rear. Tipoo had posted his men on the north side of the river in a wide semicircle three to four miles long, running roughly from the southeast to the northwest. On the sultan's right the line began below Seringapatam at some rocks dominated by the Karigaut (which the English spelled about five different ways) Pagoda, and from thence it extended to the river, ending on his left above the island at a place of worship called the Edgah. Six strong redoubts ran along this line, one of them commanding the Edgah and another the center, where a thick bound hedge gave added protection. The ground was broken everywhere with rice paddies, ravines, and streams.

All the redoubts lay within reach of the guns of the fort or of entrenchments constructed on the island. The fort took up about half the western part of the island. The eastern half held a walled village named Shar Gunjam, the tomb of Hyder Ali, buildings to accommodate pilgrims, a palace, and the beautiful Lall Baugh gardens.

The earl decided to attack at once, even though he could not depend on his allies and even though Abercrombie had still not crossed the Cauvery. But he could not besiege the city until he had driven Tipoo within it, which would also make it easier for Abercrombie to ford the river and join the operations. That afternoon the commanding general worked out his plan of attack. He decided to move at night so his enemy would not have a good view of his exposed troops charging across the plain. But that decision also meant he could not use his artillery to cover their charge, for he could not haul it over uncertain ground in the dark. Thus he would charge with musket and bayonet only. He planned a three-pronged assault. Medows would take one division of the army—two European and five native battalions—on the right against the enemy near the Edgah. Cornwallis would lead the center division—three European and five native battalions— through the bound hedge at a point just below the eastern end of the fort across the river. Colonel Maxwell, with one European and three native battalions, would take the left to strike near the Karigaut Pagoda. The earl hoped the center would break the enemy, chase the fugitives across the ford, and then follow and establish itself on the island. Maxwell should do the same, for a ford was close to the Karigaut. Once on the island, the army could begin siege operations.

Cornwallis did not reveal his plans until an hour before the attack. The allies had no part to play, much to their satisfaction. But, according to Dirom, when they learned that Cornwallis would lead the attack in person, would "fight like a private soldier," they grew very worried and feared their Company allies would fail.[41]

As the sun dropped that evening so did the temperature, from its high of 100° down to 70°. As the men made their preparations, a full moon rose. At nine o'clock the three divisions marched out, and Cornwallis found himself once again in a situation with which he was all too familiar, leading and hazarding all on an attack. As he approached the hedge, shortly after eleven o'clock, he saw firing to his left. Maxwell had already attacked and stirred up a hornets' nest. Tipoo's troops in the center heard the noise and began to mill around, creating a "universal hubub." Then they saw Cornwallis's troops and quickly started showering rockets at them. During this barrage, the earl observed that Maxwell seemed to be carrying the pagoda. Encouraged by the sight, he urged his men forward into an increasing musket and cannon fire. They reached the bound hedge and burst through to confront the enemy at close range. Without hesitation, Cornwallis ordered his men to charge with bayonet. The Mysoreans held for a while, before giving way to the dreaded British weapon. In less than an hour, they fled their camp, leaving behind all their artillery, their tents, and their stores. One redoubt stubbornly tried to hold out, but the earl's troops stormed and carried it.

Tipoo's men scurried across the river in droves, hoping to shelter in the fort. But the Company's men stuck to their heels and mixed in with them, thrusting to right and left with bayonets, clubbing their enemies with musket butts, kicking, and even using fists. Maxwell's men joined the melee, waist deep in the Cauvery, whose bloody waters began to carry corpses southeastward toward the Carnatic. On the island the surprised and befuddled defenders in their terror gave up every battery and redoubt. Tipoo, who watched with increasing anxiety, pulled up his drawbridge to prevent the English getting into his fort, although by doing so he shut out many of the fugitives. By two o'clock, the Company seemed victorious and Tipoo locked up in his fort.

But Cornwallis himself had not finished his night's work. To direct operations he had remained at the enemy's main camp with one sepoy battalion, the 74th regiment of regulars, and parts of other battalions. He was unaware of his precarious position: an error by Medows had exposed the governor general's right flank, which Tipoo could counterattack by sallying from the fort. The hapless Medows had confused his assignment. He had attacked and carried the Edgah redoubt (at some loss), but could not then move to his left along the bound hedge over ground made impassable by ravines and swamps. He had posted a strong detachment in the redoubt and then for some reason had returned clear along the rear of the army to the Karigaut Pagoda. Thus he had left his commander's right flank exposed.

Tipoo at once discerned the weakness and dispatched a large force of infantry to dislodge the governor general and retake the lost Mysore camp. The attackers swarmed forward, firing as they went. One of their bullets nicked the earl in the hand, but he took no notice of it.[42] He was everywhere, encouraging his men, chiding them, and steadying them. Soon he had them formed in a disciplined line and ordered a counterattack. His men surged forward with such determination that they drove the enemy away, fortunately for the earl, since by this time the Company's forces had almost run out of ammunition.

The action took place just before dawn. Daylight revealed

the earl's position to Tipoo's artillery, which lobbed round after round toward him. Cornwallis could not tarry any longer. Leaving a detachment in the redoubt, he took the rest of his force to the Karigaut Pagoda. The cannon fire forced such a hasty withdrawal that the British left behind tents, baggage, and artillery, although one officer managed to overturn fourteen guns into a deep ravine to prevent the enemy's recovering them.

Now, from his commanding position on the hill, the earl watched in frustration as wave after wave of Tipoo's cavalry and infantry poured out to attack the detachment defending the redoubt. Yet he could not forward a relieving force without exposing it to the fort's artillery. Without water or provisions, sweltering under a hot sun, the men in the redoubt withstood an incessant musket fire, a constant storm of rockets, and a ceaseless artillery pounding. Tipoo launched five separate assaults, during which the company commanding officer and one artillery officer were killed. But the enemy failed to carry the redoubt. Cornwallis struck his camp at four in the afternoon, moved his army forward, and after dark finally managed to relieve the beleaguered men. Bitterly discouraged, the sultan of Mysore that night withdrew all his forces from the north side of the river, abandoning all his redoubts and the cannon in them to the British.

Soon thereafter Cornwallis had Tipoo encircled. On the ninth, he dispatched the Hyderabad and Mahratta cavalry and a Company battalion in the nizam's pay to meet Abercrombie and escort him to the siege. The sooner Abercrombie could join, the sooner the entire business would end, as even the defenders realized. Rumor in the British camp said that Tipoo had offered his men an advance of three months' pay or the opportunity to leave and that many of them had chosen the latter. At any rate, Tipoo's French advisers now streamed into the British lines, including the chief engineer and the artillery commander. On the night of the attack, the Company's forces had liberated most of the British prisoners, whose tales of horror determined the British to force a surrender quickly.

On the tenth, Cornwallis decided to cross over to the island to watch the siege's progress. The beautiful gardens at some remove from the fighting contrasted with the devastation of the war all around. The governor general strolled the well-planned walks that meandered among the lovingly tended apple, pear, peach, and coconut trees, lime and orange groves, and grapevines. The soldiers, however, had marred the beauty of the place by digging up the ground and cutting trees to provide gabions and fascines to protect the sappers while they made the approaches to the fort at the western end of the island.[43] Captain Turner, who accompanied the earl, stood in awe of what the sultan had achieved in his landscaping and regretted the destruction by British troops. He appreciated the symmetry and regularity of the village streets and the beauty and splendid proportions of the palace in the center of the gardens. Though saddened at the rapid disfigurement in the gardens, he did not in the least regret that the Company's troops plundered silver from above Hyder Ali's grave. Cornwallis, more concerned with operations than with architectural beauty, returned the same day to his headquarters across the river.

Next morning, the eleventh, the commanding general heard musketry and cannon fire where he least expected it, to the rear of his own headquarters. He rode to investigate and discovered that a large body of Tipoo's cavalry had surprised his sentries and penetrated the Company artillery park. Duff drove them off quickly, and whatever their intentions might have been, they had little chance to do damage. But it later became legend that the sultan had sent them to assassinate the governor general and thus discourage the Company forces to the point of withdrawing.[44]

Instead, the British closed the ring tighter. Next day Cornwallis learned that Abercrombie had reached the Cauvery. The commanding general accordingly dispatched elements of regular and Company cavalry in cooperation with nizam and Mahratta horse to meet the Bombay troops. Tipoo tried a desperate gamble to stop the junction. Shielded from the sun under his red parasol, he personally led a force to prevent a river crossing by the reserve of the Bombay army. But he failed and retired again to his fort. On 10 February, Abercrombie brought about six thousand men to join the siege. The next day they took up their position on the extreme right in a line extending to the river and across it to the south of the island.

Tipoo's position was hopeless, but he still fought on. For

Cornwallis the affair was now routine, merely a matter of time. He arose daily at dawn to watch the siege's progress and inspect the approaches as they crawled nearer and nearer to the fort. On the twenty-third he walked amid a hail of musketry through the trenches to the first parallel, as yet unfinished and exposed. The admiring Turner noted his "utmost composure" when musket balls were "whistling all around." Indeed, Cornwallis seemed to be bothered less by them than by the flies "that torment us at our meals." But he had been under fire too many times before to worry about it now. Besides, he no doubt took satisfaction in being the besieger rather than, as at Yorktown, the besieged.

Meanwhile, Tipoo had finally had enough. For the first time, he had met a British officer who had clearly taken his measure and bested him, even on his own home grounds. Rumors of peace filled the air on 23 February as messengers scurried back and forth between opposing lines. Tipoo finally agreed to terms of surrender, and firing ceased the next day.

Now followed one of the most colorful episodes in the history of British India, an episode still enshrined in memory. As part of the surrender agreement, Cornwallis had demanded two of Tipoo's sons as hostages to ensure their father's compliance with the peace agreed upon. Reluctantly, the sultan had yielded. The time set for his sons' delivery to his enemies was ten o'clock in the morning of the twenty-sixth. As usual, delays postponed the ceremony. But at about two in the afternoon, the boys took leave of their father, accompanied by the sultan's ambassador. Grave and dignified—one seven and one eleven years of age—they had dressed for the melancholy occasion in muslin adorned with pearls and assorted jewelry. As they left the fort, Cornwallis dispatched an escort to meet them at a tent pitched halfway between the fort and the Company camp. From there they proceeded on their elephants to the earl's tent. As they passed the artillery park, Duff boomed a salute of nineteen guns, and when they reached the main encampment Cornwallis ordered his army to attention, according them full military honors.

Whatever apprehension the boys felt must have been allayed somewhat as they approached Cornwallis's tent, for they saw awaiting them there not a fierce-looking warrior but a benign-looking old gentleman. After they dismounted, this same gentleman, none other than the governor general himself, put fatherly hands on each boy's shoulders and assured Tipoo's envoy that they would never want for a father while under his care. The earl then gave each of the boys a gold watch, and they retired to tents already prepared for them.

What a splendid event to conclude a rigorous campaign! And what a scene for the soldiers, sepoy and British alike, to witness and tell their grandchildren about! Mather Brown captured the moment forever in oil. In his painting entitled *Earl Cornwallis Receiving the Sons of Tippoo Sahib as Hostages*, the earl holds the hands of both boys. On one side of the canvas Tipoo stands, looking on in supplication. On the other, the earl's staff watches in approbation. A reproduction of this picture adorns the first volume of Philip Woodruff's *The Men Who Ruled India*, an otherwise sober account of British officialdom in India. Perhaps the memory of the event has endured so well because it symbolized the way the British conceived their role in India. The natives were children who needed the fatherly care and guidance of the British in order to grow to maturity. They should be loved but watched, for without British care they could go astray.

Of course, Cornwallis himself felt much that way about Indians. On the other hand, when it came to the solid business of a peace treaty with Tipoo, he acted very much like a conventional eighteenth-century diplomat. Although Tipoo now lay at his mercy, he did not want to dictate a harsh peace that would cause his enemy to nurse a burning desire for revenge and could soon bring on another Mysore war. Certainly he did not wish to dethrone Tipoo, because in that event the British would only have to find someone else, at Company expense, to put on the throne. As Cornwallis later remarked to councillor Stuart: "If we had taken Seringapatam and killed Tipoo, which the greatest enemies to peace must have considered as the ultimate point that our success could arrive at, we must either have given that capital to the Marattas (a dangerous boon) or have set up some miserable pageant of our own, to be supported by the Company's troops and treasures, and to be plundered by its servants."[45]

A typical eighteenth-century diplomat, the earl had formulated his war aims before he went to war, indeed had thought about the peace settlement he desired as early as 1790.[46] In essence, he wanted a cash payment and a large slice of his enemy's territories, and that is precisely what the peace settlement accorded him. The Company annexed half of Tipoo's land and exacted an indemnity of about £3,000,000. All prisoners on both sides went free (save for the sultan's hostage sons). The treaty left Mysore virtually surrounded by British territory, save on the northwest and northeast, where the Mahrattas and Hyderabad gained at Mysore's expense. Cut off from the western sea because the British took the Malabar coast and from the passes through which his father had descended to devastate the Carnatic, Tipoo sultan

8. Earl Cornwallis Receiving the Sons of Tippoo Sahib as Hostages
By Mather Brown, Oriental Club.
Reprinted by permission of the India Office Library and Records, London

brooded over the terms imposed upon him for a long time before he finally ratified the treaty on 18 March.[47]

Personal tragedy, however, dampened the elation the earl must have felt over his victory. The morning after Tipoo's sons came over to the British camp, General Medows visited Cornwallis, returned to his tent, put a loaded pistol to his body, and pulled the trigger. Alas for the general, even his attempt at suicide failed! He lay in terrible agony with three bullets in his body, but could not die. No one was ever sure why he had attempted to destroy himself. Most people thought it was because of his failure on the night of 6 February, although Cornwallis never blamed him for that.[48] Poor Medows would soon quit India for good without ever realizing his desire to succeed the earl there as military commander. Instead, Abercrombie, who had performed so steadily, would acquire the coveted position.

When word of the peace spread from Seringapatam to the rest of India, the British indulged in an orgy of jubilation. On Monday, 22 April, Stuart in Calcutta organized a grand gala celebration. The guns of Fort William boomed during the day. At dinner the Company servants raised bumper after bumper to the earl. Then they brightened the Calcutta night with illuminations, each vying with the other for splendor and ingenuity in design. Government house strung up lights of different colors. A large transparent painting depicted Fame with her trumpet over a bust of Cornwallis. Beneath it Brittania received the treaty from Tipoo's sons. Hercules stood behind Brittania, and a large panoramic view of Seringapatam filled the background. The accountant general's office displayed a large transparency showing the captured forts. Lights flooded the post office.[49] Calcutta, Madras, and Bombay sent addresses of thanks to their governor general. Even Hindus and Moslems congratulated him as a person "celestial and famed all over the world as its asylum and protector."[50]

Characteristically, the earl reacted modestly. He acceded to the wishes of the inhabitants of Madras and Calcutta and sat for portraits they wished to have of him.[51] But when he heard the rumor in April that the British in Bengal hoped to give him a diamond star, he refused it. Indeed, when he returned to Calcutta in July he requested that they forego receiving him with military honors.[52] He even donated his prize money to his victorious troops.[53] But he naturally accepted a marquisate which the king bestowed upon him in the summer of 1792, after Dundas had consulted with Bishop James Cornwallis. The new marquis did not learn of his elevation in the peerage until 1793.[54]

Anticlimax

His remaining time in India would almost of necessity be anticlimactic. From Seringapatam he moved slowly back to the coast, his army ravaged by sickness as deadly as Tipoo's bullets. He did not reach Madras until the end of May. Restless, eager to go home, he wrote Stuart on 4 May that "no man ever wished to leave India more than I do," but promised to stay until his successor arrived. He fretted about his son and his son's education, and on 23 May dashed off a letter to his brother, the bishop, complaining of the tutor, who, he thought, "must worry the boy to death. A little recreation, such as parties to Lausanne or Geneva might help him get through the time, and I think Mr. Hayes in his general superintendence of good morals need not consider in too serious a light the occasional and common levities of youth." If only he could get back to Europe he could straighten things out, see his only son, heir to his name and fortune. "I am a stranger," he lamented, "not only to Brome's manner and conversation, but to his person."[55]

The change in climate enervated him when he left the cool nights of Mysore for the constant heat of the plains. He told Stuart he was "almost overcome" by it.[56] When he reached Madras, his brother William met him and was appalled at the earl's condition, for the campaign had nearly emaciated him.[57] Tired, ill, thin, he rested for awhile in Madras in a garden house offered by the nabob of Acrot and lodged the sultan's sons in a separate establishment.[58] After he had cleared up odds and ends of business in Madras, he sailed with his brother to Calcutta, where he arrived on 27 July.[59]

He wanted desperately for the government to replace him. Apparently his yearning and worry slowed his recovery. In September, Hickey thought he still looked "wretchedly thin and ill."[60] Yet the government did not replace him, and he had to carry on into the year 1793. During that time, he managed to send off a deputation to Nepal and see to the implementation of his land settlement and new justice regulations.

Cornwallis in India: The Man and His Achievements

It is fashionable today to criticize Cornwallis's work in India. He was, after all, an imperialist who believed the British superior to the native inhabitants, an indictment sufficient in itself in this postimperial age. He was an aristocrat who believed in a hierarchical society, in the virtue and necessity for that society to contain a hereditary aristocracy, a belief never popular among Americans and seriously questioned today by the British. As governor general of India, he did not compile a universally hailed record of splendid achievement. Historians have questioned the wisdom of the permanent settlement and the efficacy of his judicial and administrative innovations. His attempted reform of the army nearly caused a mutiny. Whatever saving he might have brought to the East India Company, the costly war with Tipoo swallowed. With such a record, some historians ask, why did governments and people trust him? Percival Spear, for example, an eminent Indian historian, remarked that "then as now first-class character was no substitute for third-class brains, nor did innocency of intention mitigate the effect of the blunders of ignorance." Spear sincerely believed that Cornwallis, despite all he saw around him, despite the wishes and beliefs of every one of the Company's servants, despite his coming as governor of a conquered land, should have installed Indians into the higher ranks of the Company's service. After all, the Mogul Akbar, "by special training, proper salaries and the encouragement of equal treatment, promotion and honours, bound the Hindus to the Emperor."[61]

It is doubtful, however, that either the East India Company or the British government would have allowed their governor general to emulate Akbar, even had Cornwallis wished it. In any event, both the Mogul and British empires fell, whereas Hinduism remains as a vital force. British hegemony in India nonetheless lasted almost two hundred years in a culture and environment totally different from that of Britain, which is pretty good marks for any empire. The United States, once supposedly a "melting pot," has not eliminated cultural and ethnic differences, and many today think such elimination undesirable. To put Hindus on an equal footing, Cornwallis would have had to put them on a British footing, and had he done that, he would have made them into plastic imitations of the British, turning them away from their own traditions and way of life. He did not think them British nor deem it worthwhile to make them so. He thought it proper, indeed best, to rule them in what he considered their own interest. He was an imperialist and should never be considered anything else. His brains were second-rate, not third, but then so are those of most political leaders. How many of them possessed (or possess) character?

Character, indeed, is the key to understanding the trust people reposed in the marquis. They admired him for what he was. Yet what he was also influenced, of course, what he did. And his record is far from unpraiseworthy. He was undoubtedly a successful, nearly a brilliant campaigner in India, who humbled Britain's strongest opponent there, an achievement sufficient to win the favor of a Britain that still admired martial glory. Even native Indian historians, furthermore, have praised his legal reforms. And he, more than any other individual, instilled into the Company's servants the belief that the imperial agents of a great power had duties and responsibilities to those they governed, that India was not just a treasure trove to be plucked at will, its people fit only to be milked at British pleasure.

Cornwallis possessed firm convictions which he never betrayed. He loved his family and disdained promiscuous amours. He maintained a rocklike honesty and integrity in an age that paid lip service to both but practiced neither. He was sober and dignified in a period when men fought hotheaded duels, drank themselves to ruin, and gambled away fortunes in inane, not to say insane, betting. He never stooped to trickery or backbiting, but was always open in his dealings. He possessed an abundance of physical and moral courage. Most of the English upper class had the physical courage, but very few the moral. Though an earl and governor general, then a marquis, he disdained pomposity or superfluous ceremony. He was a good judge of character and abilities and a loyal friend. He was humane, but never feared to administer stern justice when he thought it necessary. He was charitable. His leadership inspired those who worked under him. He was, in short, a gentleman in the true meaning of the term, in the meaning the eighteenth century (and, one suspects, the twentieth century as well) understood.

Undoubtedly there have been many gentlemen in history. But how many of them have occupied high office? How many men in positions of trust and responsibility, who held the fate of thousands or even millions in their hands, consistently displayed those characteristics which distinguished Cornwallis in public and private life?

The court of proprietors of the East India Company appreciated these qualities, even if he had not saved them any money. In January of 1793, they voted their thanks for his "important" and "gallant" services, and in June they awarded him an annuity of £5,000 per year for twenty years.[62] At least in the case of a fairly impecunious marquis, honesty was more than its own reward.

Homeward Bound

Finally, Shore, his successor, arrived in March of 1793. The marquis decided to stick it out until August in order to help Shore with the transition.[63] In June he learned that the French had declared war upon England the previous February, and he resolved to attack the French factories in India and to leave after that.

On 13 August he rose as usual before daybreak, mounted his horse, and rode to Shore's gardens on the bank of the Hughli. He spent the day talking with his old friend. Next day he boarded the pilot schooner and, as far as he knew, sailed from Calcutta forever. Modest as usual, he had wanted no fuss over his departure. There was "no salute, no taking leave, no ceremony whatever," as the Marquis Cornwallis left that hot, alien province he had helped attach permanently to the British Empire.[64]

He reached Madras intending to supervise in person the reduction of Pondicherry, but he found that the military machine he had done so much to build had already seized the French post. With nothing left for him to do in a civil or military capacity, he sailed from Madras for England in the *Swallow* packet on 10 October 1793.

In November, the inhabitants of Calcutta belatedly learned that the marquis had left India for good. Wishing to honor their late governor, they forwarded a petition to his successor. A simple document, devoid of rhetorical flourishes, it expressed a deep sincerity: "Resolved unanimously that an address be presented to Marquis Cornwallis expressive of the high sense this meeting entertains of his lordship's conduct during his administration of the government of Bengal, and the veneration for his private character." [65] The message did not reach the former governor general until after his landfall in England the following February. By that time, it must have been a reminder of a different world. He had left an India finally at peace, with the British position there secure. He had returned to an insecure England, gripped by fear of the French Revolution. What place would a retired servant of empire have in this new world?

Chapter 9

Flanders

The *Swallow* packet, carrying the Marquis Cornwallis, reached the bleak island of St. Helena on 15 December. After a pause of four days there, it continued on its way to England. Once in the Channel, however, it narrowly escaped the same fate as the *Greyhound*, which had carried Cornwallis home from America more than ten years before. A French frigate chased the English packet for several hours before the latter finally reached Torbay, where it anchored on 3 February 1794.

The *Swallow*'s most famous passenger, his deeply tanned face severely lined, looked nearly twenty years older than when he had left for India less than ten years previously. His right eye, damaged in a hockey game long ago, gave him more than ever a cockeyed appearance, because it opened differently and less fully than his left.[1] The marquis now shivered in the cold, of which he complained immediately.[2] Long years in India had disaccustomed him to the chill of an English winter, mild as it was in comparison to those in northern North America. He did not dally in Torbay but went directly to London, where he arrived on 6 February.[3]

The England to which he returned was not the peaceful nation he had left. His country now waged an all-out war with revolutionary France, an unremitting struggle that would monopolize Britain's energies for another twenty years. It had begun for Britain in February of 1793, when the revolutionaries, already at war with Austria and Prussia, had declared war against Britain, Holland, and Spain after executing their king, Louis XVI. Britain found it a mistake to underrate her foe's inexperienced levies:

9. Charles, Earl Cornwallis, Knight of the Most Noble Order of the Garter, Governor General and Commander in Chief in India
By John Smart, Madras, 1792.
Reprinted by permission of the National Portrait Gallery, London

already at Valmy in September 1792 they had turned back the trained Prussian army in an artillery duel fought in a fog.

The British responded moderately at first. In February of 1793, the Duke of York took a small force to Flanders to help Holland defend itself, but his two thousand men could not hope to achieve much. The British necessarily depended on the military exertions of their allies, who commanded far larger land forces. Yet the allies displayed a strange lethargy. During the summer of 1793, counterrevolution erupted in the Vendée, but the allies failed to exploit it. When the Rhone Valley exploded against the revolutionary government, the Austrians and Piedmontese stood by idly. Indeed, both Austria and Prussia seemed more interested in dividing up Poland than in defending their western frontiers. When they finally advanced, they went slowly and deliberately, in the traditional eighteenth-century fashion, with methodical sieges.

The French, by contrast, under the terror of Maximilien Robespierre and the organizing ability of Lazare Carnot, adopted the *levée en masse* and hurled swarms of half-trained but enthusiastic soldiers against the outnumbered professional armies. Attacking in dense columns, by the spring of 1793 they threw the allies back everywhere and negated allied gains of the previous summer.

The British suffered reverses as well. The government reinforced York so that by the autumn he commanded some 6,500 troops, but they were not of the highest quality. Ordered to take Dunkirk, he detached from the allied armies some 37,000 men, including his own British troops, about 11,000 Austrians, and several Hanoverian and Hessian contingents. In August he besieged Dunkirk, but in early September the French counterattacked and beat him badly at Hondschoote, forcing him to retreat toward Ostend.

Nor had the British done better elsewhere. In the same month that York besieged Dunkirk, royalists rebelled at Toulon. The British established a base there for operations against the French, but their allies sent less than half the troops needed to hold Toulon, and the Austrians in Milan did not even move. The young Napoleon Bonaparte, by judicious use of artillery, forced the British out of Toulon by the end of the year. The French, obviously, had not only held their own but had advanced.

French success particularly galled the British because they had subsidized their allies with British pounds sterling, apparently to no avail. The Prussians and Austrians preferred to spend the money in Poland rather than campaign against the French. The allies, furthermore, distrusted each other immensely and therefore would not cooperate. These factors had accounted in part for York's failure at Hondschoote.[4]

Thus, when Cornwallis returned to his homeland, British arms on the Continent had nowhere repeated the success of British arms in India. Could he do anything to change that situation? He was now perhaps England's most famous living general, a national hero, the idol even of the masses. He scarcely relished that distinction, but perhaps it would keep his name before the government. His restless soul chafed at inaction, and it remained to be seen whether the ministry might employ him in some useful capacity in an effort to reverse the military trend on the Continent.

That he hoped for new employment was evident, for after the briefest of visits to Suffolk in March he returned to London and took up lodgings in New Burlington Street. Only in the capital could he make himself easily available for consultation with the ministry. But he could not have a famous reputation without some of its consequences: in London his popularity caught up with him. On 5 April, the committee appointed by the common council of the city went in great state to New Burlington Street and bestowed upon the marquis the freedom of the city of London. The lord mayor delivered a long-winded speech for the occasion, and Cornwallis "in a very elegant manner" thanked the corporation. Then he climbed into his carriage and drove with the group to a banquet at Mansion House. This cavalcade displayed the city's command of the grand art of pageantry. Three large banners—the standard of England, the arms of London, and the arms of the lord mayor—preceded the parade, followed by city marshals, sheriffs, and other high officials, accompanied by a band. The speaker of the House of Commons joined the group at St. James's Street with his state carriage. Cheering crowds thronged the route and in Pall Mall became so enthusiastic that they unharnessed the horses from the marquis' carriage and themselves drew it to the brightly illuminated Mansion House. There Cornwallis dined in the company of the lord chancellor, the speaker of the House of Commons, and other important personages at a table that displayed such delicacies as strawberries, cherries, grapes, and green peas. Unfortunately for the victor of Seringapatam, another round of long speeches accompanied the food.[5]

Official gratitude was in its way as enthusiastic as popular hero worship. In August 1794, the East India Company bestowed on him a gift of £10,000 outright in addition to the pension of £5,000 for twenty years.[6]

Four days after his Mansion House feast, on 9 April, more serious matters engaged him. On that day he testified in the impeachment trial of Warren Hastings. Without hesitation or prevarication, he defended his predecessor. He said that no one, anywhere he went, had ever complained of Hastings personally nor had ever charged him with any "violence, cruelty, bloodshed and oppression." Indeed, the marquis emphasized that "the people in general respected him very much." Finally, when asked if he had "found any just cause to impeach the character of Mr. Hastings," the marquis answered: "NEVER."[7]

While Cornwallis feasted, testified, and marked time in London, on the Continent matters at first seemed to go better for the British. During April the government decided to subsidize some sixty-two thousand Prussians (though Prussia had already committed itself in 1792 to supply twenty thousand men for Austria).[8] Also in April, the Duke of York won some battles in Flanders. But the allies faltered. The Austrian commander, the overly cautious Prince of Coburg, failed to follow up York's success despite the fact that on 14 April the Austrian ruler and Holy Roman Emperor, Francis II, had come in person to join Coburg at Valenciennes and offer him encouragement. On 18 May the French attacked and beat the Duke of York at Tourcoing, while the Austrian army, which might have helped, did nothing. York barely eluded capture and escaped "as he frankly owned, only by the speed of his horse."[9]

Despite this reverse, the allies still would not cooperate nor coordinate their efforts. The Prussians would not serve under an Austrian general unless the Holy Roman Emperor—their nominal sovereign—personally accompanied the forces. Nor would the Austrians serve under a Prussian. Neither would serve under the Duke of York, though he gladly would have cooperated with both. This stalemate offered Cornwallis an opportunity for action. Who better to send to Europe to straighten matters out? The marquis had an outstanding military reputation and had in the past carried on negotiations with Prussia. Pitt now decided to use his diplomatic talents again. Perhaps he could prod the Prussians and Austrians to action. Of course, should Cornwallis act in a military capacity, difficulties would arise. The royal Duke of York, despite his military record, was senior to Cornwallis by six months (their generalships dated respectively from 12 April 1792 and 12 October 1792). But even though thus assured of command, York would scarcely relish the constant company of such a bright star as the esteemed Cornwallis. For his part, however, Cornwallis did not care as much about command as about striking an effective blow against the French. He distrusted the Revolution and all it stood for in the spring of 1794, when the Reign of Terror seemed to consume some of the best and bravest spirits in France. He considered the Sansculottes nothing more than a "gang of murderers on the other side of the water." If he could move the allied forces to efforts against them he would gladly do so.[10]

On 19 April 1794, Pitt outlined to the marquis his plans for that year's campaign in Europe.[11] During May they worked further on the details. At first their discussions progressed at a leisurely pace, but the situation became critical after the British lost at Turcoing and the Austrian emperor seemed ready to abandon operations entirely and return to Vienna. When the ministry learned that Christian, Count of Haugwitz, minister to the king of Prussia, would be at Maestricht on 30 May and that the Prussian General Richard Mollendorf thought a meeting there essential, it decided to dispatch Cornwallis at once.[12]

But when on 29 May he received his official instructions, the marquis found them vague and completely unrealistic. Pitt now intended Lord Cornwallis to undertake military as well as diplomatic initiatives. He should proceed to Flanders and learn from the Duke of York the allied dispositions and the intentions of Emperor Francis. Then he should try to get the subsidized

Prussians to move away from the Rhine toward either Flanders or the Meuse, the direction to be determined both by the conference between Cornwallis, Haugwitz, and Mollendorf at Maestricht and by the decisions of Francis. Having decided, after consultations with the various parties, where to move the Prussians, Cornwallis should then secure the consent of the Dutch government. The British minister at the Hague, James Harris, Lord Malmesbury, would assist in the latter area.[13]

These directions showed that Pitt did not yet understand either the nature of the war in Europe or the bitter truth that the allies were more interested in Poland than in revolutionary France. Cornwallis, of course, had not been on the Continent since the time of Frederick the Great. Even had he had more experience, the implementation of such instructions would have taxed to the utmost a man having the diplomatic skills of a Metternich. Besides, there were the military aspects of his instructions. Cornwallis supposedly should mobilize lethargic allies, inspire York, and turn the tide of war against a daring and resourceful foe who was improving his military strength every day.

Naturally things went wrong almost from the beginning. Cornwallis arrived at Maestricht on the night of 1 June. Two days later he learned from Dundas that the emperor had decided to return to Vienna, thus upsetting all previous plans.[14] Cornwallis then went immediately to the Duke of York's headquarters at Tournai, where he arrived on the fourth, to discuss the new development. There they agreed that the Prussians should march to Flanders (but would they?). Cornwallis would take a letter from York to the emperor and try to persuade him to remain with his army. Pitt, meanwhile, changed his plans, but his instructions of 5 June plunged Cornwallis into an impossible situation. The prime minister now believed that no one could dissuade the emperor from leaving, but that the sixty-two thousand subsidized Prussians could join the Dutch and British in Flanders and besiege Lisle with the assistance of a battering train. Pitt actually believed that Cornwallis should conduct the siege while York led the army covering it, thus giving a position of higher command to the marquis than to his senior, the royal Duke of York. The prime minister, fortunately for York's sensitivity, offered Cornwallis an escape. "I must however," he noted, "add that some arrangement which admits of your personal service in a way satisfactory to yourself is in my opinion more important than any one other point which I have referred to in this letter." [15]

What could Cornwallis say or do? Clearly, he could not take the role Pitt had planned for him. What other alternatives did he have in the way of service on the Continent? Pitt's schemes disregarded the difficulties of securing allied cooperation, the possibility that the Prussians might refuse to obey whatever orders York or Cornwallis gave them, and the probability that the Austrians, after Francis's departure, would be less likely than ever to act decisively.

On 6 June, Cornwallis saw the emperor, delivered York's letter, and held long conversations with the Austrian ministers—all to no avail. Francis determined to leave, and his ministers objected to the sixty-two thousand Prussian soldiers moving away from the Rhine, claiming that at least half of them belonged to the empire and should stay for the defense of Germany. [16]

Undaunted, Cornwallis tried to get the Prussians, under Mollendorf, to move from the Rhine anyway. He traveled from Maestricht to Mollendorf's headquarters. Again he failed. By 21 June, it had become apparent to him that the Prussians had no intention either of helping the British or of honoring their agreement. Accurately assessing that he could do nothing more, he requested permission to return to England. [17] He had talked to no purpose, and the bickering had only aided the French, who had captured Ypres and Charleroi and defeated the Austrians at Fleurus. As Cornwallis pointed out to Pitt, the Austrians were "much dispirited," their generals, "very incapable," and Coburg "the weakest of them all." [18] Since, however, they still distrusted the Prussians more than they feared the French, and the Prussians felt the same way about the Austrians, nothing could be done to prod them to action individually or collectively.

The government acceded to the marquis's request on 30 June, authorizing him to return to England and explain the Continental muddle. [19] Thus, by the middle of July, he could account himself well clear of the entanglements on the European Continent. [20]

After his departure the military situation deteriorated even more rapidly. Before the end of the month the French took all of Belgium. The Prussian and Austrian armies then separated. The Prussians ought now to have been willing to earn the £1,000,000 the British had given them by joining York. But they refused. By the end of September, the British government threatened to drop the subsidy entirely, and for all practical purposes that ended the alliance.[21]

Though he could do nothing with the Prussians, Pitt still hoped the Austrians would help by acting in conjunction with the British in Flanders. Pitt also had what he considered a club to force them to action. If they did not care about retaining the Austrian Netherlands, they did care about money, for their finances had begun to collapse in 1793. Early in 1794, Austria had tried to raise £3,000,000 in London by the sale of bonds based on the emperor's revenues from the Austrian Netherlands, or Belgium. As the summer progressed and the allies fared badly, few people bought the bonds: it appeared that Austria would have no revenues from Belgium because it would have no Belgium. But if the British government guaranteed the interest and the principal, investors might come forward. Pitt dangled that prospect before the Austrians as a lure to get them to act forcefully in the Low Countries.

To prod the Austrians further, he sent Earl Spencer (a Portland whig and future first lord of the admiralty) and Thomas Grenville (older brother to the foreign secretary) to Vienna. Still hopeful to give Cornwallis a command in Europe, Pitt also sent along with Spencer and Grenville the marquis's best friend, Colonel Ross. Apparently the prime minister had decided that the Austrians needed a new commanding general and that he should be the Marquis Cornwallis.[22]

Pitt's persistent efforts measured his failure to appreciate reality. The Austrians had already written off Belgium. Even if they had not done so, they would not have considered allowing a Briton to command Austrian troops. Johann Thugut, the Austrian minister, commented that for the emperor to appoint a foreign general was to "disgrace himself by proclaiming to all Europe that he had not a General fit to command them."[23]

Even beyond the difficulties presented by the Austrians, there remained the stubborn fact that the Duke of York would never acknowledge the marquis as his superior. Pitt's belief "that his Royal Highness's zeal for the service will lead him to consent to act under the command of Lord Cornwallis" was incredibly naive.[24] When York learned of the proposal, he grew hotly indignant at the implied insult to his own military capability. On 4 September, he wrote to his father, King George III, protesting in the strongest terms Cornwallis's appointment. "To say that I shall not feel this as a severe blow," he exploded, "would be to act contrary to my own character and to those principles of truth and sincerity from whence I trust I never can deviate." Should the government appoint Cornwallis to supreme command, he asked leave to retire to England.[25] George III naturally supported his son and at the same time pointed out to Pitt the wishful thinking behind his scheme.[26] Shortly thereafter, as British military fortunes continued to wane, Pitt gave up the whole idea.

The ministerial plan had kept Cornwallis on tenterhooks all through August. He had rented a house in lower Grosvenor Street in order to see Pitt frequently and learn the progress of the negotiations.[27] Though skeptical of Pitt's proposals, he could never be sure of their final outcome. To be sure, he had insisted to Pitt that he would never take command of the army over the head of the Duke of York.[28] Indeed, the episode embarrassed him so much that after Pitt had finally abandoned his notion Cornwallis wrote a long letter to York trying to explain his own role in the government's schemes.[29]

Thus Cornwallis's Continental ventures ended in fiasco, primarily because of ministerial illusions. He still lacked employment, and he wanted to work. The king seemed to bear him no grudge. And since Pitt had failed to utilize effectively the services of his former governor general on the Continent, perhaps he would now find some useful position for him in England.

Chapter 10

The Ordnance

Cornwallis had his chance for new employment when Pitt decided to reorganize his cabinet to achieve a more efficient prosecution of the war and a reduction in the number of his parliamentary critics. In July of 1794, the third Duke of Portland, leader of an opposition group of "old whigs," entered the cabinet. His associate, William Windham, also joined the government as secretary at war (head of the war office). Their defection from the ranks of the opposition turned many other former critics of Pitt into his allies. The Duke of Portland, supposedly indecisive but even-tempered, belied his reputation in his manner of gaining and exercising cabinet rank. He showed decisiveness in his refusal to enter government without the home office, which he would run firmly.[1] He would also show himself far from even-tempered in his dealing with Cornwallis. Dundas, with whom Cornwallis had worked long and well (at a distance) over Indian affairs, became secretary of state for war, a new cabinet post the prime minister had created. Finally, at the end of January in 1795, Pitt submitted Cornwallis's name to the king as master general of the ordnance.[2] Appointment came on 23 February.[3] The marquis thus found himself serving once again in an administrative capacity, this time within the cabinet.

That elite group had usually included both the commander in chief of the army (the greatest single authority over cavalry and infantry other than the king) and the master general of the ordnance (whose responsibilities included providing ordnance for both the army and navy; the control of Woolwich Academy, which turned out engineer and artillery officers; and command of the artillery and engineers). Because the events of the previous

189

summer still rankled the Duke of York, it might have proved awkward having the commander in chief serve in the same cabinet with Cornwallis.[4] Furthermore, the latter had a low opinion of York's military abilities. "If the French land," Cornwallis muttered to Ross, "I should not like to trust the new Field Marshal [York] for the defense of Culford."[5] The "very unpleasant" situation Cornwallis anticipated, however, did not arise because Pitt excluded the duke from the new cabinet.[6] Thus Cornwallis, the only professional soldier in the cabinet, became its chief military adviser.

There was need of advice. The British army was a confused and inefficient organization with various overlapping jurisdictions. Too many people had too much independent authority: the secretary of state for war, the secretary at war, the commander in chief, and the master general. Though the secretary of state for war supposedly planned the campaigns, he could not direct those people upon whom the success of his campaigns depended. He had to secure the cooperation of several different branches of the army, each independent or semi-independent, each intent on going its own way. The master general of the ordnance had responsibility for artillery, engineers, and munitions supply. The transport board supposedly provided the ships to move troops and equipment at sea, but it took directions from the first lord of the treasury, as did the commissary general, who procured the rations, animal fodder, and land transport. The commander in chief, with the rank of field marshal, commanded the cavalry and infantry and would not subject himself to the orders of any "inferior." He also held responsibility for managing the defenses of the British Isles. Though the secretary of state for war supposedly managed the recruiting, the home secretary in fact did most of that work.[7] The secretary of state for war, furthermore, did not have jurisdiction over the secretary at war, whose job of authorizing and auditing expenditures involved his office with all sorts of people, from the paymaster general of the forces to the clothiers who provided regimental colonels their uniforms to the accountants of the board of ordnance. The secretary at war also possessed final authority, even above that of the commander in chief, over troop movements in the British Isles.

Plainly, at the time Cornwallis joined the cabinet in 1795,

Britain's military establishment needed overhauling and stream-lining. Ousted ignominiously from the Continent, her army was not yet ready to implement grand strategies for fighting the French in Europe and for winning empires abroad. Fortunately, her navy, remote from the bickering at Whitehall, was in better shape. Thus, it could take the counteroffensive at sea and deprive the French and their allies of colonial possessions all over the world. When the British finally shipped a sizable expeditionary force to the Continent under the Duke of Wellington, they had fastened upon an extraordinary leader. Independent of mind and spirit, he had a talent for administrative organization as great as his tactical and strategic genius. Wellington would overcome any bureaucratic obstacles in his path. But in 1795 his supreme command and the British army's time of triumph lay in the future.

As master general of the ordnance, Cornwallis could not tackle reforming the whole army. Instead he had to concern himself primarily with what his own department could do at home. In a sense, this new position must have seemed a minor one after the complete civil and military authority he had wielded in India. Now he shared authority with other members of the cabinet and held responsibility for but one of the several branches of the military. Yet if his job gave him less power, it also demanded less work and gave him more time for relaxation. He was not a young man. He needed the time he now had to relax occasionally with his family at Culford, to grow turnips, and to shoot partridges.[8] He could alternate his work in London, where he leased a house, with rest in the country.

Nonetheless, the ordnance presented some peculiar chal-lenges. The master general wore two hats, a military and a civil one. In his military capacity, he received special military cour-tesies and retained a permanent guard of one commissioned offi-cer, one sergeant, and twenty privates.[9] He commanded the royal regiment of artillery, the royal corps of engineers, the royal mili-tary artificers (who built fortifications and did much of the heavy engineering, primarily overseas),[10] and the royal corps of artillery drivers, recently established by Cornwallis's predecessor to re-place the civilian drivers, over whom the military had not exer-cised effective control. In his civil capacity, the master general commanded the ordnance department, which had several duties.

He procured, maintained, and issued military stores—arms, ammunition, and artillery—and for this purpose had several depots in the country and overseas, each managed by a storekeeper responsible to the principal storekeeper of the ordnance board. The ordnance department had the authority to acquire land for building fortifications or for other specific reasons. It carried out topographical surveys of Britain, and the degree of details in its maps made them models of accuracy. The department was responsible for the construction and maintenance of fortifications, forts, harbors, and other military buildings, though the construction of military barracks belonged to the superintendent general of barracks. The clerk of the ordnance worked out the contracts with manufacturers or merchants for all trade supplies required by the army and navy. He then sent the estimates and expenditures to parliament. Merchants submitted their bids not only to the clerk of the ordnance but also to the surveyor general, who inspected the material contracted for and turned it over to the principal storekeeper, who arranged for its storage in ordnance depots. The ordnance had four factories at Faversham, Ballingoolig, Waltham Abbey, and Woolwich for manufacturing arms and ammunition so as to avoid shortages in the event that contractors should deliver insufficient supplies.

Woolwich also boasted a military academy that trained young men to become officers of engineering and artillery, branches of the service that required specialized skills. The academy, established by royal warrant in 1741, was under the supervision of the master general.[11] He appointed the instructors and determined their salaries, selected the cadets, was captain of the company of gentlemen cadets (which paid him a quarterly salary), established the rules of the institution, and maintained its physical facilities.[12]

Thus the master general possessed authority in several areas and a considerable amount of patronage. He shared some of this authority with the board of ordnance, a committee composed of five principal officers, three administrative officials, and several inferior officers. The five principal officers included the lieutenant general of the ordnance, second in command to the master general. At this time, awkwardly enough, Sir William Howe held the position. Howe, of course, had been Cornwallis's senior in North

America. Another principal officer, the surveyor general, was both inspector general and director general for stores. He kept the accounts on stores and certified their serviceability. He was also responsible for the repair and maintenance of all military works (except barracks). The clerk of the ordnance handled contracts, estimates in Parliament, inventories, and other matters. The principal storekeeper fulfilled what his title implied, but could release stores only with the consent of the other principal officers or the master general. Finally, the clerk of deliveries actually delivered the stores. The administrative officials included the treasurer, the secretary, and the undersecretary to the master general. A host of inferior officers completed the roster of the ordnance department. The deputy keeper of the armory held responsibility for arms in the Tower of London. The chief engineer supervised the defensive works in Britain. The master gunner of England taught the use of heavy ordnance and certified the Woolwich instructors in artillery. The firemaster taught students the use of mortars and supervised the research done at Woolwich laboratory on powder, rockets, and ammunition. Other officials included the keeper of the small arms, the storekeeper of the ordnance depots, the wagon master, the clerk of the cheque, and the purveyor.[13]

The board, created to carry on ordnance work when other matters engaged the master general, had in practice proved clumsy and inefficient. The master general could in any event overrule its decisions. Indeed, it was so inefficient, especially in wartime when the nation could not afford to await committee deliberations, that each master general had tended to ignore it and to carry on business through the lieutenant general and the surveyor general. The board had thus become a formality, giving its assent to routine matters.

The Richmond Tenure

Cornwallis's predecessor as master general was Charles Lennox, third Duke of Richmond, who held the position for just over ten years, beginning in January of 1784. Richmond was a political maverick, whom Pitt necessarily dumped when the Portland whigs took office.[14] In his decade of tenure, the duke carried out several reforms. He instituted careful budgetary procedures and tried to prevent the bribing of ordnance personnel by contractors who wanted favorable decisions. He fortified Portsmouth and Plymouth. He also created several new branches: the military artificers in 1788, whose personnel not only built and repaired fortifications but also served as sappers in siege operations; the artillery drivers in 1794; and a horse artillery armed with four-pounders to support the cavalry. Richmond was mainly responsible for the ordnance cartographic survey, initially begun following the rebellion of 1745, but allowed to lapse for many years after that. The surveys were essential to the preparation of defenses against invasion. The duke had also increased the number of government powder mills, which turned out better powder at lower cost than those of the contractors.

New Directions

Cornwallis stepped into the office in the middle of a war, with Britain fighting for survival. He could not afford as much time for reform as he wished, though he did institute some humanitarian changes, once he had mastered the techniques of his work. For the most part, however, the needs of war demanded that he use the department as he found it.

The most urgent of those needs involved the coastal defense of England. The English, at least until Trafalgar, constantly labored under the fear of an invasion by France, a fear in part justified by the French attempts on Ireland. Cornwallis, military commander of Essex and Hertfordshire as well as master general, held responsibility for the surveys and defensive fortifications of Britain. Pessimistic about the war's progress anyway—as well he might be after his Continental experiences—he soon discovered the appalling state of British defense.[15] Sir William Green, the chief royal engineer, admitted that he knew nothing of the works being repaired at Sheerness or Tilbury, which he considered the two most important fortresses in the kingdom, one the only obstruction at the Medway and the other the "water key to the Metropolis." Green added, furthermore, that he knew nothing "of the actual state of any of our other fortresses, or posts of defence, or of any military works or measures in the line of the chief engineer, for the defence of the coast, that may have been, or that are carrying on."[16]

The new master general now applied himself to correct such inexcusable laxness. He began a regular practice of consultation with the chief engineer, continued the triangulation surveys begun by Richmond, and traveled all about England to inspect the defenses.[17] Though the expected invasion never came (thanks to the navy), Cornwallis tried his best to make sure that England would be prepared to hurl the French back if they landed.

Sometimes his work on the fortifications involved him in curious situations. The populace tended to believe that the master general should not only defend English coasts against the French, but also guard English defenses from attack in the rear by English Jacobins. At one time, the marquis received a communication from Lord Sydney informing him that a former servant, whom a lady had dismissed for "keeping bad company of the Jacobin kind at Bath" and who was suspected of drilling companies "in the military exercise," had established himself in the neighborhood of Purfleet at the "head of a number of manufacturers of some sort or other." A former soldier, the man had served at Gibraltar and had been wounded in the leg during the War for American Independence. This "sensible active fellow, not well disposed," needed watching. Cornwallis received several such communications, although all such intelligence should have gone to the home secretary, whose province included internal subversion.[18] At the time, however, Cornwallis was the most eminent soldier in Britain, and apparently many people naturally turned to him for protection.

Almost as pressing as coastal defense, and intimately related to it, was supplying the British military with small arms to repel invasion. Despite all his other reforms, the Duke of Richmond had failed in this most important area. Creating new branches of the service and reorganizing administration would avail little if the soldiers of the British army lacked sufficient numbers of weapons. Richmond had simply not accumulated an adequate supply, and Cornwallis needed to work desperately to catch up.[19]

The ordnance department did not itself manufacture small arms, but depended upon purchase both in Britain and abroad. In the 1790s small arms manufacture was an unwieldy industry centered in Birmingham with branches in London. Wealthy merchant manufacturers employed different workmen to make the barrels, locks, stocks, bayonets, ramrods, and other parts of a musket in separate shops and homes. The manufacturers then assembled the parts in one central location. The industry could not expand rapidly—men needed considerable training to acquire the necessary skills—even though Britain's military demands constantly increased. Furthermore, the ordnance, supposedly the only government purchasing agent, in fact did not exercise that monopoly. It endured competition from cabinet members. Other organizations competed with ordnance to purchase for themselves the weapons the ordnance department wanted to obtain for the government. These competing organizations included the Irish ordnance department (separate until the Act of Union), the East India Company, and even the government of Portugal.

Arms manufacturers, in part because of government policy, compounded the problems, for they preferred to fill the orders of these competitors before they undertook to supply the ordnance. Though not very patriotic, their stance was understandable. Ordnance demanded a higher quality than other customers, hoping for standardization and interchangeable parts. To fulfill these requirements, producers necessarily hired the most highly skilled labor at greater expense than was necessary to make the weapons of competitors. Doing business with the ordnance was therefore not as profitable as doing business with others. Even when the manufacturers did produce the quality of muskets demanded, the government took an unconscionable time to reimburse them. Ordnance did not pay for the weapons, but gave debentures on the treasury, which honored them slowly. One London gunsmith complained in 1794 that he did not have the means to survive while awaiting payment, "which I understand is sometimes nearly six months." [20] Again, the assistant clerk of the ordnance pointed out to the treasury secretary in May of 1797 that it had not paid nearly £4,000 owed from April 1796 and for the period since then had even greater outstanding debts. [21] Arms makers, accordingly, preferred to produce large quantities of what Cornwallis contemptuously termed "trade muskets," which did not meet government standards.

Pitt and Dundas purchased for the government many of these "trade muskets," produced before the war for foreign customers. The British army ended up with all sorts of different weapons, no standardization, a resulting loss of efficiency, and no single record of all stocks on hand.

This vexing situation, as Cornwallis told Dundas, "occupied much of my attention."[22] Under the marquis's direction the ordnance tried several expedients: forcing the manufacturers to produce arms of the standard pattern; returning all purchasing to the ordnance alone; confiscating East India muskets manufactured in England and distributing them to the army; forbidding the Irish and Portuguese from buying from British producers; and purchasing arms abroad. By February of 1796, this policy had reaped some dividends. As far as Cornwallis could estimate, the ordnance had stored some 116,000 stands of arms in various locations. The master general hoped that as a result the king would refuse any more trade muskets for the army, justified in the past in any event only because of "an emergency in the public service."[23] George III granted his master general's request, and the ordnance board accordingly notified the manufacturers that it would accept none of the trade muskets after 31 March 1796. Merchants then rushed to unload on the ordnance their stocks of these weapons before the deadline. One of them sold to the ordnance some 1,772 muskets during the last week of March, 1,110 more than he had ever in the past delivered in one week.[24]

Yet the trouble continued. The war increasingly broadened in scope and demanded more weapons, for allies on the Continent, for the British regiments fighting abroad from India to Ireland, and for the militia. Trade muskets necessarily supplemented the quality arms of the ordnance. Cornwallis, furthermore, had to guard constantly against chicanery, tricks, and cabinet interference. Once when the ordnance board suspected arms makers of selling to foreign agents and smuggling the weapons out in chests marked "Birmingham toys," it asked the treasury to get the customs to stop the practice.[25] On another occasion, Pitt seemed inclined to favor an American request to purchase from the British. Cornwallis protested vigorously. He pointed out that the British had lost arms in Holland and the West Indies, that the militia needed weapons, that stocks were low, and that it would be better to give the Americans "every firelock in our store" than allow them to buy from British manufacturers.[26] When, despite such efforts, the British producers still did not fulfill its needs, the ordnance tried other expedients, including purchase from foreign manufacturers, after first testing the guns to assure their worth.[27]

Although he could not stop the proliferation of trade muskets, Cornwallis helped resolve the problem caused by Irish and Portuguese purchases of English guns in competition with his own department. The British ordnance assumed authority to purchase for Irish ordnance until both were amalgamated after the Union.[28] The arrangement with Portugal was somewhat more complex. In 1799 the ordnance refused the Portuguese ambassador's request to buy arms directly from British producers, but allowed him to purchase foreign arms imported into England.[29]

Artillery presented an altogether different problem. The British seemed to have enough big guns of high quality, but not sufficient numbers of skilled men to work them. Mastering the intricacies of handling artillery required special training. But the necessities of war did not allow time for such extended schooling. Cornwallis, acutely aware of the problem, tried several cures. He first suggested to Dundas transferring three hundred recruits from the Irish artillery to the British, offering each man who volunteered a guinea to entice him to change units.[30] Few took advantage of the offer and it was perhaps just as well, for the Irish artillery was notoriously lax and inefficient, as Cornwallis later discovered. The lord lieutenant of Ireland even termed it "miserably defective in point of science and education." The men appointed as lieutenants did not have to undergo any training or take any examination before they received their commissions and were "not very well read and practiced in their profession."[31]

The master general also hoped to incorporate recruits from some of the newer infantry regiments into the artillery. If that did not bring the royal regiment up to strength, he wished to induce men from fencible regiments to enlist, by means of a guinea bounty. If that failed also, he intended to detach them from the fencible regiments and train them as artillerymen.[32] The fencibles, however, grumbled so much at the notion of transfer that the government raised the bounty to two guineas per man. Even so, the royal regiment of artillery continued under strength. Cornwallis then tried the most desperate expedient of all, recruiting from the militia. He assembled the militia colonels, told them the problem, and threw himself "entirely on their liberality and public spirit." He asked them to send him one man for every fifty they commanded and assured them that once they had complied he would not call on them again. They would not have to become recruiting agents for the artillery.[33]

Even this plea did not bring sufficient numbers of men to the royal regiment. The militia, called out for home defense when invasion threatened, manned artillery positions. The regimental colonels therefore wished to keep their own men but have artillery officers train them in the use of the heavy guns. Cornwallis refused to oblige for two reasons: insufficient numbers of officers and distrust of the militia. He observed, in response to one such request, that if his officers trained the militia in the use of mobile field artillery and entrusted the cannon to them, they would probably abandon the guns the moment the enemy landed. The French would then capture the field pieces and turn them against the English. Militia could not be trusted to fight or even to maintain discipline. Only folly, Cornwallis believed, would put the guns in charge of such shoddy soldiers.[34]

So the manpower shortage continued during the marquis's tenure and involved him in a lengthy dispute with the Duke of York. The duke wanted the different regiments to have their own separate artillery units, leaving the royal regiment to manage the garrison artillery and heavy field guns. He wished to abolish the prevailing system, whereby volunteers from each infantry battalion, commanded by an officer or noncommissioned officer of the royal regiment of artillery, manned the battalion's few light cannon. He wanted instead to have all the artillery solely under the battalion commanders. York mustered several arguments: the shortage of artillerymen and the attitude of battalion commanders, who considered the men detached to serve the guns as temporarily taken from their command and who therefore allowed only their least useful troops to go.

Cornwallis, not surprisingly, opposed York's notion. Although he made no mention of it, as an administrator he naturally could not welcome a reduction in his own establishment. More important, he pointed out that infantry officers had no training to handle the guns and little opportunity to acquire it. British troops served all over the world, unlike Continental armies that remained for many years in quiet garrisons and could easily detach officers to receive artillery instruction. Furthermore, Cornwallis did not believe York correct in his argument that battalion commanders considered men with the artillery as detached from their command. The marquis would not deem commanders so mean-spirited and having so little regard for the service as to send their least capable people to operate such a vital part of the battalion's weaponry. Finally, he concluded, the change York suggested would cost too much money. The battalions would have to maintain not only the guns, but also the horses, stores, and carriages, which would probably necessitate the creation of a new department for the superintendence of regimental artillery. The master general estimated that the expenditure would come to £27,178 16s.[35]

Apparently Cornwallis's opposition killed York's scheme. The marquis heard no more of it. In the course of this exchange, however, he pointed out the tactical path of the future. He said that he had "ever been of opinion since I first began to think seriously on military affairs" that the army should not scatter guns about, but form artillery into brigades under experienced officers. That way a force could concentrate massive firepower on specified positions. The future Duke of Wellington, now only a colonel who had just sailed for India with Cornwallis's 33d regiment, would do precisely that in the Peninsular campaign in years to come.

Trained artillerymen required the skilled leadership of thoroughly proficient officers. Woolwich Academy schooled such officers. Both artillery and engineer officers had to know types of fortifications, mining, surveying, the construction of all types of brass and iron guns, sea and land mortars, types of wood for gun carriages, arithmetic, logarithms, geometry, trigonometry, pneumatics, chemistry, drawing, the French language, and much more. The program at Woolwich, according to the historian Richard Glover, "provided the most thorough, all-round scientific education to be had in England, if not in Britain, at the time."[36] Each cadet received the same education regardless of which branch he intended to enter.

Woolwich cadets received commissions in the artillery only

when vacancies occurred, after passing a public, competitive, general examination in the presence of the master or lieutenant general of the ordnance and the principal board officers. Their standing in the test determined their seniority in rank. Of course, these theoretically rigid standards varied according to circumstance. In wartime, when the demand for officers exceeded the supply, standards dropped. In peacetime, when the number of candidates might exceed the vacancies, rigid adherence to the standards prevailed.

Much depended on the master general, who was nearly the absolute ruler of Woolwich. Richmond in 1794 lowered the qualifications for a commission, a policy Cornwallis followed initially but later reversed. By 1798, standards had returned to the pre-1794 level.[37] To maintain them required a highly qualified and motivated teaching staff, which Cornwallis endeavored to assure. For example, he appointed the famous watercolorist, Paul Sandby, to replace Sandby's father upon the latter's retirement and authorized him to receive £100 rather than the £50 his father had earned.[38] Who better to teach drawing?

Cornwallis also controlled admissions to the academy—which numbered ninety cadets when he took office—a task that demanded much time. Indeed, after he had retired in 1802, he reflected that solicitations for admission had given him "far more trouble than all the other duties of the Master General."[39] Applications overwhelmingly outnumbered vacancies. As a general rule, the marquis accepted officers' sons who seemed qualified, on a "first come, first served" basis. He also reserved places for the children of army and navy officers who had given their lives for their country or had been disabled in the service.[40] He favored as well the applications of old acquaintances and important people. For example, he approved admission of the son of Benedict Arnold and quickly entered the son of Lord Dundas into the academy before the boy grew too old for admission.[41] Applications considered, but not immediately accepted, went on file until an opening occurred or the applicant passed the age of sixteen, the upper age limit for acceptance. To most people, however, he could offer no prospect of admission. Reflecting on it later, he thought he had always fulfilled any promises he had made of admission.[42]

Because so many qualified young men clamored for acceptance, the master general did not hesitate to dismiss cadets who did not perform satisfactorily. On one occasion he pointed out that two of them had not done their work and warned that he "could not suffer the benefits of the institution to be wasted on those who appear so determined to abuse the great advantages which are open to them, while many are excluded who would better know how to set a proper value on so desireable a situation." If they did not improve, they could expect "very serious measures." He authorized a public reading of this warning.[43]

Cadets who worked hard and completed their training did not receive commissions until they were "tall & manly enough to take upon themselves the duty of an officer." Cornwallis thought that one cadet who had finished his studies was still too short and too immature to become an officer. The marquis appointed him an assistant engineer, with pay of four shillings a day, to work with an experienced engineer officer until he matured. Then the master general would recommend him for a commission in the engineer corps.[44]

Though he had little time for experiments, Cornwallis introduced one innovation into the academy. The East India Company requested in 1796 that Woolwich permit it to enroll young men for training so as to give better service to the Company's army later. The master general favored the request, with certain stipulations. The Company would have to pay the cadets' expenses; the cadets would have to recognize their ineligibility for promotion in infantry and cavalry; and they must follow all rules and regulations, which would "on no account be deviated from." The marquis believed the Company's candidates should be at least of age fifteen. He further suggested that since Woolwich graduates could earn promotion only in engineers and artillery, the Company should order the various presidencies to forbid the filling of vacancies in these areas by other than Woolwich graduates. Finally, Cornwallis stipulated that commissions would not come more easily to Company cadets than to others. They would have to work hard.[45]

As the system finally evolved by March of 1797, the cadet enrollment increased from ninety to one hundred with the ten new positions going to John Company. The Company would thereafter get to fill two of every five vacancies until Woolwich mustered sixty cadets destined for the regular army and forty for the Company's. Schools in the neighborhood, taught by academy faculty, prepared cadets to enter Woolwich when vacancies occurred. The Company paid £100 a year for each of its cadets and 2s 6d. per day for each of its alternates at a preparatory school, as well as an initial £300 to prepare accommodations at the academy.[46] From then on, theoretically, the engineer and artillery officers who served the East India Company would possess the same expert training and skill as those who served the regular army.

Frustrations

Though Woolwich demanded time, Cornwallis did not begrudge it. Upon his decisions rested the future quality of the engineers and artillery, vital to the success of the British army, and, indeed, to the security of Britain and her empire. A number of niggling details, on the other hand, often distracted him, and their resolution seemed far less important than his other work. He looked over inventions and assessed their suitability.[47] He supplied naval ordnance (admittedly important, but, because of his inexperience with naval matters, a concern with which he did not much occupy himself). Camden pestered him to oversee the Irish ordnance.[48] Emigrés constantly importuned him, and the royal family often interfered with his work.

As master general, Cornwallis supplied the artillery for the half battalion of the French émigré army that attempted to invade France from Quiberon in June of 1795. That the incursion failed miserably did not quiet émigré assertiveness. The commander of the half battalion, Lieutenant Colonel Rotalier, badgered Cornwallis endlessly, before and after the disaster (his letters to the marquis comprise two bundles of papers). Just before the invasion, Rotalier complained that the marquis did not spare him sufficient time. "For a month," he complained to the master general's secretary, Captain Alexander Apsley, "I have presented myself several times a week at the door of Lord Cornwallis without being able to go in to him: without even being able to attain an introduction to you; without even receiving any response to several articles I have sent in writing asking justice. Nor have I had the fortune of catching him in a spare moment."[49] After Cornwallis eventually saw him, Rotalier relentlessly pushed for unavailable pay, provisions, and supplies. He complained, after the invasion, that he did not know what other plans the army had for him and his unit. He complained that he received no orders. Yet when he received orders in November of 1796 for Portugal, he insisted that he could not obey them because his troop was too disorganized.[50]

Though Cornwallis could scorn Rotalier's pretensions, he could not ignore the royal family. The Duke of York offered suggestions for the service as commander in chief, which at least gave him an official interest in the disposition of artillery. But Prince William of Gloucester simply presumed upon his membership in the royal family to try to solicit special favors. At one time he wanted Cornwallis, contrary to rules, to detach artillery or engineer officers as aides-de-camp. The master general necessarily but diplomatically denied the request: "I must therefore hope that your Royal Highness will have the goodness not to press me further to do a thing which I cannot reconcile to my public duty, & which I have on several late occasions uniformly refused."[51] The prince did not give up. He asked Cornwallis to make another exception in his favor by permitting a lieutenant in artillery to resign and reenter the service as a cornet of cavalry—at a time when the shortage of artillery officers threatened England's very security. Again the master general refused: "Nothing can be more painful to me than to thwart your Royal Highness's wishes . . . and I am sure that your Royal Highness has seen enough of the British Army to be convinced that when regulations are once broken, it is a very arduous task to restrain the abuse."[52]

Even George III made the marquis's tasks more difficult than they should have been. Cornwallis presented to the monarch the artillery and engineer commissions, which needed his signature to become valid and without which no officer could assume his official duties. Yet, according to the master general, "his majesty sometimes takes the Commissions home with him, & does not return them for some days." In one instance, Cornwallis feared that this practice would cause an officer in the artillery to miss going to an assignment in the West Indies, because the fleet would sail before the king signed the commission.[53]

Rewards

Despite frustrations, thwarted plans, and the royal family, Cornwallis managed to do his job. Perhaps the most rewarding aspect of that job was his ability to maintain a reasonably happy service with good morale. He accomplished that feat through his exercise of common sense, reward of merit, and adequate monetary provision for those people under his authority whom the government had previously neglected.

Common sense served him well during the crisis of May 1797. Government feared, groundlessly, that the artillery at Woolwich intended to mutiny. Cornwallis believed reports of their disaffection exaggerated and proved it. He visited the artillerymen personally and kept discord to a minimum. He discovered serious trouble in only three companies, one of which he transferred. And, he concluded, their discontent owed more to their sympathy with the sailors who had mutinied at Spithead than to any complaint about the artillery service.[54]

Common sense also determined him to abide by the established rules and regulations of the service, for he knew that once he began making exceptions, the pleas for special consideration would never cease. He refused, for example, to let storekeepers buy or sell offices as if they were private property.[55] He discouraged improper channels of communication.

Yet that same common sense prompted him to reward merit. He tried to get the best people into positions of importance. If in his view a hardworking official received insufficient reward for his work, he tried to rectify the situation. For example, he determined to increase the salary of the secretary to the ordnance, "an office of so much labor and responsibility."[56]

Cornwallis extended the principle of reward for merit not only to those actively engaged in the service, but also to those who had given the best years of their lives for king and country and to the families of such men as well. He sincerely believed that England owed something to the widows and orphans of officers who had performed their duties and offered their lives for England.

He did not like the operation of the pension system in the artillery and engineers. Ordnance provided pensions for the dependents of officers who had died in the service and to retired officers who had become too ill or too old to continue active. Rank determined the amount received: a general would get more than a lieutenant, as would the general's widow. Yet, unlike the cavalry and infantry, wherein a wealthy individual could buy his way to the top ranks, commissions and promotions in the artillery and engineers came only as vacancies occurred. Artillery officers and engineers did not retire at a specific age, which usually meant that they held their commissions until death. Such a system meant both stagnation in the upper ranks and difficulty in gaining promotion to them. "The Officers have no objects of either ambition or emolument to which they can look forward," Cornwallis observed, "unless they seek the latter by improper peculation. After 40 years' service they may aspire to Colonel's pay and nothing more."[57] As a result of the limited opportunities for promotion, many officers died at the lower ranks, with a correspondingly smaller pension for their families, especially since the amount was always determined according to the deceased's permanent rather than his brevet rank.

Cornwallis was unable to alter this system as a whole. But he did, for the sake of equity and humanity, bend the rules in individual cases. A Lieutenant Colonel Caddy of the royal engineers died in the West Indies in June of 1798, where his son had also died. "Had I known that Lieut-Colonel Caddy had lost a son in that cursed island of St. Domingo," Cornwallis observed, "I do not think that I should have ordered him thither." Mrs. Caddy was now left with two daughters, one of them a cripple, and her husband's pension would be only that of a captain, his permanent rank, "When her husband was so near that situation in the Corps that would have entitled her to the pension of a widow of a Lieut-Colonel." These circumstances rendered her case "truly compassionate." Cornwallis therefore overrode the rules and allowed Mrs. Caddy the pension of a lieutenant colonel with an additional allowance for each child.[58]

Whatever the inadequacies of the pension system for its military personnel, at least the ordnance provided one. On the other hand, the civilians who worked for ordnance received none at all. They benefited from no retirement plan, and Cornwallis determined to implement one in 1796. He established a regular pension fund for the families of deceased civil servants, based upon their salary at retirement. The widow of a civil servant earning £400 per year would get £50, for example, whereas £15 went to the widow of a civil officer earning between £40 and £70. The plan included three provisions: (1) that the deceased officer should have worked for the civil department at least ten years; (2) that he should have been on the ordnance establishment at the time of his death; and (3) that each civil servant should contribute one day's pay each quarter (deducted from his salary) to help defray expenses. Cornwallis further enjoined that until he could get formal approval the board should immediately act on needy cases according to the proposed plan.[59] The resulting pensions, though scarcely generous, must have seemed a godsend to impecunious and lonely widows who otherwise would have faced a penniless future, perhaps even starvation.

So the Cornwallis tenure combined frustration with reward. On the whole, the marquis compiled a record of modest achievement. He continued the map survey, strengthened the defenses, kept the British army supplied with arms and ammunition, provided an efficient and rigorous training for artillery and engineer officers for the British Empire, and instituted humanitarian reforms. These efforts had not challenged his energies as much as had India. But troubles across the Irish Sea would soon offer more scope for his talents and Britain an opportunity for great achievement—or disaster.[60]

Chapter 11

Ireland

A Troubled History

As the European situation worsened for Britain, his work at the ordnance seemed to Cornwallis ever less important. The French revolutionaries scored one triumph after another. Holland, which he had tried to defend and to cajole the allies into preserving, succumbed to French control as the Batavian Republic. In March of 1795, Prussia, on whom Britain had wasted so much money, dropped out of the war and made peace with France. The brilliant Napoleon Bonaparte, under the auspices of the Directory, rampaged through Italy and forced Austria to a peace at Campo Formio in October of 1797. The French took Switzerland and formed it into the satellite Helvetian Republic. Bonaparte early in 1798 now concentrated an army at Boulogne that threatened invasion of England herself. The 1797 mutinies of sailors in May at Spithead and in June at the Nore had shaken British confidence that she could stop the attack.

By 1798, Britain stood alone, her alliances shattered, her armies ignominiously swept from the European Continent. Could she withstand the might of ever-victorious France? To do so, she had to retain supremacy in the British Isles. Yet at the very time of mutiny at home and defeat abroad, British control seemed threatened in the one island that had never submitted willingly to her government. For the Irish, especially those of Roman Catholic faith, Britain's time of trouble spelled opportunity.

Many of the Irish hated the English and the Scots for the compelling reason that Great Britain treated them far worse than she did any other people in the British Empire. Indeed, the British record in the Emerald Isle was the most shameful in the entire history of her empire. Nowhere else the British went, in whatever corner of the globe, did they treat the native inhabitants so severely, exploit them so ruthlessly, and display such a callous lack of concern for the results of their policies. Only the Irish use of force, of violence so passionately strong as to threaten British ascendancy, finally induced the usually humane British to reexamine their Irish policies.

Bloodshed, oppression, and fanaticism bedevil Anglo-Irish history. The Normans, who conquered England in the eleventh century, used it as a base to penetrate Ireland in the twelfth. Though Normans and English blended by Chaucer's time to form a distinctively English culture, the Irish had simply absorbed the invaders from across the sea, Norman or English. The English sovereigns periodically undertook expeditions to make good their claims as kings of that island, but they at best maintained a temporary superiority. Until Queen Elizabeth I's time, the English ruled effectively only in the Pale, a strip of coastal area that stretched some fifty miles north from Dublin and included only a few towns. The English there became as Irish as the Irish, as exemplified by families like the Geraldines or the Butlers. Indeed, in Ireland, rule was exercised by heads of families or clans, like the Kildares, the Desmonds, and the Fitzgeralds. Henry VII had tried to institute stronger English control through the nominal ruler of Ireland, the lord lieutenant. The latter's deputy, Edward Poynings, authored a stringent set of laws. Poynings summoned a parliament to Drogheda in 1494, and under his guidance it passed regulations designed to ensure Irish subservience: an Irish parliament could meet and legislate only with the English king's previous approval; all laws passed in England also applied to Ireland; and the Irish parliament could not even discuss future laws unless the English king and council had first agreed.

Mere passage of "Poynings' laws" did not mean their enforcement. They never prevailed in Ulster, and Ireland continued in turmoil, with Irish chieftains defying English rule for much of the sixteenth century. Shortly before her death, Elizabeth managed to crush the rebellions, and James I came to the throne with an opportunity to lay the foundations for a wise and benevolent policy that might reconcile all parties and institute a new era in Anglo-Irish relations. He did not. Rather, he followed a course that ensured tragedy. He embittered the Irish by trying to force Roman Catholics into the Church of England and imposed a land settlement on Ulster that the Irish have never forgotten and that haunts England even today. Two Ulster lords died in exile and a third was killed in revolt, with the result that all their lands were forfeited to the crown. James then determined to "plant" northern Ireland. He might well have followed the advice of his leading officer there, Sir Arthur Chicester, who proposed that the king divide the bulk of the land among its present inhabitants, giving to each what he could cultivate. The rest could go to Englishmen who had served in Ireland (the servitors) and to English and Scottish colonists. James, as was his wont, entirely disregarded this statesmanlike proposal and followed a plan nearly its reverse. More than two-fifths of the forfeited lands went to English and Scottish settlers (the origin of the Scots-Irish), one-fifth to the church and education, and only one-fifth to the servitors and the Irish natives. In the end, the Irish received scarcely a tenth of the lands distributed. The lesser Irish chiefs, innocent of the "misdeeds" of the great lords, thus obtained only a fraction of the lands, while the mass of the natives got nothing at all. James thought of the Irish peasants as barbarians and became angry when he learned that the new settlers kept native Irish on their estates. The peasants, of course, provided cheap labor for the English, and, because they remained landless, they grew utterly dependent upon their employers. Angry, frustrated, and poor, they would willingly cut their employers' throats should the opportunity present itself.

That time came when James's reign gave way to that of his son Charles I. As a complement to his period of "personal rule" in England, when Parliament did not meet for eleven years, Charles determined to tighten English administration in Ireland. Accordingly, he sent there Sir Thomas Wentworth (created Earl of Strafford in 1640). Wentworth purged corrupt officials, made Ireland self-supporting, and even built up a small army. But in doing so he alienated all people there. He lined his own pockets. His religious policy split the already precarious Protestant minority. He tried to recover Church of Ireland (the name borne by the Anglican church in Ireland) property, an action that threatened to take over the land acquired by the new settlers. He dispossessed some English as well as Irish. In short, while in no way reconciling the disaffected Irish peasants to their masters, he also divided and embittered the masters and thereby set the stage for the next tragic chapter of Irish history, the rebellion and its crushing.

Rebellion erupted in 1641 after Strafford left. The Irish, taking advantage of England's internal dissent—for King Charles in that year confronted the Long Parliament and England edged close to civil war—arose to throw off their yoke and killed several thousand British in Ulster. Although, in 1644, Charles made · a peace with the rebels that released English troops there to fight for him in England, Ireland continued to smolder. Oliver Cromwell sternly extinguished the last of the fire. Triumphant over Charles, at the head of a victorious army, deeply committed to his Calvinistic religion, he determined to crush Catholic Irish resistance. In 1649, he sailed to Ireland and undertook military operations with a vengeance. He massacred the garrisons of both Drogheda and Wexford and followed his victories with an intensification of the program begun by the early Stuarts. He expropriated the lands of native Irish and imposed a larger English ruling class upon them. Then he returned to England to begin his constitutional experiments. The Irish had had yet another example of the harshness of English rule, but not, alas, their last.

Forty years after Cromwell's departure, another English army returned. James II, who became king of England in 1685, fled for his life in 1688. By his various policies, including his Catholicizing, he had so alienated English political leaders that they invited William of Orange, Stadholder of the Netherlands, to come and replace James. William, a grandson of Charles I through Charles's daughter Mary, had taken as his wife Mary, daughter of James II. He did not possess, of course, as good a secular claim through inheritance as James, but as a Protestant he had a better religious one. William accepted the challenging offer and managed to land a Dutch force in England. Support for James evaporated and he fled to France, ending the "Glorious Revolution." Parliament duly offered the throne to William and Mary. But James, embittered and disgruntled, did not give up, because Catholic Ireland had naturally declared for Catholic James in preference to Protestant William and Mary. In March of 1689, the exiled king capitalized on this Irish sentiment by landing there and arousing support for himself. The Irish welcomed him except in now Protestant Ulster, whose citizens armed themselves and retired to defensible towns such as Londonderry, the chief port of Northern Ireland, where they proclaimed William and Mary as king and queen. The French navy might have rendered the Ulsterite cause nearly hopeless, but it failed to act when the opportunity offered. After defeating an Anglo–Dutch fleet in the Channel, it then allowed William to sail to Ireland with a convoy of six warships instead of cruising to interdict his passage.

James, meanwhile, secure in the south with his loyal supporters, marched north. He lacked a siege train, but he blockaded Londonderry with a boom across the river Foyle to prevent relief by sea. Neither assault nor starvation would force the town to yield, and James necessarily gave up when a frigate and three ships broke the boom in early August and relieved the town. The defenders had held out for 105 days, and they never forgot it. Neither have their descendants, nor the English. Protestantism had endured and forced the retreat of Catholicism.

William now ensured victory. He landed on 24 June 1690, at Carrickfergus, with an army of about forty thousand men: English, Dutch, Danish, and French Huguenots. James had fewer men, but seven battalions of them were French regulars. The former king decided to hold a defensive position north of Dublin along the Boyne River, which runs into the sea at Drogheda, a town made famous by Cromwell's siege. Although James had a good position commanding high ground on the west side of the river, he muffed his job as a commander. On 11 July, William attacked. While his main force charged frontally, a smaller detachment crossed the river upstream and drove in on James's left flank. In the battle that followed, James suffered three times as many casualties as his opponent, and then, though his forces retired in good order, he left the field. Had James possessed any perseverance or even common sense he might have regrouped his forces and planned guerrilla-type operations against the English and thus might have changed the course of Irish history. Instead, in the moment of crisis, he folded. Before the end of July he gave up his venture and returned to France.

The battle of the Boyne solidified the English hold on Ireland and the consequent Protestant ascendancy. Ulstermen had declared for William of Orange and never, from that day to this, have they or the Catholic Irish forgotten the Boyne. Orange lodges, named after the original ruling house of William III, sprang up in Ulster. Practically every prime minister in Ulster in the twentieth century has belonged to an Orange lodge. Economic troubles have always run deep in Ireland, but religious difference in north and south has run deeper and still divides the embittered island.

William's settlement promoted additional bitterness. Fierce penal laws against Roman Catholics went into effect, which during the century to follow succeeded in their aim of ruining the Catholic landowning class. Catholics could not participate in either trade or the professions, nor could they sit in or vote for the Irish Parliament. Even the non-Anglican Ulstermen (most Ulstermen were Presbyterians) who had held Ulster did not receive the benefits of English toleration. They also could not sit in the Irish Parliament, which henceforth would be the preserve of a tiny minority of Anglicans. The British Parliament restricted Irish trade and effectively barred Irish commerce with the British colonies. Ireland could not ship cattle to England. In 1699, England forbade Ireland's export of woolen cloth, which ruined her largest industry, an industry in Protestant hands. Catholics were not only barred from voting for Parliament, but also from holding any civil or military office and from participating in the guilds. Most of the Irish were landless Catholic peasants who could not legally practice their religion. Catholics could not purchase land or inherit it from a Protestant. Land would descend intact to a Protestant child alone in a family of Catholics. But if all children remained Catholics, the land would go in equal portions to all. No Catholic could own a horse worth more than five pounds. The Irish had to tithe to the established Church of Ireland, which was in fact the Church of England. The only concessions to Ireland before the American Revolution came in 1750, when Britain allowed Roman Catholics into lesser grades in the army and in 1771, when it allowed Roman Catholics to take leases for sixty-one years on not more than fifty acres of unprofitable land. Although, under the

Hanoverians, the British tended not to enforce the penal laws against Catholics, they made few attempts to repeal or modify them until pressure forced them to reconsider.

Not until the end of the eighteenth century would the Irish have an opportunity to exert that pressure. Meanwhile, as the eighteenth century progressed, Ireland became a poverty-stricken land, totally subservient to England, the vast majority of its people deprived of civil, religious, and economic liberty, reduced to landless agricultural laborers who ground a living from the soil, or, if they were lucky, emigrated. In southern Ireland, especially, land became divided into smaller and smaller plots, farmed by more and more people, on very uncertain tenures. Absentee proprietors, many of whom lived in England, owned most of the land. By the end of Anne's reign, men of nearly pure English blood, descendants of the Cromwellian adventurers or followers of William III, comprised the Irish Parliament.

Yet even Anglican Irish landlords could join with poor Catholic peasants and non-Anglican Protestants in the eighteenth century to protest Ireland's treatment. Poynings' laws still operated, still made the Dublin Parliament entirely subservient to Whitehall. Dublin could not control the army, the purse strings, the chief executive, his secretary, or his ministers.

With so large a base of dissatisfaction built up, Ireland only awaited her opportunity to force concessions from Britain. That time came during the American Revolution. Weak on land and sea and without a single ally, Britain had neither the men nor the means to keep Ireland in total subjection. The Irish took advantage of Britain's preoccupation, just as they had in 1641 and 1688. Henry Flood, joined by Henry Grattan, led an opposition or "patriot" party in the Irish Parliament that aimed to bring the army under Irish control, to secure for the island a permanent habeas corpus act, to get permanent tenure for judges, to lift English trade restrictions, and to remove the English monopoly on church and state offices. But when Flood, who headed the fight for tax concessions, became vice treasurer for Ireland in 1775, he thereby lost his prominence as a leader. People thought the English had bought him. Grattan then took control of the movement.

Britain necessarily had to withdraw the bulk of its army from Ireland to fight in America. When it did so it deprived itself of its only means for enforcing so many odious regulations upon so many people. The Protestant ascendancy in Ireland volunteered to raise militia to replace the absent regulars. The British, lacking any alternative, accepted and even gave the new force arms. Eventually the Irish Volunteers numbered some eighty thousand men. But the Volunteers could force concessions from England as well as defend Ireland from France. Indeed, Grattan and Flood believed that the Volunteers should not disband until Ireland had won her rights.

By 1779, Britain had to heed the demands, especially because during the year a French fleet actually entered the Channel and threatened to invade England. The Irish added more impact to the situation by refusing to take British goods (Jonathan Swift had once enjoined his countrymen to burn everything English except coal). Late in the year, the harried North government yielded to circumstances. It carried through the British Parliament measures that granted Ireland the free export of her wool, woolen cloth, and manufactured glass and the right of her merchants to trade with the colonies, Turkey, and the Near East. Irish nationalists, however, deemed these measures insufficient and demanded more. In 1782, the Volunteers convened and claimed for Ireland the right to manage its own internal affairs, as expressed through an Irish Parliament. The Rockingham government, which had replaced the North one, also yielded and permitted an Irish Parliament. Acts passed by the Irish Parliament, however, required the king's signature to become law. Furthermore, Britain maintained authority over foreign and imperial commercial policy and over the appointment of the chief executive, the lord lieutenant. The Irish Parliament itself—still composed of Anglicans, although Dissenters could now legally hold office—removed the purely penal laws against Catholics. Provided they took an oath of allegiance to the crown, Catholics could lease land for an indefinite period and could even purchase, hold, and bequeath freeholds on the same terms as Protestants. They could also remain Catholics and educate their children in the faith without penalty. They had not yet acquired full civil and religious rights, but by 1782 the Irish Catholics, particularly those of the aristocracy, had advanced considerably.

When Britain found herself at war with revolutionary

France in the 1790s, her distress again became Ireland's oppor- tunity. In 1791, disaffected Protestants in Ulster created the Soci- ety of United Irishmen and established relations with the Catholic south and with radicals in England. These middle-class Ulsterites wished a share of parliamentary interests, hitherto commanded by the great landowning families. But the families, who dominated the Irish government as well as the Parliament, refused to yield their predominance, so the Ulsterites turned to Catholics for sup- port. A Catholic convention assembled in December of 1792, backed by the Society of United Irishmen. This show of strength impressed Pitt. His government in 1793 accordingly acted to al- leviate grievances. It forced the Irish government to make conces- sions that allowed Catholics to bear arms, to become corporation members, to vote as forty-shilling freeholders in counties and bor- oughs, to sit on grand juries, to take degrees from Dublin Univer- sity, and even to hold commissions in the army below the rank of general.

Neither the English government nor the Irish Parliament would concede more. Neither would allow Catholics to sit in the Irish Parliament or to secure government office in Ireland. Pitt and the British cabinet absolutely refused to heed the plea of their own appointed lord lieutenant, the second Earl Fitzwilliam, for full Catholic emancipation. Fitzwilliam resigned, and Ireland seethed again. Indeed, when he left Dublin in March of 1795, throngs of Irishmen pulled his carriage through streets draped in mourning.

The Catholics now wanted office and the reform of their Parliament, corrupt even by standards of the British Parliament. The United Irishmen in the south of Ireland, with headquarters at Dublin, so concentrated on the Catholic issue that the society became an increasingly exclusive Catholic group. Rival Protestant Orange lodges mushroomed to counter the Catholics, and the dream of a united country vanished in the Irish mist and rain.[1] That animosity which a united Ireland might have turned against the English in order to gain further concessions now turned in- ward, pitting Catholic against Protestant. The Catholics, the overwhelming majority of them penniless peasants, resented the Protestant ruling clique in Dublin and the Protestant landlords in the south, who owned 90 percent of the land. The leaders of the

United Irish movement in Dublin grew increasingly radical and republican, looking to the example of the French Revolution, and prodded Ireland as much toward civil war and social revolution as toward national liberation from the English.

Sir John, second Earl Camden, Fitzwilliam's replacement, seemed incapable of doing much about the growing discontent. Though he appeared imperious and commanding in his viceregal robes, with his high forehead, long nose, and rather disdainful look, he was indecisive in times of crisis, a captive of the ruling clique in Dublin who comprised the Irish cabinet. Though supposedly only his advisers, they in fact told Camden how to run the government. The group included John Beresford, commissioner for revenue; the lord chancellor, John Fitzgibbon, Lord Clare, and John Foster, speaker of the Irish Parliament. This cabinet was not responsible to the Irish Parliament and really consisted of those members of the privy council whom the lord lieutenant wished to consult. But he could never afford to neglect the lord chancellor and the chief secretary.[2] Thomas Pelham, chief secretary at the time, though sympathetic to further government reform, was weak and ailing, ready to be replaced by Camden's brilliant nephew, Robert Stewart, known to history as Lord Castlereagh, a cool, handsome young man of twenty-nine from a Protestant Irish family. Edward Cooke, undersecretary for the civil department, actively opposed concessions to Catholics. Indeed, his anti-Catholicism approached the fanatic. His letters breathed fire against "abominable" priests and "popish bigotry and rancour," the "sole motive" for lower-class disturbances.[3]

Since the radicals could never hope to oust the clique and establish a new social order while the British continued to back the Irish government, they therefore looked to the French for help. An Irish revolutionary, Theobald Wolfe Tone, became adjutant general to the French army. Son of a coachmaker, hardened by poverty yet still possessed of a romantic streak, Tone initially practiced as a lawyer in Belfast, but then went to America and finally to France to enlist support for his cause. On 15 December 1796, he accompanied the French fleet of forty-three ships that sailed with an army of fifteen thousand to liberate Ireland. Although the fleet made Bantry Bay, terrible weather beset them. For a week a strong easterly gale made any landing impossible.

Meanwhile, Richard White, the most important resident land-owner, organized his tenantry, who seemed to support him admirably. White's elegant manor house with its French doors overlooking the water afforded him a panoramic view of one of the most strikingly beautiful inlets in the world. But White alone, even with his loyal tenantry, could not have stopped fifteen thousand French soldiers from coming ashore, capturing his house and grounds, and sweeping forward. He needed the support of regular soldiers, and the British, caught by surprise, had none to spare him. The British general commanding in the area would not have been able to concentrate even two thousand men at Cork before 1 January. Poor French seamanship and bad weather finally prevented the French from landing, but doubtless had they done so they would have taken Cork and enormous amounts of naval supplies and stores. Had the people arisen to support them, the French might have taken all of Ireland, though whether they could have held it without command of the sea is another matter entirely.

"The Rising of the Moon"

The Bantry scare prompted the Irish government to disarm the peasantry of both north and south. Government hoped thereby to avert rebellion and civil war. The large landowners meanwhile vehemently demanded savage reprisals against peasants suspected of treasonous activities, although it was just such vile treatment of the peasants over the years that had finally driven them to such activities.

A host of spies scurried about everywhere, informing the government of possible traitors and aiding in the disarmament. Their intelligence prompted authorities to swoop into chambers where the United Irish leaders met in Dublin and to arrest them en masse. One leader managed to escape and flee overseas, and thereafter only the colorful Lord Edward Fitzgerald remained at large in the capital to continue organized rebellion. But Fitzgerald lived too openly and recklessly to retain his freedom long: he was wounded and captured in May and died in prison.

Yet, though the Dublin police could break the conspiracy and jail the leaders, they could not disarm the countryside. For this operation the government depended upon the military forces available, and those were woefully inadequate in numbers and discipline. Their commander in early 1798, Sir Ralph Abercrombie (brother of Sir Robert), an able and fearless soldier, lacked a politician's tact. In the process of the disarmament, the military committed several atrocities he could not stomach. On 26 February 1798, he sent a circular to his generals and commanding officers describing the army as "in a state of licentiousness which must render it formidable to everyone but the enemy."[4] This communication outraged the Dublin clique and disturbed the British cabinet. In March, Pitt himself expressed grave doubts about Abercrombie, whose tactics, he averred, "almost amounted to an open invitation to a foreign enemy."[5]

Yet Abercrombie had stated no more than the truth. The regular army, small in numbers with an establishment of under eleven thousand infantry and about four thousand cavalry, lay scattered all around the country.[6] Its artillery was deficient. It also lacked adequate provisions, ordnance, and ammunition. Thomas Pakenham, lieutenant general of Irish ordnance, estimated that the regulars needed eight thousand stand of light dragoon carbines, one hundred thousand rounds of carbine ball cartridges, ten thousand stand of muskets, one million rounds of musket ball cartridges, and ten howitzers with carriages and three thousand rounds of ammunition.[7] In addition to these deficiencies, leadership was poor. Men bought and sold staff appointments and bickered constantly.[8] The British government had sent over reinforcements previous to 1798, but almost all of them were Irish, ill-trained and ill-disciplined.[9] The government had also authorized the Irish gentry to raise yeomanry, who by 1798 numbered perhaps forty-six thousand men, compared to whom the shabby regulars were models of training and discipline.

Despite these handicaps, Abercrombie might have prevented rebellion had the government continued his plans and allowed him a free hand. At the end of March, the Irish privy council put the country under martial law and ordered Abercrombie to take charge of disarming the peasants, who possessed few firearms but many pikes. Unlike Lieutenant General Gerard Lake, who in 1797 brutally disarmed Ulster by torturing individual suspects to extract information, Abercrombie combined firmness with humanity. Instead of indiscriminate punishment against everyone in an area, he systematically searched out the arms. "If all else failed," the historian Thomas Pakenham noted, "troops would be sent to live at 'free quarters' in the disturbed districts." But they would use "as little actual force as possible." Though the diehard landlords in many instances opposed him, Abercrombie did his job well, especially in Queen's County and the areas in the south where General John Moore commanded.

Indeed, Abercrombie worked so efficiently that on 11 May, Camden sent the Duke of Portland, the British home secretary who had responsibility for Irish affairs, a county-by-county survey that suggested that Ireland had so quietened that general rebellion seemed unlikely.[10] Unfortunately for Ireland, however, Abercrombie could not carry on. Pressure from the Irish clique and from Pitt himself forced Camden to accept Abercrombie's resignation, which the general, seeing that he lacked the confidence of government, was eager to tender in any event.[11]

Now the command fell upon Lake, a tough-looking character with a nose nearly as distinctive as Wellington's. But he was not a soldier of Wellington's caliber, and he attempted neither to instill discipline into the army nor to disarm the disaffected in a systematic and humane fashion. He took his orders from Camden, who had given in to the gentry, who were fearful for the safety of their property. Camden told the general to stop the "free quarters" but to take "other vigorous and effectual measures." Lake gave the army its head, and the soldiers ran wild. They flogged and tortured suspects on the flimsiest evidence. They burned cabins. They refused to give those people who did surrender arms any assurance of conciliation. These measures, as one might expect, fired rather than dampened rebellion. Lake drove the peasants to wild desperation and a thirst for revenge.

The United Irish leaders in Dublin, though drastically reduced in numbers and effectiveness after the mass arrest, ordered a general rising for 23 May 1798, hoping to capitalize on the prevailing bitterness. Dubliners planned a sort of coup, inexplicably anticipating the cooperation of the British army, which they even more inexplicably supposed had abandoned its allegiance. The British had taken such effective countermeasures, however, that the planned rebellion in the capital failed utterly. By contrast, the countryside exploded—especially in the counties around Dublin, Wicklow, Carlow, and Kildare—but not in the grand manner anticipated by the United Irish leadership. Instead, the rebellion took the form of indiscriminate looting and lynching of Protestants by Catholic peasants infuriated by Lake's brutality. By early June, the rebels won most of the county of Kildare, the control of roads to Cork and Limerick and to the north through Meath, and most of Wexford, including the important towns of Wexford and Enniscorthy. Government forces desperately defended New Ross. Even Ulster, supposedly docile, suffered disturbances between 9 and 13 June, though loyalist forces, under the intelligent leadership of Major General George Nugent, defeated the United Irish. As a whole, the army showed ineptitude: it did not coordinate systematic plans to defeat the rebels, and in many instances it was routed by simple peasants.

When news of the rebellion (called "the rising of the moon") reached London, it took the cabinet aback. Camden, so assured of calm a month earlier, now prophesied disaster. He told Portland that the ministers would be "much deceived if you imagine that a rebellion so long preparing, which is fomented by party spirit and by religious animosity can be speedily put down." He concluded: "The struggle will be violent, bloody and will shake the connexion between the two countries . . . look towards Ireland as a situation extremely perilous." Indeed, it appeared to Camden so perilous that he shipped his wife and family to England for safety.[12]

Clearly, the lord lieutenant lacked the stomach to quash rebellion. Now, if ever, that office demanded strong leadership and a man who did not panic easily. To fill that need, the British cabinet turned to Cornwallis. Camden himself thought Lake's military leadership inadequate and as early as 1797 had proposed Cornwallis as commander in chief in Ireland, a position the marquis refused because it would have placed him under someone else's authority and tied his hands in the military.[13] As the Irish situation worsened, Camden's ideas went further. In March of 1798, he suggested to the British government that Cornwallis replace him as civil governor. Then in May, Camden proposed that

Cornwallis go to Ireland with the dual authority of lord lieutenant and commander in chief, a supreme authority in both civil and military affairs similar to that he had exercised in India.[14]

The ministry had already arrived at the same conclusion.[15] Indeed, as early as 30 March, Cornwallis suspected he might be asked to go to Ireland in that dual capacity, and the next day the first lord of the admiralty, Earl Spencer, thought so, too.[16] Pitt sounded Cornwallis about it in early June, and on 10 June the king agreed to the appointment. "The present Lord Lieutenant," the sovereign noted, "is too much agitated at the present hour, and totally under the control of the Irish Privy Councillors."[17] Accordingly, on 13 June an order in council officially appointed the marquis lord lieutenant and commander in chief in Ireland.[18]

Before Cornwallis could take up his new command, the British military managed to break the back of the rebellion. Although the rebels in Wexford massacred some ninety-seven loyalists by ripping them with pikes, General Lake defeated a large body of the poorly led peasants gathered at Vinegar Hill outside of Enniscorthy. This eminence rose straight up amid the flat land around it and loomed over its surroundings. That countryside, with its farms neatly bordered and the river Slaney rippling through the town, today almost resembles the peaceful midwestern countryside of the United States. In 1798, however, some twenty thousand rebels camped atop the windy hill around a tower. They had chosen that picturesque spot for a meeting place, not a fortress, for which it was by nature ill suited. Lake mustered some ten thousand men for his attack, supported by twenty pieces of artillery. The rebels had no chance. Lake demolished his foes, although, characteristically, he attacked before closing all routes of escape and thus many frightened peasants eluded capture. General Moore relieved Wexford and saved the remaining loyalists there.

By 21 June, when Cornwallis arrived unobtrusively at Dublin aboard a packet, the rebellion had subsided from a passionate explosion into a nasty guerrilla war in the bogs of Kildare and the mountains of Wicklow.[19] Camden got out as quickly as he could, and on 23 June Cornwallis escorted him in state from Dublin Castle to the quayside, where the former lord lieutenant boarded the *Dorset*. The marquis now settled down in Dublin to the tasks at hand, shunning ostentation, luxury, and the diversions of society. Indeed, he followed a simple, austere pattern of life similar to that he had lived in Bengal. He took up residence, with his aides-de-camp, not in Dublin Castle but in a lodge in Phoenix Park. He established, as he had in Bengal, a regular routine of work. He breakfasted at nine and then with his secretary attended to government work and talked to all civil and military officers who had pertinent business. He kept steadily at this work until two or three in the afternoon. Then he exercised on horseback until around six (unlike India, the climate in Ireland permitted afternoon exercise). Dinner followed half an hour or an hour later, a meal that usually found him in the company of ten or twelve people, with whom he preferred to speak on military matters. After dinner, around nine, the lord lieutenant and his aides withdrew, while the rest of the company departed, read the latest newspapers, or conversed. The marquis usually retired by eleven o'clock.

This austerity did not please the spendthrift Irish gentry, who preferred lavish displays to living within one's means. Cornwallis, however, begrudged lavish spending when protocol did not demand it.[20] The lord lieutenant's simple life highly impressed General John Moore, the best general in Ireland at the time and one of the best in British history. Moore found his commander in chief a person of "plain, manly character, devoid of affectation or pretension, displaying great good sense and observation." He marveled that Cornwallis, who had held such important positions, had not succumbed to vanity or let his distinguished record affect the "simplicity of his character or manners." Moore concluded that perhaps the marquis's character had remained the same because he had always felt himself more than equal to mastering the various jobs he had held.[21]

The present job offered him three basic challenges: to stamp out the remnants of rebellion and render Ireland militarily secure; to help the ravaged country in any way he could; and, most important in the view of the British cabinet, to effect a legislative union with Great Britain.

For the first task, Pitt prepared to give help by sending reinforcements from Britain. Cornwallis knew his military requirements, at least theoretically, before he sailed, because he had reviewed the various measures proposed for Irish defense after 1756, when his father had served as lord lieutenant.[22] Some of the first British reinforcements had arrived in time to help defeat the Wexford rebels. On 2 June, the Duke of York had promised to send over 3,197 men immediately, a figure Pitt raised to 5,000.[23] As the summer progressed, Ireland became almost a garrison state, for English militia promised more trouble than help. On 27 June, Cornwallis rushed through the Irish Parliament a bill regulating their use.[24] By that time considerable numbers of regular cavalry and infantry had arrived, and the militia would pour in (after any need for them had ceased) during September.[25]

Military expenses swelled. Lord Castlereagh, who replaced the ailing Pelham as chief secretary, estimated maintenance of the Irish yeomanry alone at £149,000 per month, and by September the militia from thirteen English counties serving in Ireland added to this already prodigious cost.[26]

A Merry Chase

The British government thus succeeded, at considerable expense, in locking the barn after the horse had been stolen. As Cornwallis told Portland in July, and as Cooke confirmed, the backbone of the rebellion had already been broken before the arrival of massive military aid from Britain.[27]

As it turned out, however, Cornwallis needed some, if not all, of these troops to stop another French design on the Emerald Isle. In August, the French managed to slip three frigates loaded with troops and arms through the British blockade and into Killala Bay. They planned to send reinforcements as soon as possible. On 22 August around eleven hundred French soldiers, led by General Joseph Humbert, disembarked at Killala and brushed aside the small force of yeomanry who opposed them. When the news reached Dublin two days later, some people panicked. Cornwallis, of course, prepared to meet the threat.[28]

The lord lieutenant decided to take the field personally against Humbert. He would be the first Irish chief executive in more than a century to lead His Majesty's troops in person against a foe. The only real danger the French presented, as Cornwallis saw it, lay not in their army, for he had more than enough men to defeat it, but in the possibility that their presence would encourage further rebellion. Humbert had brought with him large quantities of arms, powder, and ball to give to rebels who would join him.

Few volunteered. Humbert enlisted perhaps five thousand men in all. Furthermore, these recruits did not know how to use the arms he provided and seemed unwilling to learn. Some found the French food ration utterly distasteful and others liked it so well that they consumed a month's supply in a week. They pilfered, left camp when they chose, and refused discipline. One French officer grew so enraged he would have preferred to shoot all but thirteen of them.[29] Capable of little with such recruits and lacking widespread support from the peasantry, Humbert could scarcely hope to prevail without reinforcements. In late August, over-whelming numbers of troops opposed him in Ireland. His one hope, lacking reinforcements, was to try to evade the British troops and dash for Dublin, there to stir a general rising.

The French general gathered supplies for a month, left 200 men and 280 powder barrels at Killala, and on 25 August marched to Ballina without meeting any resistance. The next day, with a force now reduced to about 700 French regulars and about as many Irish volunteers, he left Ballina, intending to strike the garrison at Castlebar. To achieve surprise, he avoided the Foxford-to-Castlebar coach road, which had strong defenses at the strategic bridge at Foxford. Instead, he took a back path across a bog and over a ridge close to the top of Mount Nephin, considered impassable by the British. (How many "impassable" tracks have figured prominently in military history?)

The gamble worked. General John Hely-Hutchinson at Castlebar commanded about seventeen hundred men, mostly Irish militia, some Scots fencibles, a few dragoons, and part of a regiment of regular infantry. He also possessed what Humbert lacked, considerable artillery. Hely-Hutchinson posted his men well. Then Lake, sent by Cornwallis to take personal command, arrived the night of 26 August. Despite all this preparation, when Humbert attacked the following morning, he completely routed the defense. They ran so fast that the incident came to be known as the "races of Castlebar."[30]

Cornwallis did not panic. When he decided to take personal command, he embarked forces in a series of canal boats on 26

August and went with his suite on 27 August to take the grand canal to Tullamore. He commanded about three thousand men. At Kilbeggan he learned of Lake's defeat. On 28 August, he requested more reinforcements from Britain, a request that was promptly honored.[31] He judged he needed them in light of Lake's account. The Castlebar defeat seemed to have unhinged his subordinate, who exaggerated the danger wildly. Lake, now in Tuam, described himself as "so much distressed," he thought it "impossible to manage the militia," heard of "disaffection" among the ranks, and believed captive French officers who told him that "numbers of the inhabitants flock to the French standard."[32]

Unruffled, Cornwallis joined Lake after gathering up enough troops to bring his numbers to nearly 8,000 rank and file, many of them English and Irish militia.[33] On 2 September he drew up an order of battle consisting of four divisions: 1,700 men under Major General Colin Campbell, 1,400 under Major General John Hely-Hutchinson, 1,595 under Major General Peter Hunter, and 3,100 men under Major General John Moore.[34] On the fourteenth, he marched to Hollymount after detaching Lake to prevent Humbert's moving either to the right to the Shannon or through Sligo, which had a garrison of only 856 men and six pieces of artillery.[35]

Humbert now led the British a merry chase. But it was only a chase. Neither his landing at Killala nor his victory at Castlebar had roused the countryside. In a night and a day he marched fifty-eight miles north to Sligo. But on 5 September, at the village of Collooney, three hundred Limerick militia under Colonel Charles Vereker faced the French and stood up to them for a full hour, a defense that earned Vereker a peerage. Humbert, startled by such resistance from militia, which usually refused to fight, continued north to Dromahair. Then, thinking the midlands had risen, he swerved away from Ulster toward Dublin.[36]

Lake stayed on his heels, while Cornwallis kept his forces between Humbert and Dublin. The French general crossed the Shannon at Ballintra, but time finally ran out for him at Ballinamuck on 8 September. There he discovered Cornwallis with overwhelming numbers in his front, preventing further advance. Lake in his rear cut off retreat. The game Frenchman now turned and fought Lake for about half an hour, apparently to save face, and then surrendered.[37]

As a military campaign, the encounter with Humbert paled beside the great enterprises Cornwallis had undertaken in India and America. In Ireland the marquis commanded vastly superior numbers against an enemy scarcely stronger than a two-battalion regiment that also lacked the support of the countryside. Had they come earlier, the French might have aroused the peasants, but the rebellion had already burned itself out by the time they landed. Even then, had they been able to march to Dublin, they might possibly have stirred up sympathy. Cornwallis thought it his business to prevent the French from reaching Dublin, and he did. Humbert proved himself a dashing general in a hopeless cause, Cornwallis a cool, dogged commander. The methodical, careful commander in chief who faced the French in Ireland scarcely resembled the dashing, desperate lieutenant general who had fought in the Carolinas almost twenty years before.

On the whole, he had evolved a sound though not brilliant strategy to catch Humbert. By dividing his army in two, with each half vastly superior in numbers to his enemy, he could keep relentless pressure on Humbert and at the same time ensure that he did not reach Dublin.

Many people later criticized the lord lieutenant for moving too slowly, too ponderously. Cornwallis, had he chosen could have answered these critics by pointing out that slow or not, his campaign succeeded. He captured every Frenchman and deterred further peasant rebellion. Major General Moore, who had figured prominently in all the military movements in Ireland in the spring, summer, and fall of 1798, did not fault his chief's work. Rather he praised it. On 9 September, Moore visited Cornwallis at his headquarters at Lord Longford's, near Castle Pollard. There he conversed at length with the marquis, after which he wrote in his diary: "In fact, Lord Cornwallis was the only person in the army who always suspected the Shannon and Dublin to be the objects, and by guarding against them in time he prevented much mischief. He showed much prudence and judgment during the service. Considering the small force of the French . . . many persons perhaps thought he was over cautious, but he often said to me that in the present state of Ireland it would be unpardonable, for the chance of a little personal glory, to run the smallest unnecessary risk. The troops he had were bad and undisciplined, and if he had met with the least check the country was gone."[38] In any military appraisal, Moore's comments deserve at least as much credence as those of captious critics.

Meanwhile, two of the most prominent rebel leaders, the boastful James Napper Tandy and the more solemn and earnest Wolfe Tone, failed as Humbert had failed. Napper Tandy slipped through the British blockade in a frigate and landed at Rutland, where he learned of the French defeat. After a nostalgic evening with his old friend the postmaster, he sailed away to die in the service of the French army. Wolfe Tone embarked later than Tandy with a French fleet from Brest that hoped to land reinforcements for Humbert. Sir John Warren intercepted his force at sea and defeated it, capturing all but two of the French ships, as well as twenty-five hundred troops and Wolfe Tone, who went to Dublin in chains.[39]

The Courage of Clemency

Cornwallis had triumphed militarily. He now hoped to work out a policy that would preclude such a necessity for the future. He wanted to dampen animosities, smooth over old controversies, and promise a brighter future for all the Irish. He believed Ireland would never be secure for the British if the vast majority of the people continued to hate Protestants backed by a British government. As a first step toward overcoming that hatred, he favored leniency toward captured rebels.

The clique in Dublin disagreed. They believed the rebellion had occurred because the government had been too lenient to begin with, had "coddled" the Catholic peasantry. Accordingly, they now demanded executions for the ringleaders and harsh punishments for their followers. One anonymous correspondent even suggested sending all political prisoners to Siberia.[40] As the lord lieutenant observed, the clique were "blinded by their passions and prejudices" and talked of nothing but "strong measures."[41]

Cornwallis, despite their opposition, pushed for clemency. He and Portland agreed that a general act of amnesty, excluding the ringleaders, should be passed.[42] In July the marquis issued a proclamation promising pardon to any rebels still assembled who would acknowledge their guilt and renew their allegiance. But the general pardon he wanted arrived late and not in the form he wished. Such a document needed the king's signature. It ran afoul of so many objections in England that it did not receive the royal assent until October, and then it had too many exceptions.[43]

In other areas, however, the lord lieutenant had more authority. He forbade punishment without a trial, which usually took the form of a court-martial.[44] He had no illusions about the impartiality of courts-martial managed by Protestants bent on revenge against their Catholic countrymen, but he believed them better than the "numberless murders that are hourly committed by our people without any process or examination whatever."[45] The marquis necessarily tried some of the leaders for treason as a sop to embittered loyalists, and such people as the Sheares brothers went to the scaffold. But the few executions the lord lieutenant authorized so scared seventy-eight of the rebel leaders in state prisons that they petitioned Cornwallis on 24 July to sentence them to banishment instead of execution. They promised in turn to admit their part in the rebellion.

This proposition pleased Cornwallis, and he tried to secure the clique's approval as well, though without much hope that he could do so. Lord Chancellor Clare, hitherto a staunch reactionary, now unexpectedly helped him win that approval. The prisoners at first wanted to go to America, but the Americans would have nothing to do with them.[46] Then someone thought of Hamburg if only its citizens would take them.[47] Yet the rebels continued to languish in jail until March of 1799, when the British and Irish governments finally seized upon Scotland as a suitable place for their exile. Portland authorized the rebels' removal there as soon as Cornwallis received a letter from Scotland's lord advocate disclosing what provisions had been made for their lodging.[48] Finally, the main conspirators were banished to imprisonment at Fort George in Scotland. Lesser conspirators suffered various fates, including exile but not imprisonment in exile. Castlereagh estimated that about 410 people in all had been banished, some of whom went into the Prussian army. Cornwallis, the chief secretary estimated, had personally determined 400 cases and had sentenced 131 to death, of whom 81 had been executed by March of 1799. This estimate did not include the kangaroo courts set up by local officials or the regular courts-martial authorized by the generals. Overall, Castlereagh believed, the lord lieutenant's policy had "combined firmness with mercy."[49]

Moderate Help

His "mercy" met with opposition from much of the clique and even from Portland (though he had first encouraged an amnesty act) and the home government.[50] Cornwallis's acts of clemency stemmed from a firm conviction that British policy in Ireland must change. He believed that henceforward it would be the duty of lords lieutenant to promote measures that would benefit the entire country. They must never again let themselves be captured by the Anglican clique in Dublin. The British, through their lords lieutenant, had in the past followed a "desperate measure" by making an "irrevocable alliance" with this small party. The "desperate measure" had resulted in "eternal war" against the Catholics and Presbyterians, who together comprised nine-tenths of the population.[51] Cornwallis further believed that a lord lieutenant, even though appointed by the British cabinet, should oppose that cabinet if it proposed measures that he considered detrimental to Irish interests. Cornwallis, therefore, would try with or without the clique's approval to help in any way he could the majority of people entrusted to his care.

They most needed his help in the matter of getting enough to eat. One of Ireland's greatest disasters, the potato blight in the middle of the nineteenth century, would result in wholesale famine. But by 1799 and 1800, the island had already begun to suffer periodic food shortages, scarcity, and inflated prices. Already the potato had proved an uncertain blessing, owing to crop failures. In 1799, for example, the potato crop suffered. Dublin also lacked sufficient bread to feed its citizens. To feed "artificers and journeymen of every description," Cornwallis offered a bounty on the import of wheat.[52] Portland objected violently, arguing that the bounty would not increase the quantity imported but only profit the importer, and ordered him not to renew the proclamation.

The lord lieutenant reluctantly complied.[53] Yet both houses of the Irish Parliament thanked Cornwallis for his efforts.[54]

In 1800, all sources in the Irish government noted the scarcity of food. People in Ulster estimated in August that disease had destroyed a fourth of the stock of potatoes for winter and spring. The people would need bread. Yet wheat, as well, was in short supply. In September, Alexander Marsden, assistant secretary in the law department, wrote to John King, British undersecretary of state (to Portland), that, despite an abundant harvest, wheat could not be ground into flour fast enough. The mills, all turned by water, could not keep pace with the demand for bread.[55] Cornwallis tried several ways to increase the food supply. On one occasion he ordered a quantity of rice imported and sold at a very low price. He instituted a commissariat, forbade distilling, and inquired into the possibility of imports from America.[56] Portland, by contrast, thought that since wheat did not at present cost as much in Ireland as in England, the British navy should be supplied from Ireland with wheat and flour, an idea to which the marquis strenuously objected.[57]

Cornwallis hoped to educate as well as feed the Irish, and he argued for the establishment of a university for Dissenters at Armagh. He informed Portland that the late bishop of Armagh had bequeathed £5,000 to trustees for a university at Armagh if it could be incorporated within four years of his death. If not, the legacy would lapse. The marquis sensibly proposed a university for Presbyterians, the majority religion in Ulster, that would emulate the Church of England university—Trinity College—at Dublin. He then outlined the proposed administrative structure, teaching staff, and fellowships. But, as in many of his Irish projects, the British government would not cooperate. Portland told him in August of 1799 that the legacy should lapse. He reasoned speciously: that Ireland already had one university; that the late primate would not have approved a plan for "schismatics"; that Dissenters did not need a university because most of them enjoyed good incomes; and so on. He agreed that something ought to be done for the Presbyterians, but he could not suggest what. So the plan died.[58]

Cornwallis tendered other ideas in the civil and military

line: the possibility of an income tax, the creation of a treasury board to replace the lord treasurer, and closer correspondence between the police magistrates of Dublin and those of London, particularly the Bow Street ones. He advocated and saw effected the incorporation of the Irish ordnance with that of Britain, after political union.[59] He tried to maintain discipline and order in the army, and according to one observer, left the country's military system "in as perfect a state as the Resources of the Country and composition of the armed force will admit of."[60]

The lord lieutenant's efforts undoubtedly eased the tension in Ireland after "the rising of the moon." Neither startling nor strikingly original, they typified Cornwallis's approach to Irish government. Even had he wanted to do more, however, he would not have had the time. He had come to Ireland to quell rebellion and to secure a political union between Great Britain and Ireland. Having achieved the first task, the second now consumed his time and attention, demanding more from him than any work since his term as governor general of British India.

The Union

He deemed the union essential for the salvation of both England and Ireland, but undertook the means necessary to effect it with apprehension and distaste. The British government embarked upon a program of wholesale bribery to get the various members of the Irish Parliament to vote their legislature out of existence in preparation for the united Parliament. Cornwallis naturally found this job repugnant. It was made worse by the knowledge that he could not count on Portland's full support in the intricate negotiations with the touchy Irish gentry.

He had never been on the best of terms with the secretary of state and quarreled with him throughout his tenure. In October of 1798, for example, the marquis wrote to Pitt that Portland had "misrepresented" him to the ministry.[61] On another occasion, Portland made snide comments about Cornwallis's failure to deliver a list of representative peers to serve in the imperial Parliament. He quarreled with Cornwallis over the wording of a public announcement. The lord lieutenant disagreed with the home secretary's ideas about incorporating Irish militia into the regular army. On one occasion, Portland reprimanded Cornwallis for not always corresponding directly with him on Irish matters. "As your Excellency perfectly well knows," the duke scolded, "all communications whatever from the Lord Lieutenant of Ireland except upon matters of finance, should be made through the secretary of state for the Home Department as he is the only minister by whom the King's pleasure can be received and signified to the Lord Lieutenant."[62]

As far as he could, Cornwallis would act independently and then inform the British cabinet of what he had done when he thought it too late for them to alter his schemes. His was, to be sure, an arbitrary procedure. On the other hand, Pitt had given him the most difficult job (nearly, if not actually) in the British empire, and Portland's pedantic lectures did not help him accomplish it.

These lectures served to make an already unpleasant job even more so. In fact, Cornwallis became physically ill in Ireland, experiencing a recurrence of an ailment that had periodically afflicted him during the past thirty years.[63] In December of 1798, he told his son that his life was "as miserable as my bitterest enemy could wish." The marquis even repented he had not gone back to India, which by implication he thought more bearable than Ireland.[64] In December of 1800, he wrote to his brother William of his fits of despondency. "Whoever tells you," he growled, "of my being in good spirits, knows very little of what passes in my breast. It is the duty of persons who have so odious a part as mine assigned to them, to keep up appearances."[65] But not physical or mental fatigue, immense distaste for politicking, the obstruction of Portland, or the bigotry of the clique would prevent him from doing the task entrusted to him.

Fortunately, one of the more brilliant statesmen in English history aided him immensely. A son of the Earl of Londonderry (later Marquis of Londonderry), Robert Stewart, better known as Viscount Castlereagh, was in 1798 a young and rising politician, just approaching the age of thirty. He had known Irish politics from birth. His family had first won a county seat in the Irish Parliament in 1769, the year of his birth. They were wealthy and had married well—Earl Camden, Cornwallis's predecessor, was Castlereagh's step-uncle—but had long opposed the clique in Dublin

Castle. In 1790, Castlereagh had entered the political arena by winning one of the seats for County Down, at the staggering cost of £60,000.[66] At that time, because he came from a Presbyterian family, he had the support of many Dissenters, people who would in the future turn radical or rebel. He himself started out, if not as a radical, at least as a reformer. He advocated parliamentary reform, though he wanted to continue the imperial connection with Britain. He applauded the principles of the French Revolution. In 1789 he had become one of the original members of the Northern Whig Club in Belfast, copying Grattan's club in Dublin. His views changed as the 1790s progressed. The time he spent in England, including his attendance at Cambridge in 1788, gave him an admiration for Pitt. Undoubtedly he came to realize that he could not oppose government at the Castle without opposing Pitt, and he had no ambition to spend his days in perennial opposition. Furthermore, he visited France in 1791 and 1792, witnessing the French Revolution at first hand. That glimpse convinced him of its essential wrongness, and he came to prefer Edmund Burke's views on the French Revolution to those of Thomas Paine. By 1793, Castlereagh had become convinced of the necessity for a political union between Ireland and Great Britain. He opposed the extension of the vote to Catholic forty-shilling freeholders. He involved himself deeply in government measures to avert possible rebellion in Ulster in 1796. When Irish secretary Thomas Pelham fell ill in March of 1798, the then lord lieutenant, Camden, naturally asked his nephew Castlereagh to replace Pelham. In November the acting position became a permanent one.

With his long nose and handsome features, his hair cut short in the new fashion, Castlereagh looked every inch the imperious aristocrat. One can almost detect in Thomas Lawrence's portrait of the young man a self-satisfied disdain toward those less capable and fortunate than he. He was assuredly aloof, cold and distant in manner, even in the most heated situations, much like Pitt whom he so greatly admired. Yet, again like Pitt, he could be warm and gentle to a handful of intimates. The manner he displayed toward the outside world and his turning against radicalism had already earned him a share of hatred. That hatred grew with his status: his extraordinary abilities and connections pushed him from the relative insignificance of Ireland into the forefront

of English politics, until he finally became one of the most important men in the British government and one of the most outstanding diplomats in British history. The hatred of his enemies never
faltered. "I met Murder on the way—He wore a mask like Castlereagh." Though the poet Shelley wrote these words much later,
they reflected the feelings of many radical Irish in the 1790s.

Yet he was a better friend to radicals and Catholics than to
the clique, and without him the union might never have carried.
Cornwallis appreciated him immediately. Within three weeks of
his arrival, the marquis wrote to Portland that Castlereagh's "abilities, temper, and judgment, have been of the greatest use to me"
and that he had on "every occasion shown his sincere and unprej-
udiced attachment to the general interests of the British Empire." [67] He told Ross: "I have every reason to be highly satisfied
with Lord Castlereagh, who is really a very uncommon young
man, and possesses talents, temper, and judgment suited to the
highest stations, without prejudices, or any views that are not
directed to the general benefit of the British Empire." [68] When
Pelham resigned as chief secretary in November for reasons of ill
health, Cornwallis immediately asked Portland and Pitt to confirm Castlereagh in the position, which the ministry did. [69] Together, the lord lieutenant and his chief secretary approached the
task of affecting the union.

Union was certainly not a novel idea. At the beginning of
the eighteenth century, the Irish Parliament had requested legislative union with Britain as a way to overcome the trade disadvan-
tages imposed by their colonial status. [70] In 1751, a pamphlet advo-
cating union had appeared in Ireland and aroused discussion. Talk
about union had increased ever since. [71] Speculation mushroomed
in the 1790s at the time of Fitzwilliam's recall. Camden had advocated a union, though he did not consider himself the one to carry
it. By late April or May of 1798, Pitt seems to have given the matter serious attention, [72] and by the time of the marquis's appointment it was firm British policy to arrange the union. King George
told Pitt on 11 June that Cornwallis "must by a steady conduct
effect in future the Union of that Kingdom [Ireland] with this." [73]

By 1798, certain events favored the measure. The rebellion,
which British arms helped crush, had scared the chief Protestant
landlords. If they could not depend on British arms again, except

in a union, then they must necessarily favor it. The Catholics, on the whole, remained indifferent, but they might approve union should it bring them some relief from tithes to the Church of Ireland and the right to vote for and be elected to the Westminster Parliament. Reforms of the 1790s had included the enfranchisement of forty-shilling freeholders (though not their admission to Parliament); the modeling of an Irish treasury board on that of England; a reduction in the number of pensions; a rule preventing placemen from sitting in the Commons, including the holders of all offices created after 1793; and a denial of the vote to revenue officials. These measures had helped shift the balance of Irish political power and had favored union. Another important measure was the provision of escheatorships. The historian G. C. Bolton contends: "Hitherto it had been impossible for a member to vacate his seat during the lifetime of a Parliament. Now, as well as retiring because of ill health, residence abroad, or desire to transfer to another constituency, a member could vacate his seat whenever it facilitated official arrangements or suited the wishes of his patron. But for this provision it is doubtful the Union could have been carried." [74]

Elections in 1797 had returned a Parliament not dissimilar to ones in the past. Of the 300 members, about 50 regularly opposed government, about 50 remained uncommitted, and about 200 regularly supported government. Of these 200, 10 sat directly for government boroughs, 4 were law officers who purchased their seats, 7 were independent county members, four sat for their own boroughs, 12 had purchased borough seats, and the 163 others were attached to parliamentary connections. [75] A political crisis would decide whether they would continue to support the government in the hope of patronage or join the heads of factions in opposition.

Prominent Irish families controlled the borough and county seats, which represented a sizable investment: the borough of Gorey cost £2,300 in 1796. These seats were also the stepping stones to patronage. The "ascendancy" (prominent families with much invested) included the Beresfords, Lords Shannon and Ely, Lord Downshire, and the Earls of Belmore and Enniskillen. The Marquis of Abercorn alone controlled forty-three seats. These people supported the government when a pliant lord lieutenant did their bidding.

From their point of view, one of the best ways he could do that bidding was to use his patronage to their advantage. Government jobs, important in Britain, were even more important in Ireland. The country had a far less diversified economy than Britain, with subsequently fewer professions men could pursue and still remain in "respectable" society. Land remained a far greater measure of wealth in Ireland than in mercantile, rapidly industrializing England. No one whose rent roll came to less than £5,000 per year could hope for a peerage, and rents were the only "respectable" way to make a living aside from government jobs. The ascendancy would not stoop to trade, although they thrived in the practice of law, which then as now was a pathway to government work. They, like the Virginia planters, tended to live grandly and spend lavishly, often beyond their income. The way to recovery of their fortunes again lay in government positions, which paid well. Patronage, or the search for jobs, thus tended to dominate politics. Under these circumstances they opposed any measure, including concessions to Catholics, that might break their tight circle, challenge their control, and lead to a loss of jobs.

The lord lieutenant would have to move carefully. To get the ascendancy to vote their Parliament out of existence would necessitate compensating them elsewhere, with seats in the imperial Parliament at Westminster, with peerages, with jobs, or with direct monetary payment. Patronage, used intelligently, would help most in counties where the government and the antiunionist forces were evenly matched. Even though Cornwallis controlled patronage, however, some of his views generated hostility. Unlike the king, the British cabinet, and the ascendancy, he wholeheartedly favored concessions to Catholics, including the all-important ones of allowing them to vote for and sit in the Westminster Parliament. He urged the Catholic cause time and again. He told Portland in 1798: "If England should be obliged to make an union with a party in Ireland, instead of making it with the Irish nation, I shall sincerely lament that necessity, altho' I may consider it as a misfortune at present unavoidable. But I trust that your grace and His Majesty's other ministers will on no account consent to the insertion of any clause which shall unalterably bind the United Parliament to persevere in the exclusion of Catholics."[76] Earlier he had pointed out that "some mode must be adopted to soften the hatred of the Catholics to our government," he hoped by "advantage held out to them from an union with Great Britain."[77] In October he appealed to Pitt directly for Catholic emancipation.[78] He urged the cause so continually because, as he told Pelham, it was "the only measure that can give permanent tranquillity to this wretched country."[79] From the long perspective of history, it is abundantly clear, at least to the authors, that Cornwallis was right and almost everyone else in any position of power was wrong.

His closest ally in working for union, Lord Chancellor Clare, adamantly opposed emancipation, as did the entire ascendancy. Clare represented their sentiments when he told Castlereagh: "I should have hoped that what has passed would have opened the eyes of every man in England to the insanity of their past conduct, with respect to the papists of Ireland; but I can plainly perceive that they were as full of their papish projects as ever. I trust, and I hope I am not deceived, that they are fairly inclined to give them up, and to bring the measure [union] forward unencumbered with the doctrine of emancipation."[80]

More important than the ascendancy's opposition was the king's. George III told Pitt, after approving Cornwallis's appointment as lord lieutenant: "But Lord Cornwallis must clearly understand that no indulgence can be granted to the Catholics farther than has been, I am afraid unadvisedly, done, in former Session, and that he must by a steady conduct effect in future the Union of that Kingdom."[81]

Cornwallis's leniency toward the rebels and his disdain for the clique, save for Lord Clare, also sparked resentment. He disparaged their past achievements and scorned their selfishness. In their turn, the ascendancy, and even the minor officials in his government, disapproved his approach. Edward Cooke, for example, could find almost nothing good to say of his superior. He thought Cornwallis did not work hard enough and told William Eden, Lord Auckland: "Lord Cornwallis nobody—worse than nobody—his silly conduct, his total incapacity, and self conceit and mulishness have alone lost the question [union]."[82] Colonel Robert Ross, M.P. for Newry, lamented: "For Heaven's sake do not let poor Ireland fall a sacrifice to the madness and dotage of a very silly old Indian bitch."[83] Dr. Patrick Dueignan, a rabid Protestant, like so many of the newly converted, told Castlereagh that the "unaccountable" conduct of the marquis had "rendered him not only an object of disgust, but of abhorrence."[84] Cornwallis returned these feelings. For example, he said Cooke possessed a "narrow-minded jealousy," inexcusable in "so clever a fellow."[85] Thus he had to work with people whom he disliked and who disliked him.

Moreover, the lord lieutenant's personality and habits of a lifetime contended with the type of approach that alone could deal with those very people he already disliked. Cornwallis had ever found jobbery, persuasion, promises, threats, and all the other gimmicks of politicking distasteful. He may not have felt them beneath his dignity, for he knew as well as anyone that they formed the stuff of eighteenth-century political life, but he preferred to leave them to others. "Here I am," he told Ross, "embarked in all my troubles, and employed in a business which is ill-suited to my taste, and for which I am afraid I am not qualified."[86]

Nonetheless, he plunged into the political maelstrom, and in November of 1798 began concentrating his energies on carrying the union. He sounded out opinion. He asked for an Irish peerage for the wife of a former chief secretary. He cajoled the speaker, John Foster, an adamant opponent of union. He threatened. He dismissed from office people he could not persuade. For example, he fired Sir John Parnell, chancellor of the exchequer, and replaced him with a union supporter. He fired the prime sergeant, James Fitzgerald, as well.[87] On the whole, he dealt only with the top people, the wealthiest and most influential. Castlereagh worked with the others.

Despite their politicking, however, they did not go to extraordinary lengths to "buy" votes. They made an initial mistake in definitely promising only two peerages and intimating two others.[88] They also made other mistakes, as did the British government. Dublin Castle seemed unable to stop rumors of all sorts. Even before the British government had made its intentions clear or Cornwallis had drafted a tentative plan, people all over Ireland discussed the imminence of a union.[89] The most important people in Irish politics visited England between November of

1798 and January of 1799—Speaker Foster, Chancellor of the Exchequer Parnell, Commissioner of Revenue Sir John Beresford, Lord Chancellor Clare, and Chief Secretary Castlereagh. The British ministers showed these men tentative plans for the union, plans which the latter in turn leaked to their colleagues back home. But the various plans differed, and the British kept altering them up to the time they wished the matter introduced into Parliament.

Some features, based primarily on suggestions by Castlereagh, remained similar in all the drafts. Like Scotland, Ireland would send to the House of Lords representative lay peers (twenty-eight of them) elected for life, as well as one archbishop and three bishops. Unlike Scotland, those Irish peers not sent by their fellows to Lords could stand for election to Commons. These arrangements seemed reasonable, because more than forty Irish Lords were already members of the British peerage as well. Irish representation in Commons was not to exceed one hundred people. Yet the British did not explain how they could achieve that magic number and at the same time ensure that no one lost "property," since 118 boroughs and 20 counties sent members to the Irish Parliament. As the historian of the union, G. C. Bolton, has noted: "County members could scarcely welcome a plan which halved their numbers and exposed them to keener contests at future general elections; and borough proprietors faced a diminution of the value of their property, into which many of them had invested hard cash, and for which they might expect improved prices with the return of stability. It was one of the facts of Irish political life that boroughs were regarded as property, and no provision for compensation was adumbrated in the Union proposals." [90]

As the time approached for parliamentary debate on union, scheduled for January of 1799, opposition grew, especially in Dublin. An assembly of lawyers, called by the barrister William Saurin, met on 9 December 1798 and by acclamation supported a motion against union. To the chronically underemployed Irish lawyers the Parliament represented jobs. They usually opposed government in any event and certainly did not wish to see the abolition of the Parliament in which sixty-seven of their number sat. On 18 December, a group of merchants and bankers of Dublin met at the Mansion House and also declared against union. [91]

Pamphlet propaganda against union spread over the country. "Pamphlets swarm," Cooke observed.[92]

Yet at first government took no effective countermeasures. It did not test opinion in any of the counties or literate public opinion as a whole. Its pamphlet propaganda did not match that of the opposition. Because of such developments, the lord lieutenant began to harbor doubts about the initial success of the government's plans. Although optimistic in November, by mid-December he anticipated failure. He wrote Portland on the fifteenth that the union "cannot be carried through Parliament without allowing on both sides of the water much time for deliberation and arrangement."[93] Castlereagh, by contrast, continued to believe even in January that the measure would carry, though he knew as early as 5 January that the opposition claimed 113 members who opposed even taking the measure into consideration. On 21 January, he believed he could count on 160 to 170 members to support the government, whereas in fact he only got the votes of 104.[94]

The British planned to propose the measure to both the British and Irish Parliaments at the same time, on 22 January, when the British Parliament reconvened. Identical addresses from the king and from the lord lieutenant stressing the necessity for stronger ties between the two kingdoms would go to the respective Parliaments. The government hoped that these addresses would evoke general answers, that the Parliaments could fix a day for discussing the matter, perhaps 5 February, and that joint addresses from both houses would then request the appointment of commissioners to negotiate a union.[95]

Very little in Ireland worked as planned, although the House of Lords approved Cornwallis's address, after very little debate, by a vote of 52 to 16. The address did not fare so well in the Commons. One motion, "that the House would be ready to enter any measures, short of surrendering their free, resident, and independent legislature as established in 1782," lost by only one vote, 105 to 106. A division favoring the address carried by only two votes, 107 to 105.[96] Castlereagh now realized the hopelessness of his position. He could not prevail with such slim majorities, so he promised the House that he would not pursue the matter of union further at the present time.[97]

The government now had to change its tactics if it hoped to

round up the necessary votes. Castlereagh, indeed, admitted his own tactical failure. The opposition had fooled him, he told Portland, by attacking the address from the lord lieutenant before union was embodied in a specific bill, a maneuver that had caught him off guard. He also had not talked to all the M.P.s before the opening of Parliament. Had he done so, he might have converted some of the borough mongers from lukewarm supporters of government into enthusiastic ones. He could have done little about the men who had simply lied to him, but he might better have used a combination of threats and rewards. He concluded, guardedly, that he could carry union only by catering primarily to the greed of the members: "I should despair of the success of the measure at any future period, so weighty is the opposition of the country gentlemen in our house, were I not convinced that their repugnance turns more upon points of personal interest, than a fixed aversion to the principle of union."[98]

Castlereagh now worked with Cornwallis methodically to satisfy that personal interest. The British government promised them its full support. On 26 January, Pitt and Portland gave Cornwallis nearly a carte blanche to hire and fire, to threaten and cajole, and to use any other method deemed necessary to carry the union. "I hope it is unnecessary," Portland asserted, "to assure your excellency that whatever your decisions may be you may depend upon their receiving the unreserved sanction and support of His Majesty's servants."[99]

Backed by such assurances, Cornwallis and Castlereagh began the job of tabulating lists of pro- and antiunionists, figuring out for each individual the appropriate blandishment or inducement or penalty.[100] They believed, especially, that they needed to get a wide range of support from the various counties, which would make it appear, when the Parliament met again, that the propertied interests throughout the country supported union. Though Dublin belonged to the opposition, the government might secure favorable petitions and addresses from corporations elsewhere, as it previously had from the mayor, sheriffs, and common council of Cork.[101] Government could encourage resolutions from freeholders, convened by the sheriffs, for the freeholders represented propertied opinion. It could use the grand jury to sample public opinion. The jury consisted of twenty-three "of the most reputable freeholders in the county," and, aside from their judicial duties and administrative work, they often expressed themselves on public issues.[102] The lord lieutenant and chief secretary could undertake this ambitious program as long as they never forgot, using patronage or promises of future rewards, to concentrate on the most important people who controlled the most seats.

Cornwallis plunged into the work almost as tirelessly as his younger chief secretary. He made two exhausting goodwill journeys, one to the center and south of Ireland in July, the other to the north in October. The presence of his son, Lord Brome, made the first tour much pleasanter for him than it might otherwise have been. Brome, now a young man of twenty-five, had come to Ireland on 7 June with his wife of two years, Louisa, daughter of the fourth Duke of Gordon. Five feet seven inches tall, of a pleasant disposition but uncertain health, and in appearance more like his mother than his father, Brome was in one sense the reason Cornwallis served in Ireland. The marquis had no other son to continue the family name, so that all his hopes lay in Brome. Perhaps Cornwallis had best expressed his view toward public service and his son in a letter from India on 6 March 1787. "I have no wish for any honors," he told Brome, "but as they may offer the road for fame and reputation to you. I have no desire to increase my fortune, but as it may tend to increase your happiness. It is for you that I am toiling."[103]

With Brome there, his father could at least relieve the toil with talk about the improvements still carrying on at Culford, the cost of the new bridge's foundations, the abundance or scarcity of the partridge, and those other local matters dear to the hearts of most eighteenth-century aristocrats. Indeed, perhaps that gossip and Brome's presence alone enabled Cornwallis to carry on with a business he disliked so much. He was now getting into the seamier side of Irish politics, and he did not like it. About the time Brome arrived, Cornwallis told Ross: "My occupation is now of the most unpleasant nature, negotiating and jobbing with the most corrupt people under heaven. I despise and hate myself every hour for engaging in such dirty work, and am supported only by the reflection that without an Union the British Empire must be dissolved."[104] Partly because of this "dirty work," however, Cornwallis and his son met a generally favorable reception on the July tour. Perhaps because of the "dirty work," perhaps because of the danger, Louisa did not accompany her husband but remained behind in Phoenix Park with Lady Castlereagh. Certainly danger was always present, as Cornwallis was harshly reminded after his return. On the evening of 11 August he decided to walk alone to the Castle from Phoenix Park. During his stroll, a man disguised as a sentry on duty, supposedly a United Irishman, shot at the lord lieutenant and then fled.[105] Shortly after that incident, Brome and his wife left, probably to the marquis's mingled relief and regret.

He had no family to cheer him on his second trip in early October. But, as in the first one, he encountered a generally cordial reception. The lord lieutenant's military secretary, Lieutenant Colonel Edward Littlehales, wrote from Belfast that "nothing could have succeeded better than Lord Cornwallis's visit to this place: all classes and descriptions of persons have been forward in manifesting every mark of respect and attention to his Excellency."[106]

The two tours comprised only part of the talking and the jobbing, which continued into 1800. None of it pleased Cornwallis, but perhaps he most disliked his dealings with Lord Downshire, who controlled a following of eight members. Downshire had visited Ireland only once in the past three years and depended on his agents there, Protestants bitterly opposed to Cornwallis's policy of clemency, to see to his interests. For some time Downshire had seemed to straddle the fence, appearing open to the idea of union. The marquis tried hard to win him over, even though he disliked the work and the man. As he told Ross: "To court a proud, ill-tempered, violent fellow, raised to any importance by the weakness of former Governments, and who, if he had the power, would in a week drive this wretched country again into rebellion, is a pill almost too bitter for me to swallow. . . . Nothing but a conviction that an Union is absolutely necessary for the safety of the British Empire, could make me endure the shocking task which is imposed upon me."[107] The task became more shocking when Downshire—far from supporting union—declared openly against it by getting his regiment of militia in early February 1800 to sign a petition opposing it.[108] When he learned of this near treasonable affront, that the regiment had signed at their colonel's behest, the marquis suspended Downshire, depriving him of his command. A seemingly contrite Downshire approached Cornwallis on 7 February and said he could not understand the lord lieutenant's attitude, since Downshire had not forced anyone to sign the petition. Freeholders did so of their own volition. Cornwallis replied, in effect, that the former colonel lied and then dressed him down for his entire conduct since his return to Ireland. The legislature had already by then started debates on the union, and the lord lieutenant could not allow the impression that the militia opposed the legislature. Indeed, he did not even allow Downshire the court-martial he requested, because it would contain many officers whom Cornwallis believed "active partizans against the measure of the Union." [109] Though Portland stuttered a bit, the cabinet backed Cornwallis in his action. So did King George III, who formally dismissed the obstreperous peer from his offices (colonel of Downshire militia and governor of County Down) and ordered his name struck from the privy council. [110]

The lord lieutenant thought the arrogant colonel's dismissal one of the most important measures for union. "The turn which it has given to the public mind is astonishing," he told Ross, "and all our friends say that by this act of vigour I have saved the country and the Union." But he continued to be apprehensive and admitted to Pitt that he would not rest until the union finally became law. [111] Indeed, he went on working and working. He fired three revenue commissioners from around Dublin, replacing them with men from Clark, Cork, and Kerry who favored union. He promised patronage and peerages. Eighteen new peerages would result from his work on the union, and at least eleven of these would come from the eastern counties. [112] Even after union seemed assured, as late as April of 1800, he forwarded to London the grand jury sentiment from Armagh and Cork favoring union and also countered antiunion sentiments expressed by resolutions and addresses at the assizes.

Cornwallis kept on trying to get the Catholics to back the union. He wanted to offer them some inducement to support it, but he could get no assurance from the home government that Catholics would have any rights to participate in the new government, only the vague prospect that their best chance for more

246 / Cornwallis: The Imperial Years

rights lay in a union and a united Parliament.[113] In the end, he could only hope that wherever Protestant influence was unimportant he could at least keep the goodwill, if not the enthusiasm, of the Catholics.

The efforts continued while Cornwallis and Castlereagh counted votes. By the time they believed they had enough, Castlereagh estimated that the annual landed income in both houses of those who favored union was £1,058,200, while that against was only £358,500. For resident lay peers alone it was £606,800 to £179,000 and for commoners £268,900 to £144,500. Even the bishops and the absentee peers outmonied the opposition by £182,500 to £35,000.[114] In the end, securing the union did not involve remarkable corruption, at least by Irish standards. The Irish government, on the assumption that every former borough owner deprived of his constituency thereby lost property, promised each one £15,000 in compensation, for which every deprived owner applied. The government also offered jobs and pensions, but Cornwallis was not as lavish. The increase in his pension list was small compared to that of his predecessor. What he and Castlereagh really did was work hard, offer sufficient inducement, keep within the traditions of Irish politics, and hope for the best.

Their work came to the test when Parliament convened on 15 January 1800. Government had abandoned the idea of commissioners and now hoped to get the articles of union through the Irish Parliament and thereafter through the British one. This time Castlereagh did not intend to let the opposition beat him tactically. Though he found it difficult to determine which Irish boroughs to disenfranchise, he eventually decided to eliminate the least populous ones. In the absence of a reliable census, the records of window and hearth taxes formed the basis for determining which boroughs would have representation at Westminster. The owners of the disenfranchised boroughs, of course, received £15,000 compensation, as previously agreed.[115] The government's initial insistence that the king could continue creating Irish peerages after the union met staunch opposition in the upper house. The Irish peers feared cheapening of the value of the peerage if such honors went to minor functionaries unworthy to sit in the British House of Lords, but who might nonetheless challenge the existing Irish

peers for election as representatives to sit there. Cornwallis compromised on this issue. He agreed that the king would create no
more than one Irish peer for every three that became extinct. This
promise mollified the peers, who then supported union.[116]

Success finally rewarded all these efforts at placating injured self-interest. On 28 March 1800, Cornwallis forwarded to
Portland the resolutions of both houses in favor of union with
Britain.[117] Castlereagh, on 21 May, carried a motion for permission to bring in a bill for the Act of Union. After debate, both
houses passed the bill itself in June. In the name of the king, whom
he represented, the lord lieutenant assented to it on 1 August. He
told Ross: "There was not a murmur heard in the street, nor I
believe an expression of ill-humour throughout the whole city of
Dublin."[118] Pitt steered a similar measure through the British
Parliament.

Thus, on 1 January 1801, the United Kingdom of Great
Britain and Ireland came into existence. By provisions of the act
creating it, eighty-four Irish boroughs had been disenfranchised
and thirty-four retained, each of the latter to send one member to
Westminster, save Dublin and Cork, which would send two.
Counties returned the same number to the united Parliament as
they had sent to the Irish one. The lords elected for life twenty-
eight temporal peers to sit in the imperial House of Lords, together with four bishops serving in rotation. The Church of England
and the Church of Ireland united. The Irish received all the trade
privileges of the British, and the Catholics got nothing.[119]

Unfinished Business

The union, despite its faults, represented a very considerable achievement. Undoubtedly, Castlereagh did much of the
work, as Cornwallis frequently acknowledged. But no less an
astute observer than Lord Chancellor Clare attributed much of the
success to Cornwallis. He wrote to Camden: "Certainly Lord
Cornwallis has had much of the merit which attaches to our success in the measure. So far as he found it absolutely necessary he
did stoop against his nature to the political traffick imposed upon
him, and without committing himself in any manner to our Irish

chiefs, he continued to gain their confidence. . . . I am now quite satisfied that he has on the whole been the man of all others best selected for the crisis."[120]

Certainly the signs seemed auspicious by the time the lord lieutenant dissolved the Irish Parliament. Enthusiastic crowds greeted him on a goodwill tour throughout the island. Ultimately the union even won the approval of the Dubliners, who thronged to see him as he went in a procession from Dublin Castle to St. Patrick's Cathedral. With "cheerful countenances" they shouted, "there he is; that's he" and often said "God bless him." "Not an unpleasant circumstance," the marquis reflected, "to a man who has governed a country above two years by martial law."[121]

But despite these outward signs, the crisis remained. It would end, he believed, only when the British government made good its promises to him and when it granted the Catholics emancipation. He anticipated no difficulty in getting the British cabinet to honor his commitments. After all, its members had repeatedly assured him of their support in this matter. On 3 June 1800, the lord lieutenant wrote to Portland: "As the time is now drawing near when we shall have a difficult and heavy account to settle, it becomes necessary that I should lose no time in laying before you such part of the engagements into which I have been obliged to enter, as will require the assistance of your Grace and His Majesty's most confidential servants."[122] Shortly thereafter, the lord lieutenant forwarded to the home secretary a list of sixteen men, with their background and work, to whom he had promised Irish peerages: the titles would serve as rewards for their support as borough proprietors, as compensation for the cost of their buying seats to return government supporters to Parliament, or as compensation previously promised to veteran supporters.[123]

Portland balked, hedged, and refused much of what the marquis requested; Pitt did not even reply.[124] Cornwallis, who had pledged his honor, now threatened to resign: "When the promise was given I thought that I had made a good bargain for the public, and in the progress of the business I have seen no cause to alter my opinion; but whether the agreement was advantageous or otherwise, I am bound in honor to stand by it, and I should feel myself a degraded man if I gave my consent to its being set aside. There was no sacrifice that I should not have been happy to make for the service of my king and country, except that of honor." If the government did not fulfill its engagements, he hoped the king would be "pleased to allow me to retire from a station which I could no longer hold with honour to myself, or with any prospect of advantage to the service." [125]

Castlereagh supported his superior in indignant letters to his uncle Camden and to Cooke. He told Camden:

> I confess it appears to me that Lord Cornwallis, having been directed to undertake and carry the measure of Union, and having been fully authorized, by various despatches, to make arrangements with individuals, to which not only the faith of his own but of the English Government was understood to be pledged, will be very harshly treated, if the wisdom of his arrangements, now the measure is secured, is to be canvassed at a moment when the pressing necessities under which these arrangements were made cannot but be very fresh in the recollection even of persons on the spot, but certainly cannot be fairly estimated by those who were removed from the scene of the government.
>
> If the Irish Government is not enabled to keep faith with the various individuals who have acted upon a principle of confidence in their honour, it is morally impossible, my dear Lord, that either Lord Cornwallis or I can remain in our present situation.

To Cooke he observed satirically: "And I should hope, if Lord Cornwallis has been the person to buy out and secure to the Crown for ever the fee-simple of Irish corruption, which has so long enfeebled the powers of Government and endangered the connection, that he is not to be the first sacrifice to his own exertions." [126] Cooke, in turn, badgered undersecretary John King to plead personally for support. [127] King constantly attended Portland and might influence his decisions.

Cajoled by their servants and threatened with the resignation of a lord lieutenant and chief secretary who had crushed rebellion, carried out an act of union, and in every instance done what the British government had asked, Pitt, Portland, and the entire cabinet backed down. On 27 June, Portland assured the marquis that the government would fulfill its promises. [128] Then, for some strange reason, the cabinet that had initially balked at fulfilling Cornwallis's modest promises now went to the opposite extreme. Far from resisting Irish requests, in the remaining months of 1800 it approved Irish peerages almost on request. In December it recommended nine new baronies, none of which had much to do with the union one way or another.[129] Cornwallis marveled at the cabinet's prodigality. "Everything has been given of late with a most profuse hand," he observed to Castlereagh, "and the points which I neither asked nor recommended have been acceded to more readily than those for which the honour of my Government was engaged, and on which the success of the Union depended."[130]

The cabinet did not, however, hold out an open hand to the Catholics. Cornwallis nonetheless persisted in urging Catholic relief.[131] "I shall continue," he said in December 1800, "to press the adoption of the measure which can alone in my opinion give quiet or security to this country. When that point is either carried or rejected, I shall have no other object but that of dozing away the remainder of my days quietly at Culford."[132] He told Ross that if the British government rejected Catholic emancipation, he would resign as lord lieutenant. Should the Catholics receive their relief, however, he might stay and "endeavour to turn it to the best account."[133] He pressed Portland on the issue, and Castlereagh prepared a tract of several hundred pages urging concessions to Catholics.

Unfortunately, these concessions did not come. George III's sense of duty, which had figured importantly in the irreparable loss of his thirteen colonies, now irreparably damaged Anglo-Irish relations. At the end of January 1801, he spoke publicly against Catholic emancipation.[134] Pitt, on the contrary, drew up a memorandum urging it and requested permission to resign if the king would not concur. At this impasse, George then proposed what must have seemed to him a compromise. He would say no more about the issue if Pitt would not introduce it again. Pitt refused. On 5 February 1801, George III, with deep regret, accepted the resignation of his first minister, rather than, in his own words, "forego what I look on as my duty."[135]

Not all the cabinet resigned with Pitt, for party solidarity of the modern sort had not yet developed. Indeed, Portland, Westmorland, Liverpool, and Chatham (Pitt's older brother) had opposed emancipation, heeding the arguments of such anti-Catholics as Clare, and had urged their views on the king. Catholic relief, furthermore, was by no means popular in England. Under these circumstances, George III simply appointed a new cabinet, including in it members of the previous administration who had disagreed with Pitt. On 14 March, Henry Addington, speaker of the House of Commons (who had tried to dissuade Pitt from resigning) took leadership of the new administration.[136]

Neither Cornwallis nor Castlereagh could now remain in office. They had both committed themselves too deeply to Catholic relief. Cornwallis believed that emancipation alone would keep Ireland in the empire. According to one story, when Brome was asked who would succeed his father in Ireland, assuming emancipation failed, he replied: "Bonaparte."[137] Even Cornwallis's vehement critic Cooke had changed his views and now believed the lord lieutenant correct. He pleaded emancipation for Dissenters and Catholics in an eloquent letter to Clare in February and resigned when emancipation failed. From then on he became one of the strongest champions of the Catholic cause. Cornwallis himself agreed to remain in office only until his successor should arrive in Dublin. He would not quit in a huff, but he would certainly quit the day his successor arrived and use the time remaining to him to try, in his own words, to "tranquillize the minds of the Catholics."[138]

When he learned in March that Philip Yorke, the third Earl of Hardwicke, was to replace him, he put Dublin Castle in order for the new lord lieutenant's reception and retired to Phoenix Park. The British government, however, procrastinated, and March gave way to April and May. Finally, Hardwicke arrived aboard the *Dorset* at six in the morning on 25 May. Upon his landing, the guns on the south wall in Phoenix Park fired a salute. A parade through Dublin followed, after which Cornwallis received him in the Castle. Hardwicke was then sworn into office, invested with the collar of the Order of St. Patrick, and given the sword of state.[139]

Three days later Charles, first Marquis Cornwallis, former governor general of British India, and former lord lieutenant of Ireland, reached Holyhead. As usual with his voyages, bad weather prevented his arriving sooner.[140] But in all likelihood it had been his last such delay. Could he not, in his old age, look forward at last to a well-earned peaceful and honorable retirement?

Chapter 12

Last Calls of Duty

Frequently in the past the old soldier had proclaimed his preference for retirement over work, but then it had been a statement more of shadow than substance, uttered ritually for the sake of form. Ireland, however, had taken some of the old zeal for service out of him. It had weakened and tired him and made him periodically ill. One feels he might really have wished to quit this time. But the ministry would not leave him alone.

Amiens

He arrived in London on 27 May 1801.[1] From there he traveled to his beloved Culford for a much deserved rest, but had little time to enjoy it. Rumors circulated of a projected French invasion. Who better to organize the protection of the eastern district than the experienced general, a veteran of the Seven Years' War, the American Revolution, the Mysore War, the Flanders campaign, and the Irish rebellion? On 22 July, Cornwallis received a letter from the Duke of York recommending him to command the eastern district, a prospect that, the marquis lamented, "deranges all my plans," especially since he would enter on the new assignment without horses, house, or aides-de-camp. He would rather "have received an order to go to Egypt."[2] Nevertheless, he could not refuse the call of duty. He arrived at Colchester on Wednesday afternoon, 29 July, hired a house, and took over his new command.[3]

He was not pleased with it. Initially he had only, as he told Ross, "eight weak regiments of militia, making about 2800 firelocks, and two regiments of dragoons."[4] He set about to improve and strengthen his forces. A few weeks' work brought some success. *The Times* reported that by 17 August he commanded about eight thousand infantry, one regiment of cavalry, and thirty pieces of field ordnance.[5] He had increased the infantry, but had lost some cavalry in the process. He found the work of inspecting fortifications and managing supplies dreary and tiresome. He also found it increasingly unnecessary, for it became ever more apparent that Bonaparte did not intend to invade England. Having made himself supreme against all his enemies on the Continent, for a variety of reasons Napoleon wished to make peace, if he could get it on his own terms.

Louis Guillaume Otto, Comte de Mosley, Napoleon's agent for exchange of prisoners, had talked about peace as early as the autumn of 1800.[6] Now, a year later, it seemed an imminent possibility. Bonaparte's venture in Egypt verged on failure for want of a French fleet to supply, reinforce, or even evacuate his army there. Major General Hely-Hutchinson had already taken Cairo, and the British army now prepared to capture all French forces in Egypt.

But though the British navy had foiled him in Egypt and elsewhere, on the Continent Bonaparte reigned supreme. Austria was out of the war. Napoleon had mastered the Low Countries, Switzerland, northern Italy, and the south Italian ports. He was the ally of Spain and the friend of Prussia and Russia. Under these circumstances, the British people wanted peace. Subsidies to European allies had not stopped France, obviously, but had merely increased the costs of war and drained the Bank of England's reserves. The scarcity and high price of bread had caused a few riots.[7]

Napoleon also wanted a breather. He knew his Egyptian venture was about to collapse and he wanted time to consolidate his territorial gains and build up his navy. He, however, dissimulated better than the British. He adopted an air of arrogant indulgence toward his enemy in the hope of winning one concession after another in any ensuing peace arrangements. His invasion plan, for example, had been pure bluff. It had scared the English, although after bombarding Boulogne, Nelson had concluded that the craft Bonaparte had assembled could neither row nor sail to England.[8]

In any event, the Addington ministry, devoted to peace and retrenchment, opened negotiations in May of 1801 with Otto. So anxious were the British for peace that in London the stock market rose or fell as rumors circulated about the success or failure of the talks. On 4 September, for example, *The Times* reported a fall in stock prices when a story spread that Bonaparte had recalled Otto. He had not done so, but so intense was the concern for peace that *The Times* traced the tale to a stockbroker who had taken lodgings at Hamstead to be near the French diplomat. There he had counted couriers and watched the progress of conversations. At one point he had collared Otto's housemaid, who had told him her master was "going to leave his house,"[9] a statement, as it turned out, utterly false. But such was the desire for peace that the English watched every development. The government wanted peace, the opposition in Parliament wanted peace, and the people as a whole wanted peace.

Talks, however, dragged on through September, apparently bringing the two nations no closer to an understanding. Toward the end of the month, Bonaparte decided to break the deadlock and hasten the prospects of an agreement. He learned of the utter collapse of his forces in Egypt and instructed Otto to complete negotiations by 2 October, before the English could make much of this new development.[10]

On 3 October, Londoners learned of an imminent cease-fire and illuminated their streets that night. Throughout the month, as the rest of England learned the news, boundless joy spread. Fetes, illuminations, feux de joie, parades, speeches, and salutes gladdened the inhabitants of Bristol, Lewes, Harwich, Hull, Plymouth, Bury, Lynn, Stamford, Northampton, Chichester, Birmingham, Poole, Norwich, and elsewhere. "It is a curious fact," *The Times* reported, "that some soldiers at Ipswich actually kissed the wheels of the coach, on its return [from Norwich with news of the peace] in the evening, and many scores of them came out of the barracks on hearing the acclamations of peace."[11] The government did not authorize official illuminations until 11 October, when the French actually ratified the preliminary articles.

On that night London again blazed with lights. A mob of people passing through Pall Mall broke every window and windowframe of a bookseller's house when the owner refused to illuminate.[12] The day before, when one of Napoleon's aides-de-camp arrived at St. James's with the ratification of the preliminary articles, a big crowd, with loud cheers, unharnessed the horses and drew him in triumph through the streets.[13] Perhaps the doggerel verse of a glazier in Shoreditch best captured the popular sentiment:

Let's drink their health by way of motto:
Here's to Lord Hawkesbury and Monsieur Otto!
As I approve of the peace in toto,
May he that breaks it be shot-o.[14]

No matter how much celebrated, preliminaries were not definitive articles. To hammer out the final peace and sign the final treaty, the government had to send a person of high reputation and proven ability to Amiens, the place appointed for the formal conclusion of negotiations. To whom would the cabinet turn for this delicate but exciting mission?

Cornwallis learned early that it wanted to turn to him. Unenthusiastically, he told Ross that he felt "out of sorts, low-spirited, and tired of everything."[15] But duty called, and he, of course, accepted the new task. As he told his brother William: "I have long considered peace to be necessary for the preservation of our country, and I did not therefore feel myself at liberty to refuse the mission when it was pressed upon me, although nothing could be more disagreeable to me."[16] Toward the middle of October, the marquis left Culford for London and took up lodgings at Grafton Street. In the capital he received a ministerial briefing as well as a gala dinner with the prime minister.[17]

Cornwallis remained in London long enough to hear remarks in Parliament on the peace and to ready himself for an unduly lavish progress to France. Both the British and French governments wanted to put on a show for their people, and each made elaborate preparations. Cornwallis gathered for his trip a town coach, a town chariot, and a traveling coach. The resplendent town coach, painted yellow, with arms, supporters, crests, and the emblem of the Order of the Garter, contained reclining cushions of silk and morocco. The marquis sent on ahead twelve horses, their harnesses ornamented with silver, and their reins, tassels, and toppings decorated with silk button hangers. Although he took with him only Lord Brome and a small staff, he had sixteen servants and three king's messengers.[18]

Preparations made, he left London at six in the morning on 3 November. The subsequent journey became a sort of triumphal parade. When he passed through Canterbury to arrive at the King's Head, the populace released the horses from the carriage and drew him through the city. On his arrival at Dover, he stayed at the York House Inn. Shortly after eight the next morning he embarked aboard the *Swift* for Calais. Foul weather and rough seas tossed the *Swift* on its way to Calais, where it arrived twelve hours later. There Fort Rouge saluted Cornwallis with twelve guns, and the authorities met him with a detachment of cavalry and infantry amid the ringing of bells and a general illumination. He proceeded on foot to his hotel, Lion d'Argent, where a guard of fifty grenadiers and a picket of chasseurs honored him.[19] And so it went all the way to Paris. Bonaparte had ordered a great number of laborers to mend the roads, had stationed a relay of thirty officers at every post, and had ordered municipal officers to receive him at the entrance of every town. He reached Paris on 7 November, escorted by 150 Hussars.

In the capital, festivities mingled with business. On the ninth, Paris put on a grand festival of peace, and during his stay Cornwallis visited the Tuileries, the national gallery of paintings, and the powerless legislature which Napoleon had created to rubber-stamp his policies. The guileless British envoy also met Talleyrand, the wily former bishop who now served as the French foreign minister; Joseph Bonaparte, who would carry on the negotiations for the French; and even briefly the "First Consul" himself.[20]

His private interview with Napoleon on 28 November, two days before his departure for Amiens, proved eminently unsatisfactory for Cornwallis and foreshadowed the frustrations to come. At the meeting, the first consul suggested that the Knights of St. John should be allowed to repossess the British-occupied island of Malta, after the British had blown up all the island's fortifications. Such a proposition had not been discussed before the signing of the preliminary articles, and it was a matter over which Cornwallis had no authority to negotiate.[21]

On this tenuous note, the British envoy left for Amiens, where he arrived in early December. The nature of the place itself only increased his sense of dissatisfaction with the progress of the peace. Cornwallis found the town dreary and cold and the French with whom he dealt possessed of "all the disagreeable qualities of the old French without the accomplishments."[22] The disagreeableness of the negotiations that followed matched that of the town and of the French. Cornwallis supposedly had come to France only for a formal ceremony, easily and quickly concluded. Supposedly, he would merely sign a document that diplomats had already concluded, not turn diplomat and negotiator himself. Neither he nor the cabinet had intended, when he accepted his post, that he should engage day after day in endless talk over points already settled. He had no authority to negotiate a new treaty. But Napoleon, through his brother Joseph, kept changing his terms and upping his demands, even contradicting himself in the process. While the discussions dragged on, the first consul outfitted an expedition of ships and troops to retake Santo Domingo. He refused to discuss Germany, Italy, or Switzerland or to open them to British trade. He wanted to extend French fishing rights off Newfoundland and expected Britain, at its own expense, to restore the French fortifications at Pondicherry. He would not even agree to compensation to the Prince of Orange, one of the understandings in the preliminaries. In the face of these tactics, Cornwallis soon changed his initial favorable opinion of Joseph Bonaparte. From a "very sensible, modest, gentlemanlike man, totally free from diplomatic chicanery, and fair and open in his dealings,"[23] Joseph soon became a shifty character lacking in candor: "I feel it as the most unpleasant circumstance attending this business [Cornwallis noted], that, after I have obtained his acquiescence on any point, I can have no confidence that it is finally settled, and that he will not recede from it in our next conversation. . . . In no instance is there any show of candour in the negotiation; all consideration of what passed between your lordship [Hawkesbury] and M. Otto, and of the encouraging assurances which you received from him respecting particular points, are totally overlooked: nor, when I have urged them, has it been in my power to obtain an answer."[24] The marquis grew increasingly morose at the lack of progress, especially after Brome departed on 26 December. As in Ireland, the old swelling now attacked his legs and feet.[25]

January brought no comfort, only more affronts from the French. Napoleon met deputies from the Cisalpine Republic (northern Italy) at Lyons that month, after which he agreed to take office as president of the Italian Republic. Thus he blatantly increased French influence while allegedly committed only to peace. Now even Hawkesbury, the foreign secretary, began to rethink his position. He told Cornwallis that people formerly disposed to peace had begun to think of resuming war because of the "inordinate ambition, the gross breach of faith, and the inclination to insult Europe, manifested by the conduct of the First Consul."[26]

January gave way to February, without war and without peace. By the fifth of the month, Cornwallis prepared to break off the talks. Not only the negotiations, but life in general in Amiens, had grown intolerable for him. He now suffered through one or two dinners a week with the same dreary company—Joseph Bonaparte and his wife, a "very short, very thick, very ugly, and very vulgar" woman; the "ill-looking scoundrel" of a prefect and his "tall, plain, vulgar" wife; the mayor and his wife, and various civil and military authorities. The food and wine at these affairs, according to his private secretary, Lieutenant Colonel Miles Nightingall, was not fit for human consumption.[27] Cornwallis could not avoid these affairs and could only relieve his frustrations by riding horseback when the weather permitted. At that he was uncomfortable, for the old swelling persisted.

The French persisted as well in their stubborn course. In February, Cornwallis grew particularly incensed about the discussions concerning Malta. The French acted so contrarily as to object to the plan they themselves had initially proposed. At this point, the British ambassador wanted to quit. "It is now for His Majesty's Ministers," he wrote, "to determine whether they will on this point break off, or give way, or bring forward another plan of accommodation . . . without leaving the island in its present formidable state, to be seized by France whenever she shall think proper to do so."[28]

The foreign secretary pressed him to continue nonetheless. Hawkesbury thought some agreement on Malta could be worked out and reiterated his position that the government was "sincerely desirous to conclude the peace if it can be obtained on terms consistent with our honour."[29] So the dreary days at Amiens continued, with Cornwallis pressed by his government for a settlement and Bonaparte constantly shifting his ground regardless of understandings already supposedly reached.

In March, however, internal pressure forced the British cabinet to move quickly either to reach a settlement or resume hostilities. The government had to submit its financial estimates to Parliament, and it had to know whether to budget for war or peace. Under these circumstances, on 14 March, Hawkesbury sent new instructions to the marquis and an ultimatum to the French. The foreign secretary had drawn up the draft of a definitive treaty, "conformable to the last project delivered to you by the French plenipotentiary." Cornwallis should deliver the draft and could sign it if the French agreed to it. If, however, Joseph Bonaparte made new demands, Cornwallis should announce his departure within eight days, "unless the treaty is concluded in that time."[30]

In his attempt to get peace without the use of an ultimatum, the British negotiator had to use his own discretion for the first time in the entire negotiations. On 17 March, he laid Hawkesbury's draft before Bonaparte in a "conciliatory manner," hoping to iron out difficulties. He also explained, diplomatically, that the British had suffered enough delays.[31] A swift exchange followed, wherein the Batavian plenipotentiary acted as intermediary. Final discussions began at ten in the evening on 24 March and ended at three o'clock the next morning, each side signing a declaration binding it to sign the treaty as soon as copies could be made.[32]

The document that resulted by no means duplicated the preliminary articles. Among the many difficulties in the treaty, from the British view, the still-undecided fate of Malta stood out with prominence. British forces would supposedly withdraw to be replaced by Neapolitans, then the Knights of St. John would return, free of external influence, and finally the six major powers of Britain, France, Russia, Austria, Prussia, and Spain would guarantee the island's independence. This awkward and unworkable plan characterized much of the document as a whole. Like the peace of Versailles, it was a peace designed to ensure war. Neither the British nor the French honored the spirit or the letter of the Amiens agreement. Each intended it only to provide a breathing spell.

Even if only intended as a breathing spell, however, the peace treaty favored France. Part of Portugal's Guiana territory went to France. The Cape Colony, which the British had captured, went back to the Dutch in full sovereignty (and the Dutch were now satellites of the French). The House of Orange received no indemnity for the loss of its land. Bonaparte did not have to evacuate Dutch territory, nor the Helvetic and Ligurian Republics. The treaty of commerce with France was not renewed. J. Holland Rose, the British historian, rightly pointed out that Amiens was a failure. Britain and France would be back at war again in little more than a year.[33]

Cornwallis must share the blame for the defects in this arrangement. Perhaps he should have resigned in the face of French harassment and asked the government to send over a replacement. Yet the cabinet in any event had to make peace. Public opinion demanded it. The preliminary articles, furthermore, had conceded so much to France that what Cornwallis additionally gave away seems minor. In any event, the cabinet approved everything he did. When, at the last minute, he did not deliver their ultimatum but continued negotiations, relief overwhelmed the members. Addington dashed off a note assuring his ambassador that he was "relieved and gratified by the discretion exercised by your lordship in suspending at least the execution of the whole of the last instructions."[34] Even William Windham, who had opposed the peace adamantly, eventually concluded that no matter what the terms it was necessary at the time. Dining at White Lodge in July of 1809, he supposedly remarked: "I have for some time wished to tell you [Lord Sidmouth] that I am thoroughly convinced, if it had not been for the peace of Amiens this country could never have maintained the struggle of the present period."[35]

The resumption of war would see Britain easily regain her supremacy at sea (a supremacy retained for a hundred years) and retake the colonial empire she had given away. It would also eventually see Napoleon lose his mastery of Europe, first with his failure in Spain and Portugal, then with his loss of an army of five hundred thousand men in Russia, and finally with his loss of everything at Waterloo.

In 1802, Cornwallis could not foresee this hopeful future. He slipped back unobtrusively to England—a contrast to his departure for France—reaching London on 1 April. But to the people the present seemed eminently satisfactory. Peace, however fleeting, made the city erupt with joy, eliciting crowds, candles, and patriotic inscriptions. To that extent, and to the extent of the cabinet's helplessness, Cornwallis's mission had succeeded.

India Again

That Cornwallis did not then finally retire may well evoke wonder. He had done more for his country in one lifetime than ten men usually achieve. His work had taken him to three continents, and he had influenced the course of history on all three, albeit not in the direction he had wished in North America. Though in reasonably good health, except for the recurrence of swelling in his feet, he was now almost sixty-four years old. Surely he should at last have allowed himself to relax in the easy life of Culford, shooting, superintending his acres, watching his election interests, gossiping over old times, and being made much of by his grandchildren.

He did just that for a while. By July he was back at Culford. There he enjoyed the shooting, though his eye had lost some of its sharpness.[36] Opposition to the Cornwallis interest at an election for Eye puzzled him, but he easily won, with very little treating. His son and his brother William captured huge majorities, though William overreacted to the victory by getting drunk after the election and offering his steward £300 for expenses. "Without ever having given a vote in the H. of C. [House of Commons] for many years past," the marquis observed, "and perhaps never intending to again, no youth of one and twenty was ever more pleased [than William] at coming into Parliament." The marquis enjoyed chats with old friends, like Castlereagh, who stopped for visits. He wrote letters in a great scrawl while his grandchildren pestered him adoringly. Now, indeed, he drank to the full that cup of domestic bliss he had so often in the past told his friends he preferred to service in faraway lands.

Yet, in fact, this life soon palled. He liked Culford. He enjoyed his grandchildren. He loved to ride and shoot. He liked to survey his broad acres. But before long that life bored him because at heart he was a restless man. Despite the calm, objective exterior, the firmness of purpose, and the honesty he displayed, at bottom he was always anxious for a job, but preferably one of short duration so that he could soon move on to something else. In America, in India, and in Ireland, he grew dissatisfied after only a year or two. Perhaps after that length of time the work presented no more newness and thus no more challenge; perhaps by then he had learned as much of each problem as he thought he could. But whatever his inner reasons, like all the other restless spirits of this world, he had to keep moving. Thus, rusticating at Culford was for him an ideal more desirable in the abstract than in the reality.

Soon he wanted more than anything to return to work, to take employment of any sort that would occupy his time and talents. In August of 1803, just over a year after his return from Amiens, he jumped at the fleeting possibility of returning again to Ireland, a prospect that never materialized. In September he complained to Ross that he had too much time for meditation, considering that the Amiens treaty had not lasted and the country was again at war and again fearing invasion. "To sit down quietly by myself, without occupation or object," he moaned, "to contemplate the dangers of my country, with the prospect of being a mere cypher, without arms in my hands, if they should be realized" appalled him. He fired off a letter to the Duke of York volunteering to serve in "any part of the world." The duke's noncommittal response increased the marquis's despondency. "For my part," he complained, "I think I may now fairly consider myself as laid quietly on the shelf." He told his successor in Ireland how "mortifying" it was "after the pains I have taken to acquire knowledge and experience in my profession, to be laid aside."[37]

He experienced a revival of hope in January of 1804, when the Duke of York called him to London, but the promise proved ephemeral. "It not only appeared that there was no immediate active station prepared for me," he grumbled, "but that under the pretense of assembling a great body of volunteers of the inland counties, of which I was to have the command, at some central spot, it was the intention to put me totally in the background, when an invasion should actually take place." [38]

As the winter of 1804 gave way to summer, his prospects for action did not improve. "Brome and Lady Louisa," he wrote his brother William, "are at Hull, and I am left with the care of the children, which is, I think, a very proper occupation for an old general that is laid by." [39]

His "luck," if one can call it that, finally changed in October of 1804, when Pitt's ministry, which had replaced Addington's, sounded him out about returning to India as governor general and commander in chief. In Bengal, events had not progressed as the government wished. Shore's replacement there, Richard, Lord Mornington, who became Marquis Wellesley in the Irish peerage, had begun a policy of deliberate expansion, ably forwarded by his brilliant soldier-brother, Arthur Wellesley, the future Duke of Wellington. Under them the British had again fought a war with Tipoo Sahib and again defeated him, this time storming his capital and killing him. As a result, John Company had taken control of Mysore. Lord Mornington, furthermore, had taken over the Carnatic as well as a part of Oudh and presently intended to do battle with the Mahrattas. Pitt and the directors not only wanted to stop this expansion, but also wanted the Company to retrench and even if necessary to restore its conquests. Wars cost too much money, as did the administration of conquered territory, especially when Britain needed to concentrate her resources against Napoleon. To reverse Mornington's policy required a strong governor general, and the cabinet could think of no one more suitable than Charles, first Marquis Cornwallis.

By 23 October 1804, he was fairly sure that Pitt had decided to send him to India again. Once he knew he was likely to leave for the East, he repeated to Ross his time-honored protestation against leaving. "Nothing could induce me to return to India," he told Ross, "but the firm persuasion that it was the earnest wish of Government and of the respectable part of the Directors." He wrote to William: "When I am told that I may essentially serve my country and know by the same means I am likely to assist my family, you will agree with me, I think, that there are few enjoyments or comforts in the world for a man of sixty-six that can be put in competition with those objects."[40] One wonders why he bothered with such explanations to Ross and to William, who had heard them so often before. Yet, however familiar the phrases had become, the deep concern for the welfare of his family was genuine. Shortly before he learned of his impending appointment, he had pleaded to Pitt on their behalf: "It has I believe seldom happened in this Country that a successful service of this importance [in Ireland] has been passed by without any favorable notice. For myself I look for nothing, but when I assure you that if my Son should survive me, he will at the expiration of the annuity from the East India Company, be reduced to so limited an income as to render his situation very uncomfortable, you will not, I trust, think me unreasonable, if I prefer a claim in his favor for some reversionary official grant from the Crown, when an opening shall occur."[41]

Perhaps this plea, as well as other factors, had figured in Pitt's decision to approach the marquis. First, however, to assure himself that Cornwallis was still fit, the prime minister sent Castlereagh off to see him at Culford in December. Castlereagh responded favorably, and by 7 January 1805, the marquis held his old position again. Later in the month he sailed for India, and by 19 July he reached Madras. By 30 July he had taken up his duties as governor general and commander in chief.[42]

At first he seemed his old self. The ever-observant Hickey noted that when he landed at Calcutta he refused to allow any European troops to come out to receive him. Lord Wellesley nonetheless sent carriages, servants, a staff officer, and the "general establishment" to meet him at waterside. When he saw the cavalcade, the new governor general said to G. A. Robinson, former auditor general and now his confidential secretary: "What! What! What is all this Robinson, hey?" When Robinson then explained that Wellesley had, as a mark of respect, sent the escort to take him to government house, Cornwallis guffawed: "Too civil, too civil by half. Too many people. I don't want them, don't want one of them, I have not yet lost the use of my legs, Robinson, hey? Thank God, I can walk, walk very well, Robinson, hey; don't want a score carriage to convey me a quarter of a mile; certainly shall not use them." When he reached government house, he again scoffed at his predecessor's arrangements (it seemed the policy of repudiation began at once). He thought the sleeping apartments prepared for him too sumptuous and refused them. "They are large, much too large for me," he complained, "I should be lost in them, I should prefer a smaller place on the ground floor." In this instance, however, Wellesley prevailed and Cornwallis took the apartments, though he dismissed about a dozen sentries from different passages. "I shall never be able to find my way about," he concluded, "without a guide, nor can I divest myself of the idea of being in a prison, for if I show my head outside a door, a fellow with a musket and fixed bayonet presents himself before me. . . . Wellesley may do as he likes, but I will not be thus pestered, and must have quiet and retirement."[43]

Although he acted like the old Cornwallis, he did not look like him. The long passage and the enormous climactic change had wrecked his constitution. Hickey and everyone else who saw him were "greatly shocked to see how ill his Lordship looked and what a wreck of what he had been when formerly in Bengal."[44] Robinson noted that his health had begun to decline when he first reached Madras, "that his constitution was less equal to contend against the effects of this climate than during his former residence in India."[45]

Yet the governor general refused to heed the symptoms. He would not let ill health deter him. Though no longer able to ride, he nonetheless went out for his evening exercise in a phaeton behind "a pair of steady old jog-trot horses."[46] Despite his ill health, he soon conceived it his duty to visit the army posts up-country and proceeded there by boat. This effort weakened him still more. Though he had no specific complaint, he simply seemed to wilt away, growing closer to death with each passing day. On 23 September 1805, he managed a letter to Lord Lake, his old subordinate in Ireland, now his second in command of the Indian army. After that he declined rapidly. His mind failed him. He dozed away his life, occasionally awakening to ask a question, but constantly growing weaker.[47] When he reached Gazipore on 27 September, he could go no further. He clung to life there for a little more than a week. Then on 5 October 1805, just before the great British victory at Trafalgar, he died.

British India mourned his passing, as did the entire army,

10. Monument Erected in St. Paul's Cathedral to the Memory of
    Marquis Cornwallis
    Published for the *European Magazine* by J. Asperne, 32 Cornhill,
    1 February 1819.

for three months. In England, Castlereagh moved on 3 February 1806 that the House of Commons should erect a statue of him in St. Paul's. It still stands in the cathedral today. The court of directors of the East India Company, in mourning for several weeks, joined with the court of proprietors in voting £40,000 to the marquis's family.[48] Perhaps the most touching tribute to him resulted from a meeting in Calcutta that voted to raise by public subscription the sum needed to build a mausoleum over his grave at Gazipore. The first stone was laid on 22 December 1809, and the structure still remains. The dedicatory inscription states: "This monument, erected by the British inhabitants of Calcutta, attests their sense of those virtues which will live in the remembrance of grateful millions, long after it shall have mouldered in the dust." The inscription further praised his victories in war and his "forbearance and moderation" in peace. "Just and liberal principles," had marked his government. He had raised the salaries of "the servants of the state" so as "to ensure the purity of their conduct." Finally, he had "laid the foundation of a system of revenue, which while it limited and defined the claims of government, was intended to confirm hereditary rights to the proprietors and to give security to the cultivators of the soil."

Cornwallis would never see Culford again. He would never again shoot partridge or romp with his grandchildren. Yet, because of his sense of duty, his commitment to work, his dedication to the service of his country wherever and whenever called upon, he rests more fittingly in the soil of India than in the ground of Suffolk.

Notes

BM / British Museum, London
Br. Parl. Papers, Cols., E. Ind. / *British Parliamentary Papers, Colonies, East India*
Cornwallis Correspondence / *The Correspondence of Charles First Marquis Cornwallis*
GD / Gifts and Deposits
HMC / Historical Manuscripts Commission
HO / Home Office
IOL / India Office Library, London
IOR / India Office Records, London
NLS / National Library of Scotland, Edinburgh
PRO / Public Record Office, London
SCL / Sheffield Central Library, Sheffield, England
SP / State Papers
SRO / Scottish Record Office, Edinburgh
Rept. on MSS Var. Coll. / *Report on Manuscripts in Various Collections*
T / Treasury
WO / War Office

Chapter 1

1. Details of the controversy appear in Franklin and Mary Wickwire, *Cornwallis*, chapters 15 and 16. References appear there to other works making various arguments on the matter.

2. This episode is related in the diaries of the young officer, Captain Peebles of the 4th Grenadier Guards, stationed in New York. See SRO, GD 21/492/13, fol. 44, entries for 1 and 2 March 1782.

3. The statement to which Cornwallis and the other Englishmen aboard the *Greyhound* subscribed is found in Cornwallis Papers, PRO 30/11/7, fols. 1–2. That the agreement was honored by the British government and the Frenchmen allowed to sail the *Greyhound* away unmolested may be seen in PRO, T 29/51, fol. 21, treasury minute of 29 Jan. 1782.

4. Cornwallis's efforts succeeded. The treasury agreed to prepare a warrant to pay £400 each to the French officers in compensation for their lost baggage. Cornwallis's three letters to John Robinson on this subject, dated 12, 13, and

2

24 March 1782, appear in PRO, T 1/570, fols. 153–56. The treasury's acquiescence in the proposal to indemnify the Frenchmen may be seen in PRO, T 29/51, fols. 61 and 61b, treasury minute of 16 March 1781.

5. George III to Lord George Germain, 22 Jan. 1782, King George III, *The Correspondence of King George the Third*, 5:339.

6. Lord Chandos proposed to Rockingham a plan to ask the House of Lords to thank Lord Cornwallis for his "meritorious conduct in America" and at the same time lay the blame for his defeated endeavors on "the unwise measures of Government." Rockingham opposed the plan because the parole of honor given by Cornwallis and the other officers captured at Yorktown "should or *ought* to restrain them from answering almost every Question which can be put to them —either relative to the Campaign—or the proof it wished of the ministers' culpability." See Chandos to Rockingham, 29 Jan. 1782, and draft of Rockingham to Chandos, n.d., Rockingham Papers, SCL, R 1–1978 and R 1–1979. The actual words of Cornwallis's parole, which were quite usual, appear in PRO 30/11/93, fol. 24, and include the following: "I . . . Do pledge my faith and word of honor that I will not do or say any thing injurious to the said United States or Armies thereof or their allies, until duly exchanged."

7. Cornwallis worried that in the "hurry and agitation" right after the capitulation he had not had an opportunity to do justice to the late Major Charles Cochrane, whose head was shot off by a cannonball at Yorktown. See Cornwallis to Welbore Ellis, 12 March 1782, DunDonald Papers, NLS, MS 5375. For the request for the list of German losses see George Rose (secretary of the treasury) to Cornwallis, 25 Oct. 1782, PRO, T 27/43, p. 359. The Cornwallis Papers in the PRO contain dozens of references to the loyalist claims and pleas for help.

8. Cornwallis to Ross, 24 Jan. 1794, *Cornwallis Correspondence*, 1:163.

9. Cornwallis to Ross, 13 June 1784, ibid., p. 177.

10. See, for example, General George Washington to Sir Guy Carleton, 30 July 1782, ibid., p. 147.

11. Sir Guy Carleton to Cornwallis, 27 Oct. 1782, ibid., p. 148.

12. See Elizabeth, Countess Cornwallis to William Cornwallis, 2 April 1782, HMC, *Rept. on MSS Var. Coll.*, 6:330.

13. For these finances see PRO 30/11/280, fols. 7, 27, 32–34, and 84, and the records at Hoare's bank. In 1784, Cornwallis admitted to Pitt that he was straitened financially. See Cornwallis to Pitt, 8 Nov. 1784, *Cornwallis Correspondence*, 1:187.

14. Cornwallis to George III, 19 March 1782, and George III to Cornwallis, 28 March 1782, PRO 30/11/268, no. 11 and no. 13.

15. Charles Townshend to William Cornwallis, 6 Feb. 1782, HMC, *Rept. on MSS Var. Coll.*, 6:327–28.

16. Phillip Herrick, town clerk of Leicester, to Cornwallis, 11 Dec. 1782, PRO 30/11/272, fol. 26.

17. See Shelburne to Cornwallis, 21 July 1780, PRO 30/11/2, fols. 335–36. Countess Cornwallis noted to her son William in April that "Lord Shelburne and your brother have been upon a very friendly foot ever since he came from America." See Elizabeth to William, 3 April 1782, HMC, *Rept. on MSS Var. Coll.*, 6:331.

18. Cornwallis to William Cornwallis, 1 May 1782, HMC, *Rept. on MSS Var. Coll.*, 6:333. In his letter to Pitt of 8 Nov. 1784 (*Cornwallis Correspondence*, 1:187) the earl said that Shelburne first approached him about the post in May of 1782.

19. Steven Watson, *The Reign of George III, 1760–1815*, p. 257.

20. His feud in print with Sir Henry Clinton, however, intensified. The earl called Clinton's account of the 1780 and 1781 campaigns "a bad performance . . . not like to do the cause much good with people of judgment," when the *London Chronicle* began printing their exchanges in January of 1783. See Cornwallis to Ross, 15 Jan. 1783, *Cornwallis Correspondence*, 1:153. For the whole of this feud see the pamphlets printed by Benjamin Franklin Stevens, *The Campaign in Virginia 1781*.

21. Cornwallis to Ross, 26 Oct. 1783, and to Pitt, 4 Nov. 1784, *Cornwallis Correspondence*, 1:154, 186.

22. Cornwallis to Ross, 13 Nov. 1783, ibid., p. 156.

23. Cornwallis to Ross, 21 Nov. 1783, ibid., p. 157.

24. John Ehrman, *The Younger Pitt*, pp. 120–27, reconstructs negotiations leading to the king's statement, but John Cannon, *The Fox-North Coalition*, pp. 124–32, shows, as Ehrman does not, Pitt's direct involvement in the king's intervention.

25. The editor of *Cornwallis Correspondence* deleted the names that would have helped identify the bankrupt friend, the plight of whose daughters so distressed Cornwallis. For this story, see Cornwallis to Ross, 3 March 1784, *Cornwallis Correspondence*, 1:169.

26. See Cornwallis to Ross, 18 and 19 Dec. 1783, ibid., pp. 159 and 160.

27. Cornwallis to Ross, 2 Jan. 1784, ibid., p. 161.

28. Cornwallis to Ross, 26 Jan. 1784, ibid., p. 164. When, in February, the office of constable of the Tower went to Lord George Lennox as a military appointment, Cornwallis remarked: "This is undoubtedly a pleasing circumstance to me, as it marks more strongly my disinterested conduct, and removes Lord G. from future competition. I still cannot repent of what I have done. I certainly did not receive it as a military employment, but in the ministerial line from Lord North, and it would not have suited my character to have flown to the Crown for indemnity for the part I had taken, and endeavoured to have screened myself under a fresh tenure. Lord G. stands on other ground, and is undoubtedly as secure and free from all shackles as the Governor of Portsmouth" (Cornwallis to Ross, 6 Feb. 1784, ibid., p. 165).

29. For the proposal to send Cornwallis to Ireland see George III to William Pitt, 28 Dec. 1783, King George III, *The Later Correspondence of George III*, 1:13. See also Cornwallis to Ross, 2 Jan. 1784, *Cornwallis Correspondence*, 1:162.

30. Cornwallis to Lord Sydney, 8 Jan. 1784, *Cornwallis Correspondence*, 1:162.

31. To his confidant, Lieutenant Colonel Ross, Cornwallis wrote from Culford on 9 May 1784: "The more I turn it in my mind, the less inclination I feel to undertake it. I see no field for extraordinary military reputation, and it appears to me in every light dangerous to the greatest degree. To abandon my children and every comfort on this side the grave; to quarrel with the Supreme Government in India, whatever it may be; to find that I have neither power to model the army or correct abuses; and finally to run the risk of being beat by some

272 | Notes to Pages 13–16

nabob, and being disgraced to all eternity, which from what I have read of their battles appears a very probable thing to happen—I cannot see, in opposition to this great renown and brilliant fortune." See *Cornwallis Correspondence*, 1: 174–75.

32. Cornwallis described his meeting with Sydney in a letter to Ross, 25 May 1784, ibid., p. 175.

33. Ibid., pp. 175–76.

34. Sydney to Cornwallis, 3 Aug. 1784, and Cornwallis to Sydney, 4 Aug. 1784, ibid., pp. 179–80.

35. Cornwallis to Ross, 3 Sept. 1784, ibid., p. 181.

36. Only to Ross did Cornwallis fully unburden himself. On 3 March 1784, he wrote: "I know you will scold me for not being at least more familiar with ministers; but I cannot bring myself to it, and I see important fools every day taking the lead, and becoming men of consequence." See ibid., p. 170. Eight months later, on 3 November 1784, he wrote in complete disillusionment to the same friend of his inability to behave as so many post-seekers did: he "thought it indelicate to post up to town" upon hearing of the death of an incumbent, whose thus vacated post he hoped he would obtain (Lord Waldegrave, governor of Plymouth) and instead trusted "to the friendship of the highest powers" (ibid., 1:183).

37. Cornwallis wrote his own account of the two interviews with Sydney, as well as his personal reaction to events, in letters to Ross on 3 and 6 Nov. 1784, *Cornwallis Correspondence*, 1:182–85.

38. Cornwallis to Pitt, 7 Nov. 1784, Dacres Adams Papers, PRO 30/58/1, letter 5. This letter is misdated as 8 Nov. 1784 in *Cornwallis Correspondence*, 1:186–87.

39. See Cornwallis to Ross and to Pitt, 10 Nov. 1784, *Cornwallis Correspondence*, 1:188.

40. Cornwallis to Ross, 13 and 19 Nov. 1784, ibid., p. 189.

41. See Pitt to Cornwallis, 8 Feb. 1785, PRO 30/11/270, fols. 14–16.

42. The bundle numbered PRO 30/11/7 is full of documents relating to India just before Cornwallis took over. It contains materials relating, for example, to revenue, organization of the army, the judiciary, the government of the British possessions, and so forth. Some of these documents suggest reforms that Cornwallis later enacted. Particularly interesting is the material in fols. 267–308, entitled "Observations on the English Possessions in India, their government, population, cultivation, produce and commerce, privately communicated to the right honoble Henry Dundas."

43. He refers to his "studies" in numerous of his letters to Ross. See, for example, letters of 5 Sept., 26 Oct., and 13 Nov. 1783, *Cornwallis Correspondence*, 1:153, 154, 156. He professed himself "much amused" by the Chevalier Folard's "Traité de la Colonne" in his French translation of Polybius.

44. See, respectively, Cornwallis to Ross, 19 Sept. 1784, ibid., p. 181; undated holograph, PRO 30/11/277, fol. 22; and Cornwallis to his brother William, 1 May 1782, HMC, *Rept. on MSS Var. Coll.*, 6:333.

45. Cornwallis to Ross, 3 May 1785, *Cornwallis Correspondence*, 1:196.

46. Cornwallis to Ross, 8 May 1785, ibid., p. 197. In a subsequent letter to Ross, 24 May 1785, ibid., pp. 197–98, Cornwallis mentions plans for his trip to Prussia.

47. Numerous letters and dispatches relating to Cornwallis's diplomatic mission to the court of Frederick the Great are printed in ibid., pp. 200–214.

48. For Cornwallis's candid opinion of York, see Cornwallis to Ross, 5 Oct. 1785, ibid., p. 211. Cornwallis has a number of letters to or from the Duke of York in PRO 30/11/258.

49. Lady Mary Lindsay to Lady Campbell, 26 Jan. 1786, NLS MS 2903, fols. 34–35.

50. See Charles Townshend to Cornwallis, 14 and 19 Dec. 1775, PRO 30/11/277, fols. 27–29, 31–32; and Cornwallis's will of 5 April 1805, PRO 30/11/278, fols. 22–39; and Mr. Singleton's instrument settling the stock upon his son, PRO 30/11/277, fol. 30.

51. Cornwallis to Ross, 23 Feb. 1786, *Cornwallis Correspondence*, 1:215.

52. According to Henry Dundas, Ross's friends thought that the Company ought to settle a permanent position on Ross to compensate him for his loss, for should Cornwallis die he might go "unprovided." But the earl rejected the idea, "trusting that if his services deserved it, the publick would not fail to do justice to those he should recommend to their protection." See Dundas to Archibald Campbell, 26 July 1787, PRO 30/11/112, fols. 87–92.

53. Cornwallis to John Mitchie, 22 April 1785, IOR, Home Misc. 379, fol. 7.

54. Lord Percy to George Rose, 31 Oct. 1782, in George Rose, *The Diaries and Correspondence of the Right Hon. George Rose*, 1:54–55. Percy, as the date reveals, offered his prediction when he thought Cornwallis would go to India in a military capacity only.

Chapter 2

1. Cornwallis to Dundas, 24 Aug. 1786, Melville Papers, NLS.

2. William Hickey, *Memoirs*, 1:163.

3. J. Blakiston, *Twelve Years' Military Adventure in Three Quarters of the Globe*, 2:27–28.

4. Thomas Twining, *Travels in India a Hundred Years Ago, with a Visit to the United States*, describes Madras in 1792 in some detail.

5. See Lady Oakeley to Lady Campbell, 19 Sept. 1789, NLS, MS 2903, fols. 66–69.

6. See NLS, MS 2905, fols. 144–58, several letters of the nabob relating to this pension.

7. Description of the approach to Calcutta comes from Twining, *Travels in India*, pp. 73–75. Percival Spear, *The Nabobs*, pp. 43–65, describes both Madras and Calcutta in some detail. We have also relied on him for our impression of the two cities as they appeared in the eighteenth century.

8. Thomas Williamson and F. W. Blagdon, *The Europeans in India*. The preface, which describes the sorts of clothes to bring to India, the exercise to take, the hours of business, the diet, and the servants, with illustrations, must have been a blessing to the potential voyager to India.

9. See PRO 30/11/196, fols. 28–33.

10. *Calcutta Gazette*, 17, no. 444, 30 Aug. 1789.

11. Sir George Yonge, secretary at war, to Cornwallis, 21 June 1787, PRO 30/11/13, fols. 324–25. Despite his official interest in botany (in compliance with

his orders), the governor general may have had little personal interest in the subject. Lieutenant Colonel Kidd, in charge of the botanical garden, thought Cornwallis an "amiable and excellent Govr General," but believed him ignorant, if not contemptuous, of the worth of the botanical garden. See Kidd to Warren Hastings, 20 July 1789, BM, Add. MSS 29,171, fol. 332.

12. Extract of a public letter from Bengal, 12 March 1791, IOR, Home Misc. 380, pp. 28–29.

13. See, for example, IOR, Europeans in India, 0/5/2–3, passim. "Portuguese" was an Anglo-Indian term for half-castes.

14. Blakiston, *Twelve Years' Military Adventure*, 1:48–51; quotation on p. 51.

15. See, for example, *Calcutta Gazette*, 6, no. 141, 9 Nov. 1786; 10, no. 248, 8 Jan. 1789; and 14, no. 353, 2 Dec. 1790.

16. Hickey, *Memoirs*, 3:377, describes Mrs. Bristow. *Calcutta Gazette*, 11, no. 271, 7 May 1789, describes her theater and the performance.

17. See, for example, *Calcutta Gazette*, 8, no. 209, 28 Feb. 1788; and 12, no. 297, 5 Nov. 1789.

18. Herbert Harris to Cornwallis, 9 Feb. 1790, PRO 30/11/148, fols. 128–30.

19. Hickey, *Memoirs*, 3:292–93, describes the incident.

20. Henry Haldane to Edward Tiretta, 4 Sept. 1788, and Tiretta to Haldane, 14 Oct. 1788, PRO 30/11/26, fols. 533–36.

21. Turner to Hastings, 16 Jan. 1789, BM, Add. MSS 29,170, fols. 363–67.

22. *Calcutta Gazette*, 6, no. 134, 21 Sept. 1786.

23. Turner to Hastings, 16 Jan. 1789, BM, Add. MSS 29,170, fols. 363–67.

24. Hickey, *Memoirs*, 4:109–10, relates the story about Auchmuty.

25. *Calcutta Gazette*, 6, no. 150, 18 Jan. 1787; no. 146, 14 Dec. 1786; *Supplement*, 8, no. 174, 28 June 1787; *Calcutta Gazette*, 10, no. 258, 5 Feb. 1789; 12, no. 308, 21 Jan. 1790; and 13, no. 334, 22 July 1790.

26. For these various items see his correspondence with his agent, James Meyrick, in London, from 1787 through 1793, PRO 30/11/15, fols. 310–11; 30/11/18, fols. 499–500; 30/11/16, fols. 515–16; 30/11/23, fols. 401–2; 30/11/24, fols. 288–89; 30/11/25, fols. 418–19; 420–21; 30/11/29, fols. 301–2; 30/11/34, fols. 277–78; and 30/11/52, fols. 106–23.

27. John William Kaye, *Lives of Indian Officers, Illustrative of the History of the Civil and Military Services of India*, 1:42.

28. Hickey, *Memoirs*, 4:32, describes the barge, rowed by twenty-six men, as a cross between a European and Oriental boat. It was in rather bad condition at first, but Cornwallis eventually had it repaired. See also Joseph Price to Henry Haldane, 7 Dec. 1785 and 1 Jan. 1787, PRO 30/11/12, fols. 335–36, and 30/11/13, fols. 253–54.

29. Samuel Turner to Warren Hastings, 16 Jan. 1787, BM, Add. MSS 29,170, fols. 363–67.

30. Cornwallis to Brome, 11 Jan. 1789, *Cornwallis Correspondence*, 1:401.

31. See, for example, Cornwallis to Shore, 16 Aug. 1787, PRO 30/11/165, fols. 8–11.

32. *Calcutta Gazette*, 7, no. 361, 15 Oct. 1787.

33. *Calcutta Gazette* describes these reviews for his entire tenure.

34. At first he worried terribly about the proper ceremonial for persons of different ranks in the hierarchy of the various governments of the native states.

See Cornwallis to Captain John Kennaway, 24 Jan. 1787, PRO 30/11/166, fols. 4–5.

35. This search for such an elephant involved considerable time and expense, and Cornwallis did not find the proper one until some four months after he started looking. See Henry Haldane to Robert Lindsay, 8 Nov. 1786, PRO 30/11/11, fols. 225–26, and Gabriel Harper to Cornwallis, 8 March 1787, PRO 30/11/15, fols. 131–34.

36. *Calcutta Gazette*, 7, no. 171, 7 June 1787.

37. Captain Thomas Brown to Henry Dundas, 10 March 1780, Melville Papers, SRO, GD 51/3/312.

38. *Calcutta Gazette*, 7, no. 330, 12 March 1787.

39. Hickey, *Memoirs*, 4:93.

40. See, for example, *Calcutta Gazette*, 6, no. 145, 7 Dec. 1786.

41. Kaye, *Lives of Indian Officers*, 1:79.

42. *Calcutta Gazette*, 8, no. 201, 3 Jan. 1788.

43. Ibid., 11, no. 283, 30 July 1789.

44. Ibid., 18, no. 467, 7 Feb. 1793.

45. Hickey, *Memoirs*, 4:83.

46. Shore to Cornwallis, 10 Nov. 1793, PRO 30/11/121, fols. 54–59.

47. Spear, *Nabobs*, p. 65, says that the earl reduced entertainment. This statement appears incorrect in view of all the social amenities which Cornwallis provided or in which he participated.

Chapter 3

1. The trade to China was so flourishing that its temporary disruption in 1790 caused Cornwallis to determine to examine it thoroughly and to retain its advantages, while at the same time attempting to revive the now diminished trade of Bengal with other parts of India. Indeed, as part of the latter attempt Cornwallis abolished so many duties at the three presidencies that they enjoyed virtually free trade in 1791. This all too brief summary of a very complex development comes from Holden Furber, *John Company at Work*. A. Das Gupta, "Trade and Politics in 18th Century India," in D. S. Richards, ed., *Islam and the Trade of Asia*, pp. 181–214, traces the changes in Bengal's trading patterns. He also notes that by the end of the century, India was tending to become a single economic unit, one part dependent upon another, even though the French, Dutch, Danes, Portuguese, and country powers all had commercial control and attendant customs duties and rates of exchange over their territorial enclaves. We should note at this point that the materials relating to the administration of British India, published and unpublished, are enormous. If, however, one wishes to jump into the sources immediately, without preconceptions, and learn what the British leaders of society learned about what their compatriots were doing in India during Cornwallis's period, we suggest that the reader examine the massive compilation of documents—letters, minutes, estimates, lists, opinions, testimony—the House of Commons acquired and subsequently produced when examining the affairs of British India. The first three volumes of *British Parliamentary Papers, Colonies, East India*, compiled by select parliamentary committees and reproduced by the Irish University Press, contain these data. Information ranges from a summary in volume 3 of internal government before Cornwallis

and his reforms and their effect on Bengal to a minute examination of the entire British judicial system in volume 1, included in the second report of a select committee of the House of Commons, originally published in 1810. The Irish Press imposed its own pagination upon volume 1, but reproduced volumes 2 and 3 with original page numbers. Once one has examined this material, however, one realizes how much farther one must go to gain any understanding of British India, much less non-British India. We have examined a wide variety of materials, perhaps even more than Cornwallis actually saw, but we make no claim as experts in this complex field. Instead, we are trying to present the issues as Cornwallis and his contemporaries saw them and, under these circumstances, the solutions they advanced. Opinion, of course, will always differ on the "rightness" or "wrongness" of Cornwallis's work.

2. Arthur Aspinall, *Cornwallis in Bengal*, p. 13.

3. Joseph Gastrell to Cornwallis, 11 March 1786, PRO 30/11/137, fols. 75–76.

4. Cornwallis to Dundas, 24 Aug. 1786, Melville Papers, NLS, and Macpherson to Cornwallis, 24 Sept. 1786, PRO 30/11/9, fols. 152–69.

5. Cornwallis to Dundas, 17 Sept. 1786, *Cornwallis Correspondence*, 1:226.

6. Dundas to Cornwallis, 3 Aug. 1787, ibid., 1:337, and note 1, p. 338.

7. William Hickey, *Memoirs*, 3:344.

8. Cornwallis to Dundas, 1 Nov. 1788, *Cornwallis Correspondence*, 1:383–84.

9. Cornwallis to Dundas, 8 Aug. 1789, ibid., 1:430.

10. Cornwallis to directors, 14 Dec. 1787, PRO 30/11/153, fols. 99–104.

11. Cornwallis to secret committee, 28 Dec. 1786, PRO 30/11/156, fols. 140–41, 146, 149; to Dundas, 12 Jan. 1787, PRO 30/11/150, fols. 16–17; and to Messrs. Barton, Rider, and Henchman, 15 Jan. 1787, *Cornwallis Correspondence*, 1:253.

12. *An Abstract of Regulations in Revenue and Commerce*, regulation 31.

13. Cornwallis to Dundas, 14 Aug. 1787, PRO 30/11/150, fols. 38–45.

14. Cornwallis to directors, 3 March 1788, PRO 30/11/153, fols. 124–35; Cornwallis to directors, 1 Nov. 1788, ibid., fols. 149–76; Cornwallis to directors, 1 Aug. 1789, PRO 30/11/154, fols. 22–33; and Cornwallis to Dundas, 21 Dec. 1788, PRO 30/11/150, fols. 108–13.

15. Cornwallis to Dundas, 21 Dec. 1788, PRO 30/11/150, fols. 108–13.

16. Cornwallis to Shore, 9 Sept. 1787, PRO 30/11/188, fols. 60–62; Cornwallis to directors, 26 Jan. 1788, and 4 March 1787, PRO 30/11/153, fols. 120–21, and 55–60; and Cornwallis to James Grant, 9 March 1787, PRO 30/11/15, fols. 93–94.

17. Gabriel Harper to Cornwallis, 18 March 1787, PRO 30/11/15, fols. 141–44; Cornwallis to directors, 4 March 1787, PRO 30/11/153, fols. 55–60; C. H. Barlow to Cornwallis, 4 June 1787, PRO 30/11/17, fols. 3–6; Cornwallis to Dundas, 16 Nov. 1787, PRO 30/11/150, fols. 50–59; and Cornwallis to directors, 3 Nov. 1788, *Cornwallis Correspondence*, 1:539–40.

18. PRO 30/11/30, fol. 113, "State and Disposition of the Center Division of the Army on the Coast of Coromandel."

19. PRO 30/11/21, fols. 547–76.

20. Archibald Campbell, for example, wrote to Cornwallis in January of 1787 that "unaccountable delays" in some outstations meant that a return of Company troops for the months of September and October could not be completed at the adjutant general's office before 8 December. Campbell said that "owing to the

distance of some of our out stations, which are not less than 600 miles from head-quarters, the returns of the Company's troops are seldom collected before the 15th of the subsequent month." See Campbell to Cornwallis, 11 Jan. 1787, PRO 30/11/118, fols. 27–30.

21. Cornwallis did, however, take precautions. He sent mail in triplicate, and copies of the same letters went overland and by ship to Britain.

22. Malet to Kennaway, 2 Oct. 1789, IOL, MSS Eur. F. 149/6, p. 482.

23. Cornwallis to Campbell, 23 Dec. 1786, PRO 30/11/159, fols. 19–21. Hastings had previously set up a fairly elaborate overland postal system with stages at fixed distances and had established a number of by-laws for the post-master general and his department.

24. B. B. Misra, *The Central Administration of the East India Company, 1773–1834*, pp. 415–29, explains the background and the Cornwallis changes in detail.

25. Cornwallis to Dundas, 14 Aug. 1787, PRO 30/11/150, fols. 38–45.

26. For the Guntoor Circar see Cornwallis to secret committee, 15 Dec. 1788, PRO 30/11/157; secret and political department to Charles Ware Malet, 25 April 1787, PRO 30/11/162; Cornwallis to nizam of Hyderabad, 30 April 1788, and nizam to Cornwallis, 2 Nov. 1788, PRO 30/11/106, fols. 9–12, 13–17; Corn-wallis's instructions to Kennaway, 16 June 1788, and Cornwallis to directors, 3 Nov. 1788, *Cornwallis Correspondence*, 1:537–40, 542.

27. See Cornwallis to Dundas, 24 Jan. 1789, PRO 30/11/150, fols, 116–17, and Campbell to Cornwallis, 26 Sept. 1788, PRO 30/11/119, fol. 121.

28. Cornwallis to Archibald Campbell, 17 July 1788, PRO 30/11/159, fols. 143–45.

29. William Amherst to Cornwallis, 2 Feb. 1789, PRO 30/11/28, fols. 1–4.

30. For the whole of this episode see Cornwallis to secret committee, 16 Nov. 1786, PRO 30/11/156, fols. 1–5; Lieutenant James Anderson to Kirkpatrick, 5 Dec. 1786, PRO 30/11/12, fols. 15–34; Kirkpatrick to Cornwallis, 15 Feb. 1787, PRO 30/11/14, fols. 163–85; Kirkpatrick to Cornwallis, 18 April 1787, PRO 30/11/120, fols. 161–92; Kirkpatrick to Cornwallis, 14 Sept. 1787, PRO 30/11/18, fols. 185–96; Cornwallis to Kirkpatrick, 3 May 1787, PRO 30/11/168, fols. 35–36; Cornwallis to Kirkpatrick, 9 May 1787, PRO 30/11/168, fols. 25–28; Cornwallis to Kirkpatrick, 10 May 1787, PRO 30/11/168, fols. 21–22.

31. See Cornwallis to Dundas, 25 Jan. 1793, and to directors, 18 May 1793, *Cornwallis Correspondence*, 2:190, 558–70.

32. Cornwallis to Dundas, 5 March 1787, PRO 30/11/150, fols. 26–31.

33. Cornwallis to William Cornwallis, 27 June 1789, HMC, *Rept. on MSS Var. Coll.*, 6:344.

34. See *Calcutta Gazette, Extraordinary*, 13 Sept. 1789.

35. See Cornwallis to Dundas, 31 Dec. and 1 April 1790, PRO 30/11/151, fols. 17–23, 72–75, and to the directors, 28 Aug. 1792, PRO 30/11/155, fols. 294–305.

36. Aspinall, *Cornwallis in Bengal*, pp. 188–205, recounts the beginnings of Penang. Letters from the governor general in council of 26 March 1786 and 19 Feb. 1787 in *Br. Parl. Papers, Cols., E. Ind.*, 1:565–66, give the official ac-count of the initial settlement.

37. Cornwallis to directors, 1 Nov. 1788, PRO 30/11/153, fols. 149–76, par. 15.

38. Ibid.

39. Cornwallis to Dundas, 16 Nov. 1787, PRO 30/11/150, fols. 50–59, and Cornwallis to John Motteux, 16 Dec. 1787, *Cornwallis Correspondence*, 1:318.

40. Cornwallis to Dundas, 8 Aug. 1789, *Cornwallis Correspondence*, 1:429.

41. Cornwallis to Dundas, 13 Jan. 1792, ibid., 2:141.

42. Dundas evidently tried his best in this instance. "Upon your authority," he informed the earl, "I have recommended Jonathan Duncan. I do not know whether they [the directors] will agree to it or not: the Chairman has engaged to try it, but is apprehensive of the objections of his being so young a servant in comparison of many others. That is in truth no objection." See Dundas to Cornwallis, 20 Feb. 1789, *Cornwallis Correspondence*, 1:424.

43. Cornwallis to Dundas, 27 Jan. 1791, ibid., 2:81.

44. Cornwallis to Dundas, 4 March 1792, PRO 30/11/151, fols. 107–12. Ross prints the letter in *Cornwallis Correspondence*, 2:155–56, but omits all names. In this same letter, Cornwallis railed against other patronage appointments of the directors.

45. Cornwallis to directors, 4 Nov. 1789, PRO 30/11/154, fols. 96–101.

46. Cornwallis to Prince of Wales, 10 Nov. 1788, PRO 30/11/269, fols. 17–20.

47. Cornwallis to Dundas, 4 April 1790, *Cornwallis Correspondence*, 2:17.

48. Cornwallis to Dundas, 4 March 1792, ibid., 2:156.

49. Cornwallis to Dundas, 26 Aug. 1787, and Cornwallis to Pitt, 4 Nov. 1788, ibid., 1:290, 391.

50. Cornwallis to Dundas, 31 Dec. 1790, ibid., 2:68.

51. Cornwallis to Dundas, 24 March 1793, ibid., 2:221.

52. Haldane to Mustapha, 20 Dec. 1788, PRO 30/11/27, fol. 484.

53. Turner to Hastings, 2 March 1787: BM, Add. MSS 29,170, fols. 396–99.

54. Cornwallis to Dundas, 30 Aug. 1792, PRO 30/11/151, fols. 133–34.

55. Cornwallis to Sloper, 9 Feb. 1787, PRO 30/11/187, fols. 25–26.

56. Cornwallis to Southampton, 7 Nov. 1789, *Cornwallis Correspondence*, 1:458.

57. Cornwallis to Prince of Wales, 30 Nov. 1789, PRO 30/11/269, fols. 23–36. The earl did, however, try to blend humanitarian considerations with his conception of duty. For example, Charles Lee Lewis, one of His Majesty's company of licensed comedians, came to India on the urging of friends who told him of the fortune to be made there. Deeply in debt, Lewis believed India offered him an alternative to debtor's prison. He said he even talked to two members of the court of directors before leaving, who promised to wink at his departing England clandestinely. He then appealed to Cornwallis for employment, though he had come to India without formal permission of the court of directors. Because Lewis lacked that authorization, Cornwallis necessarily forbade his making any "public professional exhibitions whatever in this settlement." Yet the earl knew it was not entirely the man's fault, knew the directors and the whole history of British India were to blame for his misfortune. So the governor general dipped into his own pocket and sent poor Lewis 1,000 rupees "to relieve in some degree the exigencies of your present situation." See Lewis to Cornwallis (received Aug. 1788) and Cornwallis to Lewis, 9 Aug. 1788, PRO 30/11/35, fols. 304–7.

58. Malet to Cornwallis, 7 July 1791, PRO 30/11/44, fols. 324–25.

59. Cornwallis to Dundas, 14 Aug. 1787, and to the directors, 19 Aug. 1787, *Cornwallis Correspondence*, 1:283, 286.

60. Cornwallis to directors, 3 March 1788, ibid., 1:536.

61. The earl justified the raises in terms of saving the Company money in the long run. He told Dundas: "The allowance of a thousand rupees per month to Haldane my private secretary will be in lieu of all writing of contracts, & will make him by some lacs the cheapest private secretary that any governor general ever had." See Cornwallis to Dundas, 15 Nov. 1786, PRO 30/11/150, fols. 5–8.

62. Cornwallis to Dundas, 14 Aug. 1787, *Cornwallis Correspondence*, 1:281.

63. Cornwallis to Hay, 25 Nov. 1787, PRO 30/11/158, fols. 29–30.

64. Hay to Cornwallis, 25 Nov. 1786 and 5 Aug. 1787, PRO 30/11/18, fols. 229–30, and 30/11/11, fols. 191–92. Hay in fact proved a very capable and loyal subordinate. On his own he compiled a pocketbook of reference, a digest of all the important orders of the directors since 1765, for Cornwallis's convenience and use. See Hay to Cornwallis, 1 Sept. 1787, PRO 30/11/19, fols. 133–34. Cornwallis's first private letter to Hay of 26 Oct. 1786 addressed him as "Dear Sir." One year later it was "Dear Hay" and remained so.

65. Turner to Hastings, 16 Jan. 1787, BM, Add. MSS 29,170, fols. 363–67.

66. Forster to Dundas, 22 July 1787, PRO 30/11/112, fols. 78–81.

67. Thomas Brown to Dundas, 28 July 1789, SRO, GD 51/3/312, letter 4.

68. Unknown to Dundas, 29 Nov. 1786, SRO, GD 51/3/200.

69. Pearse to Hastings, 8 Jan. 1787, BM, Add. MSS 29,170, fols. 346–47.

70. Sir William Jones, *The Letters of Sir William Jones*, 2:764, 781.

Chapter 4

1. No rural statistics were then available so both figures are guesswork. See Sir William Wilson Hunter, *Annals of Rural Bengal*, p. 34, and Muhammad Abdur Rahim, *Social and Cultural History of Bengal*, vol. 2. Rahim, 2:4, estimates Bengal's area based on contemporary accounts as 551,250 square miles in the time of Akbar and 245,000 square miles in the time of Sher Shah. Under British rule, before 1874, Bengal, including Bihar, Orissa, Chota, and Assam, comprehended 248,321 square miles. Rahim, working back from the British census figures of 1872, estimates that in 1772 Bengal contained about 10.6 million Hindus and 8.2 million Moslems, nearly 20 million people.

2. Holden Furber, *John Company at Work*, p. 25.

3. The previous arrangements had failed monetarily and psychologically as well. Under the farming system, the British had perennially fallen short by over 1 million rupees of the amount they expected from taxes. The Hastings committee in its first year collected some £725,238 less than that taken in between 1766 and 1769, and £236,239 less than the average collected between 1769 and 1771. Figures are from B. B. Misra, *The Central Administration of the East India Company, 1773–1834*.

4. IOR, Bengal Despatches, vol. 14. On 12 April 1786, they expressed more forcefully their desire for a permanent settlement with the zemindars.

5. Philip Woodruff [Philip Mason], *The Men Who Ruled India*, 1:144.

6. Quoted by John Lord Teignmouth in his edition of *Memoirs of the Life and Correspondence of John Lord Teignmouth*, 1:75–76.

7. Shore to Warren Hastings, 16 Feb. 1787, ibid., 1:136. Philip Mason, a retired member of the Indian Civil Service, writing under the name of Philip Woodruff, described Shore as "not a character to arouse warmth of feeling; there is no strong love or hate, there is no passion in his life. He was fair, he was thorough, he was painstaking, he was temperate, he was honest. . . . His conscience drove him unremittingly to duties that he found mildly distasteful." See Woodruff, *Men Who Ruled India*, 1:133.

8. Cornwallis to Dundas, 24 Aug. 1786, Melville Papers, NLS.

9. Quoted in Ainslie Thomas Embree, *Charles Grant and British Rule in India*, p. 51.

10. Shortly after Grant's appointment, Major William Palmer, Warren Hastings's military secretary and confidential agent, complained that Cornwallis would have employed him "were it not for the advice of Shore, who will suffer no one but his particular friends and dependents to enjoy any credit or advantage with this government." See Palmer to Hastings, 5 March 1787, BM, Add. MSS 29,170, fols. 400–401. Palmer eventually secured a position as British resident with Scindia.

11. See Cornwallis to Grant, 20 Oct. 1786, and Grant's response of 31 Oct. 1786, in PRO 30/11/84, fols. 59–60, and 30/11/10, fols. 181–95.

12. Cornwallis to Dundas, 23 Jan. 1787 and 2 March 1788, PRO 30/11/50, fols. 18–19, 72–75.

13. W. S. Seton-Karr, *The Marquis Cornwallis and the Consolidation of British Rule*, p. 28, cites this minute as but one example of Shore's thorough understanding of Bengal revenue. For the minute of 18 June see *Br. Parl. Papers, Cols., E. Ind.*, 3:169–220. When printed here the minute comprises only 51 pages, but it still contains 562 paragraphs. Cornwallis, in a minute of 18 September 1789, lavishly praised Shore's work, commenting on the "uncommon knowledge which he has manifested of every part of the revenue system of this country, the liberality and fairness of his arguments and clearness of his style." The earl used his "powerful assistance in every branch of the business of this government" and found himself in "general approbation of the greatest part of his plan" (minute of the governor general, 18 Sept. 1789, *Cornwallis Correspondence*, 1:560.

14. IOR, Home Misc. 379–92, contains reams of papers discussing the history of the revenue collection in Bengal and suggesting the best sort of settlement to make. The Cornwallis Papers as well are full of opinions on the matter. In addition, see *Br. Parl. Papers, Cols., E. Ind.*, 3:169–498, for Shore's and Cornwallis's minutes in June and September of 1789 and February of 1790. Pages 3–78 summarize the history of British administration in Bengal and point out the effect of Cornwallis's regulations on the revenue as well as on other departments.

15. Captain Andrew Pringle to Cornwallis, 31 Oct. 1786, PRO 30/11/45, fols. 218–21.

16. Cornwallis to Dundas, 9 Aug. 1790, PRO 30/11/151, fols. 52–59.

17. Extract of Bengal Revenue Consultations, Shore's minute of 21 Dec. 1789, IOR, Home Misc. 384, p. 221, printed in *Br. Parl. Papers, Cols., E. Ind.*, 3:477–83.

18. Cornwallis to Dundas, 7 Nov. 1789, *Cornwallis Correspondence*, 1:460.

19. Cornwallis to Dundas, 5 Dec. 1789, ibid., 1:466.

20. Cornwallis to Dundas, 12 Feb. 1790, ibid., 1:493.

21. For these exchanges see Dundas to Cornwallis, 2 May 1781, PRO 30/11/117, fols. 35–40; Dundas to Cornwallis, 17 Sept. 1792, *Cornwallis Correspondence*, 2:215; John Ehrman, *The Younger Pitt*, p. 458; and C. H. Philips, *The East India Company, 1784–1834*, p. 69.

22. James Mill, *The History of British India*, 5:404–13. John Kenneth Galbraith, the Harvard economist and former ambassador to India, admitted Mill's short-comings, especially that Mill knew nothing about Indian India, and that he tended to measure everyone by his own standards in religion, marriage, customs, and even hygiene. His greatest virtue, according to Galbraith, was that he had judged British rule by British standards of the time and showed in detail the superimposition of British mores on the Indians. See "James Mill's India."

23. Seton-Karr, *Marquis Cornwallis*, passim.

24. Woodruff, *Men Who Ruled India*, 1:141.

25. H. R. C. Wright, "Some Aspects of the Permanent Settlement in Bengal."

26. Misra, *Central Administration*, pp. 185–93.

27. Anyone who doubts the massive amount of research the Company's servants did need only peruse the Home Miscellaneous Series, 379–92, in the India Office. It consists of a long series of papers discussing the best settlement for Bengal. The zemindars, of course, did not "own" the land, but in many areas the system was akin to English feudalism in the medieval period. Then the military aristocracy did not "own" the land either. They held it of others. Would not English peasants in the medieval period have welcomed a permanent settlement between the king and this aristocracy?

28. For these opinions see Brooke to Cornwallis, 8 May 1789, PRO 30/11/30, fols. 61–62; Graham to Cornwallis, 6 May 1792, PRO 30/11/49, fols. 58–61; Mercer to Cornwallis, 22 Aug. 1790, PRO 30/11/37, fols. 472–73; Bathurst to Cornwallis, 16 Oct. 1789, PRO 30/11/32, fols. 13–14; and IOR, Home Misc. 382, pp. 63–241.

29. Cornwallis to Charles Stuart, 15 June 1790, PRO 30/11/171, fols. 56–57.

30. Cornwallis to Dundas, 17 May 1787, PRO 30/11/150, fols. 32–33.

31. Cornwallis to court of directors, 2 Aug. 1789, *Cornwallis Correspondence*, 1:554.

32. Minute of governor general, 18 Sept. 1789, ibid., pp. 561–62.

33. Cornwallis to Campbell, 19 Dec. 1787, PRO 30/11/159.

34. Cornwallis to Charles Stuart, 13 Oct. 1791, PRO 30/11/172, fols. 49–50.

35. *An Abstract of the Regulations Enacted for the Assessment and Regulation of the Land Revenues . . . to 1824, Inclusive.*

36. See regulation 2.

Chapter 5

1. For these instances, see IOR, Europeans in India, 0/5/2, from 1787 to 1791, report of Colonel T. D. Pearse, 28 Feb. 1787, pp. 1–5; of a police officer, 23 Jan. 1788, pp. 11–13; and extract from Bengal Public Consultations, pp. 127–29.

2. Petition of C. L. Blundell to Cornwallis, received 27 April 1787, PRO 30/11/16, fols. 13–16.

3. IOR 0/5/3, 1794, pp. 29–32.

4. IOR, Home Misc. 380, pp. 28–29, public letter from Bengal, 12 March 1791.

5. Willes to Cornwallis, 14 Feb. 1787, PRO 30/11/14, fols. 291–92; Captain R. Baillie to Willes, 3 April 1787, PRO 30/11/16, fols. 581–84; and Willes to Cornwallis, 11 April 1787, PRO 30/11/16, fols. 585–86.

6. Welsh to Cornwallis, 14 Jan. 1787, PRO 30/11/13, fols. 280–81.

7. Harper to Cornwallis, 5 and 6 Feb. 1787, PRO 30/11/14, fols. 86–89.

8. William Farmer to board of factors at Thana, 3 March 1790, IOR G 38/8, fol. 89.

9. Phanindra Nath Banerjee, "Background to the Cornwallis Code," pp. 92–95, summarizes the Moslem law.

10. *Calcutta Chronicle*, 4, no. 161, pp. 1–2.

11. Cornwallis to Dundas, 8 March 1789, PRO 30/11/150, fols. 122–23.

12. Only the supreme court could try offenses in Calcutta, including petty offenses, but there were no English magistrates.

13. Cornwallis to directors, 2 Aug. 1789, *Cornwallis Correspondence*, 1:555.

14. See Cornwallis to Dundas, 10 Dec. 1792, Melville Papers, NLS.

15. Cornwallis to Dundas, 5 March 1789, PRO 30/11/150, fols. 122–23.

16. Garland Cannon, *Oriental Jones*, details Jones's life. A. L. Rowse, "Welsh Orientalist," is a concise little essay on Jones's life.

17. Cornwallis to Lord Brome, 28 Dec. 1786, *Cornwallis Correspondence*, 1:247.

18. Jones to Spencer, 1–11 Sept. 1787, Sir William Jones, *The Letters of Sir William Jones*, 2:764.

19. Jones to Dundas, 26 Feb. 1788, ibid., 2:791.

20. Jones to Cornwallis, 19 March 1788, ibid., 2:794–800.

21. Governor general and council to Jones, 19 March 1788, ibid., 2:801–2.

22. Cornwallis to Jones, 17 Nov. 1790, *Cornwallis Correspondence*, 2:54. Aspinall, in trying to correct the impression that Cornwallis took all his advice from Jones in the reform of justice and the police, gives Jones too little credit. Jones helped considerably, as his letters and those of Cornwallis make clear, in the judicial but not in the police changes.

23. "A Zemindar of Jessore in fact," Misra notes, "openly raided the house of a village woman, robbed her of her property and finally put her to death." See B. B. Misra, *The Central Administration of the East India Company, 1773–1834*, p. 309. Summary of previous British arrangements comes mostly from Misra.

24. This summary comes from ibid. and from Arthur Aspinall, *Cornwallis in Bengal*. Though Misra differs somewhat from Aspinall in interpretation, they go over precisely the same ground in describing factual events. We found very little to choose between them, and between our own reading of the documents, insofar as Cornwallis's contributions to criminal justice are concerned.

25. IOR, Bengal Revenue Consultations, 27 July 1787.

26. Aspinall, *Cornwallis in Bengal*, chapter 2, adduces many more examples than the ones we have cited. Misra, *Central Administration*, pp. 322–24, gives others.

27. Cornwallis to directors, 2 Aug. 1789, *Cornwallis Correspondence*, 1:535–36.

28. Cornwallis to Dundas, 8 March 1789, PRO 30/11/150, fols. 122–23.

29. Cornwallis, minute of 11 Feb. 1793, *Br. Parl. Papers, Cols., E. Ind.*, 3:109–53.

30. Dundas supported Cornwallis completely in this endeavor. See Dundas to Cornwallis, 8 Aug. 1789, PRO 30/11/115, fols. 193–201.
31. Cornwallis to the secret committee, 16 Nov. 1786, PRO 30/11/156, fols. 96–121.
32. For police regulations see "Regulations for the Police of the Collectorship of Bengal, Bahar and Orissa, passed by the Governor General in Council on the 7th December 1792," *Br. Parl. Papers, Cols., E. Ind.*, 1:178–84.
33. Aspinall, *Cornwallis in Bengal*, p. 118.
34. IOR, Bengal Public and Secret Letters to Court, public letter, 15 Sept. 1787. Summary comes mostly from Aspinall, *Cornwallis in Bengal*.
35. Cornwallis to Oakeley, 22 Dec. 1792, PRO 30/11/79, fols. 121–22.
36. Cornwallis to the directors, 6 March 1793, *Cornwallis Correspondence*, 2:562.
37. Banerjee, "Background," p. 96.
38. Aspinall, *Cornwallis in Bengal*, p. 91.
39. W. S. Seton-Karr, *The Marquis Cornwallis and the Consolidation of British Rule*, p. 95. Later, modifications would become inevitable. Litigation increased after Cornwallis left, and other matters cropped up so that after 1793 the Company would transfer revenue suits back to the collectors, impose institution fees to discourage litigation, and change the constitution of the courts to cope with increased business. Nor did Cornwallis's reforms put a stop to crime. Thuggee would not end until the 1830s and the Company, as in civil justice, would undertake to amend the Cornwallis system. Those later amendments, however, often owed as much to exterior factors as to weaknesses in the code itself. One judge in 1795 attributed the increase in litigation to back business never having been cleared up. He pointed out that "nine tenths of the causes filed since my appointment (excluding the Maal causes) have their origins from 15 years to 2, and almost the whole of the suits for land, which are the most tedious and are always contested to the last, originate in the same period. Therefore my labour since I was appointed has been generally employed in deciding causes of very old origin which the easy access to justice by the present system has invited the suitors to bring forward." See William Camac to G. H. Barlow, 11 April 1795, PRO 30/11/55, fols. 19–20. Crime may have increased after Cornwallis left, but one should remember that it occurred during a period of continued British expansion and war. Such periods offer the criminal better opportunities than times of peace and stability. G. H. Barlow claimed that the immediate effects of the system discouraged crime. In a letter to Cornwallis of 1795, he pointed out that whatever complaints existed usually owed to inefficient magistrates, and he argued that dacoity had been almost "wholly suppressed." See Barlow to Cornwallis, 12 May 1795, PRO 30/11/44, fols. 23–34. A judge of circuit for the western division of Calcutta wrote Shore that mofussil (rural or provincial) dacoity "as far as our observation extends, has certainly in great measure subsided. The instances that came under consideration were few, and not attended with the acts of atrocity, that we have noticed upon former occasions, when murder, wounding & torture were generally the concomitants of it." See John White to Sir John Shore, no date, PRO 30/11/55, fols. 62–67. Alexander Seton, judge of Bihar in 1795, wrote to Barlow in that year that he believed the Cornwallis system would benefit the native inhabitants. See Seton to Barlow, 21 May 1795, PRO 30/11/55, fols. 60–61.

40. Cornwallis to Sir George Yonge, 5 Nov. 1789, PRO, WO 40/5.
41. Yonge to Cornwallis, 1790, PRO 30/11/36, fols. 612–13.
42. BM, Add. MSS 29,202, fol. 192.
43. For the argument that the English were more familiar with Indian society in the earlier period see the excellent work by Percival Spear, *The Nabobs*.
44. Cornwallis to the directors, 7 Sept. 1791, *Cornwallis Correspondence*, 1:524.
45. Cornwallis to Ives, 24 Sept. 1788, PRO 30/11/170, fols. 113–14.
46. Cornwallis to Medows, 28 Aug. 1790, PRO 30/11/174, fols. 117–18.
47. IOR, Bengal Despatches, vol. 14.
48. Jones to Lord Ashburton, 27 April 1783, Jones, *Letters*, 2:616.
49. Jones to Arthur Lee, 1 Oct. 1786, ibid., 2:712–13.
50. Jones to Pollard, 20 Sept. 1789, ibid., 2:847.
51. Malet to Cornwallis, 28 Oct. 1787, PRO 30/11/120, fols. 287–93.
52. Campbell to Dundas, 23 May 1787, NLS, MS 3837, fols. 143–44.
53. General Order of 9 May 1792, *Cornwallis Correspondence*, 2:168–69. Ross did not print the names in his edition.
54. Cornwallis to Dundas, 14 Aug. 1787, PRO 30/11/150, fols. 38–45.
55. *An Abstract of the Regulations of Government in the Departments of Miscellaneous Revenue and Commerce*, part 5.
56. For a detailed account of Duncan's career and the establishment of the college see V. A. Narain, *Jonathan Duncan and Varanasi*.
57. John Bebb to board of trade, 14 May 1789, PRO 30/11/30, fols. 3–4.
58. Cornwallis to directors, 2 Nov. 1789, *Cornwallis Correspondence*, 1:456–57.
59. Cornwallis to Dundas, 14 Aug. 1787, PRO 30/11/150, fols. 38–45.
60. Misra, *Central Administration*, p. 107.
61. J. C. Sinha, *Economic Annals of Bengal*.
62. Jeremiah Church to Cornwallis, 30 Jan. 1787, PRO 30/11/13, fols. 26–29.
63. Anonymous to Haldane, 7 Nov. 1788, PRO 30/11/27, fols. 246–47, and Kirkpatrick to Cornwallis, 23 Dec. 1788, ibid., fols. 346–47.
64. He informed the directors only after he had stopped the traffic. See Cornwallis to directors, 2 Aug. 1789, *Cornwallis Correspondence*, 1:555.
65. See the proclamation in *Calcutta Gazette Extraordinary*, 27 July 1789.
66. G. H. Barlow to Cornwallis, 26 Nov. 1795, PRO 30/11/55, fols. 167–76.
67. Vincent A. Smith, *Oxford History of India*, p. 538.

Chapter 6

1. The exception is Raymond Callahan, *The East India Company and Army Reform, 1783–1798*.
2. Ibid., p. 6, gives figures for 1763, 1782, and 1805. We have added slightly to his figure for 1782. No exact accounting is possible and ours is a rough estimate based on the fact of expansion to 1805 and various calculations from numerous returns for various branches of the army. In 1789, for example, the army had 1,756 officers, 7,574 Europeans (excluding regulars save for the 73d regiment), 85,616 sepoys, 2,994 native staff, 8,299 lascars, 3,069 artificers, and 4,436 bheasties (water boys), comprising a total of 113,744. See PRO, SP 41/29. One immediately understands the difficulty of arriving at exact figures, however, when one examines the figures for 1794 as given to Parliament.

Appendix two to the second select committee report in *Br. Parl. Papers, Cols., E. Ind.*, 1:526, numbered His Majesty's troops at 4,854 infantry, 111 artillery, 345 dragoons; the Company's European troops of six artillery battalions and twelve infantry regiments at 8,190; and it totaled the sepoys, with cavalry, infantry, artillery, and others such as rangers, marines, and pioneers at 56,433, making an inclusive total of only 69,936.

3. Mark Wilks, *Historical Sketches of the South of India . . .*, 2:517, offers this figure.

4. Campbell to Cornwallis, 6 May 1787, PRO 30/11/118, fols. 80–90.

5. Cornwallis to York, 10 Dec. 1787, *Cornwallis Correspondence*, 1:316.

6. "It is our order," the directors stated, "that all establishments respecting native artillery or golondanse should cease, and that officers and men of these corps shall be incorporated into the Sepoy battalions, or into the Lascars attached to the artillery" (directors to president and council at Bombay, 21 Sept. 1785, PRO 30/11/9, fols. 54–61). By 1794, however, Bombay had ten companies.

7. Cornwallis to directors, 7 July 1792, PRO 30/11/155, fols. 246–53.

8. Colonel George Eyres to Cornwallis, 24 April 1790, PRO 30/11/133, fols. 80–81.

9. Pearse to Cornwallis, 23 April 1787, PRO 30/11/145, fol. 46.

10. See "State of the Rank & File of His Majesty's Troops in India after the Recruits which are on their passage shall have joined," 22 Jan. 1791, PRO 30/11/127; out-letters to the colonels commanding regiments stationed in India, 23 March 1791, PRO, WO 4/297; "Roster of the Regiments in the East Indies," IOR, Home Misc. 379, fol. 567; "General Abstracts Relative to the Company's Armies in India, in the years 1794, 1796, 1807 and 1808," from Second Report of the Select Committee on the Affairs of the East India Company, pp. 291–328, printed in *Br. Parl. Papers, Cols., E. Ind.*, 1:525–58.

11. Duke of Richmond (master general of the ordnance) to Cornwallis, 27 April 1791, PRO 30/11/43, fols. 764–69.

12. Piers Mackesy, *The War for America, 1775–1783*, p. 392 and n. 1.

13. See Campbell to Cornwallis, 4 Aug. 1788, PRO 30/11/134, fols. 57–58, and Campbell to Dundas, 28 March 1790, NLS, MS 3839, fol. 91.

14. Every one of the British knew that their military superiority alone ensured their continuance as rulers in India and that if they lost it they lost India. Yet, although regimental studies and accounts of battles in the eighteenth century exist, scholars have almost totally neglected to study the Company's army, its organization, methods of supply, growth, and similar matters.

15. Richmond to Cornwallis, 27 April 1791, PRO 30/11/42, fols. 764b–765.

16. Callahan, *East India Company*, p. 49.

17. For the plan see ibid., pp. 64–65.

18. Dundas to Cornwallis, 20 July 1786, *Cornwallis Correspondence*, 1:255.

19. Cornwallis to Dundas, 18 Feb. 1787, IOR, Home Misc 389, fols. 121–23.

20. Cornwallis to Dundas, 12 Aug. 1787, PRO 30/11/150, fols. 34–37.

21. Cornwallis to Yonge and Pitt, 7 March 1788, *Cornwallis Correspondence*, 1:344–45.

22. Campbell to Cornwallis, 22 March 1788, PRO 30/11/134, fols. 45–52.

23. Cornwallis to Sir George Yonge, 8 Sept. 1791, PRO, HO 40/5.

24. Medows to Dundas, 13 Dec. 1788, PRO 30/11/115, fols. 181–85.

25. Callahan, *East India Company*, p. 98. Again, the argument was not all in favor of the deprived Company officers. John Grattan, the adjutant general at Madras, complained to Cornwallis that when the government agreed to discontinue any more advanced local rank, the Company had an implied obligation "duly to moderate the advancement of their own officers." But, according to Grattan, they had not done so. He thought the promotions that had taken place favored the Company officers at a ratio of twelve to one and submitted documents to back this contention. In his own case, Grattan pointed out, he also suffered: "Since Jany 1st, 1783, at which time I took rank of every major of this establishment, I have been gradually superseded by two majors, fourteen captains, & one lieutenant (not including three captains now on leave, who, as is the practice of the establishment may hereafter return on their former standing with the rank of Lieut. Colonel), which two majors, fourteen captains, & one lieutenant are actually lieut. colonels, myself still remaining in the rank of major, to the manifest prejudice of my just claims of seniority." See Grattan to Cornwallis, 30 Aug. 1788, PRO 30/11/25, fols. 121–22.

26. Cornwallis to Dundas, 5 March 1787, PRO 30/11/150, fols. 26–31.

27. "Extract of a general letter from the Honble the Court of Directors to the Governor General in Council in the Secret and Military Department, the 20th August 1788," PRO 30/11/123, fols. 3–4.

28. Cornwallis to directors, 6 March 1789, *Cornwallis Correspondence*, 1:550.

29. Cornwallis to Campbell, 12 May 1787, PRO 30/11/159, fols. 61–62.

30. Cornwallis to directors, 6 March 1789, *Cornwallis Correspondence*, 1:550–51.

31. Callahan, *East India Company*, p. 221, points out forcibly the consequences of the officers' obstinacy: "The pride and parochialism of the Bengal army and its carefully preserved seniority promotion system helped make the Mutiny and its own destruction possible. Perhaps the best symbol of the ultimate consequence of the Bengal officers' victory in 1796 is the commander at Meerut in 1857: Major General W. H. Hewitt, a veteran of fifty unbroken years in India, physically feeble, and nearly incapable of grasping what was happening about him."

32. Cornwallis to York, 10 Nov. 1786, *Cornwallis Correspondence*, 1:235.

33. Cornwallis to directors, 18 Aug. 1787, ibid., 1:531.

34. Callahan, *East India Company*, pp. 75–76, justifiably points out that Cornwallis had no business harping about Company understrength when the European ranks were equally short of men. Yet the earl worried more about quality than about muster rolls.

35. Cornwallis to Colonel Fox, 10 Nov. 1786, *Cornwallis Correspondence*, 1:239.

36. Cornwallis to Fawcett, 12 Aug. 1787, ibid., 1:279–80, and to directors, 16 Nov. 1787, PRO 30/11/153, fols. 85–92.

37. Cornwallis to Dundas, 14 Aug. 1787, PRO 30/11/150, fols. 38–45.

38. See, for example, Colonel John Brathwaite to Cornwallis, 30 April 1793, PRO 30/11/52, fols. 45–46; Campbell to Cornwallis, 27 April 1788, PRO 30/11/23, fols. 89–90; and Kirkpatrick to Cornwallis, 7 June 1787, PRO 30/11/17, fols. 234–37.

39. See Colonel Norman Macleod to Cornwallis, 28 April 1788, PRO 30/11/

144, fols. 136–37; and Cornwallis to Campbell, 21 Jan. 1788, PRO 30/11/160, fol. 11.

40. Pearse to Cornwallis, 8 Feb. 1787, PRO 30/11/145, fols. 43–44.

41. Pearse to Cornwallis, 2 Nov. 1786, PRO 30/11/145, fols. 31–33.

42. Cornwallis to Pearse, 26 Sept. 1788, PRO 30/11/186, fols. 53–54.

43. Cornwallis to Campbell, 21 Jan. 1788, PRO 30/11/160, fol. 11.

44. Cornwallis to Dundas, 8 March 1789, PRO 30/11/150, fols. 122–23.

45. Ibid.

46. Campbell to Cornwallis, 27 April 1788, PRO 30/11/23, fols. 89–90.

47. Kirkpatrick to Cornwallis, 7 June 1787, PRO 30/11/17, fols. 234–37; and Cornwallis to Kirkpatrick, 21 June 1787, ibid., fols. 273–76.

48. Andrew Hunter to Cornwallis, Aug. 1787, PRO 30/11/18, fols. 243–44.

49. Colonel White to Cornwallis, 13 Jan. 1787, PRO 30/11/13, fols. 282–83.

50. See *Calcutta Gazette*, 16, no. 165, 26 April 1787, and 19, no. 220, 15 May 1788.

51. Regimental surgeon to Cornwallis, 9 May 1788, PRO 30/11/24, fol. 375.

52. Thomas Lyon to Cornwallis, 4 Sept. 1787, PRO 30/11/19, fols. 222–25.

53. See Lyon to Cornwallis, 30 Aug. 1787, PRO 30/11/18, fols. 401–10; and Pearse to Cornwallis, 2 and 3 Oct. 1787, PRO 30/11/145, fols. 29–30, 86–87.

54. See, for example, the various contracts in *Calcutta Gazette* and John White to Ross, 21 Aug. 1789, PRO 30/11/23, fols. 112–13.

55. Cornwallis to Dundas, 18 Feb. 1787, IOR, Home Misc. 389, fol. 121.

56. Cornwallis to Dundas, 16 Nov. 1787, *Cornwallis Correspondence*, 1:311.

57. Cornwallis to Campbell, 12 Jan. 1787, PRO 30/11/159, fols. 27–29; and *Calcutta Gazette*, 6, no. 152, 25 Jan. 1787.

58. Cornwallis to Campbell, 12 Jan. 1787 and 6 Feb. 1789, PRO 30/11/159, fols. 27–29, and 30/11/173, fol. 3.

59. Cornwallis to Dundas, 30 Nov. 1786, *Cornwallis Correspondence*, 1:214–15.

60. War Office, 24 April 1787, "A list of officers now in Europe who belong to His Majesty's regiments in the East Indies; with observations to their being absent from their respective regiments," PRO 30/11/16, fols. 605–6.

61. See, for example, Campbell to Cornwallis, 14 May 1787, PRO 30/11/6, fols. 57–58.

62. Cornwallis to Fawcett, 12 Aug. 1787, *Cornwallis Correspondence*, 1:279.

63. Cornwallis to directors, 15 Nov. 1786, IOR, Home Misc. 389, fol. 61.

64. Cornwallis to York, 20 July 1787, PRO 30/11/269, fols. 66–69; to directors, 18 Aug. 1787, PRO 30/11/153, fols. 67–76; and to Dundas, 16 Nov. 1787, PRO 30/11/150, fols. 50–59.

65. Colonel George Eyres to Cornwallis, 21 Oct. 1786, PRO 30/11/143, fols. 45–46.

66. Cornwallis to directors, 3 March 1788, PRO 30/11/153, fols. 124–35, printed only in part in *Cornwallis Correspondence*, 1:537.

67. Cornwallis to Hay, 18 Oct. 1787, PRO 30/11/158, fols. 23–24; and to directors, 3 March 1788, *Cornwallis Correspondence*, 1:537.

68. Michael Topping to Cornwallis, 31 March 1793, PRO 30/11/51, fols. 249–52.

69. Captain Thomas Brown to Dundas, 2 Jan. 1789, SRO, GD 51/3/312/2.

70. Lt. Col. W. Wood to Cornwallis, 27 Jan. 1790, PRO 30/11/135, fols. 47–48; and Cornwallis to directors, 3 March 1788, PRO 30/11/153, fols. 124–35.

71. Cornwallis to directors, 6 Nov. 1789, PRO 30/11/154, fols. 108–15.

72. Callahan, *East India Company*, pp. 118–20.

73. Cornwallis to Dundas, 7 Nov. 1794, *Cornwallis Correspondence*, 2:572; pp. 572–82 outline the plan. Murray, interestingly enough, compares Shore's plan for Bengal with Cornwallis's plan for all of India. See IOR, Home Misc. 451, fols. 425–40.

74. Cornwallis to Dundas, 7 Nov. 1794, *Cornwallis Correspondence*, 2:574.

75. Callahan, *East India Company*, pp. 122–26, summarizes the recommendations.

76. Ibid., pp. 127–211, outlines all these events in considerable detail.

Chapter 7

1. Act. 24 Geo. 3, chap 25, s. 32, quoted in B. B. Misra, *The Central Administration of the East India Company, 1773–1834*, p. 32.

2. IOR, Home Misc. 369, pp. 36–37, an anonymous observation.

3. PRO, SP 41/29 (unpaginated and unfoliated) contains the references to Colonel Baillie's losses.

4. Denys Forrest, *Tiger of Mysore*, offers the reader a convenient summary of events in India previous to Cornwallis's arrival.

5. See, for example, PRO 30/11/125, fols. 144–53, "Narrative of Mr. William Drake formerly midshipman of the Hannibal and other prisoners taken last war, who have lately made their escape from Tippoo."

6. Forrest, *Tiger of Mysore*, discusses these narratives in an attempt to separate fact from fiction.

7. IOR, Home Misc. 436, p. 134.

8. Cornwallis to Kennaway, 26 Aug. 1789, *Cornwallis Correspondence*, 1:436.

9. NLS, MS 3839, fol. 102, has a complete physical description of Tipoo.

10. Indeed, shortly after he landed in Bengal, Cornwallis received from Lucknow an intelligence report on Tipoo. See C. L. Martin to Cornwallis, 16 Sept. 1786, PRO 30/11/9, fols. 223–31, "A Short Account of the powers bordering on the Company's and Vizier's Dominions." See Forster to Cornwallis, 9 and 15 Jan. 1787, PRO 30/11/13, fols. 52–55.

11. Captain J. Collins to Lt. Col. Ross, 29 Oct. 1787, PRO 30/11/20, fols. 54–55.

12. See *Calcutta Gazette, Supplement*, 8, no. 184, 15 Nov. 1787.

13. See PRO 30/11/33, fols. 70, 88, 132.

14. Estimate from Alexander Dirom. Dirom, though far from reliable, condemned nearly out of hand the accuracy of intelligence gatherer Charles Lloyd. Lloyd, a former surgeon to Hyder Ali, now resided in Madras and claimed to be in contact with one of Tipoo's principal ministers. See memorandum of Alexander Dirom, 25 July 1790, PRO 30/11/35, fols. 58–59, and Dirom to Ross, 28 Jan. 1790, PRO 30/11/34, fols. 43–44.

15. PRO 30/11/128, fols. 64–66.

16. Cornwallis to name missing, 4 Nov. 1791, PRO 30/11/178, fols. 127–28.

17. Malet to Cornwallis, 28 Oct. 1787, PRO 30/11/20, fols. 272–93, enclosing extract from Governor Boddam.

18. Campbell to Cornwallis, 8 May 1788, PRO 30/11/119, fols. 39–42.

19. Campbell to Cornwallis, 26 June and 18 April 1787, ibid., fols. 71–73, 35–38.

20. Cornwallis to Edward Hay, 16 Oct. 1787, PRO 30/11/158, fols. 23–24.

21. War fever reached its height late in 1787 and then subsided.

22. Cornwallis to Medows, 20 Aug. 1790, PRO 30/11/174, fols. 111–14.

23. Minute of Cornwallis, 16 June 1788, *Cornwallis Correspondence*, 1:356–57.

24. Cornwallis to secret committee, 16 Nov. 1787, PRO 30/11/156, fols. 1–5.

25. Cornwallis to Palmer, 28 Oct. 1787, PRO 30/11/168, fols. 37–38.

26. Cornwallis to Dundas, 8 March 1789, PRO 30/11/150, fols. 122–33.

27. Ibid.

28. These lines had a rampart, a ditch sixteen feet wide and twenty feet deep, a bamboo hedge in front, and several bastions on rising ground.

29. The Dutch asserted they had taken them directly from Portugal and had never paid a cent to anyone for them.

30. Holden Furber, *John Company at Work*, pp. 243–47, describes the episode.

31. He, indeed, affirmed that he had refused to employ culprits who had embezzled large sums. See Campbell to Dundas, 11 Sept. 1788, NLS, MS 3838, fols. 214–15.

32. Cornwallis to secret committee, 12 April 1790, PRO 30/11/157, fols. 143–48.

33. Cornwallis to Medows, 23 March 1790, PRO 30/11/174, fols. 49–51.

34. Anecdotes about Medows come from John William Kaye, *Lives of Indian Officers Illustrative of the History of the Civil and Military Services of India*, 1:82–83.

35. Sydney to Cornwallis, 21 July 1787, PRO 30/11/138, fols. 176–77.

36. Cornwallis to Rawdon, 14 Feb. 1790, PRO 30/11/186, fols. 5–76.

37. Malet negotiated the treaty, which contained some fourteen articles, at Poona. Cornwallis signed it 5 July. See PRO 30/11/36, fols. 427–37.

38. For these constant admonitions to his subordinate see Cornwallis to Medows, 21 Jan. and 21 Dec. 1788; 23 Nov. 1789; 11 Feb., 20 June, 11 July, 9 Aug., and 28 Aug. 1790, PRO 30/11/173, fols. 1–2; PRO 30/11/174, fols. 7–8, 23–24, 27–30, 88–91, 101–5, 111–14, and 117–18.

39. See Colonel Thomas Musgrave to Cornwallis, 12 Jan. 1790, PRO 30/11/125, fols. 22–23; and Cornwallis to Musgrave, 1 Feb. 1790, PRO 30/11/176, fols. 23–25.

40. For Cornwallis's reflections on the proper method of campaigning against Tipoo see his letters to Medows of 11 Feb., 23, 24, 30 March, and 27 June 1790 in PRO 30/11/174, fols. 27–30, 49–51, and 92–100.

41. *Cornwallis Correspondence*, 1:480n. See also Mark Wilks, *Historical Sketches of the South of India . . .*, 2:390–400, for the detailed numbers and dispositions of this unit and Medows's troops, and Tipoo's answer.

42. Cornwallis to Medows, 25 Aug. 1790, PRO 30/11/174, fols. 115–16. Wilks, *Historical Sketches*, 2:391–92, states that Colonel Floyd, in command of the unit Tipoo damaged severely, had intelligence of the sultan's movements through an officer formerly in English service who had served Tipoo and then deserted him. Wilks avers that Floyd sent the intelligence to Medows at head-

quarters, along with the suggestion that Floyd's advance units should fall back, but that headquarters refused to believe this information and ordered Floyd to maintain his position.

43. *Cornwallis Correspondence*, 1:480, and Wilks, *Historical Sketches*, 2:408–9.

44. Cornwallis to the Duke of York, 20 Nov. 1790, PRO 30/11/269, fols. 43–46. At the time Medows made his error he had not received any direct intelligence from the Calcutta army for three weeks.

45. See Cornwallis to Colonel Thomas Musgrave, 17 Feb. 1790, *Cornwallis Correspondence*, 1:495; and Cornwallis to Captain John Kennaway, 8 April 1790, PRO 30/11/166, fols. 62–65.

46. Cornwallis to Medows, 27 June 1790, PRO 30/11/174, fols. 93–100.

47. Medows to Kennaway, 28 May 1790, PRO 30/11/36, fols. 306–7.

48. Cornwallis to Medows, 20 Oct. 1790, PRO 30/11/174, fols. 141–42.

49. Kyd's and Robinson's instructions are printed in *Cornwallis Correspondence*, 2:500–501.

50. *Calcutta Gazette*, 14, no. 354, 9 Dec. 1790. Four days earlier, the Company's servants had assembled to offer him a similar address. See PRO 30/11/213, fols. 1–2.

51. Cornwallis to W. W. Grenville, 28 Dec. 1790, PRO 30/11/152, fols. 17–20.

52. Cornwallis to Medows, 15 Dec. 1790, PRO 30/11/173, fols. 11–16; and Cornwallis to directors, 26 Jan. 1791, PRO 30/11/155, fols. 1–3.

53. Cornwallis to Abercrombie, 17 Dec. 1790, PRO 30/11/181, fols. 2–3.

54. Ibid., 24 Dec. 1790, ibid., fols. 10–12.

55. Cornwallis to Medows, 4 Jan. 1791, PRO 30/11/173, fols. 43–46.

56. Sir John Fortescue, *History of the British Army*, 3:563, makes this assertion. More important, Major Alexander Dirom, deputy adjutant general of the king's troops in India, advanced the claim in his 1793 account of the campaign, *A Narrative of the Campaign in India* . . ., pp. 113–14. Dirom said elephants had not been used much previously because their keepers lied about the amount of subsistence the beasts required. Keepers said elephants could not survive without huge daily supplies of rice, which the British were reluctant to supply for fear of the cost, but which the keepers actually wanted for themselves. Dirom said that "the elephant is not only the most powerful and most useful, but one of the most hardy animals that can be employed."

57. Cornwallis reported to Charles Stuart on 23 February 1792 that sixty-four elephants had joined the army, whereas he had put their number at sixty-seven in a letter to Sir Charles Oakeley on 20 February. See PRO 30/11/172, fols. 15–16, 17–18. Major James Rennell, *The Marches of the British Armies in the Peninsula of India* . . ., puts their initial number at sixty-seven. Roderick Mackenzie, *A Sketch of the War with Tippoo Sultaun*, 2:13, estimates sixty-five. Mackenzie's is the most thorough and detailed account of the entire war.

58. Dirom, *Narrative*, pp. 24–25, 242.

59. Duff to Cornwallis, 14 Feb. 1791, PRO 30/11/41, fols. 27–28.

60. Dirom, *Narrative*, pp. 44, 113.

61. Rennell, *Marches of the British Armies*, pp. 8–9.

62. See "List of stores dispatched to Fort St. George since the departure of the Right Honble the Governor General and commander in Chief," PRO 30/11/40, fol. 567. See also ibid., fols. 584–85.

63. See William Hickey, *Memoirs*, 4:7.

64. See Cornwallis's letters to Lt. Stewart in February, March, and April 1791, PRO 30/11/167, fols. 1–2, 15–16, 33–34, 37–38, 54–55, 59–60, and 66–70.

65. Cornwallis to Malet, 12 Feb. and 1 March 1791, PRO 30/11/163, fols. 90–91.

66. Cornwallis to Sir Charles Oakeley, 23 Jan. 1791, PRO 30/11/17, fols. 18–20.

67. Mackenzie, *Sketch of the War*, 1:228–29.

68. PRO 30/11/204, fols. 1–2, provides the basis for this estimate. It is a casualty listing for the army in the siege and assault of Bangalore.

69. Dirom, *Narrative*, p. 259.

70. Mackenzie, *Sketch of the War*, 2:7–8.

71. Cornwallis to Oakeley, 27 Feb. 1791, PRO 30/11/177, fols. 21–22.

72. See Cornwallis to bishop of Litchfield and Coventry, 23 Feb. 1791, *Cornwallis Correspondence*, 1:86. Mackenzie, who kept a meteorological account of the campaign from 19 July 1791 through 18 February 1792, recorded the highest temperatures during the day both in the sun and shade and the coolest at night. He also noted whether the days were cloudy, sunny, or windy. In September and October of 1791, the temperatures reached into the hundreds, as they did in February of 1792. But they almost invariably went down to the sixties at night, save during February of 1792, when each night the temperature remained a uniform seventy degrees.

73. Cornwallis to Kennaway, 12 Feb. 1791, *Cornwallis Correspondence*, 2:84–85.

74. See HMC, *Rept. on MSS Var. Coll.*, 6:367–68. Cornwallis's rather dry account of the event is in a letter to the directors, 20 April 1791, PRO 30/11/155, fols. 16–27.

75. Cornwallis to Stuart, 23 March 1791, PRO 30/11/167, fols. 7–8.

76. See the angry series of letters from Cornwallis to Stuart from 27 March through 12 April in PRO 30/11/167, fols. 15–16, 31–34, 37–38, 54–55, 59–60, 68–69.

77. Cornwallis to directors, 20 April 1791, PRO 30/11/155, fols. 16–27.

78. Mackenzie, *Sketch of the War*, 2:57.

79. Oldham outlined his labors in letters to Cornwallis on 5, 8, 16, 17, and 18 April 1791 in PRO 30/11/42, fols. 667, 674–75, 692–99, and 702–3.

80. Cornwallis to Oakeley, 23 April 1791, PRO 30/11/178, fols. 31–32.

81. Cornwallis to Sir William Fawcett, 19 April 1791, *Cornwallis Correspondence*, 2:90. One may follow Abercrombie's steady progress in his letters to Cornwallis from 15 January through 10 May in PRO 30/11/128, fols. 7 through 47. He took Courga pass on 25 February and completed a road for artillery by 25 March. On 6 April, he learned of Bangalore and congratulated Cornwallis, but began worrying about the lateness of the season. On 10 May he prepared to move on Seringapatam with a month's provisions, upon receipt of Cornwallis's orders. By 16 May, he had taken Peripatam to the south and west of Seringapatam.

82. Cornwallis to directors, 7 Sept. 1791, *Cornwallis Correspondence*, 2:514.

83. Cornwallis to Kennaway, 3 May 1791, PRO 30/11/166, fols. 152–53.

84. Rennell, *Marches of the British Armies*, pp. 76–77.

85. Cornwallis to Teige Wunt, 8 and 10 May 1791, *Cornwallis Correspondence*, 2:91, 506.
86. Cornwallis to Oakeley, 28 April 1791, PRO 30/11/178, fols. 33–34.
87. Dirom, *Narrative*, pp. 2–3, describes the ghastly condition of the army in even more vivid terms than did his commander.
88. Cornwallis to Oakeley, 8 May 1791, PRO 30/11/178, fols. 37–38.
89. See the description of Tipoo's army in IOR, Home Misc. 436, detailed even to his elephants, guns, and transport.
90. The earl's lengthy description is in Cornwallis to directors, 7 Sept. 1791, *Cornwallis Correspondence*, 2:516–18. *Calcutta Gazette, Extraordinary*, for 10 June 1791 prints a brief account.
91. He lost 140 Europeans, 286 natives, and 54 horses. See PRO 30/11/204, fols. 3–4.
92. Cornwallis to Abercrombie, 21 and 22 May 1791, PRO 30/11/181, fols. 55–56, 59–60. Yet, characteristically, he tried to help anyway. He sent two brigades across the ford to the west of Seringapatam, toward which he believed Tipoo was marching. Ross, in *Cornwallis Correspondence*, 2:71, asserts that Cornwallis and Abercrombie lost contact with each other because Tipoo's cavalry cut them off. Yet throughout March, April, and May, Cornwallis received regular reports from Abercrombie and knew his exact progress. Abercrombie's letters, marked with the date on which the earl received them, are in PRO 30/11/128, fols 21–47.
93. Abercrombie to Cornwallis, 24 May 1791, PRO 30/11/128, fol. 48.
94. Dirom, *Narrative*, p. 4.
95. Cornwallis to Oakeley, 31 May 1791, PRO 30/11/178, fols. 43–44.
96. Ibid.
97. *Calcutta Chronicle*, 3, no. 147, 13 Nov. 1788.
98. Dirom, *Narrative*, p. 11.
99. Mackenzie, *Sketch of the War*, 2:112.
100. Dirom, *Narrative*, pp. 7–8, 10–12; and IOR, Home Misc. 558, p. 670.
101. Dirom, *Narrative*, pp. 9–10.
102. Ibid., p. 13; and Cornwallis to Oakeley, 22 Aug. 1791, PRO 30/11/178, fols. 99–100.

Chapter 8

1. Cornwallis to Oakeley, 9 Nov. 1791, PRO 30/11/178, fols. 37–38.
2. Lt. Col. John Oldham forwarded supplies from Amboor to Cornwallis during the first campaign, and his letters give some idea of Cornwallis's demands on the depot. See PRO 30/11/42, fols. 667–703. On 17 April, for example, Oldham proposed to bring 258 casks of arrack, 639 bags of salt, 7,000 bags of rice, 9 or 10,000 sheep, and 1,200 draft and carriage bullocks.
3. See Cornwallis to Oakeley, 5, 21, 24, 25 June 1791, PRO 30/11/178, fols. 45–46, 49, 51–54.
4. Cornwallis to Oakeley, 23 July 1791, ibid., fols. 75–76. Oakeley not only sent the clothing and camp equipment on the specially built carts, but also ordered constructed, on his own initiative, a "considerable number" of eighteen-pounder gun carriages for the train coming from Bengal. Cornwallis heard of

this work and told him to halt construction if the carriages were being built of green teak. "Carriages made of unseasoned timber," he remarked, "are very unfit even for garrison, but would certainly be shivered to pieces in a few marches in the field, especially in so rugged a country as that which is the scene of our operations." The governor general added that he did not need Madras gun carriages in any event, because the Bengal government had already been instructed to provide them. He suggested that Oakeley might try to make, however, two "depressing carriages" for twelve-pounders, after the model sent to India from Woolwich. Since guns would not be put upon them except when actually needed, it would not matter if they were built of unseasoned timber. See Cornwallis to Oakeley, 21 July 1791, PRO 30/11/178, fols. 81–82.

5. Murray's detailed accounts are in IOR, Home Misc. 387, fols. 651–71.

6. Cornwallis figured that he needed 484 draft cattle to drag his 8 eighteen-pounder gun carts and an additional 58 for the spare carriages. He estimated 94 draft bullocks for his 2 twelve-pounders and 500 for his 100 platform carts. He anticipated that he would require 500 carriage bullocks for his 3,000 eighteen-pounder shot, 88 for his 600 five-and-one-half-inch shells, 70 for his 600 four-and-one-half-inch shells. He also needed bullocks for his pickaxes, broadaxes, felling axes, shovels, spades, sandbags, iron crows, rattan baskets, sledge-hammers, files, miner's tools, carpenter's tools, and ship saws. See Cornwallis to Musgrave, 13 Sept. 1791, PRO 30/11/176, fols. 47–48.

7. Cornwallis to Oakeley, 21 April and 5 June 1791, PRO 30/11/178, fols. 31–32, 45–46.

8. Cornwallis to Oakeley, 21 April and 12 Sept. 1791, ibid., fols. 31–32, 105–6.

9. Cornwallis to Charles Stuart, 11 July 1791, PRO 30/11/172, fols. 25–26.

10. Lt. William Sandys to Cornwallis, June 1792, PRO 30/11/52, fols. 227–31.

11. Cornwallis to Oakeley, 31 July 1791, PRO 30/11/178, fols. 81–82.

12. Cornwallis to William Cornwallis, 5 July 1791, HMC, *Rept. on MSS Var. Coll.*, 6:372.

13. Turner to Warren Hastings, 18 Jan. 1792, BM, Add. MSS 29,172, fols. 377–81.

14. Alexander Dirom, *A Narrative of the Campaign in India . . .* , p. 87.

15. Cornwallis to Abercrombie, 22 Nov. 1791, PRO 30/11/161, fols. 80–81. Cornwallis estimated he had forty thousand instead of fifty thousand binjarries, but in so vast a multitude one would find it difficult to determine exact numbers.

16. Dirom, *Narrative*, p. 88. Cornwallis did not calculate it quite as closely as Dirom believed, but he did stress the money he needed in a letter to Oakeley, 12 Sept. 1791, PRO 30/11/178, fols. 105–6.

17. Dirom, *Narrative*, pp. 17–18.

18. *Calcutta Gazette*, 16, no. 416, 16 Feb. 1792. See also Cornwallis to Oakeley, 1 Jan. 1792, PRO 30/11/179, fols. 1–2. The binjarries carried ordnance as well as food. The Mahrattas used them to carry five thousand eighteen- and twenty-four-pounder shot for Cornwallis a distance of fifty miles. See Cornwallis to Kennaway, 4 Jan. 1792, PRO 30/11/106, fols. 206–9.

19. See Cornwallis to Malet, 22 Oct. 1791, PRO 30/11/163, fols. 140–43; and to Kennaway, 21 Sept. 1791, PRO 30/11/196, fols. 173–74.

20. Cornwallis to Kennaway, 4 Nov. 1791, PRO 30/11/46, fols. 640–43.

21. Cornwallis to Malet, 22 Oct. 1791, PRO 30/11/163, fols. 140–43.

22. Cornwallis to directors, 7 Sept. 1791, *Cornwallis Correspondence*, 2:522.

23. Captain Alexander Read, for instance, asked for and received a detachment of six companies of sepoys to reinforce his own detachment of 746 men to convoy 15 to 20,000 sheep from his camp to Bangalore. See Read to Cornwallis, 8 June 1791, PRO 30/11/43, fols. 585–86. Cornwallis pointed out to Oakeley on 22 November 1791 an instance of Mahratta unreliability: "Although a part of our elephants went out to forage yesterday under the escort of one company of Europeans and three of Sepoys, and altho' they were at that time surrounded by Maratta foragers, nine of the elephants were, through the mismanagement of our people, carried off by a small detachment of the enemy's looties from Sevendroog." See PRO 30/11/178, fols. 133–34. For Cornwallis's idea of using allied cavalry see his letter to Kennaway, 2 Sept. 1791, PRO 30/11/166, fols. 175–76.

24. Cornwallis to Oldham, 11 July 1791, PRO 30/11/186, fols. 46–47.

25. Dirom, *Narrative*, p. 44; and Roderick Mackenzie, *A Sketch of the War with Tippoo Sultaun*, 2:144–47.

26. Cornwallis to directors, 24 Oct. 1791, PRO 30/11/155, fols. 114–23. Mackenzie, *Sketch of the War*, 2:147–51, describes the attack in detail.

27. Cornwallis to Abercrombie, 22 Nov. 1791, PRO 30/11/181, fols. 80–81.

28. Turner to Hastings, 18 Jan. 1792, BM, Add. MSS 29,172, fols. 377–81. See also Dirom, *Narrative*, pp. 23, 66–67, 69, 72.

29. Cornwallis to directors, 26 Dec. 1791, PRO 30/11/155, fols. 134–43. Mackenzie, *Sketch of the War*, 2:161–67, describes in detail the approach work and assault.

30. See, for example, Captain C. Beetson to Cornwallis, 9 Aug. 1791, PRO 30/11/44, fols. 6–7.

31. See, for example, among the many intelligence papers, PRO 30/11/47, fols. 40–41, which is a "Translation of à Memorandum sent by R [probably Read] and supposed to have been written about the 31st December 1791." Mark Wilks, *Historical Sketches of the South of India . . .* , 2:449, asserts that on the first day Cornwallis joined the army he gave Captain William McLeod, in charge of intelligence operations, "an unlimited command of means," so vital did the earl consider proper intelligence.

32. Cornwallis to directors, 4 March 1792, *Cornwallis Correspondence*, 2:533.

33. See PRO 30/11/47, fols. 36–37.

34. Cornwallis to Oakeley, 21 June 1791, PRO 30/11/178, fol. 49.

35. Cornwallis to Charles Stuart, 21 Jan. 1792, PRO 30/11/172, fols. 91–92.

36. Cornwallis to directors, 4 March 1792, *Cornwallis Correspondence*, 2:529.

37. Extract of a letter from Bangalore, 24 Jan. 1792, *Calcutta Gazette*, 16, no. 416, 6 Feb. 1792.

38. Dirom, *Narrative*, pp. 122–25.

39. There are several accounts of the final march on Seringapatam, the battle outside its walls, and the siege. The most minutely detailed is by Mackenzie, *Sketch of the War*, vol. 2. Turner, as captain of the earl's bodyguard, was with him most of the time, and his account is almost as detailed as Mackenzie's. He compiled a written day-by-day description of events for Warren Hastings, which he finally completed and sent on 1 March 1792. Turner, in his own words,

"omitted nothing" and sent "tedious detail" from an idea that "the most trivial incidents are interesting which lead to great events." Indeed, the letter (BM, Add. MSS 29,172, fols. 412–21), when transcribed on elite type, comprises fourteen single-spaced pages. Most of the detail that follows comes from Mackenzie, Turner, Dirom's *Narrative*, accounts that participants sent to the *Calcutta Gazette*, and Cornwallis's own letters and comments, especially his missive to the directors, 4 March 1792, *Cornwallis Correspondence*, 2:528–37.

40. This secure supply line enabled the commanding general to sell rice to his allies during the siege. According to Dirom, *Narrative*, p. 240, the earl acquired such a surplus that he even stopped deliveries for a while.

41. Ibid., p. 142.

42. *Calcutta Gazette*, 16, no. 418, 1 March 1792, mentions the wound, as does Mackenzie, *Sketch of the War*, 2:213. Turner, however, does not.

43. *Calcutta Gazette*, 17, no. 421, 22 March 1793, describes the gardens in more detail than does Turner. Mackenzie, *Sketch of the War*, 2:215–16, offers great detail.

44. Much later, when the war had ended and Cornwallis had returned to Bengal, he dined with Hickey at government house one evening. At that time he told the prolific memoirist that he had found proof that while the army was before Seringapatam, Tipoo had offered an enormous sum of money to any who would bring him Cornwallis dead or alive. "Thus," Hickey quoted his lordship as saying, "greatly overrating the value of my poor carcase, for which I apprehend no other person in the world would give a single sixpence." See William Hickey, *Memoirs*, 4:88.

45. Cornwallis to Stuart, 11 June 1792, PRO 30/11/172, fols. 127–28.

46. Cornwallis to Dundas, 9 Aug. 1790, PRO 30/11/151, fols. 52–59.

47. Mackenzie, *Sketch of the War*, vol. 2; appendix 3, prints the entire treaty. A copy is, of course, printed in *Br. Parl. Papers, Cols., E. Ind.*, 1:476–79.

48. See Cornwallis to Dundas, 4 March 1792, PRO 30/11/151, fols. 107–12; and Turner to Hastings, 1 March 1792, BM, Add. MSS 29,172, fols. 412–21.

49. *Calcutta Gazette*, 17, no. 426, 26 April 1792.

50. Numerous congratulatory letters appear in PRO 30/11/48, 30/11/213, and 30/11/214. The quotation is from a native address in PRO 30/11/214, fol. 6.

51. See *Calcutta Gazette, Additional Supplement*, 17, no. 435, 28 June 1792; and "Address of the British inhabitants of Calcutta to Cornwallis," PRO 30/11/213, fols. 11–14.

52. Cornwallis to Stuart, 17 April 1792, PRO 30/11/172, fols. 117–18; and *Calcutta Gazette*, 17, no. 440, 2 Aug. 1792.

53. Lt. Paris Bradshaw to Cornwallis, 27 April 1793, PRO 30/11/52, fols. 7–8.

54. See Dundas to the bishop, 30 July 1792, and to Cornwallis, 17 Sept. 1792 (received in March), *Cornwallis Correspondence*, 2:175, 216.

55. Cornwallis to the bishop, 23 May 1792, PRO 30/11/183, fols. 55–56.

56. Cornwallis to Stuart, 24 May 1792, PRO 30/11/172, fols. 123–24.

57. William Cornwallis to Lord Brome, 18 March 1793, PRO 30/11/51, fols. 58–59.

58. Cornwallis to Oakeley, 25 March and 6 April 1792, PRO 30/11/179, fols. 71–72, 77–78.

59. *Calcutta Gazette*, 17, no. 440, 2 Aug. 1792.

60. Hickey, *Memoirs*, 4:75.

61. Percival Spear, *The Nabobs*, p. 127.

62. Resolutions of the court of proprietors, 30 Jan. and 26 June 1793, PRO 30/11/215, fols. 1–4.

63. Cornwallis to Dundas, 24 March 1793, *Cornwallis Correspondence*, 2: 220–21.

64. Charles Chapman to Warren Hastings, 1 Oct. 1793, BM, Add. MSS 29,173, fols. 94–95.

65. John Bristow to Sir John Shore, 3 March 1794, PRO 30/11/213, fols. 15–16.

Chapter 9

1. The British Museum has twenty-five different engraved portraits of Cornwallis. The particular one from which we take our description was painted by D. Gardiner, engraved by J. Jones, and published on 6 March 1793. One by John Singleton Copley, published 1 September 1798, just before the marquis left for Ireland, resembles the Gainsborough of 1783.

2. Cornwallis to Dundas, 3 Feb. 1794, *Cornwallis Correspondence*, 2:235.

3. *The Times*, 7 Feb. 1794.

4. Arthur Bryant, *The Years of Endurance, 1793–1802*, chapter 4, describes these developments in detail. Sir John Fortescue, *History of the British Army*, 4:part 1, concentrates on the military situation.

5. *The Times*, 7 April 1794.

6. *Cornwallis Correspondence*, 3:562.

7. *The Times*, 10 April 1794.

8. Steven Watson, *The Reign of George III, 1760–1815*, p. 368. John M. Sherwig, *Guineas and Gunpowder*, discusses the entire British subsidy policy.

9. Fortescue, *History of the British Army*, 4:part 1, p. 268.

10. Cornwallis to Shore, 17 April 1794, *Cornwallis Correspondence*, 2:238.

11. Pitt to Cornwallis, 19 April 1794, PRO 30/11/216, fols. 3–4.

12. Lord Grenville to King George III, 27 May, and the king's reply, 28 May 1794, King George III, *The Later Correspondence of George III*, 2:212–13.

13. Dundas to Cornwallis, 29 May 1794, *Cornwallis Correspondence*, 2:239–40.

14. Dundas to Cornwallis, 1 June 1794, ibid., 2:242.

15. Pitt to Cornwallis, 5 June 1794, PRO 30/11/216, fols. 27–30.

16. Cornwallis to Dundas, 8 June 1794, *Cornwallis Correspondence*, 2:247–48.

17. For these exchanges, see Cornwallis to Dundas, 11 June 1794, PRO 30/11/217, fols. 11–12; and Cornwallis to York, 18 June 1794; Mollendorf to Cornwallis, 15 June 1794; Cornwallis to Mollendorf, 18 June 1794; and Cornwallis to Dundas, 21 June 1794, all in *Cornwallis Correspondence*, 2:250–55.

18. Cornwallis to Pitt, 2 July 1794, PRO 30/11/217, fols. 34–35.

19. Dundas to Cornwallis, 30 June 1794, *Cornwallis Correspondence*, 255–56; and Pitt to Cornwallis, 30 June 1794, PRO 30/11/216, fols. 66–67.

20. Cornwallis to York, 15 July 1794, PRO 30/11/217, fols. 40–41.

21. Sherwig, *Guineas and Gunpowder*, p. 59.

22. See Earl Stanhope, *Life of the Right Honourable William Pitt*, 2:257, and Sherwig, *Guineas and Gunpowder*, p. 59.

23. Quoted in Sherwig, *Guineas and Gunpowder*, p. 60.

24. Pitt to the king, 30 Aug. 1794, King George III, *Later Correspondence*, 2:23.

25. York to the king, 4 Sept. 1794, ibid., 2:239–40.

26. King to Pitt, 9 Sept. 1784, in Stanhope, *Life of Pitt*, 2:appendix, p. xxi.

27. See, for example, Pitt to Cornwallis, 24 Aug. 1794, *Cornwallis Correspondence*, 2:259–60.

28. Cornwallis to Pitt, 25 Aug. 1794; and to Ross, 28 Aug. 1794, ibid., 2:261–64.

29. Cornwallis to York, 8 Nov. 1794, ibid., 2:272–74. Cornwallis's account differs in one particular from the others we have read. It seems that Pitt told York that the Austrian government originally proposed Cornwallis to command the Austrian troops. Yet Cornwallis must have known that, by sending Ross, the ministry had him under consideration all along.

Chapter 10

1. See R. R. Nelson, *The Home Office, 1782–1801*, pp. 20–21.

2. Pitt to George III, 28 Jan. 1795, King George III, *The Later Correspondence of George III*, 2:298.

3. Cornwallis's appointment, with privy seal attached, is in PRO 30/11/219.

4. See York to Cornwallis, 24 Nov. 1794, *Cornwallis Correspondence*, 2:278–79.

5. Cornwallis to Ross, 21 Jan. 1795, ibid., 2:286.

6. Cornwallis used the term "very unpleasant" in a letter to Ross, 30 Dec. 1794, ibid., 2:281.

7. Captain Dale Pearson, "Cornwallis and Richmond," citing Richard Glover, *Peninsular Preparation*, pp. 28–30.

8. See, for example, Cornwallis to Ross, 20 Sept. 1795, *Cornwallis Correspondence*, 2:296. Unfortunately for the marquis's pleasure, hot and dry weather was "equally hostile to shooting and to the turnips."

9. PRO, WO 55/334, p. 56.

10. They served especially at Gibraltar and the West Indies. PRO, T 29/70, 71, treasury board minutes for the last half of 1797, mention artificers' expenses at Santo Domingo, Martinique, St. Lucia, and Bermuda. PRO 30/11/228, fols. 23–75, concern their work at Gibraltar.

11. See PRO, SP 41/36, fols. 248–49, principal officers of the ordnance to the duke of Montagu, master general, 17 March 1740 (Old Style); and SP 44/184, fols. 244–45, royal warrant establishing the school.

12. PRO, WO 34/109, pp. 87–100, "Rules and Orders for the Royal Military Academy at Woolwich."

13. See PRO, WO 55/1789 for a complete description of the duties of these officers. Arthur Forbes, *A History of the Army Ordnance Services*, chapter 5, gives a general description of the board of ordnance.

14. For Richmond see Alison Gilbert Olson, *The Radical Duke*.

15. His letters to Ross, who also became surveyor general, reveal this pessimism clearly.

16. Green to Cornwallis, 18 Feb. 1795, PRO 30/11/224, fols. 1–2.

17. Cornwallis to Green, 28 Feb. 1795, ibid., fols. 13–14. For the continued

triangulation see PRO 30/11/242, 243, and PRO 30/11/224, fols. 15–20. For Cornwallis's tours and efforts to strengthen defenses see PRO 30/11/55, fols. 272–73; PRO 30/11/236, pp. 42, 45–47, 66, 156; and PRO 30/11/59, fols. 87b–88, 90.

18. For the episode see Sydney to Cornwallis, March 1798, PRO 30/11/235, fols. 54–55.

19. According to William Windham, he never really managed to do so. See Windham to Lord Grenville, 18 Sept. 1799, William Windham, *Windham Papers*, 2:123.

20. Ezekiel Baker to the ordnance board, June 1794, PRO, WO 47/2365.

21. Assistant clerk Nettleship to treasury secretary Rose, 13 Nov. 1797, PRO, WO 46/25.

22. Cornwallis to Dundas, 17 Feb. 1796, PRO 30/11/236, fols. 191–92.

23. Ibid.

24. PRO 30/11/59, fols. 84b–85, memorandum of ordnance board, 4 Aug. 1796.

25. PRO, T 29/73, treasury board minute of 18 Oct. 1798.

26. Cornwallis to Lord Grenville, 18 Sept. 1798, *Cornwallis Correspondence*, 2:409–10.

27. For purchase of foreign arms see Cornwallis to Ross, 4 and 10 Feb. 1798, *Cornwallis Correspondence*, 2:331–32. For testing see treasury board minute for 18 Oct. 1798, PRO, T 29/73, pp. 385–86.

28. R. H. Crew, ordnance board secretary, to Thomas Pelham, Irish secretary, 14 April 1797, PRO, HO 30/373, cited in Glover, *Peninsular Preparation*, p. 52.

29. Crew to the Chevalier d'Almeida, 27 June 1799, PRO, WO 46/25.

30. Cornwallis to Dundas, 10 Feb. 1795, PRO 30/11/236, fol. 1.

31. Lord Camden to Cornwallis, 25 Oct. 1796, PRO 30/11/230, fols. 5–8.

32. Cornwallis to Dundas, 10 Feb. 1795, PRO 30/11/236, fol. 1.

33. Cornwallis to Windham, 28 June 1795, *Cornwallis Correspondence*, 2:292. For the militia see J. R. Western, *The English Militia in the Eighteenth Century*.

34. Cornwallis to Lord Rolle, 31 July 1796, PRO 30/11/59, fols. 85b–86; and to the Duke of York, 25 Nov. 1796, ibid., fols. 132b–135.

35. Cornwallis to York, 25 Nov. 1796, ibid.

36. Glover, *Peninsular Preparation*, p. 189.

37. Pearson, "Cornwallis and Richmond," citing W. D. Jones, *Records of the Royal Military Academy*, pp. 53, 63.

38. Captain Apsley to Lt. Col. Twiss, 24 June 1796 and 17 Feb. 1797, PRO 30/11/59, fols. 70b, 169b.

39. Cornwallis to Lord Pelham, 14 July 1802, BM, Add. MSS 33,109, fols. 291–92. Far more trouble came despite the fact that in his earlier years he largely neglected Woolwich. See Cornwallis to Ross, 25 May 1795, *Cornwallis Correspondence*, 2:290.

40. PRO 30/11/229 is filled with applications, each of which the marquis examined and many of which he personally endorsed.

41. Cornwallis to Arnold, 10 Dec. 1795, PRO 30/11/229, fols. 47–48; and to Lord Dundas, 28 July 1796, PRO 30/11/59, fol. 28b.

42. Cornwallis to Chichester, 14 July 1802, BM, Add. MSS 33,109, fols. 291–92.

43. Apsley to Twiss, 6 May 1796, PRO 30/11/59, fol. 48b.

44. Apsley to William Hoberton, 28 June 1796; and to Twiss, 30 June 1796, PRO 30/11/59, fols. 71b, 72.

45. Cornwallis to David Scott, 2 Nov. 1796, PRO 30/11/59, fols. 120b–121b.

46. Apsley to Crew, March 1797, PRO 30/11/237, fols. 21–25.

47. See, for example, Apsley to Samuel Bream, 18 April (no year but probably 1796), PRO 30/11/59, fol. 41b.

48. See, for example, Camden to Cornwallis, 25 Oct. 1796, PRO 30/11/230, fols. 5–8.

49. Rotalier to Apsley, 20 March 1795, PRO 30/11/225. Original is in French.

50. Rotalier to Cornwallis, 4 Nov. 1796, PRO 30/11/236, fols. 74–75. The master general also dealt with complaints from other French émigrés as well as with other refugee forces, including a corps of Dutch artillery. See PRO 30/11/227, fols. 1–10; and PRO 30/11/59, fol. 31.

51. Cornwallis to Prince William, 27 Feb. 1796, PRO 30/11/59, fols. 27b–28.

52. Cornwallis to Prince William, 9 Sept. 1796, ibid., fol. 93.

53. Cornwallis to Sir Ralph Abercrombie, 1 Dec. 1795, PRO 30/11/236, fol. 154b.

54. See Duke of York to George III, 26 and 27 May 1797, *King George III, Later Correspondence*, 2:580, 597.

55. Cornwallis to Duke of Argyll, 12 Dec. 1796, PRO 30/11/59, fol. 141b.

56. Cornwallis to Duke of Richmond, 7 March 1797, ibid., fol. 183b. The marquis's correspondence is filled with letters revealing his concern for personnel. See Apsley to Crew, 15 March 1796, ibid., fol. 30b; to Lt. General Pattison, 30 March 1796, ibid., fol. 34; to Major General Stehelin, 19 March 1795, PRO 30/11/236, p. 55; Cornwallis to Sir George Osborne, 6 April 1796, PRO 30/11/59, fol. 35b; and Cornwallis to Lord Colvill, 15 Dec. 1795, PRO 30/11/236, fol. 162.

57. Cornwallis to Ross, 24 March 1800, *Cornwallis Correspondence*, 3:219.

58. Cornwallis to Ross, 22 Nov. and 12 Dec. 1798, ibid., 2:444 and 3:15.

59. Apsley to Crew, 11 April 1796, PRO 30/11/59, fols. 38b–39.

60. Cornwallis ended his active work in the ordnance and in the cabinet in 1798, when he went to Ireland. He continued officially, however, as master general until he resigned the post in 1801. From 1798 to 1801, he left most ordnance matters to Howe and Ross.

Chapter 11

1. For a brief history of the United Irish movement see Maureen Wall, "The United Irish Movement," pp. 122–40.

2. G. C. Bolton, *The Passing of the Irish Act of Union*, p. 8.

3. Edward Cooke to William Wickham, 25 June 1798, PRO, HO 100/77, fols. 194–95. Cooke voiced these bitter sentiments only after Catholic peasants had massacred nearly one hundred Protestants at Wexford by stabbing them with pikes. Furthermore, Cooke could be kind and generous in his personal dealings with Catholics. Charles Hamilton Teeling, a Catholic United Irishman, who participated in the 1798 rebellion, recalled with fondness Cooke's treatment of him. See Teeling, *History of the Irish Rebellion of 1798 and Sequel to the History of the Irish Rebellion of 1798*, pp. 62–63.

4. Quoted in Thomas Pakenham, *The Year of Liberty*, p. 51. Pakenham's is a detailed and swiftly moving account of the rebellion.

5. Pitt to Camden, 13 March 1798, PRO 30/8/325, fols. 5–8.
6. Memorandum on the army in Ireland in 1798, PRO, HO 100/74, fols. 369–375.
7. William Elliot to William Wickham, 11 June 1798, PRO, HO 100/81, fol. 73.
8. Camden to Portland, 10 June 1795, PRO, HO 100/54, fols. 228–30.
9. Sir John Fortescue, *History of the British Army*, 4:part 1, p. 519.
10. Camden to Portland, 11 May 1798, PRO, HO 100/75, fols. 170–77.
11. Pakenham, *Year of Liberty*, p. 56; and Camden to Portland, 5 April 1798, HO 100/75, fols. 97–103.
12. Camden to Portland, 8 and 10 June 1798, PRO, HO 100/77, fols. 80–81, 104–5; and HO 100/81, fols. 61–62.
13. Camden to Cornwallis, 23 May 1797, *Cornwallis Correspondence*, 2:327.
14. Portland to Camden, 12 June 1798, PRO, HO 100/81, fols. 78–79.
15. Yet Pitt told William Windham that the marquis's appointment resulted from the "repeated Representation" of Camden. See Pitt to Windham, 12 June 1798, Windham, *Windham Papers*, 2:72.
16. Cornwallis to Ross, 30 and 31 March 1798, *Cornwallis Correspondence*, 2:335–36.
17. George III to Pitt, 10 June 1798, in Earl Stanhope, *Life of the Right Honourable William Pitt*, 3:appendix, p. xv. For Cornwallis's acceptance see Pitt to Cornwallis, 7 June 1798, *Cornwallis Correspondence*, 2:351.
18. PRO 30/11/263, fols. 11–12.
19. For the marquis's arrival see *Dublin Evening Post* for 21 June 1798; and Lord Wycombe to Lady Hollnd, 21 June 1798, BM, Add. MSS 51,682, cited in Pakenham, *Year of Liberty*, p. 263.
20. "I conclude that the expenses at Culford House must be heavy," he wrote Brome on 10 Dec. 1798. "For some time past I have lived at the park, and much within bounds, but the expence of four or five months in Dublin this winter will I am afraid oblige me to look for some aid from England. Perhaps by March we shall be able to decide whether it will be prudent to lay the foundation of the Bridge." See PRO 30/11/276, fol. 92. These expenses for Culford were prodigious. He sold considerable stock in the 1790s to pay for them and seemed even to use up the £10,000 the East India Company had given him in August of 1794, as well as the annuity of £5,000. In April of 1799, he sold stock to pay his land tax, yet not because of lavish spending in Dublin. He noted with satisfaction that his expenditures there did not exceed his income, "although my predecessor in the two first years, expended £20,000." See Cornwallis to Brome, 7 April 1799, PRO 30/11/277, fols. 61–62.
21. Sir John Moore, *Diary of Sir John Moore*, 1:329.
22. See, for example, PRO 30/11/263, fols. 1–10.
23. York to Dundas, 2 June 1798, PRO, HO 30/2, fols. 34–37; and Pitt to Camden, 2 June 1798, PRO 30/8/325.
24. Cornwallis to Portland, 25 June 1798, PRO, HO 100/81, fols. 169–70; and 27 June 1798, *Cornwallis Correspondence*, 2:355–56. See also PRO, HO 100/81, fols. 185–86.
25. See PRO, HO 100/74, for a list of the regulars and militia who landed in Ireland in 1798.

26. Castlereagh to Pitt, 7 Sept. 1798, PRO 30/8/125, fols. 17–18; and the various military papers in PRO, HO 100/82, fol. 3, and HO 100/84, fols. 467–68.

27. Cornwallis to Portland, 16 July 1798; and Cooke to Wickham, 12 July 1798, PRO, HO 100/77, fols. 242–43, 248–51.

28. For an interesting eyewitness account of the French landing and their occupation of Killala, see the diary of the bishop of Killala reproduced in W. H. Maxwell, *History of the Irish Rebellion in 1798*, pp. 255–62. For Cornwallis's source of information see Brigadier Robert Taylor to Castlereagh, 23 Aug. 1798, PRO, HO 100/81, fols. 325–26; Richard French to J. Pack, 24 Aug. 1798, PRO, HO 100/78, fols. 177–80; and Cornwallis to Portland, 25 Aug. 1798, ibid., fols. 171–72.

29. Pakenham, *Year of Liberty*, p. 307.

30. Ibid., pp. 307–11.

31. Cornwallis to Portland, 28 Aug. 1798, *Cornwallis Correspondence*, 2:394; and Portland to the admiralty, 27 Aug. 1798, PRO, HO 30/2, fols. 144–45. Portland, indeed, acted as soon as he heard of the French landing, before he even received Cornwallis's request.

32. Lake to Cornwallis, 28 Aug. 1798, *Cornwallis Correspondence*, 2:303; and Lake to Captain Herbert Taylor (Cornwallis's military secretary), 29 Aug. 1798, PRO, HO 100/81, fols. 364–65.

33. Castlereagh to Wickham, 30 Aug. 1798, PRO, HO 100/81, fols. 360–61; and Taylor to Cooke, 29 Aug. 1798, ibid., fols. 362–63.

34. "Order of the army under the command of his excellency the Marquis Cornwallis," 2 Sept. 1798, PRO, HO 100/82, fol. 31.

35. Captain Taylor to Castlereagh, 3 Sept. 1798, ibid., fols. 39–40; and PRO, HO 100/78, fol. 310.

36. Pakenham, *Year of Liberty*, p. 323; and Fortescue, *History of the British Army*, 4:part 1, p. 594.

37. Pakenham, *Year of Liberty*, pp. 325–26. Lake's report of the engagement is in Lake to Taylor, 8 Sept. 1798, PRO, HO 100/82, fols. 55–57. See also Cornwallis to Portland, 8 Sept. 1798, *Cornwallis Correspondence*, 2:402–3.

38. Moore, *Diary*, 1:324.

39. Pakenham, *Year of Liberty*, pp. 331–32, 338.

40. PRO, HO 30/2, fols. 291–95.

41. Cornwallis to Portland, 16 Sept. 1798, *Cornwallis Correspondence*, 2:406.

42. Portland to Cornwallis, 4 July 1798, PRO, HO 100/77, fols. 208–11.

43. *Cornwallis Correspondence*, 2:361–62.

44. Castlereagh to Lt. General James Stuart, 25 June 1798, ibid., 2:355.

45. Cornwallis to Ross, 24 July 1798, ibid., 2:371.

46. Rufus King to Portland, 13 Sept. 1798, PRO, HO 100/79, fols. 328–29.

47. William Wickham to Castlereagh, 10 Jan. 1799, PRO, HO 100/85, fols. 31–33.

48. Portland to Cornwallis, 3 March 1799, PRO, HO 100/86, fols. 5–11.

49. Castlereagh to Wickham, 6 March 1799, ibid., fols. 34–35, 375–76; and to John King, 23 July 1799, PRO, HO 100/89, fols. 113–14. See also Cooke to Castlereagh, 25 July 1799, ibid., fols. 115–16.

50. Portland revealed his basic attitude when he told Cornwallis to "seize

[conspirators] in every quarter of the kingdom." See Portland to Cornwallis, 3 March 1799, *Cornwallis Correspondence*, 3:72. Cornwallis also thought Portland in October of 1798 had misrepresented him to Pitt and told Pitt so directly, not mincing words: whereas Portland had spoken of "these traitors whose lives were spared on condition of their being banished," the marquis explained that had he really believed he had sufficient evidence against them to prove treason before an impartial court he would not have spared them. See Cornwallis to Pitt, 25 Oct. 1798, PRO 30/8/327, fols. 191–92.

51. Cornwallis to Pitt, 17 Oct. 1798, PRO 30/8/327, fol. 189.

52. Cornwallis to Portland, 20 Nov. 1799, PRO, HO 100/87, fols. 252–55.

53. Portland to Cornwallis, 14 Nov. 1799; and Cornwallis to Portland, 20 Nov. 1799, PRO, HO 100/89, fols. 278–81, 286–87.

54. See the addresses of thanks in PRO, HO 100/95, fols. 30–38.

55. Alexander Marsden to John King, 24 Sept. 1800, PRO, HO 100/94, fols. 169–70.

56. Ibid; Castlereagh to King, 27 Feb. 1800, PRO 100/93, fols. 139–40; and extract of a letter from Lt. Col. Littlehales to Alexander Marsden, 23 Aug. 1800, HO 100/97, fols. 128–29.

57. Portland to Cornwallis, 28 Nov. 1800, and enclosed proposal, PRO, HO 100/94, fols. 235–36, 238–40; and Cornwallis to Portland, 3 Dec. 1800, ibid., fols. 256–60.

58. Cornwallis to Portland, 29 July 1799; and Portland to Cornwallis, 31 Aug. 1799, PRO, HO 100/89, fols. 121–23, 164–72.

59. See William Alexander to Castlereagh, 1 July 1798, PRO, HO 100/81, fols. 235–36; Castlereagh to Pitt, 14 April 1799, PRO 30/8/327, fols. 33–36; S. Douglas to Pitt, 20 Aug. 1799, ibid., fols. 267–70.

60. Alexander Hope to Pitt, 25 Oct. 1798, PRO 30/58/4, no. 35.

61. Cornwallis to Pitt, 25 Oct. 1798, PRO 30/8/327, fols. 191–92.

62. See Portland to Cornwallis, 7 Feb. and 1 April 1799, and 9 Aug. 1800, PRO, HO 100/85, fols. 224–26, HO 100/86, fols. 234–37, and HO 100/94, fols. 136–38; and Cornwallis to Portland, 18 Dec. 1799 and 16 Aug. 1800, HO 100/87, fols. 279–80, and HO 100/94, fols. 149–50.

63. Cornwallis to William Cornwallis, 16 Dec. 1800, HMC, *Rept. on MSS Var. Coll.*, 6:393.

64. Cornwallis to Brome, 10 Dec. 1798, PRO 30/11/276, fol. 92.

65. Cornwallis to William Cornwallis, 16 Dec. 1800, HMC, *Rept. on MSS Var. Coll.*, 6:393.

66. C. J. Bartlett, *Castlereagh*, p. 8. There are numerous biographies of Castlereagh. This one sums up the scholarship on Castlereagh and puts his life in perspective.

67. Cornwallis to Portland, 8 July 1798, *Cornwallis Correspondence*, 2:360–61.

68. Cornwallis to Ross, 9 July 1798, ibid., 2:363.

69. Cornwallis to Portland, 7 Nov. 1798; and to Pitt, same day, ibid., 2:429–30.

70. Bolton, *Act of Union*, p. 6.

71. R. B. McDowell, *Irish Public Opinion, 1750–1800*, pp. 244–46.

72. Bolton, *Act of Union*, p. 53.

73. George III to William Pitt, 11 June 1798, in Stanhope, *Life of Pitt*, 3:appendix, p. xvi.

74. Bolton, *Act of Union*, p. 14.

75. This and subsequent analysis come from Bolton, *Act of Union*, chapter 2.

76. Cornwallis to Portland, 8 Oct. 1798, PRO, HO 100/79, fols. 27–28.

77. Cornwallis to Portland, 16 Sept. 1798, *Cornwallis Correspondence*, 2:407.

78. Cornwallis to Pitt, 17 Oct. 1798, ibid., 2:420–21.

79. Cornwallis to Thomas Pelham, 15 Oct. 1798, BM, Add. MSS 33,106, fols. 118–19.

80. Clare to Castlereagh, 16 Oct. 1798, Robert Stewart, Viscount Castlereagh, *Memoirs and Correspondence of Viscount Castlereagh*, 1:393. Vols. 1 through 5 deal with Ireland.

81. George III to Pitt, 11 June 1798, in Stanhope, *Life of Pitt*, 3:appendix, p. xvi.

82. Cooke to Auckland, 26 Jan. 1799, BM, Add. MSS 34,455, quoted in Bolton, *Act of Union*, p. 119.

83. Downshire MSS, quoted in ibid., p. 72.

84. Duigenan to Castlereagh, 20 Dec. 1798, *Cornwallis Correspondence*, 3:90.

85. Cornwallis to Ross, 25 Dec. 1800, ibid., 3:315.

86. Cornwallis to Ross, 21 Jan. 1799, ibid., 3:39.

87. Cornwallis to Portland, 16 Jan. 1799, ibid., 3:38–39.

88. Bolton, *Act of Union*, p. 101.

89. Portland to Cornwallis, 12 Nov. 1798, *Cornwallis Correspondence*, 3:436–37.

90. Bolton, *Act of Union*, p. 88.

91. Ibid., pp. 81–82.

92. Cooke to Castlereagh, 16 Dec. 1798, Castlereagh, *Memoirs*, 2:43.

93. Cornwallis to Portland, 15 Dec. 1798, *Cornwallis Correspondence*, 3:19.

94. Castlereagh to Portland, 21 and 23 Jan. 1799, PRO, HO 100/85, fols. 132–34, 136–37. See also Bolton, *Act of Union*, p. 104.

95. Bolton, *Act of Union*, p. 91.

96. Cornwallis to Portland, 23 Jan. 1799, *Cornwallis Correspondence*, 3:31–42.

97. Bolton, *Act of Union*, p. 114.

98. Castlereagh to Portland, 28 Jan. 1799, PRO, HO 100/85, fols. 162–66.

99. Portland to Cornwallis, 26 Jan. 1799, *Cornwallis Correspondence*, 3:56–57; and PRO, HO 100/85, fols. 148–53.

100. It is scarcely necessary to detail all of Castlereagh's work and the observations he made about individuals, offices, money, and other considerations. Anyone interested in the minute details of the negotiations for the Act of Union should see PRO, HO 100/85, fols. 167–75; HO 100/87; HO 100/93, fols. 121, 257–58; HO 100/96, fols. 152–53; HO 100/103, fols. 107–8; and the many papers devoted to union in Castlereagh, *Memoirs*.

101. PRO, HO 100/93, fol. 257.

102. Bolton, *Act of Union*, p. 127.

103. PRO 30/11/276, fol. 16.

104. Cornwallis to Ross, 8 June 1799, *Cornwallis Correspondence*, 3:102.

105. Editorial comment by Ross, ibid., 3:221.

106. Littlehales to Castlereagh, 9 Oct. 1799, Castlereagh, *Memoirs*, 2:414–15.

107. Cornwallis to Ross, 19 June 1799, *Cornwallis Correspondence*, 3:103.

108. "Jeffrey Foresight" to Castlereagh, 2 Feb. 1800, Castlereagh, *Memoirs*, 3:230–31.

109. Cornwallis to Portland, 10 and 14 Feb. 1800, PRO, HO 100/93, fols. 92–93, 105–12.

110. *Cornwallis Correspondence*, 3:179.

111. Cornwallis to Ross, 13 Feb. 1800, ibid., 3:189; and to Pitt, 21 March 1800, PRO 30/58/3, fols. 12–12a.

112. Bolton, *Act of Union*, p. 153.

113. Littlehales to Cook, 25 April 1800, PRO, HO 100/93, fols. 327–30; Cornwallis to Portland, 26, 28, and 30 Jan. 1799, *Cornwallis Correspondence*, 3:52, 55, 58; and Portland to Cornwallis, 29, 30 Jan. 1799, PRO, HO 100/88, fols. 71–75; and *Cornwallis Correspondence*, 3:59.

114. Castlereagh to John King, 2 April 1800, *Cornwallis Correspondence*, 3:224.

115. Bolton, *Act of Union*, p. 197; and Castlereagh to John King, 14 May 1800, PRO, HO 100/93, fols. 368–70.

116. Cornwallis to Portland, 24 March 1800; and Portland to Cornwallis, 7 April 1800, *Cornwallis Correspondence*, 3:219, 226.

117. Cornwallis to Portland, 28 March 1800, ibid., 3:222.

118. Cornwallis to Ross, 2 Aug. 1800, ibid., 3:285.

119. The act is 40 Geo. III, c. 67. Its provisions are printed in many places. A separate act, 40 Geo. III, c. 34, established a court to ascertain and pay money to corporate bodies and individuals who had suffered. The £15,000 to the boroughs no longer sending representatives went in five annual installments, to the total of £1,260,000. Whether or not a borough owner had opposed the union, he got his money. Downshire, for example, despite his notorious conduct, received £52,000. See T. Dunbar Ingram, *A History of the Legislative Union of Great Britain and Ireland*, pp. 184–87.

120. Clare to Camden, 2 April 1800, PRO 30/58/3, letter 13.

121. Cornwallis to Ross, 16 Aug. 1800, *Cornwallis Correspondence*, 3:288.

122. Cornwallis to Portland, 3 June 1800, ibid., 3:244.

123. Cornwallis to Portland, 9 June 1800, *Cornwallis Correspondence*, 3:262–66.

124. Portland to Cornwallis, 13 June 1800, ibid., 3:257–302; and Cornwallis to Pitt, 7 July 1800, PRO 30/58/3, letter 4.

125. Cornwallis to Portland, 17 June 1800, *Cornwallis Correspondence*, 3:262–66.

126. Castlereagh to Camden, 18 June 1800; and to Cook, 21 June 1800, Castlereagh, *Memoirs*, 3:327, 333.

127. Cooke to Castlereagh, 14 June 1800, ibid., 3:322.

128. Portland to Cornwallis, 27 June 1800, *Cornwallis Correspondence*, 3:271–74.

129. Bolton, *Act of Union*, p. 297.

130. Cornwallis to Castlereagh, 29 Dec. 1800, *Cornwallis Correspondence*, 3:316–17.

131. PRO 30/8/327, fols. 209–18, deal with various documents and papers Cornwallis gathered in support of his contention that the union should consider help for the Catholics.

132. Cornwallis to Ross, 14 Dec. 1800, *Cornwallis Correspondence*, 3:311.

133. Cornwallis to Ross, 25 Dec. 1800, ibid., 3:316.

134. Stanhope, *Life of Pitt*, 3:274–75.

135. George III to Pitt, 5 Feb. 1801, King George III, *The Later Correspondence of George III*, 3:483.

136. Steven Watson, *Reign of George III*, p. 402.

137. F. Bickley, ed., *Diaries of Sylvester Douglas, Lord Glenbervie*, quoted in ibid., p. 401.

138. Cornwallis to Ross, 15 Feb. 1801, *Cornwallis Correspondence*, 3:337.

139. *The Times*, 1 June 1801, describes the ceremony.

140. Cornwallis to Ross, 28 and 30 May 1801, *Cornwallis Correspondence*, 3:364–65.

Chapter 12

1. *The Times*, 3 June 1801.

2. Cornwallis to Ross, 23 July 1801, *Cornwallis Correspondence*, 3:378–79.

3. *The Times*, 1 Aug. 1801.

4. Cornwallis to Ross, 31 July 1801, *Cornwallis Correspondence*, 3:379.

5. *The Times*, 17 Aug. 1801.

6. See Lord Grenville to the king, 25 Aug. 1800, and subsequent letters referring to negotiations in King George III, *The Later Correspondence of George III*, 3:401 ff.

7. Steven Watson, *Reign of George III*, p. 407.

8. Arthur Bryant, *The Years of Endurance, 1793–1802*, p. 342.

9. *The Times*, 4 Sept. 1801.

10. Bryant, *Years of Endurance*, p. 344; and J. Holland Rose, "The Struggle with Revolutionary France," pp. 301 ff.

11. *The Times*, 7 Oct. 1801.

12. Ibid., 12 Oct. 1801.

13. *Annual Register* for 1801, p. 33, quoted by Earl Stanhope, *Life of the Right Honourable William Pitt*, 3:355.

14. *The Times*, 15 Oct. 1801.

15. Cornwallis to Ross, 17 Sept. 1801, *Cornwallis Correspondence*, 3:382.

16. Cornwallis to William Cornwallis, 10 Nov. 1801, HMC, *Rept. on MSS Var. Coll.*, 6:397.

17. *The Times*, 15 Oct. 1801.

18. Ibid., 26 Oct. 1801.

19. Ibid., 5, 7, and 11 Nov. 1801.

20. Ibid., 16 Nov. 1801. See also Colonel Littlehales to Ross, 21 Nov. 1801; Cornwallis to Ross, 8 Nov. 1801; and Cornwallis to Hawkesbury, 10 Nov. 1801, *Cornwallis Correspondence*, 3:397 and 390–91.

21. For details of this conversation see Cornwallis to Hawkesbury, 3 Dec. 1801, *Cornwallis Correspondence*, 3:399–404.

22. Cornwallis to Ross, 7 Dec. 1801, ibid., 3:406.

23. Cornwallis to Ross, 15 Dec. 1801, ibid., 3:413.

24. Cornwallis to Hawkesbury, 30 Dec. 1801, ibid., 3:420.

25. Cornwallis to Ross, 25 Dec. 1801, ibid., 3:418.

26. Hawkesbury to Cornwallis, 12 Feb. 1802, ibid., 3:457.

27. Nightingall to Ross, 10 Jan. 1802, ibid., 3:435–37.

28. Cornwallis to Hawkesbury, 5 and 12 Feb. 1802, ibid., 3:446–47 and 452.

29. Hawkesbury to Cornwallis, 12 Feb. 1802, ibid., 3:457.
30. Hawkesbury to Cornwallis, 14 March 1802, ibid., 3:472–77.
31. Cornwallis to Hawkesbury, 17 March 1802, ibid., 3:477–80.
32. Cornwallis to Hawkesbury, 25 March 1802, ibid., 3:483–84.
33. Rose, "The Struggle with Revolutionary France," pp. 307–9.
34. Addington to Cornwallis, 22 March 1802, *Cornwallis Correspondence*, 3: 482–83.
35. Quoted in Philip Ziegler, *Addington*, p. 147.
36. Description of his last years at Culford, unless otherwise cited, comes from various letters, mostly to Ross, in *Cornwallis Correspondence*, 3:494–519.
37. Cornwallis to Hardwicke, 19 Oct. 1803, BM, Add. MSS 35,743, fols. 83–84.
38. Cornwallis to Alexander Marsden, 21 Jan. 1804, BM, Add. MSS 35,746, fols. 1–2.
39. Cornwallis to William Cornwallis, 12 Aug. 1804, HMC, *Rept. on MSS Var. Coll.*, 6:405.
40. Cornwallis to Ross, 24 Oct. 1804, *Cornwallis Correspondence*, 3:521; and to William Cornwallis, 3 Jan. 1805, HMC, *Rept. on MSS Var. Coll.*, 6:406.
41. Cornwallis to Pitt, 20 Aug. 1804, PRO 30/11/277, fols. 63–64.
42. See Cornwallis to Lake, 30 July 1805, *Cornwallis Correspondence*, 3:533.
43. William Hickey, *Memoirs*, 4:318–20.
44. Ibid., 4:319.
45. George Abercrombie Robinson to Castlereagh, 25 Sept. 1805, *Cornwallis Correspondence*, 3:557.
46. Hickey, *Memoirs*, 4:320.
47. Robinson to Ross, 26 Sept. 1805, *Cornwallis Correspondence*, 3:558.
48. Ibid., 3:563.

Bibliography

The following bibliography is fuller than the select one for *Cornwallis in America*, primarily because readers are less likely to be familiar with the materials for Ireland, India, and the ordnance than with those on the American Revolution. We have chosen to organize the unpublished sources by location, the published sources by topic and type, and the secondary works alphabetically by author. We explain the pertinent document used for some unpublished sources.

Manuscript Sources

London

British Museum

Add. MSS 13,742, fols. 199–206, 207–12. Letters of General Lake in 1805 concerning the state and disposition of irregulars in India and information on provinces and princes in India west of the river Jumna.

Add. MSS 18,108, A–G. Seven maps illustrating Cornwallis's campaigns in India, 1778–92.

Warren Hastings Papers. These include Add. MSS 24,222–24,268, minutes of the proceedings of his trial, 1788–95; 29,219–29,225, papers relating to his impeachment and trial; 22,454–22,455, letters to Hastings from the governor of Madras, 1781–85; and 28,973–29,236, official and private correspondence, 1772–1818.

Add. MSS 33,106, fols. 118–19, and Add. MSS. 33,109, fols. 291–92. Two letters from Cornwallis to Henry Pelham (Lord Pelham) on ordnance matters and Irish affairs.

Add. MSS 35,743, fols. 83–84, and 35,746, fols. 1–2. One letter to Lord Hardwicke and one to Alexander Marsden from Cornwallis bemoaning retirement.

Public Record Office

PRIVATE CORRESPONDENCE

Cornwallis Papers, 30/11. These papers are the single most important source for the book. The pertinent series include: 7–58, 111–215, 262, which deal with his civil and military administration in India; 216–18, which concern Flanders; 59, 219–61, which relate to the ordnance; 263, which pertains to Ireland; 264–67, which concern Amiens; and 268–83, which contain miscellaneous papers such as wills. *List and Index Society, Gifts and Deposits*, part 1, vol. 10 (London, 1966), describes in more detail the Cornwallis Papers in the Public Record Office.

Chatham Papers, 30/8. Another important source. The most important volumes are: 102, letters from Pitt and Cornwallis to Archibald Campbell; 125, letters to Pitt in two bound volumes, the second of which contains letters to Pitt from Cornwallis and from his two brothers, the bishop and the admiral.

Dacres Adams Papers, 30/58. William Dacres Adams was Pitt's private secretary from 1804 to 1806, but his papers contain documents from 1783 to 1806. 4, letters to Pitt from 1801 to 1803, contains much information on the Act of Union and the king's illness.

PAPERS RELATING TO INDIA

State Papers, 41/29. Letters from the secretary of state to the war office, 1781–82. Unfoliated and unnumbered in this series is a disposition of the army in India.

Home Office, 50/381–85. Covers the period 1788–94. Official and unofficial in-letters and out-letters to and from the secretary at war from and to various departments. This series includes tables showing ages and heights of recruits sent to India. In 1788, they averaged in age in their late teens and in height around five feet six inches. By the 1790s they averaged in age in their early teens and in height around five feet two inches. So the recruits Cornwallis got for the regular army were—understandably in light of Continental developments—less mature in age and physique during his later years in India than they were at the beginning of his tenure.

War Office, 4/115. Out-letters from the secretary at war, October to December 1781, indexed. Includes material on the method of payment of troops in India.

War Office, 4/295–97. Out-letters from the secretary at war, 1779–92. 297, pp. 273–74, gives the augmentation of the forces in India in 1791.

War Office, 40/5. A hodgepodge of unnumbered papers for the 1780s and 1790s. These papers deal with everything from Cornwallis's order forbidding Anglo-Indians to become officers, to Knightsbridge barracks, to papers relating to Sir Eyre Coote, to deserters. Mostly they are in-letters to the war office with a lot of material relating to India, though documents also pertain to Scotland and Quebec.

PAPERS RELATING TO ORDNANCE

State Papers, 41/36, fols. 248–49. Letter dated 17 March 1740 (Old Style) from the principal officers of the ordnance to the Duke of Montagu, master general.

State Papers, 44/184, fols. 244–45. Royal warrant establishing Woolwich Academy.

Treasury, 27/46–49. Out-letters, 1795–98.

Treasury, 29/67–77. Treasury minutes, 1795–98.

Treasury, Ind. 8559–66. Treasury in-letters, 1795–98.

War Office, 34/109, pp. 87–100. These are the "Rules and Orders for the Royal Military Academy at Woolwich."

War Office, 45/36–48. Reference books to correspondence, Jan. 1795–Aug. 1798. These works list alphabetically the person from whom ordnance received a letter, the date the letter was sent and received, and the minute that describes the day on which the letter was read.

War Office, 46/23–25. Ordnance out-letters, 1794–1824.

War Office, 47/2365–78. Ordnance board minutes and in-letters, 1794–1801.

War Office, 55/334, p. 56. This royal warrant of 13 May 1686 prescribes the salutes and ceremonial due the master general.

War Office, 55/1789. This document describes in detail the duties of the principal officers of the ordnance.

PAPERS RELATING TO IRELAND

War Office, 1/407; 612; 620; 693; 767; 768; 769; 800; 922; 1101. These papers concern disaffection in Ireland, French aid in 1798, and other matters relating to "the rising of the moon."

War Office, 3/10; 13. Includes the number of forces normal for Ireland and a military survey for 1795.

War Office, 4/189; 324. Army units transferred to and from the Irish establishment and a plan for assimilating military finance to Great Britain's, 1802.

War Office, 6/131. Napper Tandy's proclamation on landing in Ireland, 1798.

War Office, 25/3220; 3247. Pay and allowances in Ireland in 1800 and report by adjutant general on Irish defense in 1801.

War Office, 30/63; 66. Defense of the south of Ireland and probable places for invasion in 1796. Sir Ralph Abercrombie's plans for the defense of Ireland, 1797–1801.

War Office, 40/11. Account of the battle of Tara.

Home Office, 30/1–2. Military correspondence on Irish affairs, 1794–97, and information on the rebellion to 1800.

Home Office, 50/4; 6; 7; 8; 379; 391; 453. Concerns the rebellion and the military situation. Includes such matters as dispatch of troops to Ireland, memorandum of defense, state of the army.

Home Office, 100/7; 11; 15; 40; 54; 67; 68. Refers to staff organization, barracks, buying and selling of staff appointments, and the disturbed state of Ireland.

Home Office, 100/73–107. Deals with all sorts of Irish affairs, 1798–1802. Some letters are printed in Cornwallis and Castlereagh correspondence.

73–74. Letters to Portland from lord lieutenant on military matters, 1798.

75–79. Private and secret correspondence for 1798.

80–82. Civil correspondence for 1798.

83–84. Military correspondence for 1799.

85–87. Private and secret correspondence for 1799.

88–89. Civil correspondence for 1799.
90–92. Military correspondence for 1800.
93–94. Private, secret, and confidential correspondence for 1800.
95–98. Civil correspondence for 1800.
99. Papers relating to Roman Catholics, 1800–1804.
100. Petitions and miscellaneous material, 1800–1802.
101–2. Military correspondence for 1801.
103. Private, secret, and confidential correspondence, January–July 1801.

India Office Records and Library

VARIOUS DOCUMENTS

Bengal Despatches, vols. 14, 15.
Bengal Letters Received, vol. 24.
Bengal Public and Secret Letters to Court.
Bengal Revenue Consultations.
Bombay Despatches, vol. 10.
Range 70, vol. 14, proceedings of committee of circuit at Krishnagar, 10–28 June 1772.
Range 52, vol. 13. Bengal revenue council.
Range 3, vol. 26. Bengal public council.
Range A, vol. 18. Bengal secret consultations.
Europeans in India, 1776–1824, 0/5/1–25. Volume 25 summarizes the details about Europeans found in the first twenty-four volumes.

HOME MISCELLANEOUS SERIES

This series, some 860 volumes, contains a vast amount of material dealing with almost every conceivable type of matter. Those volumes, and the parts of them we found most useful, are listed below.
60. Account of Tipoo in collusion with some Portuguese to foment mutiny in Goa in 1788.
68. Early British settlements in Bengal, Orissa, and Patna, and Bengal revenues before Cornwallis.
351. Revenue administration, 1769–89.
354–56. Civil offices and establishment, 1784–85.
368. Documents concerning John Holland and charges against him.
369. Correspondence relating to investigation of public offices and establishments in Bengal. Describes in detail the business of each office. Also lists houses or buildings belonging to the Company. Describes the nizam of Hyderabad in 1787.
379–92. Copious materials discussing the revenue settlement in Bengal. Documents include the reports and opinions of everyone from collectors to governors general. 387 has the letters of John Murray, military auditor general, relating to supply of the army in the war with Tipoo. Other material ranges from military accounts and regimental roles to a concise account of the Andaman islands. Many letters duplicate those found in the Cornwallis papers.
412. Legislative and judicial authority of the Company's governments in India.

414, 57–80. The opinion of Sir John Anstruther, chief justice of Bengal, on the legality of the new Cornwallis judicial regulations.

436. Reports of Captain John Taylor (on the Bombay establishment) of the war with Tipoo, as well as other military matters. Has a description of Tipoo's army.

451. Relates to Cornwallis's reorganization of the army in India.

452. Mostly correspondence between committee of Company officers and Dundas or the court of directors.

454. Other documents on the new military arrangements.

558. Mostly notes, with index, of affairs in India from the end of Mahratta war, 1780–90. Includes origins of the war with Tipoo and has an index to names mentioned in the narrative, along with biographical dates.

563. Affairs of the nizam of Hyderabad, 1784–98. A general index of Indian names (with many personal details) and of Europeans as well.

565. Abstract of correspondence dealing with Tipoo and narratives of prisoners of Tipoo.

741. Letters of Jonathan Duncan, resident at Benares, to Colonel Alexander Ross.

818. Melville papers. Some of Melville's original letters and documents from 1780 to 1818. Not as important for our study of Cornwallis as Melville papers elsewhere. They do include letters from Campbell to Melville.

MANUSCRIPTS EUROPEAN

E 60, 61. Field book of the marches of the army under the command of Major General Medows, etc., from 26 May 1790 to 27 January 1791, by A. Allan, captain of the guides to the army. Handsome colored drawings.

E 93. Observations on the state of society among the Asiatic subjects of Great Britain, particularly with respect to morals; and the means of improving, written chiefly in the year 1792 (by Charles Grant).

E 268, vol. 1. Daniell itinerary. The itinerary of the painter William Daniell on a trip from Anopshur to the Hurdwar, 18 March to 26 May 1789.

E 308. Papers of Sir Robert Grant, a commissioner on the board of control, 1830–34, and governor of Bombay, 1834–38. Important for the letters of his father, Charles Grant.

F 149/6, 65–68. Memoranda books of Charles Ware Malet. Books are like diaries. They record daily life minutely. Good for observations on geography and the customs of the Indians. Malet, resident at Poona, was both wordy and meticulous.

FACTORY RECORDS

Although these records proved of marginal value for our study, they do illustrate well how the Company's servants operated outside the traditional Bengal, Bombay, and Madras.

Anjengo
G/1. Relations with rajah of Travancore.
G/5–8. Diary and consultations, 1785–93.

Cape of Good Hope
G/9/1.

Tellicherri
G/37/6–11. Diary and consultations, 1785–93.

Thana
G/38/6–9. Diary and consultations.

Edinburgh

Scottish Record Office

Melville Papers, GD 51/3. This series deals with East Indian affairs.
    1/1–98. Letters from Lord Mornington to Melville. Some of these documents, such as 18–21 and 30, concern Cornwallis, for they deal with Tanjore and precedents for appointments by directors to offices of governor and commander in chief, 1784–97.
    30/1–21. Letters from John Bruce, Company's historiographer.
    32/1–2; 33/1–4; 35/1–2; 36; 38/1–39. These deal with everything from patronage to revenue.
    200; 208; 310; 312/1–6; 314/1–8; 318/1–2; 322; 328/1–4; 331; 332/1–4; 333; 505. A great variety of materials, from anonymous letters on public credit during Cornwallis's tenure to a sketch Major James Rennell sent to Dundas of the partition of Tipoo's dominions. Particulars are explained in more detail in *List and Index Society, Special Series, List of Melville Papers (sections 2 and 3) Preserved in the Scottish Record Office*, vol. 4 (London, 1971).
Cunninghame of Thorntoun Papers, GD 21. The notebooks of John Peebles, which describe his service in America. Notebook 13 tells of Cornwallis's stay in New York after Yorktown and his departure for Britain.

National Library of Scotland

Melville Papers. Numerous papers here as well as in the Scottish Record Office. In the National Library of Scotland, however, they are under various numbers. The library hopes to keep acquiring them as they come up for auction.
MSS 3837–39. Deal with Archibald Campbell at Madras. So extensive and detailed that from them one might almost write an account of Campbell's tenure at Madras.
MSS 3383–88. Official correspondence between Cornwallis and Melville enclosing reports from Cornwallis's subordinates.
MS 1051. Deals with the union of Britain and Ireland.
MS 5375. Dundonald Papers. Includes a letter from Cornwallis worrying that he had not had the opportunity to do justice to the late Major Charles Cochrane.

OTHER PAPERS

Many other papers have letters to or from Cornwallis or his subordinates in India or relate to Indian affairs. MS 2903, fols. 4–170, for example, provides

London and Madras gossip in letters to and from Amelia, Archibald Campbell's wife. MS 2905, fols. 144–58, contains several letters of the nabob of Arcot and the Carnatic relating to his pension to Amelia. MSS 5372–80, papers of Andrew Stuart, have two of Cornwallis's letters. Stuart was stationed at Fort St. George, Madras. We looked at a wide variety of other papers, but only a portion of them were useful for the preparation of this volume.

Sheffield

Sheffield Central Library

The Rockingham Papers contain some letters relating to Cornwallis's participation in political life after his return from America.

Surrey

Elveden Hall

The Cornwallis rent rolls are located here. Though difficult to interpret, they shed some light on his finances.

Ann Arbor, Michigan

William L. Clements Library

The most important papers we consulted here are those of Sir Henry Clinton. Though the uneasy superior–subordinate relationship between Clinton and Cornwallis virtually ended after Yorktown, the acrimony between the two men did not. After their warfare in the press over responsibility for Yorktown, however, Cornwallis seemed to dismiss the matter and seek new employment. Clinton never forgot, indeed brooded over it until he died, as his papers show.

Published Sources

Collections of Documents

An Abstract of the Regulations Concerning Criminal Justice, Civil Justice, Land Revenue, and Misc. Revenue, 1793–1824, compiled by William Blunt and H. Shakespear. 4 vols. Calcutta, 1824–28. Volume 1, *An Abstract of the Regulations Enacted for the Administration of the Police and Criminal Justice*; volume 2, *An Abstract of the Regulations Enacted for Civil Justice . . . from the Year 1793 to the end of 1794*; volume 3, *An Abstract of the Regulations Enacted for the Assessment and Regulation of the Land Revenues . . . to 1824, Inclusive*; and volume 4, *An*

Abstract of the Regulations of Government in the Departments of Miscellaneous Revenue and Commerce . . .

British parliamentary papers. The most important collection for this study is *British Parliamentary Papers, Colonies, East India*, vols. 1, 2, 3. Reprint, Shannon, Ireland, 1969–71. They cover the parliamentary sessions of 1805 through 1813. These three volumes contain the first five reports of the select committee on the affairs of the East India Company. The reports include appendices with materials ranging from the minutes of governors general to army musters. A glossary of Indian terms is in the fifth report.

The Campaign in Virginia 1781. An Exact Reprint of Six Rare Pamphlets on the Clinton-Cornwallis Controversy with Very Numerous Important Unpublished Manuscript Notes by Sir Henry Clinton, K.B., and the Omitted and Hitherto Unpublished Portions of the Letters in Their Appendixes Added from the Original Manuscripts with a Supplement Containing Extracts from the Journals of the House of Lords. A French Translation of Papers Laid before the House and a Catalogue of the Additional Correspondence of Clinton and of Cornwallis in 1780–1781: About 3456 Papers Relating to the Controversy or Bearing on Affairs in America, compiled by Benjamin Franklin Stevens. 2 vols. London, 1888.

Colebrooke, Sir J. E. *Supplement to the Digest of the Regulations and Laws Enacted by the Governor-General-in-Council for the Civil Government of the Territories under the Presidency of Bengal*. Calcutta, 1807.

Gilbert, John T. *Documents Relating to Ireland, 1795–1804*. Dublin, 1970.

Diaries, Memoirs, Correspondence, Journals, Narratives

Anderson, George. *A General View of the Variations which Have Been Made in the Affairs of the East India Company from the Conclusion of the War in India in 1784 to the Commencement of the Present Hostilities*. London, 1792.

Barrington, Sir Jonah. *Historic Memoirs and Secret Anecdotes of the Legislative Union*. London, 1833.

Beresford, John. *Letters of the Rt. Hon. John Beresford*. Edited by W. Beresford. 2 vols. London, 1854.

Blakiston, J. *Twelve Years' Military Adventure in Three Quarters of the Globe, or Memoirs of an Officer who Served in the Armies of His Majesty and of the East India Company, between the Years 1802 and 1814* . . . 2 vols. London, 1829.

Castlereagh, Robert Stewart, Viscount. *Memoirs and Correspondence of Viscount Castlereagh*. Edited by Charles Vane, Marquis of Londonderry. 12 vols. London, 1848–53. Volumes 1–4 cover the years 1798 to 1808 and deal in large part with Ireland.

Cornwallis, Charles, First Marquis. *The Correspondence of Charles First Marquis Cornwallis*. Edited by Charles Ross. 3 vols. London, 1859. Obviously, the single most important published source for our book.

Cornwallis, William. Historical Manuscripts Commission. *Report on Manuscripts in Various Collections*. Vol. 6. The manuscripts¹ of Cornwallis Wykeham-Martin, of the Hill, Purton, Wilts, Esquire. Dublin, 1909. These are the letters of Cornwallis's brother William.

Daniell, Thomas. *Views of Calcutta*. London, 1786.

Dirom, Alexander. *A Narrative of the Campaign in India, which Terminated with*

Tippoo Sultan in 1792, with Maps and Plans Illustrative of the Subject and a View of Seringapatam. London, 1793.

Fraser, James B. *Views of Calcutta*. London, 1824–25. Colored prints of Calcutta.

King George III. *The Correspondence of King George the Third*. Edited by Sir John Fortescue. 6 vols. London, 1927–28.

———. *The Later Correspondence of George III*. Edited by Arthur Aspinall. 5 vols. Cambridge, 1962–70.

Grand, G. F. *Narrative of the Life of a Gentleman Long Resident in India*. Calcutta, 1910. Grand was a collector in Cornwallis's time.

Henderson, A. J., ed. "The Irish Rebellion of 1798. Two First Hand Accounts." *Journal of the Society for Army Historical Research* 52 (1974): 34–45.

Hickey, William. *Memoirs*. Edited by Alfred Spencer. 4 vols. London, 1913–25.

Hodges, William. *Select Views of India, Drawn on the Spot, in the Years 1780, 1781, 1782, and 1783, and Executed in Aqualtinto*. 2 vols. London, 1786.

Jones, Sir William. *The Letters of Sir William Jones*. Edited by Garland Cannon. 2 vols. Oxford, 1970.

Lindsay, Lord. *Lives of the Lindsays, or, a Memoir of the Houses of Crawford and Balcarres*. 2d ed. London, 1858.

Mackenzie, Roderick. *A Sketch of the War with Tippoo Sultaun; or a Detail of Military Operations, from the Commencement of Hostilities at the Lines of Travancore in December 1789, until the Peace Concluded before Seringapatam in February 1792*. 2 vols. Calcutta, 1793.

Maxwell, W. H. *History of the Irish Rebellion in 1798; with Memoirs of the Union, and Emmett's Insurrection in 1803*. London, 1854.

Memoirs of the Life of the Most Noble Marquis and Earl Cornwallis, Viscount Brome, and Baron Cornwallis of Eye; Knight of the Garter, and a Baronet, Constable of the Tower of London, Lord Lieutenant and Custos Rotulorum of the Tower Division, a General in the Army, Governor General of, and Commander in Chief in Bengal, etc. etc. London, 1806. Author unknown.

Moore, Sir John. *Diary of Sir John Moore*. Edited by Sir J. G. Maurice. 2 vols. London, 1904.

Rennell, James. *The Marches of the British Armies in the Peninsula of India, during the Campaigns of 1790 and 1791, Illustrated and Explained by Reference to a Map Compiled from Authentic Documents, Transmitted by Earl Cornwallis from India*. 2d ed. London, 1792.

———. *Memoir of a Map of Hindoostan; or the Mogal's Empire; With an Examination of Some Positions in the Former System of Indian Geography; and Some Illustrations of the Present One; and a Complete Index of Names to the Map*. London, 1783.

Repton, Humphrey. *Sketches and Hints on Landscape Gardening Collected from Designs and Observations Now in the Possession of the Different Noblemen and Gentlemen for Whose Use They Were Originally Made*. London, 1794. Repton admitted his description came from the red book compiled while working for Cornwallis. Unfortunately, he uses Culford for only one example.

Rose, George. *The Diaries and Correspondence of the Right Hon. George Rose; Containing Original Letters of the Most Distinguished Statesmen of His Day*. Edited by Leveson Vernon Harcourt. 2 vols. London, 1860.

Scott, David. *The Correspondence of David Scott, Director and Chairman of the*

East India Company, Relating to Indian Affairs, 1787–1805. Edited by C. H. Philips. 2 vols. Camden Society Publications, 3d ser., vols. 75, 76. London, 1951.

Stewart, Major C. *Memoirs of Hyder Ali Khan and Tippoo Sultan.* Cambridge, 1809.

Teignmouth, John, Lord. *Memoirs of the Life and Correspondence of John, Lord Teignmouth.* Edited by Lord Teignmouth. 2 vols. London, 1843.

Twining, Thomas. *Travels in India a Hundred Years Ago with a Visit to the United States.* Edited by Rev. William H. G. Twining. London, 1893.

Wilks, Mark. *Historical Sketches of the South of India in an Attempt to Trace from the Origin of the Hindoo Government of that State, to the Extinction of the Mohammedan Dynasty in 1799, Founded Chiefly on Indian Authorities Collected by the Author while Officiating for Several Years as Political Resident at the Court of Mysoor.* Edited by Murray Hammick. 2 vols. Mysore, 1931–32.

Williamson, Thomas. *Oriental Field Sports* . . . London, 1807.

———, and Blagdon, F. W. *The Europeans in India; from a Collection of Drawings by Charles Doyley, Esq.* . . . London, 1813.

Windham, William. *Windham Papers.* Introduction by Earl of Roseberry. 2 vols. Boston, 1913.

Contemporary Newspapers

We looked at several of the Indian newspapers at Colindale, where the British Museum houses its newspapers. Unfortunately, Colindale often possessed only one or two issues. Among those we consulted were: *Calcutta Chronicle and General Advertiser; Asiatic Mirror and Commercial Advertiser; India Gazette or Calcutta Public Advertiser*; and *Oriental Star.* The two most important newspapers by far, however, were the two listed below.

Calcutta Gazette or Oriental Advertiser. This was the official government newspaper which came out every Thursday. Filled with local news in the 1780s, it became more sophisticated in the 1790s with foreign news and stock market reports.

The Times. The most important British newspaper in the late eighteenth and early nineteenth centuries.

Secondary Works

Aspinall, Arthur. *Cornwallis in Bengal.* Manchester, 1931.

Banerjee, Phanindra Nath. "Background to the Cornwallis Code." *Quarterly Review of Historical Studies* 9 (1969–70): 82–95.

———. "Indian Law Officer in Early British Judiciary of Bengal (1772–1793)." *Quarterly Review of Historical Studies* 4 (1964–65): 152–58.

Bartlett, C. J. *Castlereagh.* London, 1966.

Bolton, G. C. *The Passing of the Irish Act of Union.* Oxford, 1966.

Bryant, Arthur. *The Years of Endurance, 1793–1802.* London, 1942.

Callahan, Raymond. *The East India Company and Army Reform, 1783–1798.* Cambridge, Mass., 1972.

Cambridge History of India. Vol. 5. Edited by H. H. Dodwell. Cambridge, 1929. This volume covers the years 1497–1858.

Cannon, Garland. *Oriental Jones*. Calcutta, 1964.

Cannon, John. *The Fox-North Coalition*. Cambridge, 1969.

Ehrman, John. *The Younger Pitt*. New York, 1969.

Embree, Ainslie Thomas. *Charles Grant and British Rule in India*. New York, 1962.

Forbes, Arthur. *A History of the Army Ordnance Services*. Vol. 1. N.p., 1929.

Forrest, Denys. *Tiger of Mysore: The Life and Death of Tipu Sultan*. London, 1970.

Fortescue, Sir John. *History of the British Army*. 13 vols. London, 1899–1930.

Furber, Holden. *John Company at Work*. Cambridge, Mass., 1951.

———. *Henry Dundas, First Viscount Melville, 1742–1811*. Oxford, 1931.

Galbraith, John Kenneth. "James Mill's India." *Encounter* 30 (March 1968): 40–45.

Gilbert, Arthur M. "Recruitment and Reform in the East India Company Army, 1760–1800." *Journal of British Studies* 15, no. 1 (Autumn 1975): 89–111.

Glover, Richard. *Peninsular Preparation: The Reform of the British Army, 1795–1809*. Cambridge, 1963.

Griffin, William D. "Cornwallis in Search of Employment." *Studies in Burke and His Time* 11, no. 3 (Spring 1970): 1543–54.

Gupta, A. Das. "Trade and Politics in 18th Century India." In *Islam and the Trade of Asia*, pp. 181–214, edited by D. S. Richards. London, 1970.

Hunter, Sir William Wilson. *Annals of Rural Bengal*. London, 1897.

Ingram, T. Dunbar. *A History of the Legislative Union of Great Britain and Ireland*. Reprint. Port Washington, N.Y., 1970.

Johnson, Edith M. *Great Britain and Ireland, 1760–1800*. Edinburgh, 1963.

Jones, W. D. *Records of the Royal Military Academy*. Woolwich, 1851.

Law, Thomas. *Sketch of Some Late Arrangements and a View of the Rising Resources in Bengal*. London, 1792.

Lecky, W. E. H. *A History of Ireland in the Eighteenth Century*. 5 vols. New York, 1893.

Mackesy, Piers. *The War for America, 1775–1783*. Cambridge, Mass., 1964.

McDowell, R. B. *Irish Public Opinion, 1750–1800*. Reprint. Westport, Conn., 1975.

Malcolm, Sir John. *Political History of India, 1784–1823*. 2 vols. London, 1826.

Mason, Philip. *A Matter of Honour: An Account of the Indian Army, Its Officers and Men*. London, 1974.

———. *The Men Who Ruled India*. Vol. 1. London, 1953. Written under the name of Woodruff.

Mill, James. *The History of British India*. 6 vols. London, 1826.

Misra, B. B. *The Central Administration of the East India Company, 1773–1834*. Manchester, 1959.

Narain, V. A. *Jonathan Duncan and Varanasi*. Calcutta, 1959.

Nelson, R. R. *The Home Office, 1782–1801*. Durham, N.C., 1969.

Olson, Alison Gilbert. *The Radical Duke: Career and Correspondence of Charles Lennox, Third Duke of Richmond*. Oxford, 1966.

Pakenham, Thomas. *The Year of Liberty*. London, 1969.

Pearson, Dale. "Cornwallis and Richmond: A Case Study of the Master General-ship of the 1790s." Unpublished essay.

Philips, C. H. *The East India Company, 1784–1834*. Manchester, 1961.
Rahim, Muhammad Abdur. *Social and Cultural History of Bengal*. 2 vols. Karachi, 1963.
Rose, J. Holland. "The Struggle with Revolutionary France." In *The Cambridge History of British Foreign Policy* 1:216–308, edited by Sir A. W. Ward and G. P. Gooch. Cambridge, 1922.
————. *William Pitt and the Great War*. Reprint. Westport, Conn., 1971.
Rowse, A. L. "Welsh Orientalist: Sir William Jones." *History Today* 21, no. 1 (Jan. 1971): 54–64.
Seton-Karr, W. S. *The Marquis Cornwallis and the Consolidation of British Rule*. Oxford, 1914.
Sherwig, John M. *Guineas and Gunpowder*. Cambridge, Mass., 1969.
Sinha, J. C. *Economic Annals of Bengal*. London, 1927.
Smith, Vincent A. *Oxford History of India*. Edited by Percival Spear. Oxford, 1958.
Spear, Percival. *The Nabobs*. London, 1963.
Stanhope, Earl. *Life of the Right Honourable William Pitt*. 4 vols. London, 1862.
Teeling, Charles Hamilton. *History of the Irish Rebellion of 1798 and Sequel to the History of the Irish Rebellion of 1798*. Reprint. Shannon, Ireland, 1972.
Wall, Maureen. "The United Irish Movement." *Historical Studies* 5 (1965): 122–40.
Watson, Steven. *The Reign of George III, 1760–1815*. Oxford, 1960.
Western, J. R. *The English Militia in the Eighteenth Century*. London, 1965.
Wickwire, Franklin and Mary. *Cornwallis: The American Adventure*. Boston, 1970.
Wright, H. R. C. "The Abolition by Cornwallis of the Forced Cultivation of Opium in Behar." *Economic History Review* 12 (1959–60): 112–20.
————. "Some Aspects of the Permanent Settlement in Bengal." *Economic History Review* 7 (Dec. 1954): 204–15.
Ziegler, Philip. *Addington*. New York, 1965.

Bibliographical and Biographical Aids

We include here aids that have proved of special interest to our topic, and not the standard works, such as the *Dictionary of National Biography*, that are usually to be found in the bibliographies of general studies of the eighteenth century.

Alphabetical List of the Honourable East India Company's Bengal Civil Servants, from the year 1780 to the year 1838 . . . Compiled by Messrs. Dodwell and Miles. London, 1839. Lists men with dates of appointment and offices held, as well as dates of leaving office.
Hill, Samuel Charles. *Catalogue of the Home Miscellaneous Series of the India Office Records*. London, 1927. This guide to the series lists some 860 volumes. One may find duplicates of many of the same documents in several different volumes.
Hodson, V. C. P. *List of the Officers of the Bengal Army, 1758–1834*. 4 vols.

London, 1927–47. More than a list, it gives short biographies and biographical references.

Kaye, George Rusby, and Johnston, Edward Hamilton. *India Office Library Catalogue of Manuscripts in European Languages, vol. II, part II, Minor Collections and Miscellaneous Manuscripts*. London, 1937. Since there is no handlist for European manuscripts up to the middle 200s, this book is the only guide.

Kaye, John William. *Lives of Indian Officers, Illustrative of the History of the Civil and Military Services of India*. 2 vols. London, 1867.

Public Record Office Lists and Indexes, LIII, An Alphabetical Guide to Certain War Office and other Military Records Preserved in the Public Record Office. Vols. 1–56. London, 1892–1936. A marvelous guide for the history of the regular British army. It provides a guide to the war office records for the army as a whole and also for the individual British regiments. It also has a general index to all war office records.

Index

A

Abercrombie, Sir Ralph, 219–20
Abercrombie, Sir Robert, 152; in first campaign against Tipoo, 138, 147; returns to Bombay, 150; in second campaign against Tipoo, 163, 165; met by Hyderabad and Mahratta cavalry, 168, 169; joins siege of Seringapatam, 169; becomes military commander in India, 173
Addington, Henry, first Viscount Sidmouth, 251, 252, 255; his ministry wishes peace, 254; pleased with Cornwallis's work at Amiens, 260; his ministry replaced, 263
Agra, 47, 110
Ali, Nizam of Hyderabad, 45, 56, 91, 118–19, 126
Amboor, 125; supply base for combined army, 147, 155
America, United States of, 3, 6, 7, 8, 9, 15, 18, 140, 148, 179, 193; and War for American Independence, 5, 102, 121, 131; campaigns there influence Cornwallis in India, 27, 45, 133–35
Amiens, Peace of, 262; preliminaries celebrated, 254–55; negotiations for, 256–59; signing, 259; difficulties in provisions, 259–60; failure to last, 260–61; celebrated in London, 261
Andaman Islands, Cornwallis takes post in, 48
Anglicans in Ireland: privileged position of, 213; in Irish Parliament and government, 215, 217, 236–37; Cornwallis's distrust of and disdain for, 230, 238–39; Castlereagh opposes, 233
Anne, queen of England, 214
Apsley, Alexander, 203
Arcot, 23, 130; nabob of, offers Cornwallis a garden house, 174
Armagh, no university for Dissenters at, 231
Army, Austrian. *See* Austria
Army, British: pay and promotion of officers in, 98–99; hired to East India Company, 101; size of, in India, 101; artillery of, in India, 102; rivalry between its officers and East India Company's, 105–7; in war against Tipoo, 139–74 passim; in Flanders, 181–82; duties of commander in chief of, 189–90; confused organization of, 190–91; ousted from Continent, 191; deficiencies of, in Ireland, 219; expected by Dubliners to rebel, 220; Cornwallis tries to improve quality of, in Ireland, 232. *See also* Army, combined British and East India Company
Army, combined British and East India Company: size and nature of, 141; order of march, 141; plundering of, 142; enters Mysore, 142–43; takes

Bangalore, 144–45; attacks Tipoo's
rear guard, 146; its low opinion of
Hyderabad cavalry, 146; desperate
supply problems of, 147–49; defeats
Tipoo in first campaign, 149–50;
moves toward Bangalore, 150–53;
junctions with Mahrattas, 151; depends on Mahratta supplies, 153,
155–59; its low opinion of Mahratta
army, 152; takes hill forts, 159–61;
order of march in second campaign,
163; junctions with second group of
Hyderabad cavalry, 162–64; defeats
Tipoo in second campaign, 165–68;
besieges Seringapatam, 168–70;
plunders Hyder Ali's grave, 169;
Tipoo surrenders to, 170; receives
Tipoo's sons, 170–71; Cornwallis
gives prize money to, 174
Army, French. *See* France
Army, Hanoverian: in India, 102, 113;
with Duke of York, 181
Army, Hessian, 181
Army, Prussian. *See* Prussia
Arnold, Benedict, his son admitted to
Woolwich Academy, 201
Asiatic Miscellany, 78
Asiatic Society, 78
Auchmuty, at Cornwallis levee, 31–32
Austria, 179, 253, 259; its forces with
Duke of York, 181; lethargy of, in
war against France, 181; its partition-
ing of Poland, 181, 182; its troops de-
tailed to take Dunkirk, 181; its army
does not support British in Toulon,
181; British subsidy to, 182; fails to
help Duke of York, 183; Francis II
joins its army at Valenciennes, 183;
does not cooperate with allies, 183–
84; its army defeated by French at
Fleurus, 186; finances of, 187; signs
Peace of Campio Formio, 208

B

Baillie, William, 45, 102; defeated at
Pollilur, 121

Ballinamuck, Humbert surrenders at,
226–27
Ballintra, 226
Bangalore, 126, 142, 148; Cornwallis
takes, 144–45; supplies in, 145;
Tipoo's rear guard attacked outside
of, 146; Cornwallis at, 147, 153, 154;
supplies to, 159
Bantry Bay, French at, 217–18
Barlow, George, 66, 96
Barrackpore, 25, 33, 95
Bathurst, Robert, 66, 70
Becher, Richard, 61, 64
Belfast, 217; northern whig club in,
234; Cornwallis visits, 244
Belmore, Somerset, Lord Corry, second Earl of, 236
Benares, 41, 44, 58, 66; Cornwallis es-
tablishes Sanskrit college for Hindus
at, 94
Bengal, 2–6, 118, 223; Nabob
Mobaruk ud Dowlah of, 54, 80; extent of and size of population in,
59–60; lawlessness in, 75–77; types
of rupees in, 94; slave traffic in children abolished in, 95–96; size of
sepoy army in, 99; army maintains
British in, 102; wretched conditions
of East India Company European
battalions in, 107–12; East India
Company officers in, oppose Cornwallis's plans, 115; Cornwallis leaves
to fight Tipoo, 137; supplies combined army, 155, 158; British in,
hope to reward Cornwallis, 173;
events in, after Cornwallis leaves,
263
Bengal, Bay of, 47–48, 114, 148
Bengal board of revenue, 43, 61, 62,
66, 68, 70
Bengal board of trade, 64
Bengal police, 80–81; new regulations
for, 84; daroga of, 84
Bengal superior criminal court. *See*
Sadar Nizamat Adalat
Bengal supreme civil court. *See* Sadar
Diwani Adalat

Prussia, 16, 179; and partition of Poland, 182, 183; does not cooperate with allies, 183–84; desires meeting with British, 187; refuses to move from Rhine, 186; Britain threatens to drop subsidy to, 187; Irish rebels enter army of, 229; Napoleon friendly with, 253; to guarantee Malta's independence, 259

Punt, Hurry, 151; character of, 153; Cornwallis bribes to keep in the field, 162

R

Racism, British, in India, 88–96

Read, Alexander, his intelligence estimates, 125–26

Rennell, James, 139, 147

Rhine River, in British strategy, 185, 186

Richmond, Charles Lennox, third Duke of, 96, 102; his tenure as master general, 193–94; fails to supply adequate numbers of small arms, 195; lowers standards for admission to Woolwich, 201

Rising of the moon, 221–22

Robespierre, Maximilien, 181

Robinson, G. A.: goes to Madras, 137; confidential secretary to Cornwallis, 264; comments on Cornwallis's health, 265

Rockets, Tipoo's use of, 165, 166, 168

Rockingham, Charles Watson-Wentworth, second Marquis: death of, 8; makes concessions to Ireland, 215

Roman Catholics in Ireland, 208; Cromwell determined to crush, 211; harsh laws against, 213; penal laws against repealed, 215; ally with Ulster Protestants in Society of United Irishmen, 216; limited concessions to, 216; indifference of to union, 236; reforms favoring, 236; Cornwallis favors concessions to, 237–38; Clare opposes emancipation of, 238; Cornwallis tries to persuade to favor

union, 245; receive nothing from union, 247; George III opposes emancipation of, 250; cabinet divided over issue of emancipation of, 250–51; Cornwallis resigns when emancipation not granted to, 251

Rose, George, 18

Rose, J. Holland, comments on peace of Amiens, 260

Ross, Alexander, 6, 18, 30, 31, 235, 239, 243, 244, 247, 250, 252, 255, 262, 263, 264; Pitt sends to Vienna, 187

Ross, Robert, 238

Royal corps of artillery drivers, created by Richmond, 191, 194

Royal corps of engineers, 191, 204; Cornwallis changes pension system for, 206–7

Royal military artificers, 191

Royal regiment of artillery, 191, 204, 207; Cornwallis attempts to increase numbers of men in, 198–200; fears that it will mutiny, 205; Cornwallis dislikes pension system in, 205–6

Royal Society, 78

Rupee, types of in Bengal, 94

Russia, 261; to guarantee Malta's independence, 259

Ryots, 67–73, 80

S

Sadar Diwani Adalat (Bengal supreme civil court), 85, 86

Sadar Nizamat Adalat (Bengal superior criminal court), 80, 83

Sandby, Paul, 201

Scindia, 47, 118

Scotland, Irish rebels sent to, 229; its union different from Ireland's, 240

Sepoys and sepoy army, 75, 80, 81; lieutenant of a battalion of, kidnapped, 76; pay, perquisites, and promotion of officers in, 98–99; growth in and size of, 99; problems different religions present in, 99; numbers of camp followers in, 99–

28

Due 14 Days From Latest Date

JUL 3 1980	JUN 25 1981		
SEP 13 1980	JUN 14 1989		
OCT 2 1980			
NOV 10 1980			
NOV 28 1980			
DEC 9 1980	WITHDRAWN		
JAN 3 1981			
APR 16 1981			
JUN 2 1981